A Dweller on
Two Planets
Or, The Dividing
of the Way

A Dweller on Two Planets Or, The Dividing of the Way

PHYLOS THE THIBETAN
(A.K.A. FREDERICK S. OLIVER)

COSIMOCLASSICS

NEW YORK

A Dweller on Two Planets
Cover © 2007 Cosimo, Inc.

For information, address:

Cosimo, P.O. Box 416
Old Chelsea Station
New York, NY 10113-0416

or visit our website at:
www.cosimobooks.com

A Dweller on Two Planets was originally published in 1905.

Cover design by www.kerndesign.net

ISBN: 978-1-60206-311-2

Today, my brother, the masses of humanity on this planet
are awakened to the fact that their knowledge of life——
the Great Mystery——is insufficient for the needs of the soul.
Hence a school of advanced thought has arisen, whose
members, ignorant of the mysterious truth, yet know their
ignorance and ask for light. I make no pretenses when I say that I——
Theochristian student and Occult Adept——am one of a class
of men who do know, and can explain these mysteries.

——from the Preface

INDEX

BOOK I

INDEX

INDEX

INDEX

INDEX

INDEX

GLOSSARY.

Note:—Readers of "A Dweller on Two Planets" will please remember that in the Atlantean or Poseid language the word-terminations conveyed grammatical number and gender. Thus the singular was indicated by the equivalent for "a," the plural by "i," feminine by "u," while the absence of this terminal indicated masculinity.

Aphaisism—equivalent for mesmerism, but not hypnotism.

Astika—a prince.

Bazix—the name of one of the weeks of the year.

Devachan—the life after death.

Ene—terminal signifying study or student.

Espeid—Eden, Edenic.

Incal—the sun; also the Supreme God.

Incaliz, or Incalix—High Priest.

Inclut—first, or Sunday (also Incalon).

Inithlon—college devoted to religious learning.

Ithlon—any building, like a house.

Incalithlon—the great Temple.

Lemurinus, Lemuria or Lemorus—a continent of which Australia is the largest remnant to-day.

Karma—consequences growing out of one's actions in former lives.

Maxin—the Unfed Light.

Mo—to thee.

Murus—Boreas.

Naim—combined telephone and telephote.

Navaz—the night; also Goddess of the Night; also secret forces of Nature.

Navazzimin—the country of departed souls.

Ni—to.

Navamaxa—cremation furnaces for dead bodies.

Nosses—the moon.

Nossinithlon—insane asylum; [lit. a home for moon-struck persons.]

Nossura—mocking bird.

Pitach—a mountain peak.

Rai—Emperor or monarch, as Rai Gwauxln, pronounced Wallun.

Raina—a land governed; as the Raina of Gwauxln—Poseid.

Rainu [also Astiku]—a princess .

Su—he is gone.

Sattamun—desert, or wasted land.

Suernota—the Asian Continent.

Surada—to sing, or I sing.

Teka, or Teki—Poseid gold coin, value about $2.67.

GLOSSARY

Vailx—an aerial ship.

Ven—a linear unit of about a mile.

Xanatithlon—conservatory for flowers.

Xio, or Xioq—science.

Xiorain—the self-government board of Xioqua.

Xioqene—science student.

Ystranavu—the star of evening; also, when used astronomically, Phyristunar.

Zo—personal pronoun, possessive my or mine.

Rai—Emperor or monarch, as Rai Gwauxln, pronounced Wallun.

AMANUENSIS' PREFACE.

By permission of the Author, whose letter addressed to me, follows as his preface herein, and to meet the natural inquiry and satisfy, so far as any personal statement from me will, any honest inquiring mind, I humbly appear in order briefly to give the major facts concerning the writing of this —even to me—very remarkable book.

I am an only child of Dr. and Mrs. Oliver, who for many years have resided in the State of California.

I was born in Washington, D. C., in 1866, and brought to the State by my parents two years later. Prior to commencing the writing of this book, in 1884, my education had been comparatively limited, and extended to a very slight knowledge of the subjects herein treated.

My father, a well-known physician, died a few years ago, my mother surviving him. Both were daily witnesses of most of the circumstances and facts surrounding the writing of this book. But further than to state this, I do not think myself called upon to introduce my family into the work, nor, in fact, myself, except in so far as it is meet for me to stand forth and do my personal part as the amanuensis.

I feel that I am mentally and spiritually but a figure beside the Author of the great, deep-searching, far-reaching and transcendent questions presented in the following pages; and I read and study them with as much interest and profit, I imagine, as will any reader. At the same time I feel with no sense of the natural pride of an Author of such a book, that it is a work of unselfish love, and will help to the betterment of an upward-struggling world, searching ever for more light, and feed the hungry for knowledge of the great mystery of life and of the ever evolving soul, through Him who said— "I AM THE WAY; FOLLOW ME."

AMANUENSIS PREFACE.

In these days of doubt, materialism, and even rank atheism, it requires all the courage I possess to assert, in clear unequivocal terms, that the following book, "A DWELLER ON TWO PLANETS," is absolute revelation; that I do not believe myself its Author, but that one of those mysterious persons, if my readers choose to so consider him, an adept of the arcane and occult in the universe, better understood from reading this book, is the Author. Such is the fact. The book was revealed to me, a boy, and a boy, too, whose parents were mistakenly lenient to such a degree that he was allowed to do as he chose in most things. Not lacking in inclination to study, but very lacking in will-power, continuity and energy, I gained little in educational triumphs, and was pointedly criticised by my teacher as "lackadaisical, even lazy." Hence, when a little past seventeen years of age, "Phylos, the Esoterist," took me actively in charge, designing to make me his instrument to the world, that profound adept showed what seems to me a rare faith, for I was without any solid education, as generally so considered, was minus any special religious trend, and for my sole commendation, had willingness, love of the remarkable, and an uncolored mind.

For a year my occult preceptor educated me by means of "mental talks," and to such a point was my mind occupied by the many new thoughts with which he inspired me, that I paid no heed to my environment, worked automatically, if at all, studied and read not, and scarcely heard those who addressed my exterior senses. Then it was that my father determined to stop my "approaching imbecility," as he called it; for I had avoided explanations, and had said nothing of the talks with my mystic preceptor, whom even I had never seen but a few times. To parental pressure I yielded, and told my—to me—divine secret. To my relief it was not scouted, but after a long narration to both parents, they expressed a desire to hear the mysterious stranger also. This he would not grant, but permitted me to quote his words, talks and addresses, and at length I became so proficient that I could repeat what he said almost as fast as he spoke to me.

AMANUENSIS PREFACE.

A circle was formed at home, consisting at first of my parents, W. S. Mallory (now of Cleveland, Ohio), and myself, as hearers, and Phylos as teacher. Later Mrs. S. M. Pritchard and Mrs. Julia P. Churchill were present. This was in Yreka, Siskiyou Co., Cal., early in the eighties, where the MS. was commenced in A. D. 1883-4, but was finished in Santa Barbara County, California, A. D. 1886, where it has ever since remained in the manuscript, at the command of the author.

It will have added interest to many who love, or have become interested in CALIFORNIA, to know that within full view of Shasta, one of her loftiest mountain peaks, this book was begun and almost finished under the inspiration of that spirit of nature which speaks ever to those who, listening, understand.

How the Author differs from us common mortals, and how, by his occult methods, he possesses the power to dictate—"reveal"—as he has done and still does, may be better known by perusal of his remarkable record, set forth in this book—his personal history.

In 1883-4, A. D., in sight of the inspiring peak of Mount Shasta, the Author began to have me write what he told me, and, curiously enough, he dictated the initial chapter of "Book Second" first of all. Other chapters, both preceding and succeeding, were given at intervals of a few weeks, or even months, sometimes only a sheet or two, at others as high as eighty letter-size sheets being covered in a few hours. I would be awakened at night by my mentor and write by lamplight, or sometimes with no light, but in darkness. In 1886 the main work, as I remember it, was done. Then he had me revise it, under his supervision, and this work was as erratic as the other. In fact, the whole thing was as if he had the MS. already prepared when first he began dictation, and was indifferent as to what portions were written first, so only all were written. Had I been a medium in the sense usually understood by the believers in spiritualism, as I understand it, the writing would have been automatic, and I would not have been forced to clothe his converse so largely in my own language, and in that case no revision would have been necessary. But I was always conscious of every surrounding, quite similar, in fact, to any stenographer—with this lack of equality to such an amanuensis—that I was not then a shorthand reporter. Realizing how useful in taking my preceptor's teachings the possession of this art on my part would be, I learned to write stenographically, although never an expert.

Twice was the work revised, twice he had me go over this erratically written MS., which, as I have said, was mainly written backward. So strangely was it given that I had almost no idea of what it was, or with what it dealt. On one occasion, when I had written over two hundred sheets, mostly backwards, i. e., the sentences rightly last coming first, so fast and mixed that I had no idea of its sense, he bade me burn it without even reading it. This I did, and to this day I have little idea of what those pages contained, or why he had me destroy them; nor will he tell me. The book was finished in A. D. 1886, though for the purpose of publication the MS. has been thoroughly edited by a literary expert, that any errors therein due to my own limitations and mistakes in transmission as amanuensis, should be eliminated.

In the year 1894 the manuscript as finished in 1886 was typewritten in duplicate by Mrs. M. E. Moore of Louisville, Kentucky, and she has had possession of one of said copies ever since up to midsummer, 1899. The Moore copy has never been changed by even a letter since it was written, evidence whereof has been judiciously preserved. Said manuscript was copyrighted by me in 1894, and owing to an addition to the title, again in this, the year 1899.

During all this time I have not been permitted, nor able, to have it published. In the interval many of the things spoken of in the shape of scientific and mechanical rediscoveries, **spoken of in the book**, have been brought to pass. The high attainments of the Atlanteans, lost for thousands of years, following as the result of the engulfment of their great continent, have been and are rapidly being brought to light and utility; bearing out the prediction of the Author.

Witness the discovery recently of the Roentgen or "X-ray," not even dreamed of in 1886, yet in the book you will find a long treatise concerning "Cathodicity" and the amazing powers of the "Night Side of Nature," of such practical use to and so well understood by the people of that wonderful age. Also note wireless telegraphy; it, too, is herein, scattered all through and referred to in this book, precluding the possibility of interpolation. Again, regarding there being but "One Energy" and but "One Substance," now beginning to find able champions and general scientific acceptance, in place of passing it by as a chimera for the elementary hypothesis so long held by chemists. This also is an integral part of this book; though it is not more than two years since an article appeared in Harper's Magazine seriously advancing this belief of fin-de-siecle science as a novelty. These are but major examples of what was set forth in "A DWELLER ON TWO PLANETS" in 1886, together with many more predictions of the immediate oncoming of what the Author terms rediscovery of the secrets buried with Atlantis; and it is promised that we, as Atlanteans returning, are going beyond her fallen greatness, and that by slow, synthetic steps, we are coming up to surpass even those wonderful attainments, as the ever expanding and growing mind and soul of man climbs ever higher in the rounds of his evolution.

To all earnest, though perhaps skeptical inquirers, I may say that the evidence as to this book being finished in 1886, and before the latter-day discoveries became known, abundantly exists and can be clearly established, to clear away any cobwebs that might otherwise find lodgment in their minds and prevent them from accepting the book for what its Author claims—the truth.

Upon the ability of the perusers to so accept this book as history and not fiction, much depends, in lighting up the Path for their souls. I am rather in expectation of another work, but whether I will have it, or some other amanuensis will get it, I do not know. If it come as promised, it will be one for the inner eyes of those who profit by this work, and seek yet more of the counsel which will place their feet firmly on the "Narrow Way of Attainment."

In writing as such amanuensis, I am always conscious of the presence calling himself Phylos, whenever he chooses to come to me, and sometimes I see as well as hear and speak with him, though vision is rare. Clairvoyance and clairaudience would account for this. I hear—and speak or write—what is said as I am directed. Often, after being shown the mental picture, I am left largely to express it in my own language. At such times I am as fully conscious of my surroundings as at any other time, though I feel lifted as into a Master's presence, and gladly do for him the work of an amanuensis. If the good counsel and loving care I have personally received from my wise friend had been faithfully and persistently remembered and followed, instead of so largely slighted or forgotten, as often to almost fade from my memory during his absence, I should undoubtedly have been a better example than I feel that I am of the grand lessons he sets forth in this book.

I have never represented myself to any person, nor to the public as possesing mediumistic or any other quality, nor have I ever used the same at any person's request, for love or money. Whatever my talents or qualities in these things may be, they have only been used as a sacred gift. With such influences as have surrounded me in this work, I can gratefully and truly say that I have never been tempted to do otherwise, if I could; and have ever received exceedingly more good than I feel that my services have returned.

Now the question arises, do I believe this Book? Unhesitatingly, Yes. There may be points that I can accept only on faith, like any other reader, feeling that a day will come when, if I shall be faithful, I will be instructed by the Spirit to which he testifies. There certainly will be criticisms from some as to the manner of the writing of this MS., and as to the truth of

AMANUENSIS PREFACE.

my statements regarding it, as there has so often been by those who prefer to believe that all such claims are but author's fictions. I have come to personally know the truth of some of the things mentioned in this book, in the course of the fifteen years that I have had in this connection. I have had many experiences, mentally confirmatory at least, either of the direct statements of the author, or tending to strengthen the absolute confidence which I feel in him I reverence so deeply. I have often, even as "Christian" in "Pilgrim's Progress," fallen. But the Path is there. Does the sun cease to shine because fogs obscure it? Then is it not for us to follow the Path, forgetting persons, and looking to the spirit, as we read Phylos' Book?   F. S. OLIVER.

LETTER FROM PHYLOS, AUTHOR OF THIS HISTORY.

January, 1886.

Today, my brother, the masses of humanity on this planet are awakened to the fact that their knowledge of life—the Great Mystery—is insufficient for the needs of the soul. Hence a school of advanced thought has arisen, whose members, ignorant of the mysterious truth, yet know their ignorance and ask for light. I make no pretenses when I say that I— Theochristian student and Occult Adept—am one of a class of men who **do know,** and can explain these mysteries. I, with other Christian Adepts, influence the inspirational writers and speakers through an ability to exert the control of our trained, and therefore more powerful, minds over theirs, which are enormously less so. Hence, when the people ask for bread, our media give it to them. Who are these, our media? They are all men or women, in churches or out, who bear witness of the Fatherhood of God, the Sonship of Man, and the Brotherhood of Jesus with all souls, irrespective of creeds or ecclesiastical forms. Because these, our writers and speakers, have wrought for human good, so shall, and so does, good come to themselves, bread from the waters. It is proper that the leaders of the mental van should receive generous remuneration. And they do. But at this point enters a different phase. Observing the cry for more light, more truth; observing also how great is the recompense, up springs the imitator, who has no light of inspiration, no conception of the real truth, none of the laws of the Eternal. What does he? Watch! With a pen whose shaft is imitation, and whose point is not of the gold of fact, but of the perishable metal of selfish greed, this person writes. He dips his pen into the ink of more or less thrilling sensationalism, muddy with the dirt of immorality and nastiness, and he draws a pen picture illumined by the tallow-dip of lust and corruption. There is in his work no lofty aim to inspire his readers; he deals with the lowest aspects of life, and, ignorant of the inexorable penalty for sin, has no expiation to demand of his characters. While a little allured by brilliant word-painting, the reader goes to the end, he is conscious ever that the cry of his soul for the bread of infinity has been answered not even by a stone, but by a handful of mud! No good purpose is thus subserved; nothing taught of the real laws or philosophies of life; it drags down, but never elevates. Whoso shall utter thus, upon them shall come retribution, and they shall be judges upon themselves, and executioners also, out in the open sea of the soul, where their own spirit will have no mercy for the misdeeds of the soul. Other imitators there may be, who, fired with a genuine desire to do good, will mimic intuitional utterances, and, however poor the work, yet if the animus has been to do good, in the measure of that resolve shall the Most High judge that whatever is for good is not for evil. But let them beware who, for money or profit, are tempted to give stones or mud!

And now, my brother, I have another subject to speak upon. Readers of my book, "Two Planets," may consider awhile over those passages concerning the sin of the Princess Lolix and of Zailm, the legal nephew of the Emperor Gwauxln. They may say that the mention of this fact, though liable to occur as one of the varied experiences of life, is nevertheless out of place in a book whose aim is highly moral. But I

AMANUENSIS PREFACE.

ask those who know my work, is it? Is it inexcusable to speak of those grave but common crimes if the author can treat them as examples of broken law, and can place the working of such law so clearly before this unthinking world that men and women will be afraid to break it, fearful of the penalty, which can in no wise be evaded? I think it unjustifiable to keep silence under such circumstances. I have, so far from overdrawing the estimate of the penalty of crime, not given the entire expiatory picture. I know whereof I speak, for this, my brother, is my own life history, and words have no power to depict the utter misery which the exaction of the punishment has caused me! If but one soul shall be saved like misery, and similar or equal sin, or less or more error, then am I content. I have sought to explain the great mystery of life, illustrating it with part of my own life history, extracts which cover years reaching into many thousands; and the greatest of all Books has been my text. I add not thereto nor take away, but explain.* Peace be with thee.

PHYLOS.

Addendum:—I feel myself vastly indebted to many bright writers and authors for numerous quotations of which I have availed myself, without making credit at the time; it is imposible to render this award to every individual by name, hence I must do so concretely, just as the world finds itself forced to express its aggregate gratitude, not by words of laudation, but by shaping its life in conformity to the noble precepts in poetry and in prose, devised to humanity as the legacy of all the ages. As the world is helped, so has my work been; I hope I have returned help for help.

Sincerely,   PHYLOS.

---

*Revelations, XXII, 18-19; also I. Tim. VI., 8-12.

A MARVELOUS PREDICTION.

The preface is mine to say what may properly please me. It was so given me by the Author.

A subject not specifically treated by Phylos in his book, but not forbidden me by him, I feel it almost due the public to give here, most especially as it was told me by him while I was summering in Reno, Nevada, in the year 1886. I at that time embodied it in a short story, which I dated, but more to the point, read to a young lady friend, Miss S. This fact she can testify as being fact, for it was partly written under her eyes, was criticised by herself, sister and mother, and, climax, was written upon paper bought for the purpose from her father's drug and book store.

Phylos stated to me then that inside fifty years, considerably inside, he thought, mundane scientists would have discovered and applied electric forces to the astronomical telescope. Just how, he did not state, although he did give ample enough details so that one familiar with those subjects probably would have been able to seize upon and work out the idea to a successful issue. He said that electric currents **unimpressed with vibrations such as produce sound, heat and light, until resisted, would be superadded to the light vibrations constituting the image beheld through the telescope.** This would be accomplished through the media of well-known so-called chemical elements, whose then unrecognized higher powers remained to be discovered.

The result was described to me as awe-inspiring and marvelous past earthly dreams. Thus, he stated, that upon suns and stellar bodies so distant that hundreds of them only (even in this A. D. 1899) seem as a faint speck through the most powerful modern telescopes, to this electrostellarscope would, by proper amplification of the electro-luminous waves be made so plain to earthly vision that objects not visible to the unaided earthly sight would be easily perceptible on the most distant stellar body, however remote from the mundane beholder.

AMANUENSIS PREFACE.

Further, Phylos says that he did not embody this subject in his book, because Atlantis did not know of it, despite her marvelous scientific attainments. Hence it will be no "re-discovery," but a distinct step in advance of anything that Earth has known—Solomon at last outreached, so far as his time-honored saying applies to our planet, at least.

Respectfully,

THE AMANUENSIS, FREDERICK S. OLIVER.

Los Angeles, October 11, 1899.

MAP OF ATLANTIS. REFERRED TO ON PAGE 84.

BOOK THE FIRST.

CHAPTER I.

ATLANTIS, QUEEN OF THE WAVE.

"Why not?" I asked myself, pausing amidst the snow on the mountain, there so far above the sea that the Storm King was ever supreme, even while summer reigned below. "Am I not an Atlan, a Poseid, and is not that name synonymous with freedom, honor, power? Is not this, my native land, the most glorious beneath the sun? Beneath Incal?" Again I queried:—"Why not, aye, why not strive to become one amongst the foremost in my proud country?"

"Poseid is the Queen of the Sea, yea, and of the world also, since all nations pay tribute of praise and commerce to us—all emulate us. To rule in Poseid, then, is not that virtually to rule over all the earth? Therefore will I strive to grasp the prize, and I will do it, too! And thou, O pale, cold moon, bear witness of my resolve"—I cried aloud, raising my hands to heaven—"And ye also, ye glittering diamonds of the sky."

If resolute effort could insure success, I usually achieved whatever end I determined to attain. So there I made my vows—at a great height above the ocean, and above the plain which stretched away westward two thousand miles to Caiphul, the Royal City. So high was it, that all about and below me lay peaks and mountain ranges, vast in themselves, but dwarfed beside the apex whereon I stood.

All around me lay the eternal snows; but what cared I? So filled with the new resolve was my mind—the resolve to become a power in the land of my nativity—that I heeded not the cold. Indeed, I scarce knew that the air about me was cold, was chill as that of the Arctic fields of the remote north.

Many obstacles would have to be surmounted in the accomplishment of this design—for truly, what was I at that moment! Only a mountaineer's son, poor, fatherless; but, the Fates be praised! not motherless! At thought of her, my mother, miles away, down where the perennial forests waved, where snow seldom fell; while I stood on the storm-kissed summit, alone with the night and my thoughts—at the thought of my mother my eyes grew moist, for I was only a boy, and often a sad enough one, when the hardships which she endured arose to mind. Such reflections were but added incentives to my ambition to do and to be.

Once more my thoughts dwelt on the difficulties I must encounter in my struggle for success, fame and power.

Atlantis, or Poseid, was an empire whose subjects enjoyed the freedom allowed by the most limited monarchical rule. The general law of official succession presented to every male subject a chance for preferment to office. Even the emperor held an elective position, as also did his ministers, the Council of Ninety, or Princes of the Realm—offices analagous to those of the Secretarial Portfolios of the American Republic—its veritable successor. If death claimed the occupant of the throne, or any of the councillors, the elective franchise came into activity, but not otherwise, barring dismissal for malfeasance in office, a penalty which, if incurred by him, not even the emperor was exempt from suffering.

The posession of the elective power was vested in the two great social divisons, which embraced all classes of people, of either sex. The great underlying principle of the Poseid political fabric might be said to have been "an educational measuring-rod for every ballot-holder, but the sex of the holder, no one's business."

The two major social branches were known by the distinctive names of "Incala" and "Xioqua," or, respectively, the priesthood and scientists.

Do my readers ask where that open opportunity for every subject could be in a system which excluded the artisans, tradespeople, and military, if they happended not to be of the enfranchised classes? Every person had the option of entering either the College of Sciences, or that of Incal, or both.

Nor was race, color or sex considered, the only prerequisite being that the candidate for admission must be sixteen years of age, and the possessor of a good education obtained in the common schools, or at some of the lesser seats of collegiate learning, as the Xioquithlon in the capital city of some one of the Poseid States, as at Numea, Terna, Idosa, Corosa, or even at Marzeus' lower college, Marzeus being the principal art-manufacturing center of Atl. Seven years was the allotted term of study at the Great Xioquithlon, ten months in each year, divided into two sub-terms of five months each, devoted to active work, and one month allowed for recreation, half of it between each session. Any student might compete in the annual examination exercises, held at the end of the year, or just preceding the vernal equinox. That we recognized the natural law of mental limitation will be obvious from the fact that the course of study was purely optional, the aspirant being at liberty to select as many, or as few topics as were agreeable, with this necessary proviso:—that only possessors of diplomas of the first class could be candidates for even the humblest official position. These certificates were evidence of a grade of acquirement which embraced a range of topical knowledge too great to be mentioned, otherwise than inferentially, as the reader proceeds. The second-grade diploma did not confer political prestige, except in the matter of carrying with it the voting privilege, although if a person neither cared to be an office holder, nor to vote, the right to instruction in any educational branch was none the less a gratuitous privilege. Those, however, who only aspired to a limited education, with the purpose of more successfully pursuing a given business, as tuition in mineralogy by an intending miner, agriculture by a farmer, or botany by an ambitious gardener—had no voice in the government. While the number of those unambitious ones was not small, none the less the stimulus of obtaining political prestige was so great that not above one in a dozen of the adult population was without at least a second-grade diploma, while fully one-third had first-grade certificates. It was owing to this, that the electors found no scarcity of material for filling all elective positions under the government.

Some uncertainty is possibly left in the mind of the reader as to what constituted the difference between priestly and scientific suffragists. The only essential difference was that the curriculum at the Incalithlon, or College of Priests, embraced, in addition to every high-grade feature taught at the Xioquithlon, also the study of a wide range of occult phenomena, anthropological and sociological themes, to the end that graduates in the sciences might have the opportunity of fitting themselves to minister to any want, which men of less erudition and less comprehension of the great underlying laws of life might experience, in any phase or condition. The Incalithlon was in fact the very highest, most complete institution of learning which the world knew then, or—pardon what may seem to be, but is not, Atlan conceit—has known since; and for that matter, will know for centuries to come. As such an exalted educational institution, students within its halls must needs possess extra zeal and determined will-power in order to pursue, and secure graduation certificates from its board of examiners. Few indeed had found life extended enough to enable them to acquire such a diploma; possibly not one in five hundred of those who made honorable exit from the Xioquithlon—itself an institution not second to the modern Cornell University.

As I pondered, there amidst those mountain snows, I decided not to attempt too much, but a Xioqua I determined to be, if any possible chance existed; although I scarcely hoped for the possession of the eminence conferred by the title of Incala, I vowed that I would make an opportunity to compete for the other, if no occasion presented otherwise. To obtain the proud distinction would require, in addition to arduous study, the posssession of ample pecuniary means to furnish the expense of living, and the maintenance, at its highest, of an unfaltering energy of purpose. Whence could I hope to obtain all this? The gods were believed to help the needy. If I, a lad of not yet seventeen summers, who had a mother looking to me for support and the necessaries of life, with nothing that could aid me to attain my aspirations except native energy and will, might not be placed in that category, then who were the needy? Methinks there should be no more evidence of dependence necessary, and it were indeed proper in the gods to extend aid.

Filled with such reflections as these, I climbed yet higher towards the top of the sky-piercing peak, near the apex of which I stood, for the dawn was not far distant, and I must be on the highest stone to greet Incal (the sun) when He conquered Navaz, else He—chief of all the manifest signs of the great and only true God, whose name He bore, whose shield He was—might not favorably regard my prayer. No, He must see that the supplicating youth spared no pains to do Him honor, because it was for this purpose only that I had climbed alone, amidst these solitudes, up that trackless steep of snow, beneath the starry dome of the skies.

"Is there," I asked myself, "a more glorious belief than this which my country-folk hold? Are not all Poseidi worshipers of the Great God—the one true Deity—who is typified by the blazing sun? There can be nothing more sacred and holy." Só spake the boy whose maturing mind had grasped the really inspiring exoteric religion, but who knew of none other, deeper and more sublime, nor was he to learn of it in the days of Atla.

As the first glance of light from behind His shield stole through the dark abyss of night, I threw myself prone in the summit snows, where I must remain until the God of Light was entirely victorious over Navaz. Triumphant at last! Then I arose, and making a final profound obeisance, retraced my steps down that fearful declivity of ice, and snow, and barren rock, the latter black and cruelly sharp, thrusting its ridges through the icy coat, showing the ribs of the mountain which stood, one of the peerless peaks of the globe, thirteen thousand feet above the level of the sea.

For two days all my efforts had been to reach that frigid summit and cast myself, a living offering, on its lofty altar, thus to honor my God. I wondered if He had heard and noted me. If He had, did He care? Did He care enough to direct His vice-regent, God of the mountain, to aid me? To the latter, without knowing why, I looked, hoping in what may seem a blind fatuity, for him to reveal a treasure of some sort, or——

What is that dull metallic glint in the rock whose heart my iron-shod alpenstock had lain bare to the rays of the morning sun? Gold! O Incal! It is so! Yellow, precious gold!

"O Incal," I cried, repeating His name, "be thou praised for returning answer so quickly to Thy humble petitioner!"

Down in the snow I knelt, uncovering my head out of gratitude to the God of All Being, the Most High, whose shield, the sun poured forth his glorious rays. Then I looked again on the treasure. Ah, what a store of wealth was there!

As the quartz rock splintered beneath my excited strokes, the precious metal held it together, so thickly did it vein its matrix. Sharp edges of the flinty stone cut my hands, so that the blood flowed from half a dozen places, and as I grasped the icy quartz which did the deed, my bleeding hands froze fast upon it—a union of blood and treasure! No matter! and I tore them loose, unheeding the pain, so much was I excited.

"O Incal," I exclaimed, "Thou are good to Thy child in so liberally bestowing the treasure which shall enable a realization of his resolution, ere the heart hath opportunity to grow faint through long-deferred hope."

I loaded into my capacious pockets all that I could stagger under, selecting the richest and most valuable pieces of the gold quartz. How should I mark the spot, how find it again? To a born mountaineer this was no hard task, and was soon accomplished. Then onward, downward, homeward, joyfully I swung, with light heart, if heavy load. Over these mountains, indeed not two miles from the base of my treasure peak, wound the emperor's highway to the great ocean, hundreds of miles away on the other side of the Caiphalian plains. This causeway once reached, the most fatiguing part of the trip would be over, although but one-fifth of the entire route would yet have been traversed.

To give some idea of the difficulties encountered in scaling or descending this giant mountain, I must remark that the final five-thousand feet of the ascent could be made by only one tortuous route. A narrow gorge, a mere volcanic fissure, afforded foothold of the most precarious character, all other parts of the peak being insurmountable cliffs. This meager support existed for the first one thousand feet. Above this point the cleft ceased. Near its upper end a small cave existed, rather higher than a man's stature, and capable of holding perhaps twenty people. In the farther end of this rocky room was a hole—a crack wider horizontally than in the perpendicular. Entering this crevice by crawling, serpent-fashion, the venturesome explorer would find that for several hundred paces he must needs descend a rather sharp incline, albeit the crevice in the first dozen steps so widened, or heightened, that a more or less upright posture could be assumed. From the end of its descending course it twisted and again increased in size so as to form a tunnnel, ascending by tortuous windings, its walls affording sufficient support to make the climbing safe, although pursued upward at an angle of about forty degrees, while in some parts an even greater degree of perpendicularity marked the passage. In this way an upward climb of thirty odd hundreds of feet was accomplished, the sinuosities of the route greatly increasing the distance covered in a vertical rise. This, reader, was the sole method of reaching the summit of the highest mountain of Poseid, or Atlantis, as thou callest the island-continent.

Arduous as was its passage, there was more than enough room in this dry old chimney, or water-course, whichever it was, Chimney it certainly had been, originally, though now water-worn to such an extent as to render the idea of its igneous formation, de novo, merely conjectural. At one part of its course this long hole widened into a vast cavern. This led away at right angles from the chimney, and down, down, until far in the bowels of the mountain—thousands of feet it seemed in the dread darkness—he who ventured so far found himself on the brink of a vast abyss, which had no visible side except that on which he stood; beyond this, further progress was impossible except for winged things, as bats,— and bats were there none in that awful depth.

No sound came back from its frightful chasm, no brightness of torches had ever revealed its other shore—nought was there but a sea of eternal inky blackness. Yet here were no terrors for me; rather a fascination. While others may have known of the place, I had never found a companion with enough temerity to brave the unknown, and stand by my side on the horrid brink, where I had stood, not once only, but several times in days gone by. Three times I had been there, impelled by curiosity. On the third occasion I had leaned over the edge to seek a possible further descent, when the stone upon which I was—a huge basaltic block—loosened from its place, fell, and I barely escaped with my life. It fell, and for several minutes sounds of its descent came echoing back to where I stood; my torch went with it, and far adown the depths its sparks gleamed like fire-flies as it struck projecting points of the rock, ere it finally disappeared. I was left in that deep darkness, weak from my great peril, to make my way up and out—if I could. If not, then to fail and die But I succeeded. Thenceforth I had no curiosity to explore that unknown gulf. Through the chimney which led past the upper end of this abyssmal cavern—between the upper end of the outer fissure in the cliff and the summit's side, five or six hundred feet below the apex of the mountain—I had been many times; often had I been over the spot where a chance blow of my staff revealed the golden treasure, yet never found the precious store until I had asked Incal for it, urged by the pressing burden of my necessities. Is it strange that I felt absolute faith in the religious belief of my people?

It was into the dark chimney that I had to go when I left the snowy summit—out of the sunlight and fresh air, into dense blackness, and a slightly sulphurous atmosphere; but if I left the morning brightness, I also left the fearful cold of the external air, for inside the tunnel, if dark, it was warm.

At last, I came into the small room at the head of the thousand-foot crevice which would take me to the easier slopes of the lower and middle third of the mountain. In that room I paused. Should I return for another load of auriferous rock? Or should I go directly on my homeward way? At length I turned and retraced my steps. With the noon hour I stood once more beside my treasure spot. Then down again with my second load, till the weary toil ceased almost—for I was standing then at the entrance to the great cavern, four hundred feet from the little room at the head of the outer crevice—four hundred feet of pretty steep climbing. After a moment's pause I resumed the short but sharp ascent, and was soon in the little room, with only a dozen feet at most between myself and the free air. Sinuous, the long tunnel was, considered as a whole, yet it had some passages as straight as if cut by tools along a line. The four hundred feet, more or less, which separated the room where I stayed my steps, from the entrance proper of the cavern, was such a straight stretch, and perhaps on that occount as difficult to traverse as any part of the whole tunnel. Indeed it would have been impossible, except for its rough sides affording some slight foothold. Had the place been light, instead of filled with the blackness of darkness, I could have seen directly into the cavern from the apartment in which I was resting. The warm air induced me to sit or rather lie down at this point, even though I could not see, and so, as I rested there, I ate a handful of dates and sipped a little of the melted snow-water which my water-skin contained. Then I stretched myself out to sleep in the warm air.

How long I slept I did not know, but the awakening—ah! the terror of it! Blasts of air so hot as to almost scorch, swept over and past me, laden with stifling fumes, and sending back a hoarse murmur as they rushed up the passage to the summit. Howling, groaning noises came up on the fervid breath from the abyss, mingled with the sound of tremendous explosions and deafening reports. Above all other causes for terror was a glow of red light reflected from the walls of the cavern, into which I found I could look with unobstructed freedom, and through whose depths shone flashes of red and green and blue, and every other color and tint, gases on fire. For a time, fright held me fast, so that without power to move I remained gazing into the awful hell of the blazing elements. I knew that the light and heat, both momentarily increasing, and the stifling vapors, the noise and the quivering of the mountain, all pointed but one and the same meaning—active volcanic eruption. At last, the spell which numbed my senses was broken by my catching sight of a spurt of molten lava which dashed up the intervening passage, projected a number of feet therein by an explosion within the cavern behind. Then I rose up and fled—fled across the floor of the little room and crawled with insane energy of haste through the horizontal entrance, which seemed never so low as that moment! I had forgotten that I carried gold in my pockets, and the fact only came back when I felt the retarding weight of the precious rock. But with the exertion to escape came a certain degree of calmness, and the restored presence of mind bade me not throw away the treasure. Reflection convinced me that the danger, although impending, was probably not immediate. So that I again crawled back into the little room, and taking a sack which I had left there, filled it with all the ore I could carry. I undid a leather thong from my waist—a cord forty feet long—and looping one end to a point of rock at the upper end of the crevice, I lowered the sack to the other extremity of the small cord, and then climbed down after it. Shaking the loop from the rock above, I repeated the performance again and again as I descended. In this way I reached the bottom of the crevice with the larger portion of my two loads of ore. From this point onwards my route lay along the crest of a rocky ridge, not very wide, but sufficiently so to form an easy path.

I had just started along this ridge when I looked back over the way I had come. At that instant, a shock of earthquake occurred that almost sufficed to throw me to the ground, and out of the little cave, where I had slept, shot a puff of smoke, followed by a red gleam—lava. Downwards it splashed, a fiery cascade, and a most glorious sight in the gathering darkness, for the sun was not yet set. The entire mountain was west of the ridge on which I stood, and it being near night, my position was in deep shadow.

Out along the ridge I fled, leaving my sack of gold and much that was in my pockets in the safest place that I could choose, high above the bottom of the gorge, along which the lava must flow. At a safe distance I paused for rest and scanned the fiery torrent leaping down the gorge, now some distance away on my right, but in plain sight. "At least," thought I, "I have as much gold-rock—more metal than rock, it appears— left in my pockets yet, as I shall find myself well able to carry, now that the strength, born of excitement, is fled. So that even if I get not that I left behind, I have a great store of wealth. Therefore, Incal be praised!" How entirely inadequate to meet the expenses of seven years at college—and that college at the capital of the nation, where expenses were higher than elsewhere—were the twenty pounds, approximately, of gold-quartz, my inexperience could not tell me. That it was a greater treasure than I had ever possessed in my life, or even seen at one time, was an undeniable fact; therefore I was content.

A belief in an overruling Providence is necessary to most, indeed to all men, the sole difference being that men of widest knowledge require a Deity of power more nearly approaching infinity than do those of lesser experience; so those who realize the boundlessness of life, recognize a God of whom their conceptions are projected almost to omnipotence, compared to the conceptions which satisfy the ordinary human mind. Whether, then, the deity worshipped be a stone or a wooden idol, some inanimate form, or a Supreme Spirit of androgynous nature, it matters little. Those Beings who order the course of events, executing the karmic law of the Eternal God, see the faith in mortal hearts, and suffer not that that law shall ever take its course in sterness, untempered by mercy. If trust in the idol, or the animate "god," or in the Supreme Spirit of God, should be allowed to perish because of the withering forces of sorrow and despair; then would human goodness tremble for safety, and for continuation of its being. Such a catastrophe could not harmonize with God, hence, under the law, can never be allowed.

So with my belief in Incal, a belief shared by my country-people. Incal was a purely spiritual conception, and aside from the Eternal Cause—which no mind of any age of the world can sanely doubt—was existent only in the minds of his worshippers. And the faith was a noble one, one that tended to high morality, nourishing faith, hope and charity. What then though the personal Incal, symbolized by the shield of the blazing sun, was inexistent except in the brains of men? Our Poseid concept stood for us in the place of the Spirit of Life, Parent of all. That was enough to insure observance of the principles which it was supposed pleased Him best.

Surely the angels of the Most High Uncreated God, ministering then, as now, to the children of the Father, looked on the belief as it lay enshrined in my heart, and in the hearts of my fellow-men and women, and said, as they ministered: "Be it unto thee according to thy faith." The angels beholding the hope that was in me to excel among men, had chastened me with fear as I fled from the burning mountain, but there came no disaster.

Onward I ran, as speedily as the nature of the path would permit. I had life and gold; wherefore I praised Incal as I went. And the Spirit of Life was merciful, for I was not to know how insufficient for my needs was my treasure, until the sting of disappointment was removed because of having found a more abundant provision. For several miles my course lay along the knife-edged back of the ridge. In many places awful gulfs yawned beside the path, so near that I had need of my hands to aid my feet. Sometimes these cliffs extended along both sides of the trail, forming it into a narrow parapet. I was grateful for small mercies, and thanked Incal that the

god of the mountain bestirred himself not in the form of
earth-throes while I was in those perilous situations.

At a distance of three miles from the starting place my
path led me along the brink of a frightful precipice, while
above reared the wall of a second cliff. Only the light of the
burning mountain now illumined my steps. Here it was that
as I climbed cautiously downwards towards the basaltic brink,
a heavy shock threw me upon my knees and almost sent me
into the gulf. An instant later a dull boom filled the air
with an insistent intensity of sound, and I looked back in
affright. A huge spout of fiery smoke was rushing skywards,
mingled with stones large enough to be seen at the distance
I was from the spot. Below the brink where I clung, an
awful grinding and crashing was going on; the earth trembled
fearfully, and repeated shocks caused me to grasp the rocks
in desperate fear of being thrown over the edge. Off there in
front, the gorge which lay at my feet, once skirted other
ridges and spurs of the peak. Once, for a while, these ridges
and spurs had been, now they were not! I gazed upon a
scene of awful and confusing turmoil, lit by the volcanic
glare just sufficiently to be perceptible. The solid hills and
rocks seemed tossing and unstable as the waters of the ocean,
and they rose and fell in a horrid swell, grinding and crashing
in genuine pandemonium. Over all, volcanic ashes sifted in a
thick, ceaseless shower, while dust and volcanic vapors filled
the air and hung like a funereal pall over a seemingly perishing world.

Finally the mad uproar and sickening motion ceased; only
the steady glow from the still-flowing lava, and an occasional throe of earthquake telling the Plutonic tale. But I remained lying on the ledge, faint and ill. Gradually the lava
stopped running, and the light went out; the shocks came
only at long intervals, and a peace as of death filled all the
region, while the silent gray ashes sifted down, covering the
stricken land. Darkness reigned. I think I must, for a time,
have been unconscious, for when I stirred I was aware of a
sharp pain in my head; putting up my hand I felt a warm,
wet oozing from a place which smarted at the touch. I felt

about and found a jagged stone which had fallen from the
cliff above and struck me. Further motion proved the wound
was not serious, and I sat up. Already the dawn was coming,
and faint with pain, hunger and cold I again lay down to
await broad day.

What a different scene rising Incal shone upon, in place of
that of the previous morn? When I looked at the proud peak,
the red light of the sun showed that one full half of it had
been riven away and swallowed up in "some mysterious
cavern." Aye, truly:—

"Mountains rear to heaven their bald and blackened cliffs,
   And bow their tall heads to the plain."

Nearer by, where other ridges had been, and where the awful
reeling of the cliffs had occurred—right at my feet, indeed—
no more was any rocky spire, nor peak, nor cliff there forever!
Instead, was a great lake of steaming water, whose thither
shores were veiled by the softly settling ashes and clouds of
steam condensed by the cold air, a fine misty rain—the weeping of the stricken globe over its recent agony. Hushed, was
all the noise; quieted, the trembling; ceased, the fervid streaming of the lava.

That part of the ridge where I had lain had escaped, for
the most part, the general rending. But even it had suffered,
so that the path ahead of me, which I had been accustomed
to travel in my trips to the peak was gone, a huge block of
probably thousands of tons weight having slidden into the pit
below, making absolute erasure of the path, which had crossed
that very place. I sought another, and in climbing about in
the dull light, came to a part of the ridge which lay on the
far side from the sun, which, as yet, was not more than two
hours above the horizon. Moving in the deep shadow along
perilously narrow ledges—lakes of hot water below, impassa-
ble steps overhead—suddenly a dull red bar of light shone
athwart my course! Looking for its source, I saw that the
light streamed through a wide crack in the beetling cliff above.
The bottom of this crack was not far below me, and instead
of becoming narrowed out, had a floor as wide as any part of

the fissure, as if all above that point had been forcibly slidden, or "faulted" to one side—undoubtedly the real explanation. I lowered myself to the level of this floor, and finding the crevice sufficiently wide, stepped into it, heedless of the fact that at any moment fresh convulsions of the volcano might close the cleft and crush me as between the faces of a vise. I did think of this possibility, but Poseid-like, put aside fear by reflecting that I was trusting in Incal, who would do whatever was good for me.

The stricken cliff showed, here and there, veins of quartz with porphyritic sheaves, forming ledges running through the granite masses. Clear to the top, this narrow cleft extended, and though really some two or three feet wide, its height made it appear very narrow. As I paused, filled with delight at the idea that on both sides of me my eyes rested on virgin rock never exposed to the gaze of any man since earth began, I noticed that which set my pulses bounding with wild joy— right by my side, but a little in front, was a vein of yellow, ocherous-looking rock in which I saw many maculations of whitish, harder rock, which appearance was due to quartz bodies torn apart by the same shock which formed the cleft. These maculae were thickly dotted with nuggets of native gold, and with argent mineral. The ductility of the precious metals was exhibted in curious effects, the gold and silver being drawn out from the smoothly fractured surface into wires, which in some cases were a number of inches long. Again the faintness of hunger left me, and the pain of my aching head-wound was temporarily forgotten, as I chanted a hymn of gratitude to my God. Gone was the towering peak; destroyed was the sole route of access to the lofty summit which man's foot might traverse; but here, after the war of the subterranean fires was over—here was a greater treasure, nearer home, easier to reach—the excitement of joy was too great a strain on my nrves, already so weak, and I fainted! But youth is elastic, and the health of those who are without vices wonderfully buoyant. I soon recovered consciousness, and was wise enough to make my way home without stopping to waste further strength, knowing that my mountaineering instinct would be an infallible guide to my subsequent return.

I felt, in taking counsel of my mother, that her belief that I could not work the mine alone was based on actuality. But whom should I trust to aid me and take an honest share of the wealth so obtained as recompense?

Enough, is it not, that I found the necessary help? Certain professed friends entered into a copartnership with me, and for the privilege of retaining the remainder of the proceeds, allowed me one-third of the profits, agreeing to do this without requiring any labor from me; and, with some demur, also agreeing to my demand that no part of the ownership should be vested in anybody but myself. I caused them to sign a paper to that effect and to seal it with the most inviolable sign possible in Poseid, namely, to make their signatures with their own blood. We all three did thus. So much formality I insisted upon for the reason that the suspicion was irrepressible that these men proposed to claim that they themselves were the discoverers of the treasure, and that I had, per consequence, no right to any of it. Today I know that this was the case. I know that the proviso in the contract declaring that the whole mine which they, my partners, worked in the then current year was the inalienable property of Zailm Numinos, was all that prevented the intended robbery. This stipulation made no reference to the discoverer, as such, but did state in incontrovertible terms that in the possessor of that name was vested the title to the property. I would have had, in the event of a difference arising between us, no necessity to prove how I became owner of the mine; no claim that some person other than myself was the discoverer would avail the would-be defrauders, for whosoever was the first to find the lode, the fact remained that I was the owner, and possession in this event meant every advantage through the law. At least, so it seemed to my ignorance My associates were not so ignorant They knew that the contract was worthless because executed in violation of the law The day came when I knew all. I knew in later times that the laws of Poseid made every mine a tithe-payer to the empire, and that a mine worked without acknowledgment of this legal lien was liable to confiscation. It was apparent, also, that if my partners had not allowed themselves to be swayed by avariciousness into keeping secret the whole agreement, and also by working in the mine, thus rendering themselves participators in an infraction of the law, that they would have become the legally recognized owners, simply through furnishing information concerning my acts to the nearest governmental agent. But I did not know these things at the time, and the other two thought it discretion to keep silence, for the reason that they were not aware of anything excepting the fact that they were violating statutory enactments of no seeming importance. Thus was the secret kept for a later revealment.

The means having been forthcoming, the removal of my residence from the country to the city of the Rai was next in order. Our farewell to the old mountain home and our installment in the new one in Caiphul will be passed over in silence.

————

CHAPTER II.

Caiphul.

The Atlantean people lived under a government having the character of a limited monarchy. Its official system recognized an emperor (whose position was an elective one, and not in any sense hereditary) and his ministers, known by a name signifying "The Council of Ninety," and also known as "Princes of the Realm." All of these officers had a life-tenure in office, except in cases of malfeasance, which term was strictly defined and its punishment severely enforced; and from the operation of the law relating thereto, no exaltation of position was sufficient to secure exemption for offenders. No governmental positions were made elective, with the ex-

ception of one ecclesiastical office, and lesser positions in the
public service were made appointive in all cases, the ap-
pointees being held to strict account by the appointing power
—emperor or prince—who, for the use of this power was
responsible to the people for the conduct of his place-holders.
However, it is not the scheme of this chapter to discuss Poseid
politics, but to describe the ministerial and monarchical palaces with which the nation furnished its elected officers—one
for each prince, but for the emperor, three. In the main, the
description of one of these buildings, both within and without,
typifies that of any or all of the others, just as in the United
States of America and other modern lands a governmental
edifice is easily known to be such, by its general architectural
features. A description therefore of one palace will serve a
double purpose—that of presenting an idea of the most notable
residence in the great Atlantean empire—since I will describe
the main palace of the emperor; and, secondly, that of illustrating the prevailing style of governmental architecture in
the period during which I resided in Poseid. Imagine, if it
please thee, an elevation approximating fifteen feet in height,
ten times that figure in width, and that fifty times its height
represents its length. External to the plane dimensions, on
each of the four sides of the platform, which was of hewn
blocks of porphyry, an easy flight of steps led from the lawns
up to the top of the elevation. On the sides, these steps were
divided into fifteen sections, while on the ends the divisions
were only three, each being divided into lengths of fifty feet.
Between the two sections nearest the corners each division consisted of a deep quadrangular recess, into and around which the
stairs ran in uninterrupted continuity. The next, or third
section, was separated from those on either side by a sculp-
tured serpent of huge size, fashioned from sandstone, and as
faithful to life as art could make it. The heads of these
immobile reptiles rested on the green sward in front of the
stairs, while the bodies lay in full relief upon the staircases,
and reaching the top of the platform, wound about the massive columns which supported the pediments of the verandas

of the superstructural palace erected upon the platform described—columns which formed a most imposing peristyle
between the broad verandas and the steps. The succeeding
division was a quadrangle in the steps, and the next, another
serpent, and so around the building. It is hoped that this description is sufficiently perspicuous to give an idea of the tremendous parallelogram, encompassed with steps, guarded by
monstrous ornamental, as well as useful, serpent forms—religious emblems, signifying not alone wisdom, but also the
appearance of a fiery serpent in the skies of the ancient earth,
initiating the event of the separation of Man from God. Alter-
nating with these forms were the recesses, relieving what
would otherwise have been severely straight and wearisome
lines. Surmounting this was the first story of the palace
proper, its reptile-entwined peristyle holding aloft great veranda roofs, whereon were enormous vases holding earth to nourish all kinds of tropical plants, shrubs and many small varieties
of trees, a luxuriant garden which perfumed the air, already
cooled by numerous fountains playing in the midst. Above
the first story, with its flower-filled porticos, arose another
tier of apartments, surrounded by open galleries, the floors of
which were formed by the roofs of those beneath. The third
and highest tier of apartments had no verandas, although on
all sides it had promenades, formed by the roof of the portico
beneath. The same wild luxuriance of flowers and foliage
rendered the stories of equal attractiveness. In all, song
birds, and birds of plumage were welcome guests, uncaged,
but tame because they never received harm. Attendants with
blow-guns to project noiseless darts, quietly destroyed all pred-
atory species, as also they did those which, having neither
song powers, vivid coloring of plumage, nor the useful habits
of insectivora to commend them, were therefore undesirable.
Springing from the main roof of the palace, arose graceful
spires and towers, while the many jutting apartments, angles
and groined arches, flying buttresses, cornices and multifarious
architectural effects prevented any apparent heaviness in the
design. Around the largest of the towers there extended from

bottom to top a winding staircase, conducting to the rail enclosed space on its summit, one hundred feet above the aluminum sheathing, or roofing-plates of the palace. Agacoe palace was unique in the possession of this tower, differing thus from all other ministerial edifices. It may be explained that the tower had been erected as a memorial of the departure of a fair princess from the loving care of her imperial husband into Navazzamin—the shadowy land of departed souls—some centuries before my day. Such was the Agacoe palace. Its uppermost floor was in use as a great governmental museum; the middle was devoted to offices of the chief government officials, while the first flat was magnificently arranged and furnished for occupancy as the emperor's private residence. As not uninteresting, it may be noted that the yawning mouths of the stone serpents recently described, served as doorways (of the usual size) to certain apartments in the basement—a fact which gives an accurate idea of the enormous size of these lithic saurians. The monsters were made with an eye to artistic proportion, their bodies were of carved gray, red or yellow sandstone, their eyes of sard, carnelian, jasper or other colored silicious stone, while fangs for their yawning mouths were made from gleaming white quartz, set on each side of the entrance-way.

So much sawed and hewn stone forces the modern mind to wonder if the Atlanteans obtained the finished product through the unremitting toil of slaves—in which case we must have been a barbarous people, whose political autonomy was ever menaced by the uplifting forces of the social volcano which slavery always creates—or else we possessed peculiarly efficient stone-cutting machinery. This latter is the correct assumption for our machinery for that purpose—like an almost infinite variety of other implements for every sort of service—was our pride amongst the nations. Let me here make an assertion, not for argument, but to be understood in the light of subsequent chapters; namely, that if we as Atlanteans had not possessed this wide range of mechanical inventions and the inventive talent which gave us these triumphs, then neither would ye of this modern day have possesison of a like creative ability, nor of any of the results of such genius. It may be that thou canst not understand the connection between the two ages and races whilst conning this statement; but as thou shalt draw nearer to the close of this history, thy mind will recur to it with the fullness of comprehension.

Trusting that the effort has been successful to depict by words the appearance of Atlantean governmental edifices, let us next obtain an idea of the Caiphalian promontory, whereon was enthroned Caiphul, the Royal City, the greatest of that ancient day, within the limits of which, resided a population of two million souls, unencompassed by walled fortifications. Indeed none of the cities of that age were girt about with walls, and in this respect they differed from the cities and towns known to later historical epochs. To call my records of this Poseidic age history, is not exceeding fact, since what I relate in these pages is history derived from the astral-light records. Nevertheless, it precedes the histories handed down in manuscript, papyrus rolls and rock-inscriptions by many centuries, seeing that Poseid was no longer known in the earth when history's first pages were chronicled by the earliest historian using papyrus; nay, nor even yet earlier, when the sculptors of the obelisks of Egypt and the rock-inscribers of the temples cut pictorial histories in enduring granite. No longer known was Poseid, for it is to-day approaching nine thousand years since the waters of the ocean engulfed our fair land, and left no sign; not even so much as was left of those two cities hidden away beneath lava and ashes, and for sixteen centuries of the Christian era thought never to have had existence. Excavators dug away the scoriae from Pompeii, but from Caiphul no man can turn aside the floods of the Atlantic and reveal what no more exists, for were every day a century, it were even so nearly three months of such lengthy days since the dread fiat of GOD went forth unto the waters:

"Cover the land, so that the all-beholding sun shall see it no no more in all his course."

And it was so.

In preceding pages the promontory of Caiphul was described as reaching out into the ocean from the Caiphalian plain, and as visible from a great distance at night because of the glow of light from the capital. For three hundred miles westward from Numea the peninsula projected outwards from the plain, averaging almost to its extreme cape a breadth of fifty miles, and rising much like the chalk-cliffs of England, directly from the ocean to a height of nearly one hundred feet to reach a plain almost floor-like in its evenness. On the point of this great peninsula was Caiphul, or "Atlan, Queen of the Wave." Beautiful, peaceful, with its wide-spreading gardens of tropical loveliness;—

"Where a leaf never fades in the still, blooming bowers,
    And the bee banquets on thro' a whole year of flowers"—
its broad evenues shaded by great trees; its artificial hills—the largest surmounted by governmental palaces, and pierced and terraced by the avenues which radiated from the city-center like spokes in a wheel. Fifty miles these ran in one direction, while at right angles from them, traversing the breadth of the peninsula, forty miles in length, were the shortest avenues. Thus lay, like a splendid dream, this, the proudest city of that ancient world.

At no point did Caiphul approach the ocean nearer than five miles. Though it had no walls, around the whole city extended a huge moat, three-quarters of a mile broad by an average of sixty feet in depth, and supplied by the waters of the Atlantic. On the north side, a great canal entered the moat, a canal in which the outflowing waters of a large river, the Nomis, created an outgoing current of considerable swiftness. A current was thus naturally made to cause suction through the entire circle of the moat, of which the ocean supply entered at an ingress on the south side. In this manner efflux into the sea of all the drainage of the artificial circular island on which stood the city was allowed. Immense pumping engines forced fresh ocean-water through large stone pipes and conduits all over the city, flushing the drains, furnishing motive power for all requisite purposes; for electric

lighting and electric services of vast variety—but enough.
Electric service? Electric power? Indeed we had deepest
knowledge of this motor-force of the universe; we used it in
countless ways which have yet to be re-discovered in this
modern world of ours, and ways, too, which are every day
coming more and more into recollection as men and women of
that past age reincarnate in this.

It is not strange that thou art incredulous, my friend, when
I speak of these inventions which thou hast considered the
special property of to-day; but I speak from a knowledge
born of experience, seeing that I lived then, and live now;
lived not only in Poseid twelve thousands years ago, but
also in the United States of America, before, during and after
the War of the Secession.

We drew our electrical energies partly from the waves
beating the ocean shores, more largely from the rise and fall
of the tides; from mountain torrents and from chemicals; but
chiefly from what might aptly be termed the "Night-Side of
Nature." High-grade explosives were known to us, but our
employment of them was of much wider range than thine. If
thou couldst cause these substances to gradually yield up
their vast imprisoned force without fear of an explosion,
thinkest thou that thy machinery would long be propelled by
clumsy, because ponderous, steam or electric engines? If
a great steamship could dispense with its coal-bins and boil-
ers, and instead have dynamite in an absolutely safe compound
form yielding, from what a man could carry in a hand-bag,
force sufficient to drive the ship from England to America; or
to send a train six thousand miles, how long wouldst thou
see steam enginery? Yet this was a power, and a least valued
one at that, which we—possibly you, certainly I—knew in the
Atlantean life. It will be again with thee, because Our Race
is coming again from devachan to earth.

But not alone this resource of power was ours—indeed it
was to our forces of the Night-Side as an alcohol-vapor motor
is to thy steam-engines. The Night-Side forces—what are
they? At this place I will answer only by a counter-question,

namely; The force of Nature, of gravitation, of the sun, of light, whence is it? If thou wilt answer me "It is of God"— so then will I make answer that, likewise, Man is the Heir of the Father, and whatsoever is His, is also the Son's. If Incai is impelled by God, the Son shall find how his Father doeth this thing, and shall presently do likewise again, even as Man did so once in Poseid. But greater things than these which we did might ye do; ye are now, ye are then; ye are Poseid returned, and on a higher plane!

The original object for which the great moat encircling the capital was excavated had, since long centuries, been fulfilled. That purpose was purely maritime, in the days when ships had been used as carriers, before the later general use of aerial vessels; and it had served this purpose in such stead as to win for Caiphul its proud title "Sovereign of the Seas," name retained even when the original uses of its moat had become a matter of history. When the better means of transportation had supplanted the old, then the ships which for ten centuries had graced all the seas and waterways of the globe, had been suffered to decay, or had been converted to other uses. Only a few sails now roved the waters, and those were merely pleasure craft belonging to novelty-loving people of leisure, who thus indulged their taste for sport.

This radical change was, however, no reason why the masonry quays of the one hundred and forty miles, more or less, of the moat, should be allowed to go to destruction. This would have entailed the loss of valuable property, through the encroachment of the unchecked waters, as well as the deterioration of the sanitary system of the city; besides which such a course would have destroyed the beauty of the moat and its environments. Therefore, in all of the seven centuries since we ceased to employ marine transportation, no sign of weakness had been suffered to menace this great length of masonry.

A marked feature of Caiphul was the wealth and rare beauty of its trees and tropical shrubbery, lining the avenues, covering the multitudinous palace-crowned hills, many of which had been constructed to rise two, or even three hundred feet above the level of the plain. Trees and shrubs and plants, vines and flowers, annuals and perennials, filled the mimic canyons, gorges, defiles and levels which it had delighted the art-loving Poseidi to create. They covered the slopes, twined the miniature cliffs, the walls of buildings, and hid even the greater part of the steps which led in wide-sweeping banks to the edges of the moat—overlaying everything like a glorious verdant garment.

Perhaps the reader is beginning to wonder where all the people lived. Truly the query is well-timed, and the answer will, I trust, prove interesting.

In the work of altering the configuration of the surface of the great promontory from that of a plain to the more beautiful variations of hills and their intervening depressions, the scheme pursued had been to make keyed-shells of rock, of enormous strength, in the form of terraces, and leaving arched passages wherever the avenues intersected such elevations, to fill in the interiors then remaining with a concrete of clay, rubble and cement carefully tamped. The exteriors were thereafter covered with rich soil on the levels, and terraced for the support of vegetable life of all kinds. These elevations covered many square miles of the level once existent, leaving little that remained as plane-surface, except the avenues, and not all of these, inasmuch as quite a number of the thoroughfares ascended the rise between the hills, or followed the ascending bed of some canyon until they reached the ridge at the head of the latter. They then penetrated the divide and debouched upon the opposite side through an arched way, wherein tubes of crystal, absolutely exhausted of air, gave a continuous light derived from the "Night-Side" forces. The vertical faces and inclinations of the terraces, as well as the sides of the canyons, were made into rooms of varied and ample size. The entrances to these, and to the windows, were concealed under mimic ledges of rock, over which clambered vines and rock-loving plants, thus removing from view the stiff ungainliness of the metallic casings underneath. These apartments were arranged in artistic suites for the accommodation of families. The metal sheathing with which they were lined prevented moisture within, while their position under the surface insured an even degree of temperature at all seasons of the year. As these residences were designed and built by the government, the ownership was vested in the same power, and the tenants acquired leasehold from the Minister of Public Buildings. The rental was merely nominal and only sufficient to keep the property in repair, furnish the expenses of the incandescent lighting and heating service, the water supply, and the salaries of the necessary officials to attend to these duties. All of this cost not above ten or fifteen per cent of an ordinarily skilled mechanic's wages. The mention of so much detail may be pardoned, for were it omitted, only a vague and unsatisfactory conception of life in this antediluvian age would be acquired by the reader.

The great charm of these residences lay in the fact of their retired situations, which prevented the dismal appearance of masses of angular houses—an effect of extreme ugliness seen in our modern days, but seldom, or never, in our Atlantean cities. The result of this arrangement was, that to a beholder, looking from any high elevation, the city would have been conspicuous, to one accustomed to the modern atrocities of stone, brick or wood, chiefly for the absence of sky-piercing piles separated by narrow, dark, treeless and too-often filthy tunnels, miscalled streets. Here a hill, and there another and yet another, until the eye counted them by scores—there were one hundred and nineteen in all—here a lake, or there a cliff with a lake, or wooded park at its foot; gorges of mimic grandeur, little forests, so regularly irregular; cascades and tumbling torrents, fed from the exhaustless supply of fresh water belonging to the city, their banks and shores covered with those plants, trees and shrubs that love contiguity to abundant water. Such, dear friends, would have been the scene presented to thine eyes, couldst thou have gazed on Caiphul with me; perchance thou didst. And yet, Caiphul was not devoid of houses built much after the modern fashion, for the city franchise to build neat mansions here and there in situations

and styles calculated to add to the beauty of the scene, was
a privilege of which any one of means might avail himself,
under official approval. Many did so. Museums of art, edifices for histrionic entertainment and other structures not
designed for habitation were also in tasteful numbers.

I found, in going about the city, that the avenues, in certain
instances, seemed to come to an abrupt termination in some
grotto, whose interior was usually hung with stalactites pendent
from the roof. Perhaps a slight turn occurred from the
straight course, and thus prevented one from seeing through
the grotto. In these places, shaded, high-tension, airless cylinder lamps cast a soft glow throughout the interior, making
a moonlight effect very pleasing to one who came in from the
brightness of the sunlight.

While, in the majority of cases, our people were accomplished
equestrians, this mode of travel was not used except for physical culture and grace, electric transit being provided by the
government. Indeed, the social reformers of these days of
the Christian nineteenth century would have been in their
ideal land had they been Caiphalians, and this because the
government pursued the paternalistic principle so systemati-
cally as to have vested in itself the ownership of all the land,
all methods of public transit and communication, all manufac-
tories—in a word, all property. The system was a most
beneficent one, which no Poseid wanted to see disused, or
supplemented by any other. Did a citizen desire a vailx
(airship) for any use, he applied to the proper officials, who
were on duty at numerous vailx-yards throughout the realm.
Or, to cultivate the land, he applied to the Department of Soils
and Tillage. Perhaps it was desired to manufacture some
product; the machinery was for lease at the nominal rate necessary to meet working expenses and the salary of the officers
overseeing that portion of the public property. Let these sam-
ples suffice. Enough, that no political harmony exists in this
modern time of the world like that which sprung from this
paternalism on the part of our elected officials. Governmental

is a thing regarded with jealousy and semi-alarm
publics. But it is to-day a different quality from
what it was then. Ours was a paternalism closely watched and
duly checked by the suffragists of the nation, and its life was
essentially exponent of true socialistic principles.

I have not even now been so precise in details as to explain
many of the most peculiar adjustments maintained between
the political parent and its children; nor between labor and
capital. But neither can I do so in these pages with any
degree of propriety, because this is not a plea for re-adoption,
in this age of the world, of methods pursued in that remote
period. Yet, this much I can say, not inappropriately at this
juncture—that Poseid had not in my day, the modern, yet also
very ancient, annoyance of labor strikes, blocking capital and
enterprise, starving the artisan, and causing more suffering
on the part of the poor than such annoyances can ever bring
to the doors of the rich. The secret of this immunity was not
far to seek; in a nation whose government was the voice of
those people who possessed sufficient education to wield the
power of franchise; and this, too, regardless of sex, because
inborn in our national life was this principle—"An educational
measuring-rod for every voter; the sex of the suffragist is
immaterial." In such a nation, and under such a government,
it were strange indeed if industrial inharmonies could long
disturb social polity. The broad principle of equity between
employer and employee governed in Poseid; it mattered not
what a person did for another person, but the whole equation
hinged on this question: Was some service performed by one
person for another? If so, the fact that the service was or
was not accomplished by physical labor, counted for nothing.
It might be equally a service deserving compensation whether
it was a physical or a purely intellectual service; nor was it
held to be important whether the employer represented one
or more individuals, or the employee one or more people.

Our local enactments on the subject of industrial equity were
complete, and rather voluminous. While I care not to give
in detail a reproduction of what may be termed labor laws, a

few excerpts are worthy of place. It will be well to preface these with a short history of their enactment, and thus show how, in that olden time, labor troubles quite similar, and fully as menacing to peace and order as any modern industrial upheaval, were finally and equitably settled.

On the "Maxin-Stone"—to which legal code reference in full is made in the proper place—was found this vital seed of settlement of the fearful menace embroiling labor and capital, to-wit:

"What time those who work for hire shall be oppressed, and shall rise in wrath to destroy their oppressor—lo! let their hand be stayed, that they shall obey Me. I say unto them, harm not the person or the property of any man, not even though by that man they be oppressed. For are not all brothers and sisters? Are not all children of one Father, even the nameless Creator? But this I command:—That they destroy oppression. Shall things, which are less than man, rule over and oppress their masters? Seek diligently my meaning."

The students of ethics interpreted this command to mean that the oppressed industrial classes should not harm the oppressing capitalists, nor their property. The rich classes were perhaps as much victims of circumstances as the poorer people; the remedy lay, not in blind anarchy, but in eradicating conditions. This was easy, if properly attempted. The oppressed were as a thousand to one of the oppressor. The majority of them held the elective franchise, and it was determined that as the government was the people's servant, the proper method was to deal with the question at the polls, and not to employ violence against the rich. Therefore the call went forth amongst all the people to vote on the adoption of a code of industrial regulations, and to vote its respectful submission to the Raj. Of the many articles and sections, I shall insert only those that are pertinent to modern times and troubles, so that if these selections are not articled and sectioned in consecution, the reason is obvious.

EXCERPTS FROM THE POSEID LABOR LAWS.

"No employer shall demand of any employee any service outside of legal hours of work without extra remuneration."

"Sec. 4. These hours shall not be less, nor more than nine in number, for physical labor in any period of twenty-four hours; nor less nor more than eight hours for sedentary employments chiefly requiring intellectual exertion."

This statute allowed the two parties to a labor-contract to arrange to suit themselves when the working hours were to begin or end, with reference to the first hour of the day, namely, the modern noon hour. In regard to wage matters, the law was very clear. It held that as mankind was selfish by nature—that is, the lower nature—that he would operate on a basis of self-aggrandizement, the modern doctrine of "laissez-nous faire." Hence if he should not be actuated by the sense of duty to his fellow-man to treat that man right, when right was not dictated by might, then the law must compel him to be fair. It is in this that the modern Anglo-Saxon world, which is Poseid (and Suern) reincarnating, shows one mark of the slow but sure upward progress begotten of time; proves that although man moves, as does all else, sensate and insensate, in a circle, yet that circles is like a screw-thread, ever progressing around and around, but each time moving on a higher plane. Poseid must be compelled by its advanced minds to do what is fair towards the weak. America and Europe are growing willing to do rightly, fairly, because it is the part of duty. Thus we behold modern employers often doing of free-will what the ancient Poseid did because of law, namely, sharing profits with their employees.

The law then having gone to the lawmakers—the suffragists—decreed that the government should establish a Department of Commissary, the duties of which should be to collect all statistics concerning the food products of commerce; also concerning all textile fabrics necessary for clothing, and in brief, all articles necessary for the proper social maintenance of individuals. On these statistical reports was to be founded an estimate of the cost of all such necessaries, amongst which books were reckoned as mental food, and the cost of these things for a year was calculated. Upon this calculation, day's wages were estimated by dividing the annual cost into the number of days. This rate was decided anew every ninety days, as the cost of the chief staples was found to fluctuate, hence the rate was not wholly stable, and the wages of any given three months' term might probably differ from those of any previous quarter.

Let me quote:

"Sec. VII, Art. V. Employers shall divide the gross profits of business operations upon the following plan: The wage, salary or emolument of each employee shall be paid in the sum directed by the quarterly estimate of living cost determined by the Department of Commissary. From the remainder, the amount of six parts in each hundred on the capital invested shall be set aside. This increment shall be and represent the employer's net profits. From the remaining income the running expenses shall be deducted, and of any sum thereafter remaining, one-half shall be invested to provide annuities for sick or disabled, or assurance for the dependents of deceased employees. The remaining half shall be periodically distributed amongst the employees on the basis of their various compensations.

"Sec. VIII, Art. V. The whole of a body of employees is only equal to the Superintendent thereof. The Superintendent is equal to all the underlings. Hence, employers, when not themselves managers of the business, shall pay to managers a salary equal to the combined wages of the subordinates."

Truly, these labor laws and other matters have a modern sound. But civiliation in all ages, among all nations, is wont to express itself in ways which, if modern language be used to describe them, will seem almost identical; so that in ancient Atl. and in modern America the term "strike" may be properly used to designate a labor revolt; the same principle characteries all other phases; for from age to age the world makes but slow progress, and is to-day not as far advanced in its present sub-cycle, nor as civilized, as it was in olden Poseid. This may seem a hard saying, but it will presently be understood.

Such in the main, were the chief features of the industrial world in Poseid. The old-time strikes and riots out of which these laws were born disappeared and peace took its sway. The change was beneficent, indeed, yet always the strong looked to see how they might evade the law, and though they did not succeed to a harmful extent, still the wish on their part entered the sum of karma. So when the modern world of the Christian epoch came to the eighteenth and nineteenth centuries, particularly the last named, then began the reincarnation of this Poseid era, and for a time the tendency to oppression again came uppermost. But overriding this tendency now faintly appears the willingness to do right for the sake of right, which, as applied to industrial matters, has of very, very recent years been manifested—a sign of the evening after-glow of the last day, now near striking its last hour, telling of a spent age. I particularly refer to the greater willingness of man to treat his fellow rightly, without being forced thereto by legal enactments. Trutly, it is, as yet, only done because it is found to pay; but it would never have been found to pay if the reincarnated right-wardness had not induced experiments in profit-sharing to be made, in hopes of exterminating the strike iniquity, and with the idea of harmonizing society to be active in doing as it would be done by. Finally, strange and paradoxical as it may appear, this betterment is the direct child of the old-time rights extorted by might in Poseid, and to-day, reincarnated off-spring of reincarnated oppression, as in Atlantis oppression sprang reincarnate from the grave of other ages gone before, previous to the wondrous memorial of Gizeh. But to more than mention this here would be to trench upon work given unto another by the Messiah; therefore only a hint can I give now, but more later. Suffice it then, that those were ages when man was struggling, with scarcely perceptible upward motion, from our fallen ancestry. Glory be to our Father that His children surely, if slowly, are by devious ways climbing His heights; many are their fails, but they shall rise again, not suffering the enemy to triumph.

It may be a seemingly inopportune intrusion, but I must here briefly describe the electro-odic transit system of Caiphul, and the other cities, towns and villages scattered throughout the empire and its colonies. The description is of the local transit-carriages only. On each side of every avenue was a broad tessellated pavement for pedestrians. A line of massive, bottomless stone vases in which throve ornamental shrubs and foliage plants stood upon the curb, and on either side of these was a metal rail, placed at a height of about nine feet, and supported upon davits similar to those from which ship-boats are swung. At regular distances other rails crossed these main runners, rails capable of being raised or lowered to form a switch-junction—a simple lever effecting this process. These rails served as cross streets, there being in comparatively few instances any paved street underneath the rails on any but the great radiate avenues. On the maps of the City Department of Transit these main and cross rails looked like the web of a garden spider. For each transit-district there were multitudes of carriages, having aut-odic mechanism, whereby they were made to speed at tremendous swiftness with their passengers; but collisions could not occur, as the conveying rods formed a double-track system. —————

CHAPTER III.

FAITH IS KNOWLEDGE ALSO, AND IT GIVETH TO REMOVING MOUNTAINS.

There is a saying, whose origin is dim through lapse of time, to the effect that "Knowledge is power." Within well defined limits this is a verity. If behind the knowledge lies the requisite energy to realize its benefits, then only is it a true saying.

In order to exercise command over nature and her forces, the would-be operator must have perfect comprehension of the natural laws involved. It is the degree of attainment in this knowledge which marks the less or greater ability of the performer, and those who have acquired the profoundest understanding of the Law (Lex Magnum) are masters whose powers seem so marvellous as to be magical. Uninitiated minds are absolutely alarmed by their incomprehensible manifestations. On every side of me when I came from my mountain home to my metropolitan abode, I found inexplicable wonders, but natural dignity saved me from appearing ignorant. Little by little was I to acquire familiarity with my environment, and thereby gain a knowledge of the things which have been referred to since I first mentioned the exchange of country life for urban surroundings. But these attainments of pleasing authority over nature demanded a special course. That course of study had not yet been determined upon by me, prior to my introduction to the city, for it seemed that the part of wisdom was to concentrate my energies upon specialties, and not to scatter force by attempting generalities. To this end I determined to live for a more or less extended period without seeking admission to the Xioquithlon, and resolved to devote the interim to observation. I had been an extensive reader of books, which I obtained from the public library in the district where my mountain home had been. From these I had gained no inconsiderable understanding of social polity. The fact that there were but ninety-one elective offices in the gift of the people, while there were almost three hundred millions of Poseidi in Atl and her colonies, and according to a late census which I had seen, thirty-seven—nearly thirty-eight millions of electors held First Degree diplomas, thus entitling them to hold elective offices—disposed me to think it extremely improbable that such a high preferment would ever fall to my lot. But if I could scarcely expect a ministerial office, I yet felt that I might, if I fitted myself therefor by gaining a prime diploma, attain to a high political level and hold an appointive position, and some of these were almost equally as honorable as a councillorship. What special subjects should I concentrate upon? Geological research was very attractive to me, and by its numerous branches offered wide and alluring fields of opportunity. Then again, philology was almost as much so; my ability to acquire foreign languages was not inconsiderable, as I had found from studying a little volume descriptive of a land known as Suernis, a strange country, and of the language of which many examples were given; these I had without effort learned perfectly from once reading.

Several months of city residence at length found me determined to acquire all the geological knowledge that I could, for it was a study which I believed Incol had directed me to make, as also a knowledge of mines and of practical mineralogy. As co-efficients I purposed to thoroughly ground myself in synthetic and analytical literature, not alone of my native Poseid, but also that of the Suerni and Necropanic languages. Thus have I named the three greatest nations of pre-Noachian (pre-Nepthian) times. One of these nations was effaced from the earth, but the other two have, after terrible vicissitudes, survived till today; of them I will speak later.

The reasons which induced me to choose the curriculum which I have menetioned were, that as a geologist and coordinate scientist I hoped to make new discoveries of value, and to place them in book form before the world—at least before the Poseid peoples, who esteemed themselves most of the world—an end scarcely to be attained otherwise than by this course of study. The influence which I hoped to gain through such publications, might lead to my becoming Superintendent-General of Mines—a political place not second to any other appointive office. There certainly would be other studies required of me if I entered the race for a prime diploma, but the ones cited were the most agreeable, and would constitute my chief aspiration. As an aside, I may remark that those studies then selected, and afterwards mastered, led my nature to assume a bent which resulted, not many years ago, in my be-

ine-owner in the State of California—and a suc-
oo. It so much more firmly fixed my linguistic
leanings that, while a citizen of the United States of America,
I was a master not alone of my native tongue, but also of
thirteen other modern languages, such as French, German and
Spanish, Chinese, several dialectal varieties of Hindostanee,
and Sanskrit as a sort of mental relaxation. Please not to
regard this confession as due to boastfulness; it is not. I
but make it in order to show thee, my friend, that thine own
powers are not matters of heritage only, but re-collected ac-
quirements from some one, or it may be of all of thy past lives;
also to give thee a hint of profit,—to-wit:—that studies to-day
undertaken, no matter how near to the evening of thy days,
will surely bear fruit, not alone in they present earth-
life, but in the experiences of subsequent incarnations
also. We see with all we have seen, we do with all we have
done, and we think with all we have thought. **Verbum sat
sapienti.**

In the next chapter I purpose devoting some pages to a
consideration of physical science, as understood by the Poseidi;
more especially will I refer to the prime principles upon which
it was based, inasmuch as neglect to do this would necessitate
the taking of many statements **ex cathedra** which otherwise
might be clearly understood at the moment.

—————

CHAPTER IV.

"AXTE INCAL, AXTUCE MUN."

In their consideration of natural laws the philosophers of
Poseid had come to the conclusive hypothesis and working
theory that the material universe was not a complex entity,
but in its primality extremely simple. The glorious truth,
"Incal malixetho," was clear to them, that is, that "Incal
(God) is immanent in Nature." To this they appended,—
"Axte Incal, axtuce mun,"—"To know God is to know all

worlds whatever.'' After centuries of experimentations, re-
cording of phenomena, deductions, analysing and synthetizing,
these students had arrived at the final proposition that the
universe—not here dwelling on their wondrous astronomical
knowledge—was, with all its varied phenomena, created and
continuously kept in operation by two primal force-principles.
Briefly stated, these basic facts were that matter and dynamic
energy (which were Incal made externally manifest) could
readily account for all things else. This conception held that
only One Substance existed, and but One Energy, the one being
Incal externalized, and the other His Life in action in His
Body.* This One Substance assumed many forms under the
action of variant degrees of dynamic force. Because it was
the basic principle of all natural, and all psychic, but not of
spiritual phenomena, allow here a postulate with which not
a few of my friends will find themselves at least partially familiar, perhaps wholly so. Commencing with dynamic energy as
first sensibly manifest in the example furnished by simple
vibration, the Poseid position may be outlined as follows: A
very low rate of vibration may be felt; an increase of rate
heard. For example, first we feel the pulsing of a harp-string,
and then if the rate of vibration be increased we hear its
sound. But substances of other sorts, able to endure greater
vibratory impulses, manifest under more intense action—following sound, first heat, then light. Now again, light varies in
color. The first color produced is red, and thence, by a constantly augmentation vibratile energy, orange, yellow, green
blue, indigo, violet—each spectrumband being due to an exact
and definite increase in the number of the vibrations. Succeeding the violet, further augmentation gives pure white, more
gives a gray, then more extinguishes light, replacing it with

*NOTE—As, in its outgoing impulse the Created draws away from
the Creator, it looks back to its origin and notes its progression-marks;
that is, its multiplied realizations of its increasing separation from its
Source. The greater this separateness, the greater the field (Matter)
wherein these points appear, because the divine element in the Created
has noted more points, or, in other words, more things, more material
objects, as being between it and its source. Only when we look back at
these things we have sensed, these thought-forms of God, do we perceive
matter, for when we look forward to reunion with Him, matter disappears,
giving place to Spirit.

electricity, and so on through an ever increasing voltage until the realm of vital or psychic-force is attained. This may truly be regarded as going inward from those manifestations of nature, of Incal or God, or the Creator, which are external; as going toward the internal from externality. A very brief study will show thee that the laws of the physical world continue inward to their spiritual source; that they are, truly, but prolongations the one of the other. But, ere entering into the realm of vibration, whose doorkeeper is sound, we find that the One Substance vibrates in viriant, but definite dynamic degree, and that thence arise each and all of the diverse forms of matter; in short, the difference between any given substances, as gold and silver, iron and lead, sugar and sand, is not one of matter, but of dynamic degree solely. Do I weary thee, my friend? Bear yet a little longer, I pray thee, for it is an important matter. In this dynamic affection the degree is no loose limitation, for if the vibratile rate be a shade variant— lower or higher than in any special material which may be under notice—the variation will be different in appearance and in its chemical nature; thus to proper substantial entities definite if enormous vibration per second may be imparted. and the resulting substance (for light is substantial) is, say. red light,* but if one-eighth greater it will be orange, and if more or less, then the resultant must inevitably be a reddish orange, or a yellowish, respectively. It thus appears that certain definite degrees exist as plainly as mile-posts, and that these major degrees are absolute. In other words, the One Substance is not as readily kept between these greater definitions as upon them—a fact which explains the tendency of composites, or intermediate affections, to decompose into the

---

*NOTE.—Red-light is stated to occur at 395,000,000,000,000 vibrations of that "ether" which by Phylos is termed the last form of matter below where matter ceases and mind begins. And the highest visible light vibration is placed at 790,000,000,000,000. So says science. But Phylos says: "Vastly higher than the high purple range where light ceases ordinarily to be visible, the One Substance again vibrates visibly. As a synchronous harp-string that responds to key of low C, for example, struck on another harp, will also respond to every C in the whole register, be it low, or middle, or high, so the One Substance responds at 831,000,-000,000,000; at, again, the next octave of vibration, and again at the next. where it becomes visible as the fatal Unfed Light, called in Atla the "Maxin," and again, by the Tchin as the "Vis Mortuus."

difinite or simple elements; chemical compounds are not as
stable as chemical primaries. The modern "wave theory,"
that sound, heat, light and correlatives are but forms of force
is only half correct; they are this, but they are more also.
They are, in brief, affections of the One Substance by specific
degrees of the One Energy, and except that the rate of this
affection is vastly greater in the case of electricity than in that
of lead or gold, there is no difference between these widely
diverse appearing things. This is the energy by the Rosicrucians named "Fire," that which gives entrance to that
mysterious realm of nature penetrated only by the adept,
thaumaturgist, magician. Call these students at whose will
all nature bends obedient, by whatever name best pleases thee,
only bearing ever in mind that the real Magian never speaks
of self or works, and is not known by his fellows to be what he
is, save an accident hath revealed the secret. To this membership belonged He at whose command the winds and the waves
were stayed on tempestuous Galilee. But He spoke not of
Himself. Of that sublime brotherhood I will relate much ere
long. No better proof is needed that all the variant manifesti-
tions are but variants of the odic force, the Rosicrucian "Fire,"
than this:—offer resistance to an electric current, thereby reducing or diverting it against an opposing force—and thou
hast light; oppose to this (arc) light a combustable obstruction,
and flame results. So mightest thou go on to the discovery
soon to be made by the world of science, that light, all light,
of the sun, or from any source, can be made to yield sound;
upon this discovery hinge some of the most astounding inventions that thine age hath even dreamed of in its visions. But
the primal discovery in this wonderful link, first of the sequence
will be the greatest of all, and so heralded. And this will be
warranted, for the fact that it will be but a reincarnate unfoldment will not diminish its importance to mankind, nor the
credit of its re-discoverer. In brief, the truths of our Father's
Kingdom are eternal; have ever been, will ever be existent,
and only the discoverers themselves will be new to the fact.
The fact not being a new one in itself, nor new even to the

world, but only to this age of it. Poseid knew that light gives
out sound when correctly resisted. It knew that magnetism
gives rise to electricity in the same manner, and for the same
reason. Thus, the load-stone exhibits magnetism; revolve it
in the field of a dynamo, and so cut the current and pile it
upon itself, so to speak, and electricity develops. So, resist
this and light appears; this, and heat comes; again resisted
properly, and sound results, then next energy appears as
pulsing motion. But these various processes may be "short-
circuited" and all of the intermediate phenomena cut out.

Have I been wearisome in this discourse? If so, and I
suspect that I have, the reward is at hand.

The Poseidi found that in the realm beyond magnetism were
yet other forces, superior and more intense of pulsation, forces
operated by the mind. And Mind is of our Father, and is
the constantly creating source of all things whatsoever. Were
the perpetual **Vis a tergo** of divine creation to cease for one
instant, in that instant the Universe would cease to exist.
Now wilt thou see the sublime beauty of the Altan postulate not
long since repeated: "Incal malixetho. Axte Incal, axtuce
mun." For down from His heights, marking the descent by
"forcefalls" as a river marks declivities in its bed by cata-
racts, comes this supreme power; comes far, oh! very far
adown its course to the cascades of magnetism, electricity, light,
heat, sound, motion—and far off where the bed of this Divine
stream becomes nearly level, exhibits those little ripples of
material differentiation which thou termest chemical elements,
insisting on there being sixty-three, when there is but One:

From this knowledge came all the wondrous triumps of that
old age, and one by one they are emerging to-day after their
long oblivion, till to-morrow they shall awake in crowds, and
press to re-discovery by threes and fours, and then by platoons
and companies and legions, till all the treasures of Poseid shall
be again on earth, in air, and sea. O, bright to-morrow of time,
and fortunate thou who shalt open thine eyes upon it and its
marvels: And yet, although so fortunate, still shalt thou
find it well behooves thee to temper all things by the spirit, and

not to let the march of physical discovery outstrip the advance
of the soul. O, sad shall be found any day wherein man ap-
proacheth the arcane treasury of his Father from the side of
the blind physical eye; for if by this the whole world shall
be gained, what shall it profit if it lose the soul?

Having thus acquired insight into a new realm, if it be
new to thee, let me ask, and answer thou me: How explainest
thou these two great phenomena, heat and light? They are
not easy to explain; cold and darkness are not merely the absence of heat and light.

Having given the basis thereof, now will I show a new philosophy:

I have said that the Atlans recognized Nature in its entirety
to be Deity externalized. Their philosophy asserted that force
moved, not in straight lines, but in circles, that is, so as
always to return into itself. If the dynamism operating the
universe acts in circular progression, it follows that an infinity
of increase in vibration possible to the One Substance would
be an untenable concept. There must be a point in the circle
where extremes meet and run the round again—and this we
find between cathodicity and magnetism. As vibration brought
substance into the realm of light, it must carry it out. It does
so. It conveys it into what the Poseidi termed "Navaz, the
Night-Side of Nature," where duality becomes manifest—cold
opposing heat, darkness light, and where positive polarity
opposes negative—all things antipodal.   Cold is as much a
substantial entity as heat, and darkness as light.   There is a
prism of seven colors in each white ray of light; there is also
a septuple prism of black entities in the blackest gloom—the
night is as pregnant as the day.

The Poseid investigator thus became cognizant of wondrous
forces of nature which he might bend to the uses of mankind.
The secret was out, the discovery being that attraction of
gravitation—the law of weight—had, set over against it the
"repulsion by levitation;" that the first belonging to the Light-
Side of Nature, and the second to Navaz—the Night-Side; that
vibration governed the darkness and the cold. Thus Posied,

like Job of old, knew the path to the house of darkness, and the treasures of the hail (cold). Through this wisdom Atlantis found it possible to adjust weight (positiveness) to lack of weight (negativeness) so evenly that no "tug of war" was manifest. This achievement meant much. It meant aerial navigation without wings or unwieldly gas-reservoirs, through taking advantage of repulsion by levitation opposed in over-matching strength to the attraction of gravitation. That vi-bration of the One Substance governed and (composed) all realms was a discovery which solved the problem of the con-veyance of images of light—pictures of forms—as well as of sound and heat, just as the telephone thou knowest so well conveys images of sound, only in Poseid no wires or other sensible material connection was required in the use, at what-ever distance, of either telephones or telephotes; nor even in caloriveyance, that is, heat-conduction.

To digress a little, it is to the employment of these and the higher forces of the night-side that seemingly magic feats of occult adepts, from the Man of Nazareth down to the least Yogi, are indebted for their possibility. •

And now, let me close this chapter by saying that when modern science shall have seen its way to the acceptance of the Poseidonic knowledge herein outlined, physical nature will no longer posses any hidden recess, any penetralia, for the scientific investigator. Not earth, air, the depth of the seas nor those of interstellar space will hold secrets from that man who approaches from the God-ward side, as did Poseid. I do not say that Atl knew the very all; it knew more than this day has yet uncovered, but not all. Yet, the search commenced then by them might be continued now by thee, for America, my people, thou wert of Atlantis Of either I can sing, "My country, 'tis of thee."

CHAPTER V.

LIFE IN CAIPHUL.

The new life presented very many novelties to my mother and myself, coming into the midst of urban environments from the mountains, as we had so recently done.

After learning more about its conveniences, I very readily harmonized myself with the new requirements. My attire I altered to suit the city styles, while my bearing being reserved, I was enabled to appear at ease, an appearance supported in continually increasing degree by the fact that I steadily gained in self-command.

The indoor life of a student, when I had enrolled myself for attendance at the Xioquithlon, proved so enervating to one accustomed to unhampered freedom, that I found myself obliged to follow some scheme which would afford me needed exercise.

After some thought, together with fortuitous information which I gained, I went to the District Superintendent of the Department of Soils and Tillage, and requested that official to show me some piece of land which I might cultivate, not necessarily for profit, but for exercise, telling him that I was a student.

The Superintendent, with official indifference, laid before me a platted map of the lands adjacent to Caiphul.

In speaking of distances I have consulted the probable convenience of my readers, and used feet, yards, miles, and so on, as nominal quantities. I refer to this now, remembering that our system of measurements was founded on a principle similar to the modern Gallic or metric system. But its unit was not the ten-millionth part of the terrestrial quadrant. Instead, it originated from the great Rai of the Maxin Laws. As previously remarked, this monarch had introduced all conceivable reforms, and among others was this of replacing with a uniform system of measurements the clumsier, though not wholly unscientific method previously in use. The circumference of the earth at the equator, as determined by astronomers, had served as a basis, just as the modern metric system of a fraction of the quadrature of the earth's north and south polar division does today. But this standard was not regarded with unfailing confidence; it was feared some error had crept into the original calculation, and while if it had, the rod of gold used as a register would have served all purposes, being unchangeable, still such is the human wish to be as perfect as possible, that, as I have said, the fear of an error annihilated confidence. Every man who chose to do so, set up a private standard, based on any scheme which suited himself, a condition of things which led to deplorable fraud throughout the empire.

The Rai of the Maxin instituted a system so admirable that it was immediately accepted as absolute authority, more especially as no man doubted that it came from Incal.

The Rai had a vessel constructed of material which underwent the smallest known contraction or expansion under the influence of cold or heat. This vessel was interiorly a perfect hollow cube, of the exact size of the Maxin-Stone. A massive tube was also made of the same substance, some four inches in interior diameter. Into the cubic vessel was poured precisely enough distilled water, of a temperature of 39 degrees Fahr., to fill it, and leave no bubble of air within the hollow. This water was then drawn off through a faucet into the tubular vessel, the same low temperature being carefully maintained. The exact height of the water was then graven on a rod of the same metal of which the vessels were made. The next step was to heat the water to 211.95 degrees Fahr., both this and the other process being performed at the sea-level on a uniform summer day. Under the heat, the water expanded in an appreciable degree, and the almost boiling point was marked as in the other instance, and the difference on the rod between the two graven lines was made the unit of lineal measurement, from which all other measures were derived—that of weight being the weight of the hollow cube full of water at 39 degrees --|-- Fahr. I use the Fahrenheit thermometrical scale because to thee our Poseid scale would be meaningless.

Pardon this digression, since it reveals another of the phases of life in that long-past age.

To return to the Superintendent's office. This person, having laid before me a map of unrented areas—it will be remembered that there was no owner of land except the government—turned to other business, leaving me to study the plat at pleasure. Running my eye over the printed descriptions, I found that a tract of about five acres, on a part of which was an old orchard of various kinds of fruit trees, was to be had at a distance of some eight "vens" (nearly the same number of miles) from the city, but farther up the peninsula. Its former tenant had leased it for a period of fifty years, but by reason of his death the property was left vacant, and was consequently again for disposition.

The fact that students were often hard-pressed for means on which to live was taken into account by the government, which in all of its dealings with this class allowed better terms than were accorded to any other social division.

The property under consideration attracted me from its description, viz:—"An area of approximately eight ven-nines (five acres) with a dwelling of four rooms, spring water piped over the house; one ven-nine devoted to garden-flowers, and six to fruit trees fifteen years of age. Terms (with all conveniences) to students—one half of the fruit-crop, and all perfume-flowers grown, delivered to the Agent of Soils and Tillage Department. To other persons than students, four tekas per month (ten dollars and twenty-three cents.) Not leased for less than one year."

I concluded to lease the place, for I learned that "all conveniences" meant vailx transportation, telephotic (naim) service, and a caloriveyant instrument, which latter would save fuel, energy to be converted into heat for cooking and other purposes being transmitted by the "Navaza"—a range of material forces denominated in these, thy modern days "earth-currents", but also including those of the higher ether, a range which ye shall yet find and utilize as did Atl, for are ye not Poseid returned? I have said it. Ye lived then; ye live now.

Ye used all these forces then; ye shall ere long use them all again.

Having decided to take the property shown me, I so stated to the official, whereupon he furnished me with a blank contract, helping me to properly fill it out. As a glimpse into that long-fled epoch, I give a copy of this leasehold: —

"I,................years of age, of the ..... sex, and by occupation a ...... do covenant with the Department of Soils to lease block ...... in district ...... described as follows: .... And I do agree to take this .... for ...... years, the same being smiled upon by the Most High Incal."

I took the place for a term of eight years, expecting to be a resident of Caiphul during at least that period of time, as a student at the Xioquithlon.

It seemed no small thing that I could have conveyance by vailx from my leasehold to the Xioquithlon, and thus enjoy a daily trip through the air. Vailx, like the modern cab, might be sent for by telephone, and respond for service in a short time after the call.

It was customary with all new-comers in the city to make a visit to the Agacoe palace and gardens as early as might be convenient after their arrival. Two hours in each week the Rai (emperor) sat in the reception hall, and during these two hours visitors thronged the corridors and passed in double ranks before the throne. After this ceremony all who chose were free to wander unrestricted through the gardens, visit the menagerie—where every known species of animal was kept— or to go through the grand museum or the royal library. With many it was a pleasureable custom to frequently spend the day at Agacoe, on which occasions lunches were brought and a quiet picnic held under the great trees beside fountain, lake or cataract.

I must now return to that time when my mother and myself were wholly unfamiliar with city usages, in order that the reader may accompany us through scenes of novelty. Let us begin with the visit to Agacoe.

An acquaintance at that moment gained, guided us to the palace taking us with himself in a car into which he ushered us. At this time these cars were a novelty to me, and consequently their manipulation became a subject upon which to inform myself.

Our friend took a small coin from his purse and dropped it into an aperture in a glass-fronted box at one end of the car. The coin could not miss falling in such a way as to rest in the bottom of a glass cylinder, a very little greater in diameter than the money itself. Two metal points which projected into the lower end of the cylinder, but did not approach each other nearer than a quarter of an inch, were in the bottom of the tube. When the coin fell upon these a little bell rang, and our friend then raised a lever in the carriage, which lever had a lock-bar over it until the bell rang. This bar had, with the closing of the circuit by the coin, automatically slipped back, at the same time ringing a bell as above noted, thus releasing the lever. When the latter was raised the car moved suddenly but easily out of the station. It swung from its over-head rail, only the peripheries of its large suspensory-wheels being visible, for together with their axles they were mostly hidden by a long metal case which extended from one wheel to the other, and within which a low, humming whirr could be heard- a sound produced by the mechanism of the motory apparatus. The plan of making the passenger do duty as engineer and conductor also was a good one, seeing that the processes required so little knowledge or trouble. As we left the car at the main entrance depot below Agacoe terrace, our friend replaced the lever, the bell rang again, the coin dropped from sight into a strong box underneath, and the vehicle was ready for other passengers. At the grand entrance—a gate which was a marvel of architectural beauty—our friend bade us adieu, entered a car which hung from another track, and was soon disappearing at lightning speed to some yet more distant destination. Glancing at the directory which hung above that particular line, I saw that it bore the legend in Poseid characters, "Aagak mnoiinc sus,"—that is "City Front and Grand Canal,"—to make a free translation. Wishing to inform myself concerning our friendly guide, I asked some one who had interestedly watched the arrival of our little party, who the gentleman was. The reply given was:—

"A great preacher, who foretells the destruction of this continent, and bids all men so live that they will not fear to meet One who, he says, is the Son of Incal, who shall come upon the earth in days yet very far off. He says that this Son of God shall be the Savior of mankind, but that many shall not know Him until He shall have been put to death. Twelve shall know Him, but one of them will deny Him in the hour of His last peril. Indeed, it is a subject of very exceeding interest, albeir one I do not very well understand; yet, as Rai Gwauxln—Incal be good to him!—showeth this preacher all favor, and saith of him, 'He speaketh verities'—therefore is he. attentively received by every one."

Reader, even in that far past age of the world truth was dawning, and this, in the morning of the cycle, was a first ray of the bright sun of Christianity, the orb which even yet is not arisen in the fullness of its glory. I had that morning ridden in the same car with the first prophet who announced the coming of our Lord Jesus Christ, exhorting all of his hearers so to live that their souls might be turned as virgin soil to the rising Sun of Truth, and thereby be made ready to receive the Master when, after the death of their then possessed corporea! bodies, they had returned to earth from Devachan as reincarnated souls. Sowing the seed by the wayside! It fell on me when at a somewhat later period I heard the prophet speak in impassioned eloquence to the specially assembled Xioquithli (students). I know it fell on fallow soil, when I compare my life now with the lives past; yet, for long, the seed lay dormant, and while it did so the bitter experiences of sin and error arose and swept my life outward on a wave of scorching fire, which required another incarnation to heal the scars it left.

As we stood beneath the portal at the grand entrance to Agacoe, we—unsophisticated mountaineers!—could not know when a uniformed guide accosted us, that the emperor, on his throne half a mile distant, was in that same moment perfectly aware of our personal appearance, and also of the very words we used, and our tones.

To me the soldier said:

"And thou, whence comest, and what is thy name?"

"I am called Zailm Numinos, and come from Querdno Aru."

"This visit—is it thy first, or hast thou previously been here?"

"Not ere this; neither I, nor my parent here by my side."

"So! I will provide thee a conductor. Thou wilt find him at yonder gateway. One more question, an' it please thee;—thy mission in Caiphul?"

"I am come to study xioq in the Inithlon; my mother doth purpose to keep our house."

" 'Tis well. Thou mayest go."

This colloquy occurred at the great portal giving entrance to the terrace above. The sentry sat behind a richly wrought gate of bronze metal and gold, very slight, but all sufficient to bar unwelcomed progress. At his back was a large mirror in the heavy arch of the portal. This reflector was suspended by two burnished copper rods in such a manner as to prevent it from touching the side of the niche at any point. Could I have looked behind it, I would have seen an arrangement of metallic cords much resembling those of a piano, together with much other mechanism which at the time would have meant nothing to my untutored mind. How was I to suspect that this brightly polished metal sheet, in which as in a calm lake, the whole interior of the archway was reflected, was an ingenious automatic messenger? That some one of the myriad wires behind it was vibrant to every possible inflection of the voice, or to any sound whatever, and that when I spoke, every briefest sound I uttered was sped along the natural earth-currents which sprang from nature's Night-Side responsive to the control of man, and heard by the Rai on his throne. No more did I dream that, simultaneously with this tell-tale, our imaged reflection was likewise conveyed to the same august presence. But such were the facts.

A few steps brought us to an inner gate made of fenestrated iron plates which, upon the pressing of a button at the side, arose between standards to give passage beneath. At this point we found the guide whom the guard had provided. I deemed his silence an indication of gruffness, not knowing that he had received orders, ere we came unto him, which directed him to conduct us to the royal presence, and needed from us no repetition of our wishes. His quiet remark:—"I understand"—when I began to tell him what we desired, prevented more words on my part, for I felt a sense of injured pride at his reserve, so different from the freedom of my mountain associates; and there were so many of these haughty city people! I determined to give this man a lesson, and considered how I might best let him know that I thought his manner overbearingly out of place for one in his station. That he already possessed all necessary information concerning us I did not imagine, since, if the distance from his post to the outer gate was not great, it was obviously too far for our low-spoken tones to have been heard. The unsuspected mirror had done its work here also, although we knew it not.

"Come," said this haughty fellow, "I will conduct thyself and mother."

"Mother!" I thought. "How does the fellow know that one so fair and so young looking is my mother? She might be my sister, or even my wife, for aught he knows to the contrary." The supposed presumption of the man nettled me, for I was proud not only of my mother's youthful appearance, but also of my own fondly-fancied mature looks; I had not infrequently been told that I looked seven or eight years older than I really was. Had the foolishness of such a pride in my personal appearance been fairly presented to me, instead of feeling an ill-defined resentment at a seeming presumption, I would have laughed at its absurdity, and put it aside as unworthy of one having such high-aimed ambition. As it was, it merely resulted in stiffness of demeanor as a retaliation for the imagined overbearance, and, mostly to my own detriment, caused somewhat of an obliviousness to sights and surroundings I had better

have noted at the time. Though I did not laugh then, by reason
of the obtuse view caused by my ignorance, I have laughed
since, as I looked back over the record of the past. So many
thousand years as have since elapsed may make it seem
laughter at long range, but, " 'Tis better late than never," fitly
applies here!

We seated ourselves as directed, in a car of lighter build than
those used on the public avenues, and also of a different shape.
It was not until we were fairly in motion that I realized how
absolutely different was its construction and propulsive
method. Well-used as I wished to appear to all these novel
things, I gave a tell-tale start when the conductor touched a
lever and the vehicle rose into the air like a soap-bubble,
steadied itself, and then darted up the incline to the edge of the
level ground surrounding the palace. Here we left the cigar-
shaped vehicle, and entered a car which ran upon rails. When
we were again in motion, we made a half circuit of the building, and then shot across the plateau directly into the dark,
yawning mouth of one of the great stone serpents Instead of
ascending at the same angle as did the body of the reptile, our
car glided along on a horizontal plane. As we entered, a sudden illumination lit up the gloom, where an instant previous
all had been darkness. From this pleasant surprise my attention was attracted to the brilliancy of the walls about us,
which seemed to flame with red, blue, green, yellow and all
other tinted flashes of fire, so that I can find no simile more
fitting than comparison to the sun-lit dews on the myriad webs
of morning lawn-spiders I forgot my own haughtiness, and
asked concerning the cause of this dazzling effect, and was answered that the masons had finished the walls with a mortar
in which colored grains of glass had been incorporated.

In the midst of our admiration our horizontal progress
ceased, and I saw that we were at the bottom of a sort of well,
around the sides of which the track coiled in upward spirals
until it seemed to cease just beneath a ceiling vaguely visible
from the light cast upward by ourselves as we swiftly circled
the incline. As we came directly beneath the ceiling a sweet-

toned bell rang twice, and immediately afterward the entire ceiling slid noiselessly aside, allowing our carriage to pass through Behind us the well again closed automatically, and we found ourselves in a splendid apartment, of which the size was not apparent, owing to the many swinging screens of carmine silk—the royal color—as well as to the foliage plants which made miniature sylvan vistas The flowers and songbirds, the fountains and perfumed air, with the cool shade after the heat outside—for we had not been long enough in the elevator-well to become cool—all made what seemed a paradise. The ceiling of this great room was visible only here and there, being in most places hidden by pendant vines. Through all this harmony of vision, trembling in the air, over, under, around-about were sounding entrancing musical cadences, to which, as to an inspiration, the birds replied in rivaling chorus. In and out, amongst this edenic scene of color, sound and scent, past choice statues and fairy, graceful fountains, our car glided with a noiseless speed which from its even motion aided the illusion that we remained still, and all the vision of delight shifted about us as about a center. And this was a marriage of art and of science; from their union sprang the fair dream, a triumph of human skill and knowledge!

In every direction cars were coming, going, or at rest, containing people dressed as for a gala-day, the various distinguishing colors of their turbans denoting their social rank. Poseid, like other countries then and since, had its social castes—as the governmental, the literati and ecclesiastics, the artisans, a limited military, which served as a police and sanitary corps, and so on through the usual familiar list. The apparel of all classes was fashioned in the same general style, until it came to the head-dress—all of the people wore turbans—which article of raiment differed in color according to caste Thus, the turban of the Sovereign was of pure carmine-hued silk; of the councillors, a wine-red, and of lesser officials, a pale pink. The turbans of the soldiery were deep orange for the ranks, and lemon-chrome for the officers. Pure white marked the priesthood, and gray the scientific, the literary and artistic classes. Blue distinguished the artisans, mechanics and laborers, while green denoted all who, for any reason, either immaturity or educational lack, did not enjoy the right of suffrage. Nothwithstanding that these caste-indices were strictly adhered to, they resulted in good rather than otherwise, for caste conceits did not find place among those who wore any color but green, since dignity of labor was a feeling of such vigor that there was no envy of one class by another. As for those who perforce wore the green, those who did so because of not having come to their years of majority would grow out of the color, while those who lacked sufficient education to entitle them to another hue, felt the stigma attaching to their grade to be a reason for extra efforts to attain a more honorable station in life.

While I had been studying the various topics presented for thought, our car was deftly made to avoid collision with that of a lady who came swiftly onwards, apparently heedless of her course, while she was putting in place a loose end of her gray turban, showing as she did so the flashing rays from a ruby, a gem that only royalty might wear. Our car wheeled into an augmenting procession of carriages, and presently carried us into a second apartment. But the royal maiden of the gray turban and ruby—my thoughts were still with her! How radiant was her beauty! 'Twas my first sight of the Princess Anzimee—but I must not anticipate!

The apartment into which we were now come was smaller than the one we had just left, but yet of no mean extent. Everything here was of brilliant, flashing carmine, except an elevation in the center of the room. This was of circular black marble steps, or small terraces, the top, which was twelve feet across, being surmounted by a dais of some dark wood, upholstered in black velvet.

It should here be remarked that black was a representative hue, and included the symbolism of all colors, thus denoting, as used on the throne, that he who sat there belonged to every class; and this was the fact, since Rai Gwauxln was not only sovereign and chief of the army; one of the high priests; a literate; scientist, artist and musician, but was also well acquainted with the duties of artisans and machinists.

In front of the silver railing which surrounded the throne our carriage stopped out to one side of the moving line, obedient to a gesture of the emperor. The guide bade us alight, and opening a little gate directed us to ascend the steps of the dais to the feet of the Rai. My heart beat fast as I obeyed, and though pale with causeless trepidation, I had myself well enough under control to offer the support of my arm to my mother, and I think I never walked more proudly erect in my life. At the top of the steps we knelt and waited the command to rise again, nor had we long to wait.

As we arose Rai Gwauxln said quietly:—

"Zailm, thou art young for a student so ambitious as I know thee to be."

"If it please thee to have me so, I am happy," I made reply.

"Hast thou learned what the primary schools for the young have to teach? For this must be ere thou couldst gain admission to the Inithlon."

"I have done even so, Rai."

"May it please thee, Zailm, to confide to me what studies thou dost chiefly prefer?"

"Zo Rai, I count it an high honor to speak. Of my own fancy I have not chosen any studies. Yet I do not doubt that Incal hath Himself ordered my preference, indicating geology above all else. Also He hath given me a natural disposition, which, if I consult, points that I study languages and literature. I am not yet decided, but think well of these branches of xioq. But geology He directed through a wild experience."

"Thou dost interest me, lad. Yet this is an hour of state duties, and I must not neglect my people who come before me to pay respects to their monarch. Take, therefore, this pass, and at the fourth hour come again to the portal at which thou didst enter into Agacoe. I bid thee welcome."

I took the present, and on my way down the steps of the

marble terrace, saw that it bore the inscription, "Rai's presence. Permit bearer."

We had with us a packet of dates and pastries, and were therefore under no necessity of leaving the gardens for luncheon. Our guide took us again in charge, and after learning that we desired to remain within the grounds about the palace, threaded our conveyance through the mazes of the building once more, letting us out of the carriage beside one of the pillars of the peristyle. From the point where we alighted, and where we parted from the guide, I looked about to ascertain the direction of the grand entrance, and seeing that it was in the east, I escorted my mother to a seat under the shade of a giant deodar, or, as they were called in after centuries, "Cedars of Lebanon." On a bough over head sat a mockingbird, or, as we call them, a "nossuri"—signifying "songster of the moonlight"—in reference to the habit of these lovely, gray-coated birds to fill all the still, moonlit air of night with their wondrous melody. Not that they do not sing by day; indeed, the bird was even then singing, but the naming these "nossuri"—from "nosses" (the moon) and "surada" (I sing) was a distinctive Poseid ornithological term.

At the appointed hour we went to the place designated, and presenting the passport, were shown into a conveyance, and after again ascending the eminence, the guide ushered us into a small apartment of most luxurious appointments. By a table almost hidden by books sat the Rai, listening to a well-modulated voice which was relating the latest news of the day, but the owner of which was not visible. The Rai turned as the usher announced us, dismissed the servitor, and bade us a fair eventide. Then he turned to a case shaped something like that pleasing instrument, the modern music-box, and turned a key in it with a soft snap. On the instant the voice of the unseen speaker ceased in the middle of a word, and I knew as we complied with our sovereign's request to be seated, that I had for the first time heard one of the vocal news-records of which I had so frequently read.

During the ensuing hour I related the story of my life, its
hopes, sorrows, triumphs and ambitions, in answer to the questions of the genial yet not seemingly old man to whom any living person might pay homage and suffer no loss of dignity, because his regal courtesy showed how very manly a king, or how
kingly a man might be.

I told how each new fact had but added to my appetite for
yet greater knowledge. Then I recounted the experiences of
my trip to the summit of Rhok, a recital interrupted as I made
mention of the name of the mountain. "Rhok!"—exclaimed
the imperial listener—"Dost thou mean to tell me that thou
didst ascend that awful height, in the night, alone—a mountain which all our maps assert to be inaccessible, except to
vailx?" "Perchance, Zo Rai, that the only route was known
to but a few of us mountaineers; I have read that it was
thought inaccessible; but—" I hesitated, whereat the Rai said,
quickly:—

"Yea, speak! 'Twas to judge of thee that I have listened to
thy recital, for well do I know all thou hast told me. I could
have told it ere thou didst, and can tell all the rest thou wilt
say; I have desired to hear thee to judge of thee; thy story I
have known ever since I saw thee first. I am a Son of the Solitude," he added. I was silent, for the thought abashed me—
that he already knew all. Seeing this, he said:—"Go on, my
son. Tell me all; I wish it from thy lips, for I am interested
in thee for thyself."

Thereupon I resumed the interrupted narration, and described my rendition of homage to Incal, and the petition for
His aid; His quick granting of my prayer; then of the eruption
of the volcano and the peril in which it had placed me. At this
the Rai remarked:—"Then thou wert eye-witness to that outburst of the terrene forces? I have been told that it wrought
great local changes, and that there is now a lake of extensive
size where before none was, at the foot of Rhok; it is nine vens
across."

I was still unsophisticated enough not only to be curious as
to whether the Rai had seen the eruption—for I did not un-

derstand the significance of his being a Son of the Solitude, and as to his knowing about all my adventures, though I did not doubt that to be a fact, I took it to be due to a keen judgment of possibilities that this knowledge was his—but as an addition to my unsophistication I asked the Rai if he had seen these things.

"Artless youth!"—said the Monarch, smiling—"I do not often find so frank a person! Thou art indeed a son of the mountains! But thou wilt not long remain thus, I fear me, in this thy present environment! I will answer thy question even as thou askest. Know, then, that no large convulsion of nature can occur that is not immediately automatically recorded, both as to its approximate extent, and its location, and a photic exhibition of every portion of the affected locality shown forth afresh from instant to instant. All I had in this case to do to see this depiction was to go into the proper office, which is in this building—and there the whole scene was before me quite as vividly as it could have been to thee, for I was able to see the outburst, and also to hear it, by means of the naim. Truly, what I saw lacked one element which doubtless made it a little more vivid to thee than to me—that of bodily peril; but as to me this element was nil—thou wilt some day know why— therefore the scene lacked for me no element that mere presence could have added."

I marvelled greatly to learn of such instrumentalities concerning which Rai Gwauxln had informed me, and pondered with delight the prospect that I also might some day personally know and have access to them. The Rai resumed:—

"Thou saidst that thou didst find treasure of native gold in two separte places. Didst thou ever seek to recover that which thou didst obtain before the eruption occurred? No? It matters little. Zailm, it is said that ignorance of the law is not valid excuse for its infraction."

The demeanor of the Rai had become one of great gravity, and I felt a foreboding not at all agreeable.

"Still I am convinced that thou didst know nothing of the

involved violation of the statutes when thou didst fail to report the finding of the treasure. I shall not, therefore, punish thee. But—'' Here the emperor paused, lost in thought, while I, not till then aware that I had done anything wrong in the view of the law, paled so visibly with apprehension that Gwauxln smiled a little, and said:

"But they who now work this mine, and they who receive the gold-dust and ore shall not so escape. With them it is conscious crime, made worse in that they not only ignore the statute, but do also defraud thee. Of thee I will require only so much expiation as may be in demanding their names of thee.''

This command I perforce obeyed, yet thought with regret of the wives and children of the culprits. Innocent these; must they suffer likewise with the real transgressors? The Rai seemed to know my thoughts; or if he did not, he at least spoke in accord, asking:

"Have, then, these men wives, families?''

"Yes, it is true!'' I replied, so earnestly that once again the monarch smiled—and encouraged, I begged him to be lenient for the saks of the innocent.

"Knowest thou aught of our punitive system, Zailm?''

"Very little, Zo Rai; I have heard that no malefactor ever comes from the hand of justice without being better, but I imagine the treatment to be very severe.''

"As to severity, no. And as to the other, if men are made better who have erred, so they will not be apt to again err, would not that redound to the advantage of the families of the criminals? Behold I will have these men brought before the proper tribunal, and thou shalt see the process of reformation. Methinks thou wilt thereafter desire to learn anatomy, and the science of reformatory punishment, as an addition to thine other studies in Xio. Furthermore I assure thee that thou shalt in no case suffer confiscation of that mine, but shalt possess it; and if thou wilt give it to the national treasury, while thou art a student thou shalt in no wise feel a lack of money. Afterward, when the years of study have passed over thy head, if thou art successful as a student, lo! then will I make thee superintendent of that mine. And if thou dost so use as to prove thyself faithful over its few things, I will make thee master over many things. I have spoken."

Rai Gwauxln touched a service-button, whereupon an attendant entered, to the guidance of whom he entrusted myself and mother, bidding us:—"Incal's peace be with you both."

So ended an audience which influenced the course of the years and bent life's great twig, making me feel a proud consciousness of being a repository of the trust of a revered friend, a consciousness which has ever proven most potent in this world of trials and temptations.

CHAPTER VI.

NO GOOD THING CAN EVER PERISH.

As antedating the reign of Rai Gwauxln, attention is called to a period of time embracing four thousand three hundred and forty years, inclusive of the main events of Poseid history. This interval, notwithstanding its long duration, had been singularly free from internecine wars, and, while not wholly unmarked by marital events, was certainly more peaceful than any subsequent world-epoch of equal length occurring within the one hundred and twenty centuries whose lapse furnishes the incidents of this history

At the initial date of the period referred to, the Poseidi—a powerful, numerous race of mountaineers, semi-civilized at best, but of splendid physique—had swept down "like the wolf" and had, in many sanguinary contests, finally conquered the pastoral people of the plains—the Atlantides. The war was long and fierce, consuming years in its duration. The admirable valor of the hill-tribes found almost its equal in the desperate courage of their primitive foe; one body of combatants fought for life, and like the Sabines, for the preservation of their women against capture by mate-seeking tribes, while the other warred for conquest, and like the Romans, for wives. It was superior strategy which finally gave victory to the Poseid hosts.

As time went on, racial coalition obliterated all distinctions, so that the union resulted in producing earth's greatest nation. Inconsequential civil wars had several times made a change of political complexion, so that Poseid had seen itself governed by absolute autocrats, by oligarchic and by the theocratic rule; by masculine and by feminine rulers, and at last by a republican monarchical system, of which Rai Gwauxln was the head, when I lived as Zailm, in Atlantis.

Gwauxln was of a long line of honorable ancestors, and his house had several times furnished successful candidates whom the people had placed on the throne, during the seven centuries that the present political system had ruled.

Such is the synopsis of the history of Poseid which I gathered from a volume drawn from the Agacoe library. I might relate other scenes, other features, of that long historic period, and show how Poseid came to found great colonies in North and South America, and in those three great remnants of Lemuria, of which Australia is but the one-third left to the world by that cataclysm which sunk Atlantis; also of how Atl founded certain large colonies in eastern Europe at an age when there was no western Europe, and in parts of Asia and Africa. But I will not do so here, although by-and-by reference will be made to our Umauran possessions, when such reference is relevant to the subject-matter of this history.

Fatigued with late reading in the absorbing history, I arose and went out into the quiet ravine in which our abode was situated, and my tired eyes rested upon a scene which in the glorious moonlight was one of fairy-like beauty.

In the bed of the ravine, quite near, was a miniature lake, but none the less a lake in seeming, because it was in fact only a good-sized pond. Bits of shore, then steep banks, flower-hidden; the song of the nossuri, and the calls of various other birds and furry-folk of the night-time, intermingled with the soft plash of falling water—the voice of the cascade which fed this lacustrine gem. Somewhere out of the night came the sound of flutes and harps and viols in harmony, rising in swelling cadence or lulling with dreamy languor, as the light breeze rose or fell. Over all shimmered the silvery rays of Nosses, round as a shield in her soft brilliancy, and oh! so beautiful! Presently, I turned from the lake, and looked down the ravine along which a few people were yet moving, despite the lateness of the hour—the fourteenth since the beginning of the day at meridian. Here and there the gleaming white rays of householders' lamps were observable, shining from underneath some seeming ledge, revealing the presence of quaint windows or door-ways. But not on these did I gaze over-long. I could not, with the wonderful Maxt—the greatest tower of human construction in the world, rising in the perspective. In the very mouth of the canon it seemed to ascend, with nothing between itself and me to interfere with the view. Although apparently near, it was in truth over a mile away from my dwelling.

In this year A. D. 1886, chemists count the process costly which produces the metal, aluminum. In that day, forces arising from the Night-Side rendered inexpensive the production of any metal which might be found in nature, either native, or as an ore. As it might be done to-day didst thou but know how —and that day is not far off when thou wilt again uncover the knowledge—so, in that time, we transmuted clay, first raising its atomic speed so that it became white light of a pale illuminating power and then reducing it to the, so to speak, chemical "mile-post" of aluminum, and this at a cost not nearly so great as in this modern day it takes to get iron from its ores. The mines of native metals, as gold, silver, copper, and so on, were valuable then, as now, requiring no processing save smelting. But a metal which might be obtained from any ledge of slate-rock, or a bed of clay, was so inexpensive as to be the chief base metal in use.

Of aluminum was the giant tower of the Maxt constructed. I could see its base from where I stood; an enormous cube of masonry; then the superstructural round shaft of solid metal of the tower proper, a dully white, tapering column, lit by lunar rays. From base upward, my gaze traveled until it rested on the top, an apical point nearly three thousand feet in height. Entranced by this crowning triumph of the scene, I gazed at the heaven-piercing shaft; sentinel over the garden city, warding off the lightnings when the lord of thunder was abroad; and all my thought was of its grandeur, and its majectic beauty.

> "How often, oh, how often,
> "In the days that have gone by— — "

I have stood and gazed on some scene of loveliness, or of sublimity—handiwork of God, or possibly of man—God in man! And, as I have looked, my soul sang with praise, and my breath was the breath of inspiration. Always in such an experience, the soul, be it that of man or beast, takes an advance step. However, much a soul may be steeped in sin or misery,—synonymous terms—an inspiration breaks over it, and bears away a little of its sordidness, a little of its pain and fever.

So, therefore, the glories and marvels of Atlantis the Great were not in vain. Thou and I, reader, lived then, and before then. The glories of those long-dead centuries seen by us have lived enshrined in our souls, and made us much, aye, most, of what we are, influenced our acts, soothed us with their beauty. What, then, though the forms of the dim, mysterious past are effaced from all existence save in the record of the great book of life, the soul? Their influence lives, and forever. Shall we not, then, strive that our labors may ennoble, may live in soul and in spirit, and be looked back upon by ourselves and others, even as I, here, look back upon the record of my dead, but ever living past? It is a great joy thus to have attained the eminences of the spirit which enable me to scan the history of lives from which I passed through the portal of the grave; lives which now I am returned to gaze upon through the eyes of a different personality, a personality strung, greatest one of a chain, like pearls upon a thread, teaching me I AM I! Smoky, some of these pearls; black, others, or white or pink, aye, some are even red! Could tears add to their number, I would have more; oh! so many more, for the white ones are so few, and the smoky, the black and the red, so many. But my pearl of great price is my last life. Of white is it; and by my Master was it cut cruciform. When He gave it me, He said, "It is done." Verily so! It marks the junction of finity with infinity. So is it the period set to all time, for me, save I elect.

CHAPTER VII.

CONTAIN THYSELF.

It was in the time of the annual respite from study that I made my advent to the capital city. In this vacation the Xioqua and the Incala participated, the majority seeking their homes first, for a season, but generally, soon returning to the capital, in order to enjoy the special pleasures of the resting time. But some went over the ocean to Umaur, or to Incalia, that is, South or North America, respectively; others went only to the more distant provinces in Atl itself.

Thus far the reader has had to guess what sort of religion the worship of Incal was; it may even have been inferred that Posiedi were polytheists, from my reference to the various gods of this and that title, class or grade. Truly, I have said that we believed in Incal, and symbolized him as the Sun-God. But the sun itself was an emblem. To assert that we, despite our enlightenment, adored the orb of day, would be as absurd as to say that the Christians adore the cross of the crucifixion for itself; in both cases it is the attached significance that caused the sun, and causes the cross, to be held in any sort of regard.

The Atlantides were given to personification of the principles of nature, and of the objects of the earth, seas and skies; but this was purely a result of the national love of poetry, and could be mainly traced to the favor which popular fancy had accorded to a chronological epic history of Poseid, wherein the chief men and women figured as heroes and heroines. The powers of nature, such as wind, rain, lightning, heat and cold, and all kindred phenomena were gods of various degree, while the germinal principle of life, the destroying one of death, and other of life's greater mysteries, were characterized as the greater gods; but each and all were but offspring of the Most High Incal. It was an epic related in metrical measure and rhyme, constituting a poem whose every line exhibited the master touch of genius. Its authorship was lost in the night of time. It was supposedly the work, however, of a Son of the Solitude. There was an addendum embracing later events and epochs, but it was a markedly inferior work, and was not valued as highly as the body of the poem.

As a fact, the worship of Incal never included anything other than the adoration of God as a spiritual entity, and the "gods" had no portion in the religious services held on the two Sundays of each week, that is, the eleventh and the first days, for with the Poseidi a week consisted of eleven days, just as a month comprised three weeks, and a year eleven months, with one or more "leap-year" days at its end, as the exigencies of the solar calendar might require, these days being a regularly recurring holiday season, as New Year's Day is now. That so many gods and goddesses seem to have been venerated was due to the national influence of the epic history spoken of, and it was but a habit of mind to speak of them at all.

In our monotheism we differed little from the religion dominating the Hebraic civilization: we recognized no divine trinity, nor any Christ-spirit, neither any savior except the endeavor to do the best we knew in the sight of Incal. We considered all mankind as the sons of God, not any one mysteriously conceived person as solely His son. Miracle was an impossible thing, for all things we deemed rationally referable to uncontravenable law. But the Poseidi did believe that Inca had once lived in human form upon the earth, and had cast off the gross body of the world to assume that of unfettered spirit. He had in that time created mankind, and as the Poseidi were evolutionists, that word, "mankind" embraced all the lower animals too. In course of time beings of the genus homo, were evolved, one man and one woman, and then Incal had placed woman spiritually highest, and above man, a position which she had lost through an attempt to enjoy a fruit which grew on the Tree of Life in the Garden of Heaven. But in doing this she had, according to the legend, disobeyed Incal, who had said that His highest, most progressed children should not enjoy this fruit, for whosoever did should surely die, because no mortal being could have immortal life and also reproduce its kind. The legend read: "I have said unto my creatures, attain perfection and study it evermore, and such is endless life. But whoso enjoyeth this tree, can not contain self."

The form of punishment meted out was the rationalistic— as the woman's attempt was to attain forbidden pleasures, and she did not, uninstructed, know how. Her hand slipped from its grasp on the fruit, and its side was torn out, so that its seed dropped on the earth and became flint-stones, while the fruit still adhered to the tree, and became of the likeness of a great, fiery serpent, whereof the breath scorched the hands of the culprit. Feeling the pain, she let go her hold on the Tree of Life, falling prone upon the earth, and never fully recovering from the injury. Thus man became the superior being through the development of his nature by the necessity he was under of preserving his mate and himself from the cold and kindred conditions which came along with the flint-stones. (The last Glacial or Ice-age.) Having fallen back into these material conditions, reproduction of species was a necessity once more, and so the law of continence supposedly commanded by Incal, was broken. Death thus entered again into the sum of human reckoning, and until the Word be observed, no man could know a deathless condition. CONTAIN THYSELF! On this dependenth all knowledge; no occult law is so great as this. Use all things of this world as abusing none. (I. Cor. vii., 31.)

Such was the popular belief regarding the creation of human-

kind by Incal. The higher priests held to a religion which was
virtually Essenianism, although for obvious reasons, the popu-
lace were not aware of this fact. The date of this fabled occurrence was theologically supposed to have been precedent at
least a thousand centuries, and some semi-authorities set it at
even a more extended period than that.

Incal, the Father of Life, was not supposed to punish His
children except that He made the laws of nature self-executive,
—His imminent will, and if any one transgressed these, the
guilt was inexorably punished by nature;—it being impossible
to set in motion a cause without a consequent effect; if the
cause was good, so also was the consequence. And in this they
were undeviatingly correct; no mediator can avert for us the
results of our misdeeds.* The Poseid nation believed in a
heaven of good effects for those who put good causes into
operation, and there was a region filled with bad effects for the
wicked; the two places were adjacent, and those who were
neither wholly good, nor wholly bad, were supposed to live
on a middle territory, so to speak. But both of these post-vital
conditions were included in the Shadowy Land, as the word
"Navazzamin" may be translated, literally, "A country of departed souls."

Though the religion of Incal was one based on cause and effect, nevertheless a slight inconsistency appeared in the more
or less prevalent belief that He was supposed to reward the
very good.

To-day, my friend, thou standest on the threshold of a new
unfoldment. The religion of to-day is even yet tinctured by
this concept of an omnipotent, but man-like, Creator, heritage
of a dead antiquity. But thou art living in the final years of
an old Human Cycle, the Sixth. While I choose not at present
to explain what this means, I will do so ere I bid thee God's
peace. But I will say that humanity's new conception of the
Eternal Cause will be more lofty, more sublime, purer, wider
and more of an approach to boundlessness, than anything of
which the long gone aeons of time have ever dreamed. Christ

---

*NOTE.—Do not confuse "undoing" with "atonement." Christ atoned;
we must undo.

is indeed risen, and cometh unto His own, who ere long shall
know Him as no exoteric man hath ever known Him. And,
knowing Him, they shall know the things of the Father, and
do them, because it is written, "I go unto my Father."

GLORIA IN EXCELIS!

Faith shall soon be knowledge. Belief shall be twin with
science, and the Word shall blaze as a sun of glorious new
meaning, for true religion means "I bind together."

RESURGAM CHRISTOS.

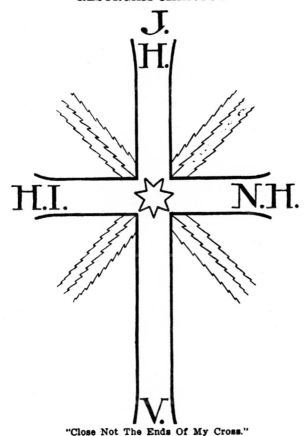

"Close Not The Ends Of My Cross."

The Exoteric Church hath closed the ends of His Cross. Wherefore they are exoteric, and shall not ever be esoteric until they open the ends of that Four-Way Path. Open thine eyes and thine ears.

--- --- --- ---

CHAPTER VIII.

A GRAVE PROPHECY.

It was about the first hour of the first day in the fifth month which had passed since I began attendance at the Xioquithlon, and as it was the week of Bazix, it was consequently the thirtieth week of the year, and near its close, there being but three weeks left in B. C. 11,160.

With the Poseidi, the day, as the reader has seen, commenced at meridian, making twelve o'clock till one, the first hour. From this hour in the last day of each week until the end of the twenty-fourth hour in the following, or first day in the next week, all business was suspended, and the time devoted to religious worship, such observances being enforced by the most rigid of all laws, custom. To-day, A. D. 1886, there are those who argue that if a man is engaged all the week at sedentary labor, on Sunday he is obtaining natural recreation by going zealously into athletic sports, or upon a fatiguing excursion. But I submit, that as the body is the externality of the soul, that, therefore, as the soul is, so will be the body also. Ergo:— if the soul is of God, then to return to the Father as often as possible is to be re-created, or rested, or refreshed. Perhaps not indoors; no, rather amidst His works, but ever with unartificial, natural thoughts of Him uppermost. Hence I am to-day not less in favor of Sabbath observance, whether it be the seventh day or any other of the seven days of the week as now constituted, or the eleventh and first, as in Atla. Still, I shall

not argue my preferences, and will only make a re-statement
of the well-known physiological law that a periodic day of rest
is necessary to health, happiness and spirituality. In Atla any
person was free to employ the morning hours even of the
eleventh day in any manner most agreeable, whether at work
or playful relaxation. With the first hour, however, an enormous and very sweet-toned bell pealed forth with an intense,
reverberant boom, two strokes, paused a moment, then rang
four times more. Thereupon all occupations ceased, and religious worship commenced. On the following day the great
bell struck again, and throughout the length and breadth of a
great continent other bells pealed synchronously. It was even
so in the populous colonies of Umaur and Incalia, the difference
in time being calculated, and one man in the great temple of
Incal in Caiphul attended to this sweetly-solemn duty. Then
the season of worship was over, and the rest of the Inclut (first
day) was devoted to recreations of every sort. This is not to
be construed that the worship was of a gloomy nature, or severe; not so, nor was it continued through the night, any
further than that every light allowed during that interval was
rendered carmine red by blending the atomic speed of the odic
force, so that it was the element of light, and that of strontium
combined; this being done at the odic depots.

About the third hour after the Sun-day had ceased, a peculiar event occurred in my Poseid existence. As I walked
leisurely homeward, not yet having summoned a vailx, but proceeding under the dreamery calmness of the influence produced
by the music of a choice concert given to the public in the Agacoe gardens, I met a stately old man, also on foot. I had often
met him on former occasions, and, by his wine-colored turban,
knew him for a prince. Upon meeting him now, the current
of my thought was altered, and I determined not to go home
at once, but to remain in the city for a time, perhaps all night.
Just as I came to this determination, the older man smiled, but
without stopping went on his way. I then noticed that much as
he resembled the prince I had in mind, he was not that person,
and it must have been an illusion, for the turban of this man

was pure white, not tinted. And somehow I felt that he had
wished to speak to me, but for some reason had not. If I should
happen there later in the day, I might meet him again, and
learn what he had to say.

Pondering these thoughts, I went into a cafe in one of the
grotto-tunnels, where an avenue pierced a hill, and after or-
dering a luncheon, waited for it to be served. During the dispatch of the refection, a xioqene, or student with whom I had
become friendly, strolled in, bent on the same erand. The repast over, we proceeded to the moat, where we took a water-
sailer held for hire by a poor man who made his living from
the rental of these craft to those who liked this seldom-indulged
pleasure; the common mode of conveyance was by vailx. The
breeze being fresh, we sailed out into the ocean through the
exit-flow of the Nomis river—the great river which made a
complete circuit of the city, traversing the moat and then
emptying into the ocean. On account of this extended trip I
was unable to be again on the avenue until after nightfall.
When I neared the spot where my meeting had occurred with
the white-turbaned stranger; this time in a car, which I
checked from running overfast—I saw his commanding figure
standing in full view in the bright light of the tropic moon.
It was quite a part of my expectations thus to see him, and
this time I inclined my head in courteous recognition. As I
did so the stranger said:

"Stop! I would speak with thee, lad, with thee alone."

Almost mechanically I nearly stopped the car, in obedience to
his gesture to descend, and setting its lever so that the vehicle
would move at about the pace of a slow walk, I let it go, knowing that if no one took advantage of the paid carriage, it soon
would reach some station, and there be stopped automatically.
When I stood before the priest, as I judged him to be, he
said:—

"Thy name, I understand, is Zailm Numinos?"

"Truly it is."

"I have seen thee oft-times, and am informed concerning
thee. Thou hast a laudable will to excel, and to attain high

honors among men. Thou art yet a boy, but in a fair way to
succeed as a man, as success is commonly counted. A boy thou,
conscientious at present, regarded with favor by thy sovereign.
Thou shalt succeed, and shalt come into places of high honor
and profit, and continue well-thought of by all thy fellow-men.
Yet thou shalt not live the full term allotted to man on earth.
In thy shorter period shall come to thee a knowledge of love.
Thou shalt experience the purest affection man is capable of
feeling for woman. Yet, notwithstanding this, thy love shall
not be a love crowned in this life period. And thou shalt love
again, wherefore thou shalt weep because of it. Thou shalt
work some good in the world, but alas, much evil also. And
because of an overshadowing destiny, unto thee shall come
much sorrow. By thee unto another, shall deep misery of
anguish come, and unto the uttermost shalt thou pay therefor,
nor come out thence until thou hast done so. Yet, behold, not
in this life shall much be required of thee. When thou thinkest
least to do sin, then shall thy foot stumble, and thou shalt
commit a sin which shall be unto thee a pursuing fate, inexorable. Even now, in the days of thine innocence, thou art tread-
ing upon the steps of thy destiny. Alas! that it is so. Once
thou camest near to the realization of thy death; and death is
but the least portion which shall overtake thee;—but thou didst
awake and flee out of the caverns of the burning mountain unto
safety. Yet at last thou shalt pass into Navazzamin, the world
of departed souls, and lo! I say unto thee thou shalt perish in
a cavern. Me, even me, shalt thou behold as the last living
being upon whom thy Poseid eyes shall ever rest. But I shall
not seem then as now, and thou wilt not know me for the one
who shall smite the evil-doer who will then have enticed thee
to thy doom I have said. May peace be with thee."

Much I marveled at first to hear these words, thinking that
perhaps the speaker was one escaped from the Nossinithlon
(literally the "Home for Moonstruck" or crazy persons), and
this despite the introductory circumstances under which we
had met. But as he continued speaking, I knew that this was
an erroneous judgment. Finally, amazed, I gazed on the

ground, knowing not what to think, and filled with an indefinable fearsomeness. As he ceased utterance, and bade me peace, I raised my eyes to look him in the face, to find to my bewilderment that not a soul was in sight, but that I stood alone in the great plaza surrounding a fountain whose jet seemed like molten silver in the moonlight. Dumbfounded, I looked about on every side. Had I been dreaming? Certainly not. Were the words of the mysterious stranger true, or false? Time will satisfy thy curiosity, my reader, as it did mine.

CHAPTER IX.

CURING CRIME.

During the subsequent four years after my strange meeting with the tall and straight, white-haired old man who had prophesied concerning me, events one after another shaped themselves in harmony with his forecast. In all that time we never met, indeed I met him but once more before my death.

Before going further I must recall and finally dismiss from the scene the partners in my gold-mine, and also, the one who bought the gold, knowing the act to be unlawful.

Several months had elapsed since the interview with Rai Gwauxln in his private apartments, when a youth wearing an orange-hued turban, and upon its front a gold-mounted garnet pin—denoting him to be a guard in the imperial service—entered the geology-room in the Xioquithlon, and going to the instructor-in-chief, spoke in a low tone. Rapping on his desk for attention from the ninety or more students in session, in the minerals class, the chief asked if a Xioqene named Zailm Numinos was present.

I arose in my place in response to the question.

"Come forward."

The other Xioqeni looked interestedly on, as I went up, not without some trepidation, for I well knew what service was represented by the messenger, and there seemed to be a sternness in the tones of the instructor not at all pleasant.

"This courier desires that thou wilt go with him before the Rai, who has so commanded. He is at the Tribunes of the Criminal Court, and thou art needed as a witness."

Remembering what the Rai had said, I was considerably reassured by the import of the words addressed to me, and no longer specially apprehensive, went as required. Arrived at the Court of the Tribunes, I saw my mining partners there in custody, along with the incriminated purchaser of the gold. The judge of the court sat on the judicial divan on its raised platform, and by his side sat, in simple dignity, Gwauxln, Rai of the greatest nation of the earth; but he was nevertheless studiously observant of the fact that the judge was, as such, entitled to the place of first rank while in the hall. Several spectators were in the seats provided for the public in the auditorium.

There could be but one verdict concerning the malefactors— "Guilty as charged." This opinion was reached very quickly, and by the culprits admitted to be a just one. Immediately, an officer took the prisoners into another part of the building, where was a well lighted apartment, fitted with various portable and stationary instruments. He was accompanied by all persons present.

A chair with a head-clasp rest, and with other rests, clasps and straps for the limbs and body of the occupant, stood in the center of the room. A guardsman seated and firmly strapped one of the prisoners in the chair. This preliminary attended to, a Xioqa approached bearing in his hands a small instrument of which, from its general appearance, I knew the nature to be magnetic. He placed the two poles of this in the hands of the condemned man, and after a brief manipulation a slight, purring sound was heard from the instrument. Immediately the prisoner's eyes closed and his every appearance indicated profound stupor; he was in fact magnetically anaesthetized. Then

the operator carefully felt all over the head of the unconscious
man, and this examination concluded, ordered the attendant to
shave the entire cranium. When this order had been obeyed,
he made a blue mark upon the shaven surface in front and
above the ears. Feeling further, he made the Poseid numeral
$\mathbf{Y}$ (or 2) above, and a very little back of each ear. These op·
erations done, he gave his attention to the spectators, but, on
being spoken to by Rai Gwauxln, he paused long enough from
making his proposed address to the audience to call me to his
side from where I stood outside the railing. Then he spoke:

"In the prisoner I find that the predominant, most positive
faculties are those which I have marked one and two; these
are—number one—a grasping desire to acquire property, and
his disposition is to do all things secretly, as may be seen from
the exceeding prominence of the organs of secretiveness. While
the skull does not extend upwards very high, but at number
two is very wide between the ears, I should infer that here we
have a very acquisitive individual, lacking conscientiousness
and spirituality, and therefore the moral nature, almost wholly.
As he has also a very destructive temperment, we have withal,
a very dangerous character, one which I marvel has
so managed as not ere this to have exposed himself to
this office for correction. Why any one should hesitate, even
voluntarily, to undergo corrective treatment causes me much
wonder. It is something, I suppose, explicable on the theory
that one on the low moral plane of this poor fellow is unable to
see the advantage of being on any higher plane, but is able to
see the immediate advantages due to the pursuit of nefarious
methods. He is, in short, a man who would not hesitate at the
commission of murder, could he see any immediate gain in it,
and be wholly oblivious of after consequences. Is this true,
Zo Rai?"

"It is," replied the emperor.

"My diagnosis of the case," continued the Xioqa, "having
been confirmed by so high an authority, I will now apply the
cure."

He summoned an attendant, who wheeled out another magnetic apparatus contained in a heavy metal case. Having placed this in a satisfactory condition of activity, the Xioqa next applied its positive pole to that place on the head of the patient marked by the figure one, and the other pole he placed at the back of the neck. He then took out his timepiece and laid it on the metal case of the instrument, near a dial, the pointer of which he adjusted. All was then still, except the low-toned conversation in various parts of the room, during the ensuing half-hour. At the end of this time the Xioqa arose from his seat and changed the positive pole to the other side of the head, where the duplicate figure was marked. Then again a half-hour's quiet, broken only by the exit of some of the spectators and the entrance of others. When the half-hour had again elapsed, the operator changed the pole to the place marked "two." This time only half an hour was given to both sides of the head. I had been told by the emperor to remain. He had only staid a few moments after the beginning of the operation which was not new to him. At the end of the work on the first man he was taken from under the influence of the magnetic anaesthetizer by merely reversing the poles of the instrument at a second application. The Xioqa lectured upon the theme afforded by the operation while the first patient was being removed. To the considerable audience that had, by this time, assembled, he said:

"You have seen the treatment of those mental qualities which tended through their predominance to warp his moral nature, something but partially developed. The process has been to partially atrophy the vascular channels supplying that portion of the brain where are located the organs of greed, and of destruction. But mark well this point; after all is said, the soul is superior to the physical brain, and, it is in the soul, the nature of the man, in which these criminal tendencies inhere—the brain and other organs being the seat of psychic expression—the business office, so to speak. Hence, merely to have mechanically hypnotized this subject would not accomplish our purpose. Hypnotizing is an indrawing, and the cerebral blood-vessels contract and become partially blood-less; indeed, they may become fatally empty; this art is a very dangerous one. But the opposite effect is produced in aphaism (Poseid equivalent for the modern word "mes-merism"). The brain is filled with blood, and the rever-sion of the instrument cessated the hypnotic and initiated the aphaic process. It is at this moment that the mind of the operator may assume control of the mind of the subject, and suggest to the erring soul a permanent cessation of the error. This man has been so treated, doubly treated, since not only has the blood supply been partially cut off which went to those organs where was the seat of his weakness, but with my will I have impressed his soul to cease its sin, and I have supplied it with a work to execute which will have a counter action. He may be slightly ill for a few days, but his tendencies to sin will be gone. It requires a superior mind, which has gone wrong in several directions, to make a successful evil-doer, and where the lower nature, chiefly a perverted sex-nature predominates, there will be found the criminal. Atla has no debauchees, for if a person show such dispostion, the state takes the waywarl one in hand and operates upon the proper organs. But I need not dilate upon these subjects any fur-ther."

The first man having been taken away to receive careful nursing, the next of my whilom partners was placel in the chair. Examination of the cerebral development revealed that he was more weak than wicked; an habitual prevaricator, and of libertine tendencies; one whose skull was mostly behind and above the ears. I need not pause to describe his treatment; it was on the lines of the other; mesmeric suggestion was the chief cure.

As I went to my home that evening, I resolved to add the science of prophylactic penology to my chosen curriculum. I did so. By practice of the knowledge of men then acquired I interfered with the karma of not a few individuals, but as the result has proven, the interference was in no case injurious, so that I have not today to answer for any harm done. I have sometimes wished that I had submitted myself for treatment at the hands of the State, for it would at least have prevented the commission of errors which have wrought much misery to me, and to others by me. That I did not, is as well, not only on the principle that in our Father's kingdom whatever is, is best, but also because no one can in any way whatever shirk the responsibilities inbound in character by the karma of all preceding incarnations. To have so submitted myself for correction would have been an evasion of the ordeal, a sort of cowardly attempt similar to the act of the self-murderer who seeks to avoid trouble on earth by suicide, and who in every case escapes nothing, not one jot nor tittle of the law of God. Instead, he piles his miseries and penalties mountains higher and prolongs through inexorable karma, and other earthly incarnations, his anguish. Thus it is with those who die by self-destruction; but those who die by unavoilable causes, involuntarily, are not visited by such penalties. So the Poseid culprits who could in no wise avoid the treatment, were benefited, whereas for me, voluntary submision would have sown dragon's teeth for my pathway. Penalties, observe, concern not those who know and, knowing, do God's will.

CHAPTER X.

REALIZATION.

The government was accustomed to keep systematic track of the more prominent Xioqeni to whom it gave free tuition, but the supervision was never irksome, indeed, was scarcely felt to be maintained by those under this paternal surveillance. Those who, besides being bright and studious, were approaching the last years of the collegiate septerm, were admitted to those sessions of the Council of Ninety not of an executive or secret character. There were some especial favorites who, being bound by strict vows, were not excluded from any meetings of the councillors. Not one of the many thousand students, but esteemed even the lesser privilege most valuable, for beside the honor conferred, the lessons in statecraft were of incalculable advantage.

In the latter half of my fourth year of attendance there came to me one prince Menax, who desired to know whether I would accept the position of Secretary of Records—a position which gave opportunity to become familiar with every detail of Poseid government. He spoke:

"It is a very important trust indeed, but one which I am happy to offer thee, because I feel that thou art capable of filling it to the satisfaction of the council. It will bring thee into close contact with the Rai, and of all the princes; also it will clothe thee with some degree of authority. What sayest thou?"

"Prince Menax, I am aware that this is a very great honor. But may I ask why thou hast given so great opportunity to one who supposes himself almost a stranger to thee?"

"Because, Zailm Numinos, I have thought thee worthy; now do I give thee all chance to prove it true. Thou art no stranger to me, if I be much of one to thee; I feel a trust in thee; wilt thou not prove it well founded?"

"I will."

"Then hold up thy right hand to the blazing Incal, and by that sublime symbol declare that in no case wilt thou reveal aught that taketh place in secret session; nothing of the doings in the Hall of Laws."

This vow I took, and in taking it, was bound by an oath inviolable in the eyes of all Poseidi. Thus I became one of the seven non-official, unenfranchised secretaries, who were entrusted with the writing of special reports, and the care of many important state documents. Surely this was no small distinction to confer on one out of nine thousand Xioqeni, and a man, as yet, unenfranchised in a nation of three hundred million people. If in some sort, I owed it to merit, yet I was not more worthy than a hundred other of my fellow-students. It was due fully as much to personal popularity with the powers that were, a popularity, however, which had not been mine had I not in all things shown the same solid determination which had governed my actions on the lone pitach of Rhok, the great mountain.

Prince Menax continued, saying:

"I would have thee attend at my palace this night, it being convenient, as I have somewhat to say unto thee. I would prove to thee thine error in believing thyself unknown to me, merely because thou art one of a large concourse of Xioqeni, each in pursuit of knowledge. I do know thee. From me, and not, as thou hast always imagined, from thy Xioql (chief preceptor) did the invitation issue to thee to attend the sessions of the councils-in-ordinary. The Astiki (princes of the realm) are always much interested in deserving Xioqeni; hence the reason of many little duties falling to thee for execution. But I will not say more at present, as I hinder thy studies. Remember then, the appointed eighth hour."

Menax held the highest ministerial office of all the Astiki, being premier, and, in short, the Rai's chief adviser. My opinion of myself rose in degree when I felt that I was held in such high favor; but it rendered me full of gratitude, and not self-conceit; it was true self-esteem, not vanity.

Although this was not my first visit to the palace of this prince, I could by no means claim familiarity with the interior of his astikithlon.

Winding my best green silk turban about my head, and sticking in it a pin set with gray quartz, through which ran veins of green copper; thus denoting my social rank; I stepped to the naim and called for a city valix, as thou wouldst call for a cab. The vessel soon came, and though small in size, was ample for the conveyance of two, or even four, passengers. Bidding my mother good night, I was soon speeding on my way, and the conductor leaving me to my own company, I sat listening to the furious patter of the torrents of rain which rendered the night inclement in the extreme.

The palace of Menax was not far distant from the inner quay of the moat where that great canal nearest approached my suburban home, not indeed, ten miles away, and therefore the aerial trip consumed only about the same number of minutes ere the bottom of the vailx grated a little upon the broad marble floor of the vailx-court, announcing arrival at my destination.

A sentry came up to demand my business, and having learned it, a servitor was summoned to escort me into the presence of Menax.

A number of officers of the prince's suite were in the great apartment, sedulously engaged in doing nothing in particular, an occupation in which they were aided by several ladies resident at the palace. Prince Menax himself was lying at length on a divan drawn up in front of a grate full of pices of some refractory substance heated by the universal force.

As the attendant conducted me before the prince and prior to my presence being announced, I had time sufficient to enable me to notice a group of officers and ladies, gathered about a woman of such exceeding grace and beauty that even her evident sorrow and distress, together with the distance of the corner where she sat, could not wholly conceal it. Her attire, her features and complexion, denoted that she was other than a daughter of Poseid, inasmuch as she had not their dark eyes, dark hair and clear but distinctly reddish complexion. She who sorrowed, and was in distress, was the reverse of all this, as nearly as my hasty glance could discern at the distance between us.

Menax said, in salutation:

"Thou'rt welcome. 'Tis well. Be seated. The night is tempestuous, but I know thee well; having promised, thou art come."

He was silent for several moments, and gazed steadily into the glowing grate; then said: "Zailm, wilt thou attend and take part in the competition in Xie in the nine days given to the annual examination of Xioqeni?"

"I have so intended, my Astika."

"Thou art privileged to waive examination until the last year of the sep-term."

"Verily that is so in all Xioqeni?"

"I approve most emphatically of thy determination. I did after that way myself, when I was a student. I hope that thou wilt pass, that thou mayest be joyful at thy success, though it shall not shorten thy years of study. But after the examination, then what? Thou wilt have a month wherein to do as thou shalt fancy. Would that I had thirty-three days' respite from my duties! Menax paused in meditation, and resumed:

"Zailm, hast thou any preferred plan for the occupation of that vacation?"

"None, my prince."

"None? 'Tis well. Would it please thee to do me a service, and go into a far country in fulfilling the kindness? The brief duty completed, thou mayest remain there such time as thou desirest, or go whither fancy may beckon."

I was not averse to doing as he desired, and as the duty took me to a land barely mentioned hitherto, the account of my long-ago vacation trip may be prefaced by a description of Suerins—now called Hindustan—and Necropan or Egypt, the most civilized nations not under Poseid supremacy.

When nations seek to make religion absolutely dominant in their affairs, the result is sure to be fraught with disaster. The theocratic policy of the Israelites was a case in point; and as the reader will ere long perceive, Suernis and Necropan were examples yet earlier in the history of the world. And the reason is, not that religion is a failure; the force of this record of my life must convey the truth that I think nothing is better than pure religion undefiled. No, the reason why a successful theocracy can not permanently thrive is that the attention of the promoters must be given to things spiritual to render the spiritual successful, and the things of God's Kingdom can never be the things of earth. Not, at least, until man is fully developed in his sixth or psychic principle; has become purified, by the fire of the Spirit, from all taint of animality.

Suernis and Necropan were possessed of a civilization which I now perceive to have been peer with our own, though so different. But because it possessed scarcely a salient point in common with that of Poseid, therefore the people of the latter country regarded it with a sort of scorn * when discussing it amongst themselves. But they were very respectful in their demeanor towards these poeple, for reasons that shall presently appear.

The differences in the two coeval civilizations lay in the fact that while Poseidi tended to the cultivation of the mechanical arts, to sciences having to do with material things, and were content to accept without question the religion of their ancestors, the Suerni and Necropani paid but little heed to anything not mainly occult and of religious significance—practical principles truly, occult laws having a bearing on materiality—but none the less were they careless of material objects except in so far as the proper maintenance of life was concerned. Their rule of life was summed in the principle of taking no heed of the life about them, but neglecting the present they strove after the future. The vital principle of Poseid was to extend her dominion over natural things. There were those who philosophized over the spirit of the times—Poseid theorists—and these drew a prognostic picture of Atlantean destiny. They pointed out the fact that our splendid physical triumphs, our arts, sciences and progress, absolutely depended on the utilization of occult power drawn from the Night-Side of nature. Then this fact was put side by side with the fact that the mysterious powers of the Suerni and Necropani owed their existence to this same occult realm, and the conclusion

---

*It hath been ever thus; the seed sown in the Acre whereof the corners are marked by posts of which the first hath but one side, the second five sides, the third six sides, but the fourth again only five.— hath ever been scorned by man. That seed groweth a tree seventeen-branched. So was Suern. In another day it would be watered by Poseid; later it must be in Poseid. Yet again this would be after it was pruned by its Sower. Then it must grow till the day's end, and become great in the next day. But greatest at the end of that day. I have spoken a riddle that whoso unfoldeth it proveth him of the Tree I have spoken, and filled with **deathlessness.** Hear, O Israel! Seek, O Manasseh, and Ephriam, seek! Land of the Starry Flag, open thine eyes, and thou, too, O Mother land!

was that in time we also would grow careless of material progress and devote our energy to occult studies. Their forebodings were extremely gloomy in consequence; yet, while the people listened respectfully, the failure of these prophets to suggest a remedy rendered them in some degree objects of secret contempt. Any one who shall find fault with an existing state of affairs and be confessedly unable to substitute a better, is sure to meet with public ridicule.

We, as Poseidi, knew that the mysterious nations across the waters were possessed of abilities which virtually dwarfed our attainments, such as our power to traverse the aerial or marine depths, our swift cars, our sub-surface sea ships. No, they did not boast such conveniences, but they had no need of them to carry on the course of their lives, and therefore, as we supposed, no desire for such apparatus. Perhaps our scorn was more affected than real, for in our more sober thought we acknowledged, with no small admiration, their supremacy.

What though we could speak with, and see, and hear, and be seen by those with whom we wished to communicate, and this at any distance and without wires, but over the magnetic currents of the globe? Truly, we never knew the pangs of separation from our friends; we could attend to the demands of commerce, and transport our armies in war times with a dispatch which could pass around the world in a day; all this as long as our mechanical and electrical contrivances were at hand. But what availed all this splendid ability? Shut one of the most learned Xioqui in a dungeon, and all his knowledge would be as naught; he could not, deprived in such a way of implements or agencies, hope to see, to hear or to escape without external aid. His marvellous capabilities were dependent upon the creation of his intellect. Not so with Suern or with Necropan. How to hinder one of these people, no Poseida knew. Shut in a dungeon, he would arise and go forth like Saul of Tarsus; he could see to any distance, and this without a naim; hear equally without a naim; go through the midst of foes, and be seen by none of them. What, then, availed our attainments if opposed to those of Suernis and Necropan? Of what use our instruments of war even against such a people, a single man of whom, looking with eyes wherein glittered the terrible light of a will-power exerted to hurl in retribution the unseen forces of the Night-Side, could cause our foemen to wither as green leaves before the hot breath of fire? Were missiles of value here? Of use, when the person at whom they were aimed could arrest them in their lightning path, and make them fall as thistle-down at his feet? What, even, was the value of explosives, more awful than nitro-glycerin, dropped from vailx poised miles above in the blue vault of heaven? None whatever; for the enemy, with prescient gaze and perfect control of Night-Side forces we knew not of, could arrest the falling destroyer, and instead of suffering harm, could annihilate that high ship and its living load. A burned child fears the fire, and in times past we had sought to conquer these nations, and failed disastrously. Repulse was all they sought to effect, and successful over us in this, we had been left to go in peace.

As the years stretched into centuries, our ways likewise became those of defence only, never offensive any more, and owing to this change on the part of Poseid, friendly relations arose between the three nations.

Atla had learned at last so much of the secret as to wield magnetic forces for the destruction of its foes, and had dispensed with missiles, projectiles, and explosives as agents of defense. But the knowledge of the Suerni was still greater. Greater because our magnetic destroyers spread death only over restricted areas circumjacent to the operator; theirs operated at any desired point, however distant. Ours struck indiscriminately at all things in the fated district; at things inanimate, as well as animate; at men, whether foes or friends; at animals, at trees—all were doomed. Their agencies went out under control, and struck at the heart of the opposing force, not destroying life unnecessarily; nor even molesting any of the enemy except the generals and directors of their forces.

Of all these facts concerning the Suerni, I had long before learned. Prince Menax asked me that I oblige him by going

on a mission to that people. I had never seen the land of
Suern, and having a desire to do so, felt well pleased that it
was to be gratified. After consenting to do as requested, I
asked the prince concerning the proposed duty, saying: "If
Zo Astika will tell his son what is required, he will satisfy a
growing curiosity."

"Even so will I do," answered the prince. "It is desired
to send unto the Rai of Suern a present in acknowledgment oi
certain gifts sent by him to Rai Gwauxln. While there can
be but small doubt that these gifts were sent to induce our acceptance of seven score women, prisoners of war, who seem to
be much in the way of Rai Ernon of Suern, nevertheless we
cannot regard it as necessary to throw us a sop, and while the
women will be allowed to remain, or go whither they will so
that they go not where forbidden by Suern, we choose to regard
the gift of gems and of gold as a gift, and make due return
for it. So saith the council in quorum assembled. It seems
that these women are members of certain strong forces of
foolish invaders whose country lies far to the west of Suern.
These people very unwisely made war upon the terrible Suerni.
They had never experienced, nor beheld exerted, the wrath
wherewith Incal arms His children of Suern—a wrath which
moweth its foes as the scythe of the reaper layeth the grass.
Now, Ernon hath a fertile country, and these ignorant savages
longed to possess it, wherefore they sent unto the Rai of Suern
a challenge of war. To this Ernon replied that he would not
make fight; that those who sought him with spears and with
bows, and came arrayed in armor, would find him, and therefor
be sorrowful, inasmuch as Yeovah—as the Suerni are pleased
to name Him whom we called Incal—would protect him and
his people of Suern, and this without strife and bloodshed.
Thereupon the barbarians returned derisive language, and declared that they would come upon his land and destroy his
people with the sword. So they gathered a numerous army,
even ten score thousand fighting-men, and many camp-follow-
ers, and these, led by a dauntless Astiki, swept east by south to
devastate the realm of Suern. But wait; there is in this room

one who can doubtless tell more than I, and tell it better.
"Mailzis!"—addressing his body servant—"conduct hither
yon fair stranger."

Mailzis obeying, the foreign woman whom I had seen as I
entered the apartment of the prince, arose in an easy, graceful
manner which commanded my admiration. Arranging her
attire in a not at all hasty way—quite, in fact, the reverse of
one obeying a superior—she approached Menax. Arising def-
erentially, the prince said:—"Lady, art thou minded to recount
to me that which thou hast told to my sovereign? I know that
thy narration is vastly interesting."

During these remarks the stranger had looked not at the
Prince, but at me. Her eyes had been riveted on my face, not
boldly, but intently, though obviously quite unaware of the
fixity of her gaze. None the less there was such a magnetic
power in it, that I was compelled to look away, strangely
abashed by the glance, but feeling that yet it folowed me, although I saw it not. It occurred to me that the fact of the
lady's reply being couched in the Poseid language was indica-
tive of her possession of a good education.

"If, Astika"—said she—"it be a pleasure to thee that I do
this that thou askest, it is also one to me. It is also much of
a pleasure to me to repeat it to the youth thou favorest. I
would, however, that the maid, thy daughter, were not here"—
she added, sotto voce, with a glance of antagonism toward
Anzimee, who sat near us, engaged in perusing a book, apparently, but, as I fancied, not in reality. This jealous under-
tone was not heard by Menax, though Anzimee heard it, and
presently arose and left the apartment in consequence. This
action I regretted, and the cause of it I resented, as the Saldu
quickly saw, and because of it bit her lip with vexation.

"It cannot be agreeable to stand; wilt thou seat thyself at
my right hand, and thou, Zailm, change thy seat, also, and be
at my left?"—said Menax, re-seating himself on the divan.

When this arrangement had been made, we were ready to
listen to the recital. At this moment the valet, Mailzis,
respectfuly approached, and being asked his wish, said:

"It is the desire of thine officers, and of the ladies of the astikithlon, to be also present at the narration."

"Their wish is granted; bring also the naim, and place it near us, that the editor of the Records may take account, too."

Availing themselves of his permission, the petitioners were soon grouped about us, some on low seats, others—higher officers—more familiar with their prince, stretched themselves on side and elbow in front of Menax upon the rich velvet rugs on the marble floor.

CHAPTER XI.

THE RECITAL.

"Mailzis," said the Prince, "some spiced wine for us."

In the enjoyment of this truly refreshing, because unfermented beverage, we listened to the following thrilling narrative:

"Thou art, I think, acquainted with my native country, since thou hast had commercial intercourse with the Sald nation. All here have likewise heard of how our ruler sent a great army against the terrible Suerni. Ah! how little we knew of those people!" she exclaimed, clasping her small, patrician hands in an agony of terrified retrospection.

"Eight score thousand warriors had my father, the chief, under his command. One-half as many more were followers of the camp. Our cavalry was our pride, veterans tried and true, and ah! so lustful after blood! Such splendid armament had we; glittering spears and lances—oh! a wondrous array of valiant men!"

At this eulogy of such primitive weapons her listeners were unable to repress a shadowy smile. For a moment this seemed to disconcert the princess, but not for long, for she continued:

"In this splendid, powerful fashion—ah! how I love power! —we came, taking loot as we proceeded towards the Suern city.

When we arrived near it, after many days, we could not see it, as it was in a lowland. But we felt assured of an easy victory, since captives whom we took informed us that no walls or like defenses existed, and that no army was gathered to meet us. Indeed, we nowhere found walled towns in all Suern, nor met with resistance, hence had spilled no blood, but contented ourselves with torture of the captives, by way of amusement, ere we set them free."

"Horrible!" muttered Menax under his breath. "Heartless barbarians!"

"What saidst thou, my lord?" asked the girl, quickly.

"Nothing, my lady, nothing! I but thought of the splendid march of the Saldan host."

Though seemingly somewhat doubtful of the accuracy of this statement, the Saldu nevertheless continued her recital.

"Arrived, as I have said, we stayed our march on the brink of a shallow, but wide defile, wherein the Rai was soun warlike and unwise as to have his capital, and sent a messenger to announce our errand and offer him favorable terms of war. In answer there came with our flag-bearer a solitary, unarmed old man. Elderly is a better word. He was tall, erect as a soldier, and had a dignity of mien that made him splendid to look upon. Aye, he looked as power incarnate! I ought to hate him, but he is powerful, and I cannot choose but love him! If he were younger—I would woo him to be my mate."

At this unexpected remark we looked at the fair speaker in amazement, not unmingled with other emotions, while Prince Menax asked:

"Astiku, hear I aright? Woo a man? Is it customary amongst thy people to give unto woman the love-making? I had thought myself versed in the customs of every nation, ancient and modern, yet knew not this fact. However, strange things are to be expected of—well, a race which has but numbers to entitle it to recognition at the hands of people like the Poseidi."

"Why not be frank, Zo Astika? Why not say what thou thinkest—that civilized nations like thine consider such a

race as the Saldi beneath them so far that even their customs
are well nigh unknown to thee?"

Prince Menax flushed deeply in ashamed confusion, for he
was unaccustomed to prevarication, and replied:

"Candor is best, I admit; but I desired to avoid wounding
thy feelings, Astika."

With a ringing laugh, full of amusement, the Astiki said:

"Zo Astika, allow me to tell thee that in Sald, either sex is
free to woo its chosen one. Why not? It is sensible, methinks.
I shall follow our custom in this respect, if chance ever pre-
sents. My chosen one must be pleasing to look upon, and
must be courageous like unto the lion of the desert, yea! even
the deserts whence he came unto the continent of Suernota.
Ah, me; yes, if chance offers,"—she reiterated, with a little
sigh.

At length she resumed wearily, sadly:

"The Astika—my father, chief of our armies—said to this
grand old man;

" 'What saith thy ruler!'

" 'He saith:—'Bid this stranger depart least my wrath
awake, for lo, I shall smite him if he obey me not! Terrible is
mine anger.'

" 'What ho! And his army; I have seen none,' said my
father with the laugh of a veteran to whom despised resistance
is offered.

" 'Chief,'—said the envoy, in a low, earnest tone—'Thou
hadst best depart. I am that Rai, and his army also. Leave
this land now; soon thou canst not. Go, I implore thee!'

" 'Thou the Rai? Rash man! I tell thee that when the
sun hath moved one other sign, that thy courage shall not save
thee, unless thou wilt now return and collect thine army. Else
will I then send thy head to thy people. There is but this option. After that length of time I will strike and sack thy
city. Nay, fear not now for thy personal safety; I cannot hurt
an unarmed foeman! Go in peace, and by the morning I will
attack thee and thy army. I must have a worthy foe.'

" 'In myself is a worthy foe. Hast thou never heard of the

Suerni? Yes? And thou hast not believed! Oh, it is true!
Go, I entreat thee, while yet thou canst do so in safety!'

" 'Foolish man!'—said the chief. 'This thine ultimatum?
Then be it so! Stand aside! I go not away, but forward.'
Then he called unto the captains of the legions and com-
manded:

" 'Forward! March to conquer!'

" 'Withhold that order one moment; I would ask a question,'—said the Rai.

"Agreeably to this request our men, who had sprung to
place at the word, were now halted with arms at rest. In the
very front ranks of the Saldan army as it stood on the little
eminence overlooking the Suern capital, and the great river
flowing near, was the prime flower of our host. Veterans they
were, tried and true, men of giant stature, two thousand strong
—leaders of the men less seasoned. I shall never forget how
grand looked that array, no, never! So strong; the very
mane of our lion-power, every man able to carry an ox on his
back. The sun was caught on their spears in a glorious blaze
of light! Looking upon these men the Suerna said:

" 'Astika, are not these thy best men?'

" 'Aye.'

" 'They are the ones of whom it hath been told me that they
tortured my people, merely for amusement? And they called
them cowards, saying that men who would not resist—to them
should they serve death, and they did murder a few of my
subjects?'

" 'I deny it not,' said my father.

" 'Thinkest thou, Astika, that this was right? Are not
men who glory in shedding blood worthy of death?'

" 'Possibly; if so, what matter? Perchance thou wouldst
have me punish them for such action?—said my father, scorn-
fully.

" 'Even so, Astika. And thereafter depart hence?'

" 'Aye, that will I! 'Tis a good jest; yet have I not humor
for jesting!'

" 'And thou wilt not go, though I say to remain is death?'

" 'Nay! Cease thy drivel! I weary of it.'

" 'Astika, I am sorrowful! But be it as thou wilt. Thou hast been warned to leave. Thou hast heard of the power of the Suern, and believed not. But now, feel it!'

"With these words the Rai swept his outpointing index-finger over the place where stood our pride—the splendid two thousand. His lips moved and I barely heard the low-spoken words:

" 'Yeovah, strengthen, my weakness. So dieth stubborn guilt.'

"What then befell so filled all spectators with horror, so wrought upon their superstition, that for full five minutes after, scarce a sound was heard. Of all those veteran warriors not one was left alive. At the gesture of the Suernis their heads fell forward, their grasp was loosed on their spears, and they fell as drunken men to the earth. Not a sound, save that of their precipitation; not a struggle; death had come to them as it comes to those whose hearts stop pulsing. Ah! what frightful power hast thou, Suernis!"

> "For the Angel of Death spread his wings on the blast,
> And breathed in the face of the foe as he passed."

Sennacherib was unknown then; the Salda princess knew not of the poem; but we do, my reader, thou and I; that is enough.

While describing the action of the Rai of Suern, the princess had risen to her feet from her place by the side of Menax, simulating at the same time the fatal gesture of Ernon of Suern. So apt had been this mimicry that the group of listeners on our left had involuntarily cowered as her arm swept over their heads. The Saldu noticed them shrink, and her lip curled with scorn.

"Cowards!"—she muttered. A Poseida overheard the words, and his cheek flushed, as he said:

"Nay, Astiku, not cowards! Consider our involuntary shrinking as a compliment to thy descriptive powers."

She smiled, and said:—"Perhaps so." Then, overcome by her apostrophe to the dread strength of Yeovah as invoked by Ernon, a strength which even proud Atla feared—she sank back in her seat weeping.

A little wine revived her, and the narration was resumed.

"After the horrible silence that fell on all who had witnessed the awful sight, the women—wives and daughters of the higher officers—began shrieking in affright. Many of our men, as soon as they could realize that the stories they had heard and discredited were no idle tales, fell to the earth in an agony of puling terror. Ah! then, then could ye have heard supplications to all the gods, great and small, in whom our people place trust. Ha! ha!"—laughed the princess, bitterly, contemptuously—"Appealing to gods of wood and metal for protection against such awful power! Faugh! Since I may not live in Suern, being banished, I would not live again in the land of my nativity! I want no more of people who idolize insentient objects and defy them. No, Astika," she said in answer to a question from Menax—"I never worshipped idols; most of our people do, but not all. I have not proved an apostate. But I do worship power. I ought to hate Ernon of Suern; but I do not. Indeed, I would, if permitted, live in his presence and idolize his wondrous strength, which works death to his enemies. Not so permitted, I would rather remain with thy people, who are a goodly race, and, if not equal to the Suerni, are yet better and more powerful than mine own, ah! far more so.

"My father knew better than to imagine this some trick of a wily people—knew now, after this bitter lesson, that the reputation accorded them by travelers was no idle fabrication of wonder-mongers. But he did not cringe before the Rai—he was too proud-spirited for that. While we gazed, stupefied, on the awful scene of death, another and not less frightful, but more ghastly thing happened. We that were alive—all our host except the two thousand stood between our dead and the river west of the city. Rai Ernon bowed his head and prayed —what dire alarm that action caused our people!—and I heard him say:

" 'Lord, do this thing for thy servant, I beseech thee!' "

"Then, as I gazed on the victims, I saw them arise one by one, and gather up each his spear and shield and helmet. Thereafter, in little irregular squads they marched towards us, towards me. O! My God!—and passed on to the river! As they passed I saw that their eyes were half-closed and glazed in death; the movement of their limbs was mechanical; they walked as if hung on wires, and their armor clanked and clanged in a horrid, mocking ring. As, one by one, the squads came to the river, they walked in, deeper and deeper, till the waters closed over their heads, and they were gone forever— gone to feed the crocodiles which already roared and snarled over their prey adown the stream of Gunja. No one to lead, none to carry; each going as if alive, and yet somehow dead, this ghastly procession to the river, a thousand paces distant, so completed the horrible sense of fear that desperate terror possessed the great army, and they fled, leaving behind all things, and soon only a few faithful soldiers were left in sight; these remained with their commander and his officers of staff, ready to share with him the death which they expected would be meted out to all who remained. The women also did not all flee. Then spoke Rai Ernon, saying:

" 'Did I not tell thee to depart, ere I punished thee? Wilt thou now go? Behold thine army in flight! Its rout shall not cease, for thousands shall never more see Saldee, because they will perish by the wayside, yet not a few shall reach their homes. But thou shalt never more go home, neither thee nor thy women. But they will not stay in my land nor their own, but in a strange country.' "

"That haughty, but now humbled soldier, my father, bent on one knee before the Rai, and said:

" 'Mighty Rai, what wouldst thou with innocent women? Thou saidst my warriors were guilty; I admit it, nor except myself. But these, my women—they have harmed no man. Thy words lead me to believe that justice is thy ruling principle; thine acts do likewise, for when thou mightest have struck us every one, thou didst no more than make example of a few guilty ones. I implore thee, then, have mercy on my women; perchance on my officers also.'

" 'On thy officers, yes; they are faithful unto thee, though they expect but death as their reward. Bid them depart with what still bides of thine army. They are unused to caring for the needs of the body, wherefore they will of a surety all perish, except I save them. Having power, I will use it mercifully. None shall perish by the wayside; not one shall hunger, neither thirst, nor suffer any sickness, O Yeovah! all the way home, nor lose his way, though none shall have to eat any food all the way. And about them shall wild beasts rave, and though not one have a weapon, no animal shall harm him, for the spirit of Yeovah shall go with them and be their shelter and their safeguard. Yea, more also, shall He do—for he will enter into their souls, so that they that are warriors shall be henceforth His prophets, and shall uplift their people and make of their name one which shall go down unto all ages; a famous race of educated men shall they be, and astrologers, telling of God by his works of heaven. Yet shall a further day come some six thousand years hence when the men of Chaldea shall again try to prevail over my people, and again shall fail, even as now, but thou shalt long have been with thy fathers asleep from a second life, and safe in the Name* whereby I work, ere this second attempt. Callest thou innocent, women who voluntarily came in all the insolence of supposed power and invincibility to murder my people? Innocent! they who came to see the rapine of my cities and to revel in the sufferings of my people? Innocent! Nay, not so! Wherefore I shall retain with thee these wives and these maidens. Behold! I have said thou shalt not go hence; neither these women yet awhile, but thou—thou shalt never go again from this land. I will put thee in a prison which has neither bars nor gratings nor any wall; yet thou canst not hope to leave it.'

" 'Dost thou mean that we are all to die, Zo Rai?' asked my father in a low, sad voice.

" 'Not so; Zo Astika, thinkest thou I condemn murder, yet

*Yeovah or Jehovah.—Ed.

would myself do it needlessly? No. Having said that thou
canst not leave Suern, neither is it possible for thee thereafter,
though neither bolt nor bar hindereth, nor any man watcheth
or keepeth thee.'

"It was piteous to see the partings between those who were
to go and those who must stay. But then, such are the fortunes of war, and the weak must obey the strong. I had rejoiced in our fancied strength, nor cared who fell by it. Power,
aye, power! I think, after all, that I felt a grim satisfaction in
beholding thee, Power, my god, work so swift destruction!"

The princess said these last words musingly, apparently lost
to her surroundings as she sat with clenched hands, admiration
depicted on her beautiful face and her glorious blue eyes with
their far-away look, but oh! so heartless, so cruel, after all,
Queenly in figure, commanding in personality, beautiful, won-
derfuly beautiful, the world now, as then, would call the
Princess Lolix; indeed she bore a most startling likeness to
thine own fair American women. But these are not like her,
really. She, lioness-like, sided ever with the triumph-power.
But the real American maiden, sympathetic, true as steel,
graceful as a bird, sweet as a rose just blown—like Lolix in
these three last traits, but ceasing to parallel her further, for
she of today clings to her father, her brother, her lover, come
sunshine, come storm, success or adversity—faithful unto
death. Such have their reward.

There came a day when Lolix was altered to be all that the
fair modern maidens are. But it was not till after years.
There are some kinds of roses which, while in tender bud, seem
all thorns; but what marvels of beauty are they when they have
at length opened their hearts to the sun and the dew!

It appeared that Prince Menax had not heretofore heard
Lolix speak at length, but had for some reason waited this
experience until I might listen. Consequently it was a revelation to him to hear one so fair, and even so sweet, reveal so
heartless a nature as she exhibited in her speech, which was

quite as much retrospective meditation, on her part, as recital. After some moments, Menax said:

"Astiku, thou hast related that his Majesty of Suern did not by thee and thy companions as thou didst anticipate, reasoning from the national custom of thy people to devote female prisoners of war to lust and ministrations to man's base passions."

"Astika Menax, thou'lt not esteem me disrespectful if I shall henceforth call thee friend? I will confess it to have been very much of a surprise that Rai Ernon did not so do. I could not have complained, for such are the vicissitudes of war. Instead, however, he declared that neither he nor the Suerni had any use for us; wherefore he sent us into a foreign land. Is that our destiny here—such a hard fate?"

"No! never so!" replied Menax, his lip curling with disgust at the bare imputation. "Here thou shalt be supported by the government until perchance Poseid citizens shall choose wives of thy number; ours is a people of strange tastes, sometimes!"

"Thou art sarcastic, Astika!"

Save that the prince slightly raised his eyebrows, he vouchsafed no reply to her remark; even this notice was so faint that if I had not been closely watching his face, I should not have perceived it. After a more or less extended silence, Menax said that they were hindered from evermore returning home to Salda, because—

"No longer my home!" quickly interrupted the lady.

"Then the land of thy birth!" said Menax with some asperity, as he again lapsed into silence.

Lolix then arose and, clasping her hands, vehemently exclaimed:

"I have no wish evermore to see my native land. Henceforth I choose my lot in Poseid—to call it home!"

"As thou wilt," said Menax. "Thou art certainly a most strange woman! For love of power thou forsakest gods and home and native land. Are the others, thy captive friends— nay, hold! perchance not friends, seeing that they are fallen under misfortune!—are these as thyself, these women, forgetful of their country?"

Bending her lovely head, the princess fixed the gaze of her glorious blue eyes upon the upturned face of her critic. Two drops—tear-drops—fell from beneath the long sweeping lashes, her lips quivered, and she clasped her little hands together with the words:

"Ah! Astika, thou art cruel;" then turned away and walked sobbing to the seat where first I had seen her.

Thus was the unblown rosebud mistaken for a thistle blossom.

As for me, a strange mixture of feelings possessed me, a commingling of wonder and approval. I wondered what sort of a nature it was that could be so heartless and thirst so greatly after power as to leave every natural tie for the sake of following it, and yet was so essentially feminine as to be pained at the expression of a very natural reprobation of such conduct. I pitied her because she was so ingenuous, and was so sincerely honest in and through all her soullessness, and had so artlessly narrated her later history, evidently expectant of approbation, and felt so hurt at the contrary effect produced. Finally, approval divided my emotions, because the prince had given a really merited rebuke, and one which, though its smart was keen, could not fail of a salutary effect. My reflections were interrupted at this point by Menax, saying:

"Zailm, let us go into the Xanatithlon* where all is quiet and beautiful among the flowers. We shall be alone there, thou and I. I would dismiss these people of my palace, but prefer not to disturb you Saldee maiden."

CHAPTER XII.

THE UNEXPECTED HAPPENS.

A very few steps took us into the great conservatory, or Xanatithlon, where bloomed all manner and species of flowers.

*Building for flowers.

In the midst, was a fountain whose three lofty jets sprang into the arch of the great dome, and sparkled during the day in the sun-rays as they filtered through the thousands of panes of many-colored glass. Now, however, when the dull roar of the rain falling on all without, mingled its tones with the dulcet plash of the fountain, that object of beauty was flashing in the rays of numerous electric images of the Day King.

Intermingled with the myriads of natural flowers were many hundreds wrought in glass so perfectly that only close examination by sense of touch might say which were produced by Flora and which by the artist. These illuminants were suited in kind to the natural flowers of the plant, tree or vine on which they hung; on the plants there were but few, on the trees, higher above the floor, the number increased, while on the vines that clambered over arches and pillars, or swung pendent between high points overhead were a great multitude, casting throughout this floral paradise a soft, steady glow which was most delightful.

In the midst of these pleasant environments we seated ourselves on what to the eye seemed a pile of moss-covered rocks with cosy depressions amongst them—very comfortable, since in reality they were easy springs, whereon grew moss originally furnished by silk-worms.

"Sit here, closer to me, my son,"—said the benign old prince, drawing me down into a hollow beside that occupied by himself.

"Zailm,"—he began—"I hardly know why I called thee this night; why I waited not for a time. And yet I do know, too; I had a mission to confer upon some one fitted to perform it. There are others more experienced, yet I choose to give it to thee; thou knowest what it is."

Very evident to me was it that this was not what actuated the Astika in his choice, and that it was not for this that he had asked me into the conservatory. He had relapsed into silence, which he presently broke by asking:

"Hast thou ever heard that my wife gave me a son, and that both wife and son are taken by death? Aye, one son, and a daughter. Praise unto Incal, I have her yet! But my son, the pride of my life, is gone unto Navazzamin, the destiny of all mortality. My son, oh, my son!''—he sobbed.

When his emotion had somewhat subsided, he resumed:

"Zailm, when I saw thee, at thy first speech with our beloved Rai—four years ago, was it not?—I was astonished at thy likeness to my dead boy, and I loved thee then, Zailm! Many a time have I gone to the Xioquithlon to note thee at work in thy studies. Always have the summonses thou hast received at divers times to attend at this astikithlon had for their prompting motive sight of thee! Yes, sight of thee, lad, sight of thee!''—he murmured softly, gently stroking my curls the while.

"Few days have passed that I have not at some time seen thee, either personally or by naim; yes, I have gone at night, and stood by thy window, that I might gladden my heart with the sound of thy voice as thou hast sat reading to thy mother. I have watched thee, and been proud of thee, Zailm, for in every way thou hast seemed as my own; thy triumphs in study have made joyful my days, as has also the skill with which thou hast performed governmental commissions—for thou wert as my son! Then come and live here, lad, for I want thee near me, in this mine old age. Together will we float down the stream of life, thou and I! Perchance I go first out across the great ocean of eternity; then will I await thee in the dim land of dreams, where is no more parting, neither pain nor sorrow. Come, Zailm, come!''

To this tender appeal I replied:

"Menax, I have often wondered, during the years of my abode in Caiphul, what meant thy favors to me. Thou hast ever been more kind to me than any other, yet have ever been reserved and distant, yea, more so than others who could not care overmuch what befell me. Now all is plain. I have looked on thee with affection and loving reverence, and treasured thy kindnesses, and acted according to thy few words of advice. Yea, Menax, we will together go hand in hand to the shadowy land of departed souls, thou for me, or I for thee, waiting the other's coming, whichsoever the Harvester of Souls shall first garner.''

We arose and tenderly embraced each other. As we parted our clasp, I beheld the only child of the prince, enframed in clustering vines that twined caressingly around her lovely form. As I looked upon her I thought of that other girl, the Saldu to whose story I had so recently listened. Nearly the same age, neither of them more than a year my junior, but so widely different from each other as types of womanly beauty. It is difficult to describe a person in whom the deepest interest of the heart is centered, and the greater this feeling, the more difficult will be the portraiture. At least, it is so in my case.

The reader is aware how the brown-haired, blue-eyed, queenly girl of far away Sald appeared, how delicate her fair complexion, how high-strung and sensitive her nature, yet withal, how cruel! But how can I picture her whom I loved, her with whom the hope of a chance meeting, even at a distance, made a great part of the pleasure I felt in going to the palace of Menax. She whom I had loved and enshrined within my heart nearly as many years as I had resided in Caiphul— how can I describe her?

If the Princess Lolix was on the threshold of womanhood, so was this fair one, the Princess Anzimee. Slight, delicate, womanly, the daughter of a long line of patrician ancestry; my senior and superior in the ranks of study at the Xioquithlon, if my junior in years; I loved her, yet carefully concealed the fact. Each of my friends who reads this will know what I feel when I avow unwillingness to describe Anzimee, and bid each to place in this Poseid life-frame the picture of his own best-loved one.

"Each heart recalled a different name,
But all sang 'Annie Laurie.' ''

Prince Menax caught sight of his daughter at nearly the same moment as I did, and a look of mild surprise overspread his face at her presence, when he had supposed the Xanatithlon deserted. Seeing this expression, the Rainu came forward and, kissing her father, said:

"My father, have I intruded? I heard thee and this—this youth enter, but knew not that thou didst desire privacy, so kept my seat and continued my reading."

"Nay, my pet, thou hast no need of excuse. I am, indeed, rather glad that thou art here. But what, may I ask, wert thou reading? It will not be well for thee to study too hard, and this, I suspect, was, or is, thy meaning when thy word is 'reading.'"

With a sweet smile dancing over her face and lighting her gray eyes, she replied: "Thou wouldst make an excellent reader of the hidden mind! I was indeed studying, but the end justifies the labor. Whosoever shall acquire a deep knowledge of the science of medicine shall be in a position to relieve even those in the agonies of mortal pain, and to cure those less gravely afflicted. Is it not a work for Incal then, as well as for His children, and is not such an act done for the least of these, something done also for Him?"

Two girls—Lolix of Sald, and Anzimee of Poseid! A wide continent separated their two countries, but a yet greater distance was between the daughters of the two lands. Lolix, with no sympathy for those in pain, no sorrow for those in mortal agony; Anzimee, at the very antipodes of such traits of character.

For a full minute there was silence, while Menax looked at the noble-hearted, dainty speaker. Then, clasping my hands with his right, and those of Anzimee with his left, he said:

"My child, unto thee I give a brother—one whom I deem worthy to be such; Zailm, unto thee I give a sister more precious than rubies; and unto Thee, Incal, my God! all the song of praise which fills my breast for Thy blessings to me." Here he dropped the hands that had touched together for the first time, and lifted his own to heaven.

How the touch of that little hand thrilled me ere it was withdrawn. Was I worthy of all this love? No sin yet stained my fair fame, and I felt at that moment entirely deserving. If ever it blotted my record, sin was yet to come; but with disquiet I thought of the strange prophecy on that night of long ago; for an instant only this feeling possessed me, and then it fled.

I was much given to the habit of analyzing men and motives; it was a second nature, so to speak, to consider every question in every possible aspect. So, even now, I was querying myself as to the meaning of this latest experience. I knew that for Menax, who had so winningly asked me to be his son, I entertained the most profound respect and affection. My life would not have appeared to me too great a price to pay, if for it I could have bestowed commensurate benefit on him; and I loved life, too; there was nothing morbid about my nature, unless exceeding love for my friends be a sign of morbidness. I dwelt a little upon what my adoption meant socially and politically. Thou needest not be told what it must have been to my ambition thus to be placed in so high a niche as I would thenceforth occupy in Atlan estimation as the legal son of a high councillor, who by marriage was the brother of the Rai. All this time, while considering the situation, I was reserving as a choice sensation the pleasure of examining what was the kind of love I felt for her who was my sister—by adoption only, it is true—but who, herself the pet of inner circles, and the adored of the people of Caiphul, would appear before the world as my sister the moment Rai Gwauxln should officially approve his brother's course.

Ought I to feel pleasure or vexation? I looked at her whom I had dreamed of as my wife in case Incal in His goodness should see fit to grant me exaltation to high places. Could I hope to realize the dream, after this unexpected turn of fortune? If I had come to my high place by a different manner, then I could have hoped for the hand of Anzimee. But now! My great fortune semed like an apple of Sodom, bitterness to my mouth. For I was her brother, legally, if not by consanguineous ties. There was a chance that things were not so dark as they semed, since such adoptions among the lower classes were frequent, yet did not act as a bar to marriage. So, thus again, the sun came from behind the clouds.

The characteristic most marked in the appearance of the girl before me was the simplicity of her attire. That evening, her glory of brown tresses was caught in a loose, unbraided fall at the back of her shapely head by a plain golden clasp. A long, flowing robe clothed her slender, girlish form. No costume could be more artistically, tastefully simple than this colorless, diaphanous fabric, tinged just enough with blue to seem pearly white. Shoulder-tips of pure carmine indicated the wearer's royalty. Her dress was gathered at her throat by a pin made of a golden bar whereon flashed large rubies, grouped about a center of pearls and emeralds, the whole heightening the color of her cheeks so as to make her seem some lovely human rose-bud. Rich, as it was quiet, the attire added nothing to the girl's own sweetly dignified loveliness. The pearls—emblem of her rank as a Xioqenu; the emeralds—mark of her not yet having attained political voice; the rubies—gems of royalty, worn only by the Rai, or one of his near relatives. Gwauxln's own sister was Anzimee's mother and the wife of Menax.

Poseid derived her greatness from her educational superiority—a greatness which recognized no sex in its learned ballot-holders. But if Atlantis owed all things to knowledge, it was none the less true that Atl's people of ability would not have been what they were had it not been for their wives, the sisters and the daughters, and more than all, the mothers of our proud land. Our grand social fabric was founded on and built by the efforts of sons and daughters who, for centuries, had respected the lessons inculcated by fond, true, patriotic mothers. Next to that paid to his Creator was the homage which a Poseida accorded to woman. We loved our Rai, and the Astiki; we respected them as much as ever rulers in this world have been respected; but we honored our women more, and Rai and prince, sovereign and subject, were proud to acknowledge the holy influence which made all our glorious land of freedom one great home. America, thou art beloved by me even as was

Poseid. Foremost amongst nations, art thou so because of woman—and Christ. Thou wilt keep in the van because of them, and eclipse all the world beside when the happy karmic day shall have arrived which places woman not below, not above, but by the side of man on the rock of esoteric Christian education, the granite of knowledge and faith, which withstands the winds and storms of ignorance. Built on such foundation, the National house shall not fall; built on other, great shall be the fall of it. Here is wisdom:—myriad serpents are in a man; in thee; keep them. Now ye are slaves. Be ye masters instead. But, alas! this Way is narrow; few will to find it.

CHAPTER XIII.

THE LANGUAGE OF THE SOUL.

"Zailm, my son, thou heardst the narration of the Saldu, Lolix. As thou knowest, it is from things arisen out of the occurrences by her related that thou goest on a mission to Suern. It is not a hard task, merely to make return of acknowledgement for the gifts presented, and disavowal of our intent to keep as prisoners the people whom Rai Ernon sent hither. We will give them asylum, but Rai Ernon must not think that we permit their presence for any purpose except to do him a favor. Concerning other business; on the morrow it is Rai Gwauxln's pleasure that thou attendest at Agacoe. But wilt thou not remain here this night?"

"My father, I fain would stay; but is it not duteous that I go unto my mother this night, and set her at ease? She hath an infirmity of nervousness than can not well withstand my absence at night."

"Thou are right, Zailm. Yet soon it must be arranged that thy mother be domiciled in some pleasant part of this astikithlon; so that thou shalt be under thy father's roof at night."

I then departed from the prince and from the sweet girl who had been with us during a part of the evening, and went forth into the night. The rain had ceased, and the clouds, rolling across the sky in sullen blackness, had but one rift in their gloomy mass. In this single rent shone a great white star, which at times flashed red. As I looked at it, down close to the horizon, seeming that moment risen from old ocean's phosphorescent waters, visible from Menax Heights, I thought of the past; for this star had flashed brightly upon me while I awaited the sunrise on Pitach Rhok. So many years it seemed since that morn! Today this star is called "Sirus"—we named it "Corietos." As I looked upon it, it seemed an omen auspicious of success—past, present and to come. Raising my hands toward it, I murmured:

"Phyris, Phyrisooa Pertos!" which is: "Star, O star of my life."

It seems a little singular that the language which is translated thus should have a similar sound and import as today used by the people of my home-planet. At that old day I raised my hands aloft and exclaimed: "Star, O star of my life!" To-day I turn awhile from precipitating this history in astral word-things, turn to my Alter Ego, and say: "Phyris, Phyrisa." This is her own dear name, and signifies "Star of my soul." Peculiar, is it not, that twelve thousand years should pass, and I, member of another race of human beings, in another mansion, find so little change in the language of the soul?

CHAPTER XIV.

THE ADOPTION OF ZAILM.

When, according to request, I arrived at the Agacoe palace on the next morning, I proceeded directly to the private office there occupied by Prince Menax, expecting to find my father alone. But in this I was disappointed, as Rai Gwauxln was there with him. The two were in conversation when I entered, and did not cease, evidently not regarding me as an intruder. At last I heard the Rai ask:

"Should we not now go to the Incalithlon?"

"If it please thee. And thou, Zailm, accompany us."

A palace car was summoned by the Rai, and came rolling along into our presence without any person to operate it; came in at the door of the office, which opened to allow its passage precisely as if some court page had opened it. It wheeled into the room and came to a stop in front of us. All this was done exactly as if under a guiding hand. But no visible hand was there. This was the first time I had ever seen any exhibition of occult power on the part of Gwauxln; indeed I never saw many examples of his power, notwithstanding his high adeptship. Like all true adepts he was exceedingly chary of such object lessons, disliking to show his knowledge before those not posessed of sufficient common sense to know that any acts of the sort were but examples of the control of nature through an understanding of higher laws than the ordinary mind perceives in its natural surroundings; but I was not one who saw anything miraculous in the occult; if I understand not the process, I did understand that it was but the operation of some unfamiliar law. Hence Gwauxln was not averse to allowing me to witness his power at times.

The car conveyed us to the vailx-landing outside, where we found a vailx of small size, into which Rai Gwauxln courteously assisted first Menax, then myself, and himself entered last. Here was a spectacle worthy of note; the ruler of a mighty nation without the display of a single attendant, not more deferential to rank than to those of inferior station. True, as a Xio-Incali, Gwauxln had command over mechanical service which was more regal far than a retinue of menials could be.

Like father, like son. Gwauxln, who was as a father to his people, was copied by them in his demeanor. They, too, were simple in habits, courteous in manner, and, though in many

cases wealthy, and luxurious in their habits in life, were entirely unostentatious, as their Rai set them example.

The great temple of Incal was distant several miles, but a few
minutes sufficed to bring us to its huge structure. Outwardly
the Incalithlon was shaped like the Egyptian pyramid of
Cheops, not quite so high, but covering an area of twice as great
extent. No windows pierced its sides, and sunlight or that of
day never entered its interior. Besides a number of small
apartments, the building contained one vast hall where was
space for several thousand worshippers. The Poseid habit of
copying nature was followed in this sanctuary with extraordinary faithfulness. Instead of straight walls, or alcoves, or
the ordinary arrangement of interiors, the enormous auditorium
was in faithful semblance of a cave of stalacttes and stalagmites.
In placing all this calcite, utility was consulted with regard to
the stalagmites so that too much floor space should not be occupied by them. But the stalactites, being pendent from the
marble ceiling, had been placed as thickly as space allowed,
and sparkled like stars in the light from the incandescent
lamps swung midway between them and the floor below. From
the latter point of view these lamps were concealed by broad
concave shades so that their glow was wholly invisible from
beneath, but shining upwards was reflected from myriads of
sparkling white needles, filling the temple with a steady and
soft, but powerful light that seemed to emanate from no
special point, but from the air itself—a light well adapted to
religious meditation.

We left the vailx and entered the unimposing but ample portal, and proceeded across the hall to the Holy Seat, in the back
of the sanctuary. Within it we found Mainin, the Incaliz, or
high priest, a man of wondrous attainments of knowledge, second to none in fact. To him we all made courteous obeisance,
and then Prince Menax said:

"Most holy Incaliz, thou knowest, in thy great wisdom, upon
what errand thy sons have come before thee. Wilt thou fulfill
our prayer by granting us thy blessing?"

The Incaliz arose and bade us to follow him into the triangle of the Maxin, or Divine Light, in front of the Holy Seat. Deferring the relation of our subsequent action, I will describe this especially sacred part of the temple. It was a raised, triangular platform of red granite, several inches higher than the floor of the auditorium, thirty-six feet between its points. In the very center of it was a large block of crystal quartz, upon the perfect cube of which rose the Maxin. This seemed aflame, in shape like a giant spear-head, and it cast a light of intense power over all things around, yet one could look at its steady, unwavering white glow without desiring shade for the eyes, even though these were not strong. Over three times the height of a tall man it stood, a mysterious manifestation of Incal, as all spectators believed. In reality it was an occult odic light, and had stood in that one spot for centuries. It had witnessed the grander development of Poseid and its capital city, and had seen the original temple of Incal (a small architectural structure, unworthy of a great people) torn down, and the present Incalithlon built around it. It made no heat, did not even warm the quartz pedestal; yet for any living being to touch it was fatal in the instant of the rash act. No oil, no fuel, no electric currents fed it; no man tended it. Its history was peculiar, and can not fail to interest thee, my friends.

Many hundred years previously there had been for four hundred and thirty-four days a ruler over the Poseidi who possessed wonderful knowledge. This wisdom was like that of Ernon of Suern. No one knew whence he came, and not a few were disposed to question his statement, while all were in doubt, as to whether his meaning was figurative or literal when he said:

"I am from Incal. Lo, I am a child of the Sun, and am come to reform the religion and life of this people. Behold Incal is the Father and I am the Son, and He is in Me and I am in Him."

He was asked to prove this claim, whereupon he laid his hand upon a man born blind, and the man received his sight and saw with the doubters that his deliverer stooped to the pavement of the triangular platform, and with his finger drew a square five and a half feet either way. Then he stepped out-side of the lines indicated, and at once the great block of quartz appeared, a perfect cube, in the place. Standing by its side he placed his finger upon the rock, and blew thereon with his breath. As he withdrew the finger the Maxin, or Fire of Incal sprang up, and thus had Cube and Unfed Fire remained during all the centuries since.

It is needless to say the proof was satisfactory, and there-after the mysterious stranger revised the laws and provided then the code which had ever since governed the land. He had said that whosoever should add to or take from his laws, that person should not come into the Kiugdom of Incal until "I am come on earth for the final judgment."

No one had ever desired to disobey, it would seem, or at least no change had ever been made. The laws which this Rai had given were written by him with his finger upon the Maxin-Stone, and no work of sculptor's chisel were better done. They were also written upon a book of parchment leaves, and this he placed under the Unfed Light itself, which thereafter sprang from the surface of the Book; this had remained ever since, unharmed, unscorched. The wonderful writer had placed it there in sight of all the people who could enter the new Tem-ple built in place of the old one. As he did so, he said:

"Hearken unto me. This is my law. Behold it also written on the Maxin-Stone. No man shall remove it, lest he die. Yet after centuries have flown, behold! the Book shall disappear in sight of a multitude, and no man shall know its place. Then shall the Unfed Light go out, and no man be able to rekindle it. And when these things have come to pass, lo! the day is not far off when the land shall no more be. It shall perish because of its iniquity, and the waters of Atl shall roll above it! I have spoken."

Once, in the history of Poseid, a Rai had come to doubt whether a man would surely die if he tried to withdraw the Book of the Unfed Light. He conceived the idea that as the Maxin sprang from the top of the Book alone, and not from its sides, that removal might be possible. So therefore he forced a malefactor to attempt the deed, fearing after all to try it himself, although in the tyrannous policy which he followed, he cared not whether the man died or not. That was a day of growing darkness and wickedness, when men had somewhat forgotten the Great Rai, Son of Incal. The unhappy wretch was made to grasp the Book, and withdraw it if he could. He found it impossible to move it, but yet was not destroyed by the Maxin. Grown bolder, and urged by the Rai, he tried harder. He pulled, and then his grasp gave way, and one hand passed through the Maxin. The member was instantly destroyed, cut off, gone, while the monarch, standing many feet distant, fearful of approaching near, was stricken in that same instant by an outleaping flash of the Maxin, and no one ever saw him more!

That one example was sufficient! The error of their ways suddenly became very apparent to the evil-doers, and administration of the laws was again in accord with their spirit, as with their letter. The day of the "Dismal Prophecy" had been looked for as the decades passed into centuries, but its time was not yet come, and though many alarmists set days when it would surely come, it came not, and the Unfed Light continued. According to the law bodies of all souls which had passed into Navazzamin were cremated. This even included some animals. Those dying at a distance from Caiphul were incinerated in some one of the multitude of Navamaxa (furnaces especially for dead bodies) which the government provided all through the provinces, and if the incinerated body was that of a human being, the ashes were taken to Caiphul and cast into the Maxin, as a ceremonial act. Those of the departed from Caiphul were taken as they lay in death to the Incalithlon, and being raised to the top of the Cube, were let fall face forward into the Unfed Light. In either case, whether as incinerated ashes or unaltered forms, the result was the same; that is, while there was no flaming, no smoke, no tremor of the Maxin, nevertheless the instantaneous disappearance of the object occurred at the second of contact with the marvellous Unfed Fire.

Hence it had been sung by poets as the "Gateway" to the country which each soul must discover for itself. To die, without in some manner passing into the Maxin, either in corpus personae or by the ashes from prior incineration, was thought to be the most frightful calamity by the greater number of the people.

It might appear that people of such scientific erudition would not be so seemingly childish in religious conceptions as this. As a verity it was not childishness.   Instead, it was an insistence upon such entire destruction of the earthly casket of the soul, as to render certain the freedom of the real person from all earthly restraint in entering into Navazzamin.

Not that many people understood the esoteric significance of the rite; no, they but understood so much of the real meaning as the Incali had given them through comparing the earth-leaving soul to the seed which, sprouting, leaves behind it every fragment of the shell.

To return to the Incalithlon, and the ceremonial of my adoption by Prince Menax.

As we stood beside the Maxin-Stone, Gwauxln bade me kneel, and then, placing his hand upon my head, spoke, saying:

"In harmony with the laws of the land, made and provided in such cases, Astika Menax, a Councillor of the land of Poseid, hath a wish to adopt thee, Zailm Numinos, for a son unto his name, in place of one departed hence into Navazzamin. Wherefore, as thy Sovereign and his, I, Gwauxln, Rai of Poseid, do declare it to be as prayed for by Astika Menax."

The Incaliz completed the ceremonies by placing his right hand upon my head and his left upon that of Menax as we knelt before him, and invoking the blessing of Incal upon us both. As he removed his hands, he addressed me thus:

"Be thou erect in the sight of Incal, that no man may accuse thee truthfully. This do, and thy days shall be long. But even as thou shalt fail, so then shall thy time be shortened. May the peace of Incal be with thee."

Not one of the three hearers of the Incaliz understood him to mean that my days would be short because I would fail in rectitude, but only as a warning were the words taken. Yet I knew afterwards, all too late, what prescience guided Mainin in his words. Knew in a flood of bitter memory, which recalled how recreant I had been to the high resolve on Pitach Rhok to be successful, as a result of being true to my divine, God-considering selfhood. But all this came, as I thought, too late. Too late was it when I lay in a dungeon awaiting death, from which no mortal could save me, and dreamed that my soul sat on a verdureless shore looking across a limitless ocean, and crying, "Ah! where is the hope of my years!" Bitter and fiery was the remorseful agony, but my name was still on the Book of Life; still there, and not erased as I feared. Karma is inexorable and severe, my brother, my sister; but our Savior hath said: "Follow Me." "He that hath an ear to hear, let him hear." "Be ye doers of the word, and not hearers only."

As we turned away, an Incala, who had been present, began playing on the great organ of the temple; then the silences of the vast auditorium responded as no human voice could make them do.

"On the winds the bells' deep tones are swelling—"

The echoes rang again and again as the thundering voices of the great organ pealed forth, thrilling the soul with its mighty harmony. Rays of many-hued lights, some brilliant, some soft-tinted as those of a spectroscopic image of the moon, played from point to point in exhausted air-tubes, and as the colors changed, so did the notes of music—for every ray of light, whatsoever its source, is a pulsing choral note, if developed rightly. Thus the stars sing.

The Rai did not go with Menax and myself, when the conclusion of our business was reached, but remained with the Incaliz Mainin. With him Gwauxln was more familiar, his friendship more deeply intimate than with any other human being. And the reason was that both he and Mainin were Sons of the Solitude, and had been youths together in the days ere public favor had marked the one for Rai, the other for Incaliz —these both being elective positions, the office of High Priest being the only ecclesiastical office which could be filled by popular vote. And this exception was because it was considered true justice to allow the people to consult their own desires in this matter of choosing one whom all believed to be the most eminently good and perfect example of moral life, to be over them in this highest spiritual office.

But in the days of their youth neither had seemed to expect the preferment which the years had in store, and after the long course required of Xio Incali at the Xioquithlon, both had bidden the world of men adieu and had gone forth into the solitudes of the vast mountains, where only the Sons of Incal had abode, of all mankind. These men were the Theochristic or Occult Adepts of that olden age,—the Yog-Vidya of their time. They were indeed chary of their wisdom, then as now; but to Gwauxln and Mainin they imparted it without stint. They had no families then, nor do these students of God, of Nature, deviate now from the same celibate principles. None who hope to achieve their deep knowledge will mate.*

After years had flown, so many that men had almost forgotten them, Gwauxln and Mainin did what few had ever been known to do—returned to the haunts of ordinary humanity. My father, Menax, had been but a babe when Gwauxln went away, and the latter's sister was not then born. Yet when Gwauxln came back, the silvery threads of age already gleamed in the hair of the Prince Menax, while as for the Rai that was to be, he looked a little more mature, but otherwise unchanged from the youthful semblance of the days of yore. In the interim, his sister had come to the world, grown to womanhood, wedded Menax, and after bringing into life their son, Soris, and their daughter, Anzimee, had gone into the undiscovered country through the Maxin gateway. Mainin, too, was of a similarly youthful appearance.

Both of these "Sons of the Solitude" came back, giving as their reason for return that their presence was needed, and both were eventually chosen by the people to fill the respctive positions which we have seen them occupying, positions rendered vacant by the death of the incumbents. It is only now,

*I. Cor. vii., 3-4-5-7-8-9-29-31-32.

after twelve thousand years have slipped into eternity through the back door of time that I have come to know how much Mainin had to do with those events, and how wholly in the dark concerning his real character was Gwauxln, and every other Son of the Solitude.   Not to anticipate, is it strange that Rai Gwauxln felt more pleasurably intimacy possible in his intercourse with Mainin than with any other person connected with his daily life? Or that he felt his finally exposed treachery more keenly than any one else could? I think not.

———————

CHAPTER XV.

A MATERNAL DESERTION.

On leaving my farm-home that morning, I had told my mother all that had transpired, and said that she should have an escort to the palace, whither, after my recent change of fortune, I expected her to go and live, in accordance with the instructions of Menax.

What an anomalous position was this.   Here was I, son by adoption of one of the Imperial Princes, and by virtue of being recognized brother of his daughter, Anzimee, I was a nephew of my sister's uncle, Rai Gwauxln.   Yet my mother was not related to any of these royalties, and had seen none of them, except the Rai, often enough to enable her to be sure of recognition should she meet them again.   But I rejoiced when I thought of the opportunities she would presently have of more intimate acquaintanceship.

Having sent the promised escort for her, what was my surprise on returning to the palace, at learning from my father that instead of coming she had sent a message in writing.   I hastily broke the seal and read, in her fine Poseidic chirography, the simple command:

"Zailm, come to me.
        PREZZA NUMINOS."

I went. Somehow an icy feeling of apprehension was about my heart, a presentiment of something harrowing. When I arrived at the house, my mother, looking, as I thought, rather pale, said:

"My son, I cannot go to the palace. I have no desire to do so. I am overjoyed at thy success in life, then, in thy high place. I may not go with thee. Thou art easy in the midst of noble society—I could never be so. Perhaps thou wilt say that for me thou wilt give it up and remain with me. Do not do so. Lest thou feel thus, it is best that thou shouldst endure the pain of knowledge now rather than hereafter. Listen: I have cared for thee during the years of infancy and boyhood, and seen thee arrive at man's estate. Thou needest not this care now. I will go back to the home of the mountains—"

"Mother, talk not so!" I interrupted.

"Hear me through, Zailm! I will go back to the mountains with my husband, he whom thou knowest not, a good man, a lover ere I married thy father, and whom, having wedded this morning, the notice of it hath doubtless by this time been published abroad. An Incala who came past very opportunely, performed the simple ceremony. My other husband, thy father, I loved not, but did detest, for it was a marriage arranged by my parents against my will, but alas! with my consent, fool that I was to give it! Thou art the fruit of that union, and to me came unwished. For thy father was disliked, abhorred, but dying, left you heritor, not of my dislike—that were too unjust:—but, must I say it?—an object of indifference. I have not been a lacking mother, for, as a matter of pride, I concealed my feelings. In a way I even love thee; I love my friends; 'tis nothing deeper. I have now to bid thee good-bye, having said which it is necessary to—"

I heard no more, for I had falled unconscious upon the floor. Was this the mother I had idolized? For whom I had striven so hard in the earlier years and later, in Caiphul, ere a new object to work for arose, and led me thenceforth with greater determination in the form of a double ideal—love of mother, and love of Anzimee? O Incal! My God! O my God!

At last I came out of the horrid dream into which, without regaining consciousness after my swoon, I had passed, a heated nightmare of brain fever.

"Mother!"

As I uttered the loved word, Astika Menax, who sat by my bedside, turned away, his eyes brimming with tears.

"Nay, Zailm, be not troubled! Thou hast been ill near unto death with brain fever these two weeks. I will tell thee all, tomorrow, perhaps. Thou camest very close to going to await me in the Shadowy Land; but not long wouldst thou have had to wait, my light—for it would have been but a little while ere I rejoined thee, lad!"

The story is not long. My mother, being told that good care should aid her in nursing me, said that she would not remain at all, as she doubted not that the skilled care of Menax's private physician could do as well, or better, for me than she. Wherefore she had gone with her husband to their mountain home. From the hour in which Menax told me this, at the cost of much pain to himself, the subject was dropped, and never again referred to by any one.

Once, when I went near to the place of my birth, and sent a messenger to ask if I was welcome, he came back to my vailx and said that a man met him at the door. To him the message was given, and he said: "Say to thy master that my wife bids him come." I went, but could see that she would rather I had not come. She gave me her hand, but did not offer to kiss me, as a mother is wont to do. Her manner—but spare me details of this last meeting, and last time I ever saw my Poseid mother. She acted wisely in not going to the palace, constituted as she was; it is a painful subject; let it be dropped.

———————

As soon as my health permitted me to go on my mission to Suernis—which was not until the new year had begun at the Xioquithlon, from attendance at which the Xiorain forbade me until the next year—Prince Menax took me to his private office.

"The Xiorain has ordered wisely,"—said Menax. "Oh! these younger minds, they are full of promise for the future! No scheme was ever better than this in which the students govern themselves, and on all questions concerning educational matters, even to the distribution and use of the educational funds provided by the government, and the selection of tutors—their word is law."

On the table in Menax's office stood a lovely vase of malleable glass, into which, while fused, powder of gold, silver and other colored metals were mixed, together with certain chemicals which rendered the whole of various degrees of translucency, from nearly opaque to perfect transparency, the various range affecting the metals as well as the glass, and appearing in different parts of the same object. The beauty was not second to the value of the costly product. Menax pointed to the tall vase, and I read upon it this inscription, formed with rubies:

"To Ernon, Rai of Suern, I, Gwauxln, Rai of Poseid, return this in token of thy appreciation of the Poseidi."

If any reader desires to see a fac simile of the original legend in Poseid chirography, the desire is here granted:

Turning from the vase, I asked:

"When shall I go upon this mission, my father?"

"As early as health and convenience permit, Zailm."

"Then be it the day after the morrow."

" 'Tis well. Take any company thou mayst choose. There are none who cannot get leave of absence from the Xiorain, I think, shouldst thou wish fellow students for companions; at least they can probably obtain a vacation of a month, and thou wilt scarcely care to stay longer than thirty-three days. Take also this signet ring, whereby I delegate

thee my deputy, being confident of thy discretion in its use;
its powers are those of Minister of Foreign Business. And
take escort of courtiers, also.''

To this I replied that I would not take a retinue, such as a
staff of officers, since from the story of Astiku Lolix, I judged
Rai Ernon to be one who would look with scorn upon such a
useless appanage. This pleased Menax greatly, and he
proudly said:

"Zailm, thy language pleases me! I see thou art wisely
politic, and dost consider well the probable idiosyncracies of
those with whom thou hast dealings.

During my illness Anzimee had shown much solicitude, and
as I learned from the regular nurses, all the while I was outside the realm of consciousness, she had permitted no one else
to care for me except when she was utterly fatigued, and not
long then. As I convalesced, her presence was not bestowed
upon me except at intervals. I took advantage of one of these
visits to let her know that I was aware of her kindness during
my delirium. She flushed, then said:

"Thou knowest that I am studying the science of therapy;
what better chance to experiment could an eager student have
than thou didst furnish me?"

"Yea, verily," I answered, but felt that there was a deeper
reason than the experimental proclivity, and that the indulgence in the latter was extremely, lovingly cautious!

To Anzimee I outlined a plan for getting the greatest possible amount of pleasure from my trip, after the state business
at Ganje, the capital city of Suernis, should have been attended
to. It was three years since I had been away from Caiphul to
any greater distance than going to Marzeus involved. I
showed her the route I purposed to take; together we scanned
the map, and I pointed out that from Caiphul on the extreme
western cape of Poseid, my course would be east by north
across the continent, the intervening ocean beyond it and between that point and further land. Then still on east across
the country of Necropan, which country—now called Egypt,
Abyssinia, etc.—then embraced the entire continent of Africa,

under one government similar to that of Suern, and was inhabited by a people of kindred powers, but not nearly so
far advanced.

Africa was then not more than half its present size, while
Suernis, which also embraced all of Asia, was much different
from what it is today, but was a name more distinctive of the
peninsula of Hindustan.   Leaving Necropan, the route would
be acros the sea to India, or, as we knew the names, across the
"Waters of Light" (in reference to their phosphorescence) to
Suernis. From Ganje, capital of Suernis, our course was still
eastward across the Pacific ocean, as it is now named, to our
colonies in America, called "Incalia" by us, because in that far
antipodal land, the Sun, Incal, was fabled as making his bed
by that epic heretofore mentioned as the basis of Atlan folk-
lore.

From Southern Incalia (modern Sonora) I intended to go
northwards and skim hastily over the desolate ice-fields of the
arctic regions.   What is now Idaho and Montana, Dakota,
Minnesota, and the Dominion of Canada were then covered
with vast glaciers, the rear-guard of the glacial epoch, which
was slowly retreating, very slowly, even in so late a day,
geologicaly speaking, as the days of Atl, reluctant to end its
frigid reign.   The trip could thus be made to afford novel and
pleasing contrasts—tropical, semi-tropical, temperate and
frigid.

"Would our father object to my going also, Zailm?" asked
Anzimee, wistfully. "I have not been away from Caiphul in
five years."

"Indeed, no, little girl. He bade me invite whomsoever
should please me, and I know of no person who doth please
me more than thou. I have already asked a goodly company
of our common friends."

So Anzimee went also. When everything was arranged, our
party consisted of nearly a score of young people congenial
to each other; a couple of officers of the staff of Menax, with

the necessary servitors, and conveniences for a month's absence. Our vailx was of the middle traffic-size—these vessels being made in four standard lengths—number one, about twenty-five feet; number two, eighty feet; number three, something like one hundred and fifty-five feet, while the largest was yet two hundred feet longer than the third size. These long spindles were in fact round, hollow needles of aluminum, formed of an outer and an inner shell between which were many thousands of double T braces, an arrangement productive of intense rigidity and strength. All the partitions made other braces of additional resistant force. From amidships the vessels tapered toward either end to sharp points. Most vailxa were provided with an arrangement allowing, when desired, an open promenade deck at one end. Windows of crystal, of enormous resistant strength, were in rows like port-holes along the sides, a few on top, and others set in the floor, thus affording a view in all directions. I might mention that the vailx which I had selected for our vacation trip was fifteen feet and seven inches in its greatest diameter.

At the appointed time (the first hour of the third day, as agreed with Menax) my invited guests assembled at the palace, from the roof of which we were to take our departure. How careful I was of my lovely sister, and how proud of her beauty.

The princess Lolix, whom we had ever treated as a guest at Menaxithlon, came up to the platform where the ship lay, curious to see our preparations for departure. It seemed ever new to her to behold an aerial vessel leave terra firma. Not that anything of her wonder was expressed; she made it a point of pride to appear surprised at nothing, however novel or marvellous it might really be to her experience. Indeed, hers was a calm, even temperament, not easily aroused. I had not, in the five or six weeks since hearing her story, again seen her exhibit so much of any sort of emotion as she had that evening when I had observed that my attentions to Anzimee disturbed the Saldu, and I knew that the effect must be deep because of her inability to keep its appearance wholly secret.

Considering that we were bound for Suernis, Lolix was not invited to go, as she otherwise might have been. But I did not forget to bid her a cordial and respectful farewell.

The current keys were set, and, just as the vailx trembled slightly ere leaving the roof, Menax sprang upon the deck, thereby considerably astonishing me, for I had no idea that he intended accompanying us. In reality he did not, but to all questions he preserved a smiling silence.

Long as was our silver-white spindle, we had soon risen so high as to make us seem a mere speck to people on the earth beneath. Then for half an hour we flew at moderate speed through the high abyss, when a young lady called attention to an approaching vailx, following in our wake. Prince Menax, seated in a deck chair by my side, looked over the rail at the surface, more than two miles beneath, then he drew his heavy fur cape more closely about his shoulders, looked back over the hundred miles, more or less, of our course already covered in the half hour, and remarked that the other vailx was rapidly gaining on us.

"Shall I give orders to the vailx-man to increase speed, that we may enjoy a race?" I asked of the company, which clad in arctic clothing, was occupying the passing time in sightseeing round about us on the open deck.

"Nay, not so, my son," said Menax.

I said no more, for it at that moment dawned upon me that the pursuer followed us by the prince's order.

Menax now arose, bade the company good bye and a pleasant trip, and then, Anzimee having arisen also, he put his arm about her and came back to me. As I stood up he passed his disengaged arm around me and thus we stood for some moments. Then releasing us, he ordered the two deckmen to throw grapples across to the other vessel, which at that moment grated alongside. The next instant he stepped on board the other vailx and signed to loose grapples. Thus we parted, high above the green earth, two miles beneath, he to return, we to go onwards.

CHAPTER XVI.

THE VOYAGE TO SUERN.

Before us lay a pleasure trip during which we should travel many thousands of miles. We proceeded slowly when we came above the base of the huge bulk of Pitach Rhok, the mighty mountain, and ascended somewhat, so that we should be on a level with its high point. When at the place, nothing would suit the company except a stop on the summit, and together we all placed foot in the snows on the pitach, which thing was done chiefly to please Anzimee, who said that the place was very interesting on account of what had there happened to me.

Then, again, we were under way, descending from the higher altitudes in order to better view the thickly inhabited, though mountainous country beneath us, between Pitach Rhok and east Poseid.

At the approach of sunset a dull roar arose to the ear, and soon the long white shore of old ocean flashed beneath a moment, and in a little time was far behind, with the waters, lead color in the twilight, beneath, behind, before and on both sides, no land in sight, and over one thousand miles east the country of Necropan. Without going at a full rate of speed, we could not expect to be above that land in less than two or three hours. But as it would be dark ere reaching it, we slackened speed to an hundred and fifty miles per hour, closed the deck and went into the salon, where incandescent lamps lit up the darkening night-glooms.

A trip by vailx could never prove so monotonous as a journey in even the fastest of ocean steamships so often is today. The variety of scenery, the wide views possible, for altitude was dependent wholly on pleasure, the external cold being unheeded by people who sat in a parlor warmed by means

from Navaz, and furnished with air of the proper density by
the same Night-Side forces—all this tended to prevent ennui.
Then too, the rapid transit changed the aspect of things beneath so fast, that the spectator looking backwards gazed upon
a disolving view. As an aside, the currents derived from the
Night-Side of Nature permitted the attainment of the same
speed as that of the diurnal rotation of the earth, e. g.: supposing we were at an altitude of ten miles, and the time the
instant of the sun's meridian; at that meridian moment we
could remain indefinitely, bows on, while the earth revolved
beneath, at approximately seventeen miles every minute. Or,
the reverse direction keys could be set, and our vailx would
speed away from where it was meridian on the surface beneath,
at the same almost frightful rate,—frightful to one unused to
it, as my reader is now, but one day will not be, if, as I hope,
he or she will live to see vailxi rediscovered. Nor need the
life be a very long one ere then.

While we had such preventives of ennui, we lacked not
commoner means of enjoyment. We had our naima, in the
mirrors and vibrators of which our friends, however distant,
could appear in image of form and of voice, life-sized and
with undiminished vocal volume. The salons of the great
passenger vailxa had libraries, musical instruments, and potted
plants, amongst the flowers of which birds similar to the modern domestic canary darted about.

At about the tenth hour it was reported that Necropan was
beneath, and at this surprising information—because at the
speed I had ordered, we should have been at least six hours
longer in coming to that country—I enquired of the vailxman
his reason for increasing speed without orders.   No good
reason being given, I severely reprimanded the conductor, and
ordered that a descent be made to terra firma, in order that
we might travel by day over the Wasted Land, as our word
Sattamund may be translated, which is the Sahara desert of
to-day. This great waste some of our party had never seen,

and to allow them the privilege we settled down to spend the night on an elevated ridge, high enough to be above malarious influences, for we were near where modern Liberia lies.

> "The proud bird—The Condor of the Andes,
> Tnat can sail thro' heaven's unfathomable depths,
> Or brave the fury of the northern hurricane
> And bathe his plumage in the Thunder's home,
> Furls his broad wings at nightfall, and sinks down
> To rest upon his mountain crag."

Though we called it Sattamund, or the Wasted Land, yet it was not such an arid region then as it is now. Water, if not as abundant as it was in Poseid, was abundant enough to give a wealth of tropical trees of the hardier sorts, sufficient at least to hide the nakedness of the slopes and hills of that old sea-bed. There were even a few saline lakes there, broad and blue, and it was around these that the population was centered. But the same dread catastrophe that overtook fair Poseid laid its terrible hand upon Necropan, and its beauty of verdure went out from the land, because the geological changes withdrew all the water from the surface, and hid it so that only artesian augers could find it. The same mighty throe rent the rocks through and through in South-west Incalia, and today there is in that arid region scenery most fantastic, weird past the power of my pen to describe—where flows the Rio Gila, the Colorado, and Colorado Chiquita. But I will reserve the description, and when it is given it shall be in other words than mine, so that thou and I, my friend, shall together have the pleasure of enjoying a fine word-painting.

In Poseid and Suern, and wherever civilization extended its sceptre, it was the universal law, and mankind's pleasure to obey the heavenly mandate which the general accordance with the solar life spirit taught us required the planting, instead of careless rejection of all seeds of goodly flower or fruit, for shade, for beauty, for utility, wherever it chanced that a favorable spot offered, either in the habitats of man or in the untrodden wilderness. Indeed, in such trips as our party was then taking, it was a matter of religious significance to take great quantities of seeds, and to scatter them from the vailx-decks at nightfall, both as an offering to Incal, as His sublime symbol set in the west, and also that the dews of night might insure germination, and this ceremony was also held to be an acknowledgement of the Goddess of Increase—Zania. Thus the wilds came to bloom as the rose; and today the world is heritor of that sowing of seed; the indigenous cereals,—the wheat, for the origin of which many ingenious but insufficient theories have been put forth, and the varieties of palms that make the tropics famed for the grace of their cocoas and dates, and every genera of the Chamaerops. And these things are because man, woman and child found pleasure in that olden time in "planting seed by the wayside." Go thou and do likewise, that the waste places may become full of beauty, and be a joy forever. All hail to Arbordays, which fulfill the injunction of Christ; they will surely make a return, and some an hundred fold. A small pocket now and then will hold many a seed for planting, and though thou heedest not its sort, so that it be goodly, yet the Father hath said:—"It shall bring forth after its kind."

THE STORM.

The morning dawned clear and cloudless, and was altogether so delightful that we essayed scarcely any forward progress, moving slowly in order that the deck might be uncovered and the company allowed to sit out in the fresh air and warm sunshine.

Down below, a couple of thousand feet at most, we saw, through good glasses, various forms of human, animal, bird and plant life; and sounds came up to us in drowsy, musical monotone, as our vailx hovered above. Towards evening the winds began to blow, rendering it unpleasant to remain so near the ground. The repulse-keys were set, and presently we were so high in the air that all about our now closed ship were cirrus clouds—clouds of hail held aloft by the uprushing of the winds, severe enough to have been dangerous had our vessel been propelled by wings or fans or gas reservoirs. But as we derived from Nature's Night-Side, or in Poseid phrase, from Navaz, our forces for propulsion as well as for repulsion. or levitation, therefore our long, white, aerial spindles feared no storm, however severe.

As the windows, being frosted over, obscured our view, and as the night promised furious weather, we had recourse to books, music and to conversation with one another, and, through the naim, with our friends at home in far-away Poseid. No authority had Murus (Boreas) over the currents from Navaz. The evening had not far advanced when it was suggested that the storm would most likely be heavier, and the wind wilder nearer the earth, and so the repulse-keys were set to a fixed degree, making nearer approach to the ground than was desirable impossible an as accidentl occurrence. We might, if it were generally agreeable, take advantage of our privilege and enjoy the sensation of being in the midst of the storm, ourselves safe and under full speed,

"And brave the fury of the Northern hurricane."

The partial novelty might make us sleep better, when, the evening passed, we should have gone to our state-rooms. I. therefore, approved the plan, and gave orders to the conductor to descend to a height of about twenty-five hundred feet. Down we dropped. Our lights were made low in order to produce a partial gloom, the better to enjoy the full fierceness of the tempest, and we sat near the windows where we could hear, if not see. To the eye naught would have appeared outside save entire blackness; to the ear the loud beating of the rain upon the metal shutters was plainly, delightfully apparent. Against the sharp points of prow and stern the wind howled and shrieked like an army of demons. At times when the vailx was struck broadside by some counter-blast, it would careen and tremble, but it kept on its way, determined as a thing of life. The experience was enjoyable, if not entirely novel, for it spoke to us of the power of man over matter, and taught us of the things of God—Incal to us—Master of all things and of ourselves—who by Him had this authority over the elements.

When the sensation had become monotonous the lights were increased to proper brightness; again we turned to books and games and music, as we once more sought the upper regions of the atmosphere, which were quieter compared with those of the half-mile plane.

Anzimee and a girl companion sat apart from the rest of the company in a retreat formed of flowering vines draped across one corner of the main salon. In a short time she came from her nook to where I sat, wrapped in meditative obliviousness. Touching my shoulder as she came close, she said:

"Zailm, thou dost sing; it would please me if thou wouldst take thy lute and come to where Thirtil and myself have chosen seats, and sing to us."

She bent over my shoulder, blushing slightly, looking so altogether lovely that I simply sat and gazed in silent appreciation of her beauty.

"Come, Zailm, wilt thou?"

I arose promptly enough when I saw a shade of disappointment cross her face, a she interpreted my silence to mean unwillingness, and I said:

"Lo, Anzimee, I am but too pleased to comply, but how could I move?"

Unsuspiciously, she asked:

"Move? and why not?"

"Hast thou ever seen a bright humming bird," I replied, "which, poised at a flower beside thee, kept thee still, almost afraid to breathe, lest it be alarmed to flight? Even so I could not move, lest—

"There, there now! If I were not used to reading one's earnestness or other emotions in the eyes, I would say thou art a sad flatterer. But—come."

"What shall I sing, little friend?"—I asked of Thirtil, a demure, sweet little maiden, an art student, half-serious, half-frivolous in temperament.

"Oh, dost ask me? Well, something, something"—with a mischievous glance at Anzimee—"from thy heart!"—she laughingly replied.

Anzimee blushed, but made no other sign, merely dropping her long lashes as I looked at her, while I said, "Truly! Then from my heart—this" (a popular favorite. by the way):

"Ere the heart can know its own,
    Ere the doubts of life are o'er,
Love in our hearts must have grown
    To the heights of heaven's shore.
Truly, love is sought in vain
    In other place than in the heart;
True love always hath its pain,
    When from purity we part.
May we cease from every strife,
    While in lovely verse enshrining
Incal's blessing in our life;—
    With His peace it e'er entwining.
Song is melody divine,
    When the music of the soul;
'Tis betrothing thine and mine,
    While the centuries unroll.
Yet our hearts are young and gay—
    Seeking ever fairest bowers
Where shall bloom from day to day,
    All the beauty of the flowers.
There is one of all the rest,
    That alone for me is blooming;
Deep the tendrils in my breast,
    Find forever their entombing.
Shall I pluck it while in bloom—
    Ready for the gardener's gleaning?
Could I take forever home
    What unto me, is no dreaming?
Yea, beloved, we shall rejoice
    In His blessing evermore;
List'ning to the gentle voice,
    That as One—we do adore."

Thus it was within the vailx, song and pleasure; without was the storm, risen up after us. Into the teeth of the furious gale plunged our long spindle, giving no sign exteriorly—even had any one been there to see—of the light and warmth. laughter and song, of the human freight and song-birds within its staunch shell, amidst the flowers—a drifting bit of the tropics, safe from boreal blasts. No sign, save only the gleam of the crimson fore and aft lights.

While the others retired for the night to their various state-

rooms, I remained in the vacated salon until the announcement was made to me that we were above Suernis. No landing could be made, however, in the face of a gale blowing
eighty miles an hour—such an attempt would have resulted in
being dashed to pieces the instant we reached the ground.

In order that we might be wholly out of the range of the
influence of the storm, I gave directions to rise above the
level of the disturbance, if such a region of calm existed within
reach, and there set the keys so as to stop all propulsion. Receiving this order, the conductor augmented the repulsion
force by means of the levers of degree, and we rose steadily
up, up, up—above the clouds, above the rush of the hurricane,
into a clear, calm atmosphere, intensely cold, almost thirteen
miles from the earth's surface. Could we have had a view
unobstructed by storm-clouds, we were just about high
enough to afford us a horizon of three hundred and fifty miles.
Soon after this order I went to my room to bed. With the
morning the storm had not decreased in fury; and occasional
flurries in the air above us proved that the storm-area on the
surface must be of vast extent. The cold outside was too intense to consider, even for an instant, the opening of the deck;
the sky was almost black in the depth of its blueness; the sun,
shorn of much of its dazzling brightness, appeared strangely
dim, and the stars were visible. The steady motion of the
air-dispensers as their wheels and pistons worked to maintain
the interior air at a normal pressure was painfully apparent in
the awful stillness, while the fizz of the air escaping through
the fine crevices around the windows and edges of the deck
made such a noise that I ordered the set-screws tightened and
the ventilator-pipes opened. Had the frost not hindered vision
through the windows, and, with the clouds, prevented a view
of the earth's surface, a sight most peculiar would have been
presented. The view toward the extended horizon would have
made the apparent union of earth and sky seem almost on a
level with us; but directly beneath, the full separation from the
solid globe would have seemed, not like a ball, but like a huge
bowl, ornamented with landscape scenes in its interior. As,

however, we could not see; our songs, our reading, and our conversation went on, whilst the very faint beams of Incal, coming through the frosted glass, were supplemented by the same knowledge which gave us heat and air and position, to defy the cold and the rarefaction and gravitation knowledge of Navaz.

At home in Poseid there was no storm, but Menax, at the naim, told us that the weather office anticipated one, the one of which we at that moment awaited the abatement. We waited until the sun set in the west, and came in sight in the east twice.

Several times the Saldu appeared at the end of the salon, seeming in the mirror of the naim as real and present as if, in verity, a third of the globe did not separate us. Once, only, she spoke, and then in a whisper to me, as I stood near the naim:

"When, my lord, wilt thou be at home? A month? 'Tis long, 'tis long!"

A report of even the smallest events of our trip was furnished the news office, and was printed upon the discs of the public vocaligraphs—to use a word of modern sound—and long before any landing was effected by us on the soil of Suernis, our fellow countrymen were acquainted with the story of our enforced suspension between heaven and earth, while biding the abatement of the storm. Speaking of the vocaligraph leads me to remark that the social superstructure of Poseid was maintained upon the broad basis of equitable laws laid down by the great Rai of the Maxin-time through the influence of free speech as made and molded by church and school, and expressed through the millions of vocaligraphs, the three rendering secure the integral homes which, aggregated, formed the nation.

At last the storm king withdrew his forces, and the time had come for our descent. Down we swept from the vault of heaven, into Ganje, capital city of Suern.

Hast thou ever been in the ancient and long deserted city of Petra of Seir? That very peculiar city at the foot of Mount Hor, a city hollowed from the living rock? Quite likely not, for the followers of Mahomet make it hard to visit the place. But if thou hast read thereof, then thou hast some idea of Ganje, in old Suerna, built in the cliffs of the river banks.

Such details as embrace the manner of our reception are too trivial to fill this record. Suffice it that it was suited to the friendly international relations of Suern and Poseid, and to my station and rank as a high deputy. Rai Ernon was far less interested in the vase, and in the other gifts of gold and gems, than in the captive Saldani whom the tokens commemorated, particularly in the Saldu, Lolix the Rainu. I was startled at the monarch's close knowledge of the whole affair in all its details, and of my sickness and other incidents which were not matters of public note; but I betrayed no such feeling, since it was but momentary, and passed as soon as recollection of Ernon's wonderful occult powers came to me.

Speaking of the Saldui, but especially of Lolix, he said:

"I did not send the Chaldeans unto Gwauxln as objects of lust, neither as a retributive punishment, that by exile from their native Chaldea they might atone to Suern for their fathers, sons, brothers, or husbands who worked harm to Suernis. No doubtless they were not more blamable than is a tiger which hath a similarly destructive nature, but by the laws of Yeovah we find that ignorance of the law never exempts a wrongdoer from penalty. Law says in regard to sin: 'Thou shalt not.' And the penalty lies alongside, inexorably, and is dealt out unsparingly for disobedience. Law, therefore, appears not to be retributive, but educational. Having felt the punishment, no one, either man or animal, is apt to try the error twice out of curiosity. Nature makes no penalty easy, saying: 'When thou hast learned, then the punishment shall be more severe.' If a babe fell over a cliff, its death would be the result, though its innocence knew nothing of sin, just as surely as a knowing man might meet the same fate deliberately. Now the Chaldean women needed to learn that

conquest, bloodshed and pillage is a sin.   The Chaldean nation needed a lesson also.   It received it, in the death of its
prize soldiery.   But such examples need finish; a diamond in
the rough is surely a diamond, but how much doth the lapidary
increase its beauty and value!   To not release unto them those
women was to that nation what the faceting is to a gem.
Thinkest thou not that I am right?''

"Even so, Rai," I responded.

For several days we remained in the capital, and during
this time were escorted over it by no less a person than Rai
Ernon himself.

It was a strange people—the Suerni.   The elder people
seemed never to smile, not because they were engagd in occult
study, but bcause they were filled with wrath.

On every countenance seemed to rest a perpetual expression of anger.   Why, I pondered, should this thing be?   Is it
a result of the magical abilities they possess?   By what seems
to us of Poseid mere fiat of will these people appear to tran-
scend human powers, and set at naught the immutable laws
of nature, though it can not be said that Incal has not limited
them as surely as He has limited our chemists and physicists.
The Suerni never lift their hands in manual labor—they sit
at the breakfast or the supper table without having previously
put upon it anything to eat, or elsewhere prepared a repast;
they bow their heads in apparent prayer, and then, lifting up
their eyes, begin to eat of what has mysteriously come before
them—of wholesome viands, of nuts, of all manner of fruits,
and of tender, succulent vegetables!   But meat they eat not,
nor much that is not the finished product of its source, containing in itself the germ for future life.   Hath Incal exempted
them from His fiat as Creator of the world, which all men
suffer?—"In the sweat of thy face shalt thou eat bread."   It
is less onerous, certainly, on those who walk His paths, or
even those who partly do so, and whose rule of life is continence.   Such are more powerful, have occult powers that no
eater of meats can ever hope to attain, but surely they are
not wholly exempt; it must be somewhat toilsome to perform

such magic feats as these. None ever got something for nothing. These people gaze upon the foes who come to menace them in their homes—and they are not!

> "It passed o'er
> The battle plain, where sword and spear and shield
> Flashed in the light of mid-day—and the strength
> Of serried hosts is shivered, and the grass,
> Green from the soil of carnage, waves above
> The crushed and moldering skeleton."

What Poseida could do these things? Rai Gwauxln, Incaliz Mainin, but no more, at least none known to the public even by repute. But no man of all Atl had ever witnessed much display of such power on the part of either, and with the masses it was mere repute. I was favored beyond most Atlanteans, in this respect.

I noticed in our visits in and about the capital a thing which cast a shadow over me—that his people did not love Ernon, however much they respected him, and feared his power. That the Rai was aware of my knowledge of this dislike was obvious from his conversation.

"Ours is a peculiar people, prince," he said to me. "During many years, centuries even, it hath had to reign over its rulers come from the Sons of the Solitude. Each and every one hath striven to train his subjects so as to fit some future generation for initiation, as an entire people, into the mysteries of the Night-Side of Nature, deeper than thy people of Poseid have ever dreamed of going. To this end moral codes have been insisted upon as a co-efficient of tuition in operative magic. But the endeavor hath never produced the end sought; only here and there hath an individual arisen and progressed; soon every one of these hath fled away from the less energetic people, and gone to the solitudes, to become one of the 'Sons' of whom thou mayst have heard; generically we term these students 'sons;' specifically we would have to refer to them as 'sons' or 'daughters,' for sex is no bar to occult study."

It had long been a matter of interest to me to learn all I could of this band of Nature students—Incalenes, as they were sometimes called, from Incal—God and "ene"—to study. Thousands of years later, in the time of Jesus of Nazareth, these were called "Essenes." But Atla, which possessed such a wealth of literature, had, with a single exception, no books on the subject. In that exception—a little volume printed in ancient Poseidonic—the details were very meagre; yet its perusal had been of great interest to me. As I now listened to Rai Ernon, my interest was re-awakened, and I thought I might one day become a candidate for admission to the order, if—but that "if" was of a large size. If the study renders the student so wrathful in soul as I see the Suerni are, then I will have nothing to do with it. The seed was planted, however, and grew a little when I learned that the angry gloom was not due to occult study, except in the sense that the lower nature was rebellious against the purity of the study, and cast up the mud of anger, rendering turbid the clear waters of the soul. It grew still more when the Rai remarked later on that "the girl Anzimee would one day be an Incalenu." But the growth was not great in that olden time; it was reserved for a life to come, when decades upon decades of centuries had flown, till now!

The Rai continued: "Ye of Poseid, dip a little into the Night-Side, and behold! out of it ye gather forces which open the pentralia of the sea, and of the air, and subject the earth. 'Tis well. But ye require physical apparatus; without it ye are nothing powerful. Those versed in occult wisdom need no apparatus. That is the difference between Poseid and Suernis. The human mind is a link between the soul and the physical. Every higher force controls all those lower. The mind operates through odic force, which is higher than any speed of physical nature; hence controls all nature, nor needeth apparatus.

"Now I, and my brother 'Sons' before me, have striven to teach the Suerni the laws which govern the operation of this force. Through this knowledge Yeovah lendeth His children strength. Hand in hand with this knowledge are physical acts—powers that come early in the study. So far have they gone, but will no farther go.

"Morality aids serenity of soul; hence it is profitable to the Incalene, above all things, to be moral. But man is an animal in his corporeal self, and the passions thereof are pleasant. Love is of twofold nature—love of God and of the Spirit, pure and undefiled, and love of sex, which may likewise be pure, though if the dominion of the animal in man be over it, and not so that of the human, it shall cause the man to sin, for then it is lust. I have sought that the Suerni may know the law, so that they may be the masters, not the creatures, of circumstance. But because they know a few things of magic, and in the greater feats were aided by the 'Sons' dwelling amongst them, lo, they are content. And behold! they rebel against punishment on account of the lustful nature they do indulge, and curse me mightily because I exact obedience to the law, and penalty for the infraction thereof; and they curse my brother 'Sons' who do aid me,—therefore is their wrath which it hath so troubled thee to witness. My people do things strange in thy sight, O Poseida, yet have no wisdom why it is so, and work their wonders heedless of Yeovah. Wherefore they are a brood of sorcerers, and do not work white magic, which is beneficient, but black magic, which is sorcery. It shall work them exceeding woe. I would, O Zailm of Poseid, have taught these my people faith, hope, knowledge and charity, which same make pure religion undefiled. Have I not done well? Gwauxln, my brother, have I not done well?"

Rai Ernon was sitting in the salon of the vailx, and now addressed Gwauxln of Poseid, whom I saw in the naim as I looked around.

"Verily thou hast even so, my brother," said Gwauxln. For some moments the noble ruler was silent, and I could see tear-drops falling occasionally from beneath his closed eyelids. Then he opened his eyes and began a most touching apostrophe to, and in some sort against his people.

"Oh, Suernis, Suernis! I have given up my life for thee!

I have striven to lead thee into Espeid (Eden) to teach thee of its beauties, and thou wouldst not! I have tried to make thee van of all nations and thy name synonym with justice and mercy and love of God, and how hast thou requited me? I would be as a father to thee, and thou didst curse me in thy heart! Keener than knives is ingratitude! I would have led thee to the heights of glory, but thou wouldst rather lie in wallow of ignorance, like swine, content to do what are marvels to other people, but thyself all ignorant of their import. Thou art an infidel, ingrate race, believing not in Yeovah, content to live by the little thou knowest, too slothful to learn, more ungrateful to Yeovah than to thy Rai! O, Suernis, Suernis, thou hast cast me off and made my heart to bleed! I go. From thy midst the 'Sons' go also, a mournful band of disappointed men. And thou shalt become few where thou art many, a derision before men and a prey to the Chaldeans—yea, thou shalt dwindle and shalt wait until the centuries—even ninety centuries, are fled into eternity. And in that day thou shalt suffer until the time of him who shall be called Moses. And of them it shall be said: 'They are the seed of Abraham.' And behold, even as now the Spirit of God is abroad in the land, immanent in the Sons of the Solitude, and ye do mock It, so in a remote day shall His spirit become manifest, and shall incarnate as the Christ, and so shall the perfect human glow with the Spirit, and become First of the Sons of God. Yet shalt thou even then know Him not, but shalt crucity Him; and thy punishment shall go down the ages until that Spirit eomes again in the hearts of those who do follow Him, and find thee scattered to the four winds! Thus shalt thou be punished! From now until then shalt thou earn thy bread by the sweat of thy face. Thou shalt no more have the regal power of defense, less thou use it for offense. I will no more restrain thee. My people, oh, my people! Ungrateful! I forgive thee, for thou canst not know how I love thee! I go. Oh! Suernis, Suernis, Suernis!''

At the last word the noble ruler's voice lowered to a murmur, and he buried his tearful face in his hands, and sat

bowed in silent grief, except for a sigh of sorrow which once
or twice he uttered. Several Suerni had heard his words, and
these now left the vailx very quietly and went to the city.

"Rai ni Incal."

I turned to the naim as these words were uttered, and noted
that a great shade of sadness rested upon the face of our own
Rai, Gwauxln, as he looked upon Ernon—like himself, an
Adept Son.

"Rai ni Incal, mo navazzamindi su," which being translated, is—"To Incal the Rai; to the country of departed
spirits he is gone!"

Startled I looked around at the Suern Rai, who still sat
silent as before, in the same position. I spoke to him, yet he
gave no sign. Then I bent and gazed through his fingers into
his fine gray eyes. They were set, indeed, and the breath of
life was fled. Yea, verily, he had gone, even when he said
"I go."

"Come unto me, Zailm," commanded Gwauxln.

I went to naim and stood waiting.

"Are thy friends all within the vailx?"

"Even so, Zo Rai."

"Take then thy guards and seek the palace of Rai Ernon.
Call upon his ministers to come before thee, and tell them that
their Rai is deceased. Tell them that thou wilt take his body
in charge and carry it unto Poseid. Amongst the ministers are
two elderly men and sedate; these are Sons. They are of that
body of disappointed men who go forth from Suernis according to the words of Ernon. These two will know that thou
speakest truth when thou sayest that Ernon of Suern hath
left his Raina in my hands to govern as I shall decide is most
wise. But the others will not know, and the Sons will leave
to thee the telling of the facts. Great shall be the anger of
them that are not Sons, so that they shall try to destroy thee
by their terrible power, disliking to be told that they are de-
posed from authority. Nevertheless, this do and fear not; be
of good cheer, for how shall a serpent bite if it hath lost its
fangs?"

When, according to these orders, I had the court before me,
I spoke as directed by the Rai. It was received with a courteous smile by the two who by their demeanor I recognized
as the Sons of the Solitude. But by the others great anger
was shown.

"What! and thou, Poseida, offerest us such indignity? Our
Rai is dead? We are pleased! But we, not thou, will attend
to the funeral rites. As to the government of Suern, we
laugh with scorn! Begone! We are our own masters. Leave
us our ruler, and thou, dog, leave this country!"

For reply I repeated with emphasis the assertion of my
authority. I confess to having felt an inward fear when the
brow of one of these never-smiling men clouded with intense
anger, as he pointed his finger at me, and said:

"Then die!"

I did not outwardly shrink, though half-expecting to perish
on the spot. Neither did I feel any death tremor, though the
menace, ever before fatal, was not withdrawn. Gradually
the minister's fury gave place to surprise, and he dropped his
arm, gazing at me in amazement. I ordered my guards to
manacle and take him to the vailx. Then I said:

"Suern, thy power is fled. Thus said Ernon. He hath said
that henceforth thou shalt earn thy bread by the sweat of thy
face. Over this country Poseid shall rule. I, special envoy of
Gwauxln VII, Rai of Poseid, do depose all ye that are here
from rulership, except those two who offered not scorn, but
courtesy. While they remain, which will not be long, I will
make them governors over Suern. I have spoken."

Indeed I had spoken, and that, to so great an extent, unau-
thorizedly. I was in an agony of doubt lest Rai Gwauxln
should rebuke me. But I would not reveal my real weakness
to these ingrates. Instead, I took a roll of parchment and
wrote from memory the form of commission of governors
of provinces in Alta, appointing one of the Incaleni to the
office. This I sealed with my name as envoy extraordinary,
following that of Gwauxln as Rai, using red ink, for which I
sent a messenger to Anzimee at the vailx. My reason for ap-

pointing one of the Sons as Governor was that only one would
serve. The other chose to ask passage to Caiphul in my vailx.
Then, giving the Governor his commission, a document which
he received with the remark, "Thou art a man, indeed, not
longer a boy;"—words which, though so kindly meant, fell on
heedless ears at the time, for as I made my return to the vailx
I felt actually heartsick at what I feared had been the acme of
indiscretion on my part. I called for Rai Gwauxln, and when
he responded I told him what I had done. He looked grave,
and said merely the words:

"Come home."

Imagine now my distress. Not reprimanded, nor com-
mended, but without any explanatory clue whatever, I was
ordered home. Then it was that I sought Anzimee, and having
found her in her stateroom I told her all the story. Our Rai
was known to be one who could be severe in his punishments,
although these took the form of disgrace meted out, as public
dismissal from office for being unworthy of trust. Anzimee
was very pale, but said hopeful words:

"Zailm, I see not but that thou didst right well. And yet,
why was our uncle so gravely reticent? Let me give thee a
potion; lie here on this couch, and take what I give thee."

She poured a few drops of some bitter drug, put in a little
water, and handed the cup to me to drink from. Ten minutes
later I was asleep.

Then she left the room and, as I afterwards learned, called
her royal uncle to the instrument, where she laid the case
before him. He was troubled at the effect of his words upon
me, an effect not intended, as he told her, and one which would
never have occurred if he had not at that time been engaged
in solving the very abstruse political problem presented by the
new aspect of affairs through the decease of Rai Ernon. What
further he said was: "Be not worried because Zailm is called
home for no purpose of punishment, since I am well satisfied
and called him for quite another reason."

I slept for hours, and when I at last awakened, Anzimee,
sitting beside me, told me all that Gwauxln had said. As it

was then nearly night, I concluded to go to my own room and prepare for the evening repast. On the way I met the Son who was going to Caiphul with us. To this person it seemed a great novelty to travel as he was then doing, although his remarks on the subject were few.

It was, as I reflected upon it, something of a novelty to be piercing the air at the rate of seventeen miles each minute, a mile above the earth. I tried to fancy how it would seem to one like my passenger to be doing this thing; but after five years of familiarity with it as a means of travel, I had poor success in attaining a sense of his feelings concerning the experience.

As we traveled westward, the sun seemed to remain as it was when we left Ganje, for its speed, or that of the earth, rather, was the same as our own. We had been on the way for five hours, and had covered considerably over half of the distance home, the whole journey being something like seven thousand miles. The remaining two thousand miles would occupy some three hours for transit, a length of time which seemed to my impatient desire so long, that I paced the floor of the salon in very fretfulness. I have seen, since the days of Poseida, a time when a vastly slower progress would have seemed swift—but then the past had a veil obscuring it so that comparison was impossible—

"Man never is, but always to be blest."

CHAPTER XVII.

RAI NI INCAL—ASHES TO ASHES.

On a bier in front of the Holy Seat, by the eastern face of the Maxin Stone in the Incalithlon, lay all that was of the earth, earthy of Ernon of Suernis. In the triangle were gathered a few who were asked by Rai Gwauxln to be present, and

. . . . one the mysterious light which required no fuel, nor
for its tall taper any human keeper. High above, hung the
white stalactite ceiling, casting down from its many points the
radiance of the lights which no one could see from below.

"Close his eyes, his work is done."

Beside the restful form stood Mainin, the Incaliz, his hand
on the shoulder of the dead Rai. After the mighty organ had
sounded a mournful requiem, Mainin made the funeral speech,
saying:

"Once more has a most noble soul known earth. How hath
it treated him who gave his life to the service of its children?
Verily, Suerna, thou hast done a deed which shall clothe thee
in sackcloth and ashes for aye! Ernon, my brother, Son of
the Solitude, we bid thee adieu in great sorrow of soul; sorrow
not for thee, for thou art at rest; but for us left behind. It
shall be until many years ere we know thee again incarnate.
As for this, thy poor clay, over it we will say final words, for
it hath done its work and is committed to Navazzamin. Ernon,
brother, peace be with thee evermore."

Again the mighty organ played in solemn sadness, and while
attendants raised their bier upon the cube of the Maxin, the
Incaliz raised his hands to heaven and said:

"Unto Incal this soul, unto earth this clay."

The body, bound with light bands to the bier, was raised
with it to an erect posture, trembled a moment in that position, and fell forward into the Maxin. There was no flame,
no smoke, not even ash left behind the instantaneous disappearance of body and bed.

The funeral was over. As we who abode in Caiphul turned
to depart, we saw that which no man then living had ever
before beheld in the Incalithlon. Back of us, in the auditorium, stood groups of grey-habited men, cowled like monks of
Rome. There seemed great numbers of them, collected in
groups of seven or eight amongst the maze of stalagmite pillars which supported the roof. As we gazed, these men faded
slowly from sight, until over four score of Caiphalians seemed
indeed small in number in the vast hall where so recently had

been hundreds of Incaleni—Sons of the Solitude in astral form, gathered at the funeral of their brother. Yea, verily, had the Sons come to witness the impressive ceremony where all that was mortal of their dead fellow was restored to the keeping of the elements of nature.

> "But no man knows that sepulchre,
> And no man saw it e'er,
> For the angels of God upturned the sod
> And laid the dead man there."

———————

CHAPTER XVIII.

LE GRAND VOYAGE.

Rai Gwauxln directed me to attend at Agacoe ere resuming my vacation trip, although it was all arranged previously to the funeral of Ernon that my action in Suern was to his satisfaction.

When I obeyed the Rai, which was almost immediately, for we were all ready to resume our journey, Gwauxln, in the presence of his ministers of state affairs, tendered me the position of Suzerain over the land of Suern. I was vastly surprised, yet felt that I might accept, and in conducting the affairs of that country render good service. But the fact that I was yet an undergraduate at the Xioquithlon made me hesitate. At last I spoke, saying:

"Zo Rai, I am sensible thou hast done thy servant a great honor. Nevertheless, my liege, feeling that I have not thus far acquired the full knowledge I desire, being yet but a Xioqene, I ask thy permission to refuse the office."

Gwauxln smiled, and said:

"Even so. But the governor thou didst appoint shall execute thy duties for the three years intervening—the four years, I would say, since I would not that thou shouldst study at all this year—and thereafter thou shalt legally assume active

duties. I have an object in this besides mere form; I believe
that that man who hath an object, a direct goal, in view, is
more likely to win success than one without. It is a good
stimulus. I do therefore appoint thee Suzerain over Suernis,
and dismiss thee to thy journey of pleasurable recreation with
thy friends as soon as thou shalt sign thy name to this document. That is well written, though thy hand shakes a little
because of thy nervousness. Be calm." This last he said as,
trembling slightly, I wrote the desired signature.

Once more we were on our travels.

Anzimee, the elf, persisted in calling me "My Lord Zailm"
when she had learned the story of my imminent suzerain
duties.

Our course was again eastward, although now farther south,
for we did not propose to visit Suernis this time, but intended
to proceed instead to our American colonies, as in the original
route we had planned to do after leaving Suernis.

We crossed equatorial Necropan (Africa), then the Indian
Ocean and the present East Indies—but then colonies of Suern
called Uz—then onwards above the wide Pacific, still eastward.

"Umaur! the coast of Umaur!" was the cry that called our
little company to the windows to look at a dark, serrate line
that bounded the eastern horizon. It was the distant range of
the Andes, appearing almost on a level with our vailx, which,
two miles high above the ocean, shot towards the hazy, black
line. Below was the broad mirror of the blue Pacific, apparently waveless because so far beneath us.

Umaur, land of the Incas in a far later day. Umaur, where,
in eight centuries more they must find a refuge who should
be so fortunately fated as to escape from Poseid, ere—"Queen
of the World" no more—she sank beneath the waves of the
Atlantic. Eight centuries, whose lapse would see the proud
Atlantean become so corrupt that his soul no more reflected the
wisdom of the Night-Side, because the calmness of morality
being fled, the key to nature's pentralia would have been lost,

and with it his dominion over the air and the depths of the sea. Alas, poor Atl!

But Umaur lay ahead of us, and ignorant of the misdeeds-to-be of our national posterity, we in our vailx stood gazing on the coast we were so rapidly approaching, and commented upon its majestic mountain ranges as seen through the telescopes.* Here we beheld a land where, after thousands of years, the conquering Castilians would come, led by Pizarro, and find a race under the rule of Incas, a name preserved through the many centuries from the day when their remotest ancestors fled from sunken Poseid, calling themselves "Children of the Sun."

Umaur was the region of the quarries of Poseid, and of many of its rich mines of mineral wealth. Here, too, were vast plantations, and east of the mountains were regularly planted groves of the rubber tree, the genuine Siphonia Elastica of botany. Here also flourished the Cinchonas, as well as many other trees now indigenous to South America—colonized plants from Poseid. Until planted abroad by Atlanteans these vegetable treasures never grew outside of Poseid, and to-day the wild forests of peculiar South American trees and shrubs are the direct descendants of our regularly cultivated farm and plantation products in Umaur. In that olden time the Amazon river ran within dykes across the continent, and the trackless

---

*NOTE.—When thy science shall, like Poseid, approach Nature from its Godward side; when, instead of ascending to that key-force of all Nature, the Odic force, from a synthesizing of environing phenomena —thou shalt look from Odicity adown all the river of Energy, then wilt thou have all that Poseid had (being thyself Poseid returned), even its vailx, its naim, and its telescopes. Not such crude instruments as thine are, were the telescopes of Atl. Not the most remote star which sends a beam of faintest light across the depths of space, but that star could be brought so near to us in seeming, that had so minute an organism as a leaf been lying on the "ground" of the star, it were visible to our eyes. Dost thou refuse credence? Con this proposition:—that light is not alone a reflection or refraction of force from a substance, but is a prolongation of every substantial form. for as much as only One Substance exists, though many are the dynamic variations thereof; these are mistaken by thee for different substances. There is but ONE SUBSTANCE: Light from Arcturus, let us say, is the prolonged substance of that star. Machine-made electricity is per contra, unimpressed. formless force. One can be made to reinforce the other—the Formless to acquire the image of the Formed. Dost now see the principle of our telescopes? Thy mind jumps far to the van, and I hear thee ask, "Is Mars inhabited? Is Jupiter? Is Saturn, Venus?" Ah! my friend, I will not answer yea nor nay, for when the Poseid view of Nature reappears on earth, thou wilt KNOW: Seek and ye shall find; but seek correctly. Walk the cruciform Way.

sylvas of Brazil were then drained areas of tilled soil, such
as the adjacent territory of the Mississippi is to-day. Some
day this river, "Father of Waters," in the north, will sweep
unresisted, undyked, across the lowland, which, even now, its
surface is above in altitude. It will do this, because these
things are certain to be, in the mutations of the coming centuries. It will do this, also, because history repeats itself;
think not that thou shalt inherit, reincarnate the glories of Atl,
and escape its shadows. All things move in cycles, but the
circle is that of the screw-thread—ever around and around on
a higher plane each time. But that time when these things
shall come to pass, and no man be able to say nay, is yet far
away on the horizon of time future, as far as is the grand
recession of the Amazon on the horizon of the past.

From the great orchards and plantations and homes of
Umaur, in the north of that continent, to the desert wilds of
its southern parts, where one day trouble was to overwhelm
me—and thence north along the eastern coasts, we took our
way, leaving the doings of the millions of our colonists—the
Umauri—to the imagination of the reader.

Successively we came to the Isthmus of Panama, then over
four hundred miles in breadth; to Mexico (South Incalia) and
to the immense plains of the Mississippi. These latter formed
the great cattle-lands whence Poseid drew most of its supplies
of flesh-foods, and where, when the modern world discovered
it, enormous herds of wild progeny of our ancient stock roamed
at will. Buffalo, elk, bear, deer and mountain sheep—all off-
spring of the remotest ages. I regret to see them so wantonly
slaughtered as they are; surely so old a stock might be spared.

To these broad valleys were to come, in later centuries, in-
vading hordes in boats, and over the far northern isthmus
where now are only vestiges of its former existence—the Aleu-
tian Islands. They came from Asia, then, as now, to a large
extent the home of semi-barbarians, except where the sway of
Suernis had extended a civilizing influence by sending out the
tribes which, in a later day, were to occupy so large a niche
in history under the name of the Semitic races. But the bar-

barians who went into Incalia, occupying the North American
plains and lake region—a future age should come which would
find these hordes gone from the earth forever; and, later still,
curious people digging from archaeological remains would
say: "Here lived the mound-builders."

Still farther north than this, in the present "lake region,"
were large copper mines, whence we obtained much of our copper, and some silver and other metals. A cold region was this,
far colder than it is to-day, for it lay in the edge of the retreating forces of the glacial epoch, an epoch not over until much
more recently than geologists have hitherto thought, and even
still think.

To the west lay what in early American days were called the
"great plains." But in the days of Poseid they had a far different appearance from that which they bear to-day. Not then
arid, nor very sparsely inhabited, though vastly colder in winter, owing to the nearness of the vast glaciers of the north.
The Nevada lakes were not then mere dried up beds of borax
and soda, nor the "Great Salt Lake" of Utah a bitter, brackish
body of water of its present comparatively small size. All
lakes were large bodies of fresh water and the "Great Salt
Lake" was an inland sea of fresh floods, bearing icebergs from
the glaciers on its northern shores. Arizona, that treasure-
house of the geologist, had its now marvelous desert covered
with the waters of "Miti," as we called the great inland sea
of that region. Verdure was on all the slopes of all the hundreds of square miles not covered with lovely bodies of water.
On the shores of Miti was a considerable population, and one
city of no small size—colonists all, from Atl.

Reader, dost thou remember a promise given in previous
pages, wherein I looked forward to a treat in scenic depiction,
saying it was from another pen than mine? I redeem it now,
for already the geologist is after me for having declared Arizona the scene of a lake or inland sea so vast as Miti, and so
recently as twelve thousand years ago. I am reminded that he
has decided from evidence afforded by erosion and weathering
of the rocks in that amazing region, that while the Arizona

desert was undoubtedly a lake or a sea-bed since the palaeozoic time when it was the site of a shallow ocean, nevertheless that lake was certainly "of an age older than the Pliocene, being probably in the Cretaceous epoch." My friend, no. Those gorges and stupendous canons are not merely the gradual product of time and water and weather. Per contra, they are of sudden formation, the rending and cracking apart of the strata in a similar, but on a far more vast scale than the volcanic out burst at Pitach Rhok, described in the first chapter of this history. The Arizona wonders, and the gorge of the "Grand Canon of the Colorado" were the result of an awful dance of the solid crust of the globe. Even now the lava-beds of the rectangle between the parallels 32 deg. and 34 deg. north latitude and 107 deg. to 110 deg. longitude west from Greenwich, in the Mt. Taylor and Mt. San Francisco region, have few parallels on earth as regards size. All over this hideous work of destruction, when the sea Miti had fled away into Ixla (Gulf of California) the rains and torrents of eleven thousand winter seasons, and the dessicating, powdering influences of as many torrid summers have smoothed and chiseled and wrought the ruptured, ragged surfaces into yet more fantastic shapes, and claimed the whole work as its own, denying the hand of Pluto as the major worker. And the geologist seems to have admitted the claim, and placed the lake-time far back, in order to allow a sufficient term for the execution of the gigantic work. And it is not so, for I saw that lake, only twelve thousand years ago. But now for the literary treat; it is taken from a very modern pen, but it is so faithfully descriptive of the appearance of the region to-day that I desire to enjoy its perusal with my readers.. The words are those of Major J. W. Powell, U. S. Army:

"The canon walls are buttressed on a grand scale, and deep alcoves are excavated; rocky crags crown the cliffs, and the river rolls below. * * * The sun shone in splendor on the vermillion walls, shading into green and gray where the rocks were lichened over; the river filled the channel from wall to wall, and the canon opened like a beautiful gateway to glory.

But at evening, when the sun was going down and the shadows were settling in the canon, the vermillion gleams and roseate hues, blended with tints of green and gray, slowly changed to brown above, and black shadows crept over below—then it seemed the shadowy portal to a region of gloom. * * * Lying down we looked straight aloft through the canon cleft and saw that only a little of the blue heaven appeared overhead—a crescent of dark blue sky with but two or three constellations peering down upon us. I did not sleep for some time, as the excitement of day had not worn off. Soon I saw a bright star that seemed to rest on the very verge of the cliffs overhead. Slowly it seemed to float from its resting place on the rocks, out over the canon. At first it appeared like a jewel set in the brink of the cliff, but as it moved out I almost wondered that it did not fall. In fact, it did seem to descend in a gentle curve, as though the sky, in which the stars were set, was spread across the canon, resting on either wall, and swayed down by its own weight. The star appeared to be really in the canon, so high were the battlemented walls. * * * The morning sun was shining in splendor on their painted faces. The salient angles were as if on fire, and the retreating angles buried in shade; the rocks, red and brown, blazed from their setting of deep gloom below, but above all was vermillion fire. The light above, made more brilliant by the bright-tinted rocks, and the shadows below, made more gloomy by the sombre shades of sunlessness, increased the apparent depth of the awful canons, and it seemed a long, long way up to the world of sunshine—and was a mile!"

Even the wide waters of the Miti, set about with towering peaks in the olden days, beautiful as a dream, were not more grand and glorious than these awful gorges come to take their place.

From the city of Tolta, on the shores of Miti, our vailx arose and sped away north, across the lake Ui (Great Salt) to its northwestern shore, hundreds of miles distant. On this far shore arose three lofty peaks, covered with snow, the Pitachi Ui, from which the lake at their feet took its name. On the tallest of these had stood, perhaps for five centuries, a building made of heavy slabs of granite. It had originally been erected for the double purpose of worship of Incal, and astronomical calculations, but was used in my day as a monastery. There was no path up the peak, and the sole means of access was by vailx.

_____

In the neighborhood of twenty years ago, more or less, counting from this Anno Domini 1886, an intrepid American explorer discovered the famous Yellowstone region, and while on the same expediton went as far west as the Three Tetons, in Idaho* These mountain triplets were the Pitachi, Ui, of Atl. Professor Hayden, having arrived at the base of these lofty peaks, succeeded, after indefatigable toil, in reaching the top of the greater peak, and made the first ascent known to modern times. On its top he found a roofless structure of granite slabs, within which, he said, that "the granite detritus was of a depth indicating that for eleven thousand years it had been undisturbed." His inference was that this period had elapsed since the construction of the granite walls. Well, the professor was right, as I happen to know. He was examining a structure made by Poseid hands one hundred and twenty-seven and a half centuries ago, and it was because Professor Hayden was once a Poseida and held a position under the Atlan Government, as an attache of the government body of scientists stationed at Pitachi Ui, that he was karmically attracted to return to the scene of his labors long ago. Perhaps knowledge of this fact would have increased the interest he felt in the Three Tetons.

Our vailx alighted upon the ledge without the temple of Ui just as nightfall came on. It was very cold there, so far north, and at such an altitude. But the priests within the heavy, well-built edifice never suffered cold, for Alta, drawing upon Navaz, had Night-Side forces at its call. The primary cause of our

_____

*The Three Tetons are situated in north-western Wyoming. but Wyoming as a territory, was not in existence at the time referred to having been formed in 1868. from parts of Idaho, Dakota and Utah. A small part of the Yellowstone Park is in Idaho.—King's Hand-book of United States.

visit was our desire to pay devotion to Incal as He arose next
morning. All night the brilliant beams of light from our ruby-
colored lanterns flashed the tidings, to such Posedi as might
look our way, that a royal vailx was in the region. Next morning after sunrise our vessel lifted and departed for the east,
that we might visit our copper mines in the present Lake Superior region. We were conducted in electric trams through the
labyrinths of galleries and tunnels. When we were about to
leave, the government overseer of the mines presented each of
our company with various articles of tempered copper. To
me he gave an instrument, similar to the modern pocket-knife,
which I retained to the day of my death, and always valued
highly on account of its extra fine temper, which kept a keen
edge, good enough to shave with, and rarely required to be
sharpened. The Poseidi were adepts in this now lost art of
copper tempering. In return I gave the overseer a nugget of
native gold. He asked me whence it came, and when I told
him, remarked:

"Any specimen from the famous mine at Pitach Rhok will
be highly prized by an old miner like thy servant, more especially as it is presented by the discoverer of the mine himself."

Thus had the mine, found by me when an obscure lad, returned riches to the pick and shovel which had rendered it
famed throughout the civilized world.

After taking counsel among ourselves, we decided not to
make the farther northern trip, for every one of us had seen
the Arctic ice-fields at least once, while some of us had been
there several times. Instead, we concluded to remain in Incalia
for a week longer, and spend the eleven days thereof in visiting,
more at our leisure, the great territory where, although of
course we did not know it, the Anglo-Saxon was one day to
found the glorious American Union. History is said to repeat
itself; I believe it does. Certainly races follow in the track of
preceding races, and as the most important and populous part
of all the North American colonies of Poseid had its habitat
west of the great chain now known as the Rocky Mountains,

so also the grandeur of America will be upheld by the western and south-western States of the American Union.

Man likes pleasant places to live in; he likes those lands where mother nature is amiable and laughs with abundant harvests upon slight provocation; man likes to live in a fruit-land, and where shall he find anything more to his mind than this same south-west and west of the Incalia of yore? Along the ocean shore, and back to the Sierra Nevada mountains is the region where, under Poseid dominion, lay a province not second in beauty to the lake region along the shores of Miti. And it has retained its fair charm, while that of the other has given place to drifting sands and cactus and the mesquite, and has tenantry of the Moloch lizards, rattlesnakes, and prairie dogs. It is no more the

"Union of lakes and union of lands"—

that it was in that olden time.

When we finally left Incalia, that we might return home to Caiphul, the last of our colonial lands visible was the coast of Maine, for we journeyed eastward, then south.

For change we decided to forsake the realms of the air for those of the deep where the shark is king. Like all vailx of the class to which it belonged, ours was constructed for both aerial and submarine service, the plates of the sliding deck and the other movable parts of the hull being capable of very close approximation by means of set-screws and rubber washers.

To settle straight down into the ocean would be too much like a landing on terra firma. But being at a height of two miles, more or less, the conductor was directed to gradually reduce the repulsion current, thus diminishing our buoyancy so as to bring us into the water ten miles distant from where the slant commenced. He was further ordered to do this while maintaining a speed which would, though very slow for a vailx, be really swift—that is, he was to cover ten miles in as many minutes.

When we struck the water at this rate of progress the shock which the entering needle experienced, was sufficiently great to cause its inmates to stagger, and little exclamations were made by the ladies.

As soon as we entered the water the repulsion was made nil, and its opposite, a degree of attraction greater than that of water to the terrestrial center of gravity, was set up, whereby we were enabled to sink to a considerable depth, despite the air contained in the vessel. The lights outside the windows were started, our speed modified to suit the element, and then we all gathered in the salon by the windows, darkness within and the waters lit without, enabling us to see curious tribes of Neptune which crowded about the strange illumination in their midst.

While thus engaged and while listening to the delighted words of an enthusiastic ichthyologist, I heard a familiar voice in the darkness. I knew it for that of my father Menax, and accordingly went to the naim. He could not see me because I stood in darkness; but I could see him in the great mirror—for at home he was in the light and his image was so transmitted, so that I saw not only himself, but his immediate surroundings, just as a person outside a lighted window at night beholds everybody and thing in the interior, himself unseen.

"My son," said the prince, "thou shouldst not have allowed thy love of novelty to cause thee to act so unwisely as thou didst in entering the ocean at even the slow rate of a ven (mile) per minute. I fear that thou hast a vein of reckless daring in thy nature which will some day bring thee misfortune. Incal punishes the reckless by allowing His broken laws to exact their own penalty. Be cautious, Zailm, be cautious!"

After the submarine experiences had become tedious, the opposite course of a rapid but graduated augmentation of repulsion was imparted to our vailx—a procedure not dangerous, as the other had really been—and soon our long spindle shot out of the water like some great bubble, then rose to where the raz, or repulse indicator, was set for its government—only a few hundred feet above the surface of the ocean. There, putting aside the closed deck, we sat in the bright sunshine and enjoyed the pleasant ocean breeze, which blew in the same southern direction in which we were going. Desiring to reach home by the next day, when the afternoon grew cool we closed the deck, arose high in the heavens so as to lessen atmospheric resistance and made the quickest speed we could towards the south. This, I should remark, was not nearly so great as either an eastern or western course would have allowed. Thus, travelling either due east or due west, we could proceed at the rate of a degree of longitude every four minutes. But north or south we cut the earth's currents, and just in proportion as a vailx-course deviated from east to west, in that proportion was its speed lessened, until going due north or south we could only travel at the comparatively slow rate of some hundred miles each hour.

We saw that if we travelled home by the straight course, we would not reach Caiphul under two days, and, having set our desires on reaching it by the next morning, the prospective delay was so tedious that we decided to run in on an angle. That is, we would head our vailx south-east for the Necropan coast, thence south-west for Caiphul, and though the extra distance would be several thousand miles, the increased speed attained would allow us to reach our destination in time to take our breakfast at home.

> Beautiful Caiphul,
> There's no place like thee;
> Queen of Atlantis
> And Queen of the Sea.

CHAPTER XIX.

A WELL-MET PROBLEM.

Work awaited me upon my return to Caiphul—work to which I might attend without harm to my delicate health, in fact rather tending to its improvement, furnishing a proper degree of mental stimulus, without involving any of the severe tension of study.

On the day of my arrival home, Menax said to me in a way which set me to thinking:

"I understand that the people of Suern have lost the power which they have hitherto had of providing themselves with food by seeming magic. It must be a terrible problem to them how to meet the cravings of hunger."

Whether Menax designed these words for the purpose of arousing me to a sense of my duties in the premises or not, I had at the time no idea. But I pondered the situation very earnestly. It occurred to me that these people had few if any cultivated fields like our own; that they probably had no adequate knowledge of the arts of husbandry, tillage and like requirements, and, finally, that they were not possessed of muscles trained to effort. In fact they must be, in all matters of this sort, a kind of overgrown children. The more I dwelt on the problem, the more startling the situation seemed. I saw that they would, for at least a year, require to have provision made for them. They would also have to be taught the methods of agriculture, horticulture, and care of cattle, sheep and other useful domestic animals. Later, it would be necessary to teach them such other arts as mining, spinning and metal working. In fact, here was an entire nation of eighty-five millions of people coming to school to me for tuition in the arts of life. As the full force of the position came to my realization, it staggered me. Ah, poor me! I fell upon my knees on the greensward of the gardens and prayed to Incal. As I arose I turned and found Gwauxln regarding me with a most peculiar glance. His face was as grave as possible, but his splendid eyes were full of laughter.

"Dost thou feel equal to the task?" he queried.

"Zo Rai," I replied bravely. "Thy son is hard pressed. Equal?. Yea; if Incal will give me guidance."

"Well said, Zailm. Thou shalt call upon the resources of Poseid to aid thee, and they shall be at thy service."

Not to be prolix, the schools were established, the food and raiment stations were placed in given districts, and the people of Suern—the great peninsula of modern Hindustan, with parts of Arabia—were taught the means of comfortable self-preservation and dependence upon their knowledge. Not all of this was done, that is to say, supervised by me, but the initiation of it, and during three and a half years the practical work of it was conducted by me and my vice-suzerains. Perhaps I was not grateful to Incal; perhaps I never thought a second time, in these days of prosperity, of the prayer of the moneyless and unknown youth upon Pitach Rhok. But perhaps I did, too. I rather think that I was never for one moment forgetful of that morning and its vows. Yet, it is a strange fact that human nature may swerve aside from what it knows to be the undeviating line of right; may be keenly conscious of every infraction, and still be able to feel that it has been true to its vows. Moral lapses are the most frequent, those sins which are not strictly direct infractions of communal equities, but rather of the Magdalen type. Strange, also, is it that mankind is seldom lenient to the victims, though generally quite sparing of censure for the real criminal. There can be no true justice in a decision on any subject in the world until, in crimes of this sort, equal penalty is meted regardless of sex. Does my proposition seem too sweeping? Consider then this: human justice is a system; if it be faulty in only one particular it is faulty in all things, since justice means perfection, and that is not perfection which hath a blemish.

In the history of the Judaic race the later records of the deserving portion of the people of Suernis may be found. Verily, my people, we have seen glory together, and long suffering. We have stood together since before the age that is and, that which passeth, was! My seed of strong effort was sown in fallow soil, and it returned more than a hundred fold. The end is not yet; the harvest is not garnered, nor the Chosen People come yet into their reward for the Great Tribulation since Ernon of Suern ceased to strive for them. The way was long, but they shall come at last from out the desert they entered so long ago, and Yeovah will give His children rest!

As Rai Ernon had said, the Saldee general never returned to his native land. He wandered about the city, little noticed by the people, and made his chief abiding place at the vailx of a certain Poseid commissary stationed with others at Ganje.

One day, having become quite friendly with the latter, the Salda asked that his friend give him the pleasure of an ascent into the air; he had never experienced a ride on a vailx, and was desirous of so doing. At the time the commissary was busy, and promised to do as requested on the morrow. Accordingly, after dinner next day, which meal was served on the open promenade deck of the vailx, the ascension was made. The general had taken too much strong wine, and was rather unsteady in his motions. One of the party was a Suerna who had been one of Rai Ernon's counsellors. The general stalked to the taffrail of the vailx to look down into the nether air. Standing near was the Suerna. Neither liked the other, and the Salda, also excited by wine, became quarrelsome. The Suerna, the same, by the way, who had been so amazed by the failure of his occult powers when he made his attempt to kill me, gave the general a sly push, and he fell against the rail. Being heavy, his weight bent it so as to cause a still further loss of balance, and he fell over the side, catching the rail with both hands in a very agile manner. Here, unable to raise himself, he hung, calling for help in an agony of terror. The Poseid captain was not a bad man, but he was somewhat stupid, as a result of a fall on his head, and while able to give satisfaction as a commissary, he was not able to rise higher than some such subordinate position. He had, previous to his injury, been a talented man, and was even yet an inventor of some small note. This was a talent that did him small service now, however, because so many others outranked him in the same direction. He had finally come to be a lunatic on the subject, and was ever seeking to utilize force, or to economize power. While the captain was standing in stupid indecision, the Suerna stepped in and pushed him aside, himself grasping the terrified Salda by the arm. The next instant the ex-counsellor and the Salda general were swinging, whirling towards the earth, over a mile below. Then the Poseida looked over at them as they fell, and, his mind all occupied with his favorite mania for invention, exclaimed:

"What a waste of force! If only they could fall on some mechanism adjusted to raise a weight!" How it happened, the commissary never knew, he averred, and for lack of witnesses, together with his obvious stupidity, the court excused him.

When I learned of the event it was through the governor, whom I had appointed, who reported having relieved the captain from command of his vailx and commissarial office, and the placing of another Poseida in his place. The Salda was the father of Lolix, and I thought it well to break the news as gently as possible to her. How was I astounded, after having done so, to hear her calmly say:

"Prithee, how doth this concern me?"

"Why, thy father,—" I began, when she interrupted me with:

"My father! I am glad. Shall I, who love courage, feel aught but displeasure at his cowardice in the face of death, wherefore he was moved to cry out in terror like a child? Faugh! I call no coward father!"

I turned away entirely horrified, silent for lack of words to express my feelings. Perceiving my action, Lolix came to me, and resting her small, white hand on my arm, looked up into my face, so that my gaze was directly into her glorious blue eyes.

"My Lord Zailm, thou seemst offended! Is it so? Have I said aught to cause thee offence?"

"Gracious gods!" I exclaimed. Then remembering a former estimate of mine, that the Saldu was only a child in certain respects, I said:

"Offended me? Not so, Astiku."

Then she slipped her hand through the bend of my arm and walked beside me. This little experience was the beginning of a longer one which, while very sweet for a length of time, yet culminated in anguish there in Atlantis, and phoenix-like, arose from the ashes of the dead centuries, only a few short years ago. Verily, "the evil that men do lives after them."

Because it was so very obvious that her heartlessness was only that of undevelopment, I was not disgusted with Lolix. I reproved her, indeed, but instead of turning away in unreasoning wrath at its existence, I sought to induce a perception of the enormity of such an offense as cruelty of heart.

According to the custom of her people, Lolix wooed me to wed her. Of course I could not accede, pleasant thought it was to have this beautiful girl doing her best to win my regard. I could not, while I loved Anzimee. Of this love for my sweet, womanly little sister, I never told Lolix, disliking possible contingencies. But I did worse—I told her an untruth, for I said that the Poseid law forbade marriage with those of alien birth.

"Never an exception?" queried Lolix.

"Never one. Death is the penalty."

This was another falsehood, for in Poseid the death penalty was never inflicted, it being forbidden by the law of the Maxin book.

"Well, then, it matters nothing. Thou art young and strong, and of good courage and handsome. Wherefore I love thee. If the law forbid, it is all the same. None but ourselves need know."

The last barrier was fallen. Conscience slumbered. Thoughts of Anzimee were put aside as one would shun an accusing angel. Did I think of Pitach Rhok and my days of sinlessness? Or of the mysterious stranger whom I had heard in awe in the first of my life at Caiphul? Yea, I thought of these things. I thought of Incal, and I said:

"Incal, my God, if I am about to do wrong in thy sight, in disregarding the laws of society and marriage, smite me dead ere I sin."

But Incal smote, not then, but afterwards through the ages. He smote not then; conscience slept the sounder, but passion awoke.

CHAPTER XX.

DUPLICITY.

The year during which I was not permitted to study passed quickly and uneventfully, except that complications deepened on account of Lolix. My affection for Menax became almost reciprocally great as his love for me, which was limitless. But I did not tell him that, which heavier and yet heavier, weighed upon me as time lapsed—the secret affair with Lolix. To have done so would have been best, yet I dared not, for it would have lost me all that I most prized. At least I so feared then.

As time went on I began to query my position. Did I love this beautiful girl? Not as I loved Anzimee. "O, Incal, my God, my God!" I moaned in anguish of soul. Conscience slept yet, but stirred restlessly. The fact that Anzimee was my adopted sister did not prevent her becoming my wife, for the law of consanguinity was not violated. But my own acts barred the way.

My scheme to domicile Lolix in a palace on the far side of Caiphul from Menaxithlon was successfully carried out without exciting the suspicion of any one, not even arousing the jealousy of Lolix. Duplicity, duplicity!

Then I wooed Anzimee unrestrained by the presence of her who would have been a dangerous factor had she even suspected that the daughter of Menax was not my sister by the ties of consanguinity. But my days began to be filled with fear, for I had sown dragon's teeth; the denouement of such affairs as have evil for a guide is invariably sorrow and bitterness. Suppose Lolix did not tire of me?—and I had neither the heart nor the will to do anything to cause her to do so—nature-laws were ever liable to cause a revealment of the facts which would be fatal to my hopes; and though I often cried in agony of soul that I was an unhappy wretch, conscience still slept.

But mine was not a character to be deterred from my resolves by danger. If I was engaged in a game of skill with the Evil One for opponent, I would play to the best of my ability. So I determined to be rid of Lolix, a determination that was late, for the fruit of our sin was come and a home secretly provided—for I would do no murder. These plans were carried out—all fortunately, as I thought, without any man being the wiser. But how to be rid of the really lovable woman, Lolix. Only a year remained ere I would enter examination for my diploma at the Xioquithlon. If successful, I meant to ask Anzimee, whom I knew loved me in return, to be to me all that the honored name of wife conveyed.

At evening, or of an afternoon, nothing pleased Anzimee better than to walk alone, or with Menax, or myself through the palace gardens, under the spreading palms and festoons of flowering vines which canopied all the walks, forming long, cool tunnels of green, gemmed with Flora's most radiant hues. From the breaks in these verdant walls we could see the mimic lakes, hills, cliffs and streams, and beyond these could look out over palace-capped, vine-draped Caiphul and its half thousand hills, large and small. Walking amidst such scenes by the side of her who was so dear, is it strange that my soul was at such times eased of something of its burden of sin and woe?

So long did I defer action in the case of Lolix that I came to fear to take any course except to let events order their own settlement. Yea, I lost confidence in my ability to solve the dangerous problem, fearful lest I should make a bad matter worse. Thus the days slipped by and the examination ordeal was close at hand. Neglect Lolix I did not, could not, nor had I desire to do so. Very often I was with her; indeed, with a strange blindness to the wrong involved, I divided my leisure between Lolix and Anzimee. I sometimes feared that Mainin, Gwauxln, or perhaps both, knew of my secret. They did, too, for their occult vision was too keen to allow them not to know the facts. But neither made any sign—not Mainin, for he cared not how much secret evil went on, as we shall see ere long. Nor Gwauxln, not because he, like Mainin, did not care, but because he was merciful and knew that karma had more dreadful punishment in store than any man could possibly inflict, and his mercy forebore to add to my penalty. So the cancer remained hidden from public gaze, and I knew not that the noble ruler was a sad spectator of my misdeeds. I do not wonder at his sad demeanor when with me as manifested in the last year of my studies.

Anzimee had postponed the time of her examination in Xio until the year in which I was to graduate, and hence the festivities which always followed the examination as a mark of rejoicing over the success of those who received diplomas, included her in the honorable list, for she had passed with high credits.

A dinner was given by the Rai to the successful contestants, and this feast inaugurated an extended season of high social dinners, balls, parties, concerts and theatrical performances—all in the same honor. Anzimee, arrayed in a robe of grayish silk, with her heavy coils of dark hair fastened apparently by a lovely rose, and upon her shoulder a pin of sapphires and rubies—was presented by Gwauxln at the state dinner to the new Xioqi as the "Ystranavu," or "Star of the Evening." This was a social distinction akin to the modern "Queen of the Ball."

Knowing that Rai Gwauxln would lead his niece to the table and be her escort, I took Lolix, as I had a right to do, for I was a graduate and the possessor of a diploma, and all such might choose a companion, who might or might not be a graduate. Lolix, for my sake, had studied hard during the last three years, and was now in her second year at the Xioquithlon, to which she went from the lower schools. I was growing proud of the girl, and felt most tenderly towards her; indeed, I would have been a most despicable person had I not, after her sacrifice for me. Several times I found Gwauxln looking intently at me—I sat not far from him—and once, as he passed me after the feast, he murmured sadly:

"Oh, Zailm, Zailm."

As may be imagined, this address did not increase my peace

of mind. But that night passed without any further disquiet, as so many others had done.

As I walked with Lolix in the great hall of Agacoe, I remarked the many glances of admiration bestowed upon her beauty by the many gentlemen we met; nobles of high degree. She had indeed grown to have a loveliness of face and figure, and best of all, of character, which was no longer heartless, but very gentle since her sad experience of secret motherhood and consequent disbarment from its innocent joys, since the child might not be known as hers. She had had offers of honorable marriage, and refused them, knowing even as she did so that the fact of their proffer was a proof of my having spoken falsely when I told her that the laws of Poseid forbade our marriage. But her love for me, if it suffered, was faithful and knew no lessening. And she kept the secret well, and the more closely for my sake, wretch that I was! As I looked upon her, I felt that she was very dear to me. But Anzimee was more so, and therefore the hideous tragedy went on. I knew that from love of me, Lolix had first repressed heartless remarks, then taken an interest in relieving suffering for its own sake, and so had become transformed from a beautiful thorn tree to a glorious rose of womanly loveliness, with few thorns indeed. Had I really any conscience deserving the name, that I did not come out before the world and take Lolix as my wife after all this boundless love for me? No, not in Poseid. Conscience had not slept; it had never been existent; it was yet to be born, and grow in a later time. Thus did the nemesis of judgment still withhold her stroke.

CHAPTER XXI.

THE MISTAKE OF A LIFE.

Comparison is good mental exercise. It is due to the reader and to myself, as well as to Anzimee and Lolix, to indulge a

present mood prompting me to make an analytical comparison
of these two women.

What was it that fixed so unalterably my desire to wed Anzimee, and not Lolix? Both were gentlewomen—the first by
nature, the second by—yes, by nature, also. I was, however,
about to ascribe the sweet charity of Lolix to the perception
on her part of the misery she would feel, placed in like situation with those who suffered in very fact. But the ability to
so perceive could arise only from its existence in her nature.
No, it was her nature finally developed. Both women were
refined, intelligent, and both were beautiful, though of types
as widely variant as a blush rose and a white lily. Anzimee
was a born daughter of Atl; Lolix was one by adoption. A
small difference, surely, since both were in full accord with,
and equally sensitive to the good, the beautiful and the true,
in the polished refinement of erudite Poseid. Truly, the relations between Lolix and myself were wrong, but she was not on
that account less dear to me, nor was my regard for her less
tender and loving. Her companionship had become a part of
my life. If I had a sorrow, or was despondent, she interposed
her sympathy and cheered me. My anxieties were also hers;
my joys her joys. In everything but name she was my wife.
Then why did not I acknowledge the fact before mankind? Because karma ordered otherwise. I loved Anzimee also. Through
this love karma operated to annul its own tendencies to espouse
Lolix. And the mode of this operation was exhibited in my
recognition of Lolix as possessed of every requisite to make
me happy except in her one lack—that of psychic perception
of the relation of the finite to the infinite. Absurd? No.
That my soul craved such an ability on her part, and found it
not, but did find it in Anzimee, was evidence of the growth of
the frail seedling of interest in the occult life of the Sons of
the Solitude, which had been somewhat matured by the words
of Rai Ernon of Suern, years before. Sayest thou that if a little such interest worked such error in life that deep interest
would make for the losing of the soul, wherefore thou wilt
have none of it? Not so. It was the not being true to the

ideal at that time gained, true with all my soul, that did the mischief, just as in the myth of Lot's wife—she had never been turned to salt had she obeyed, not curiosity, but the higher injunction.

Lolix had no dimmest perception of this psychic link between the things of earth and the things of infinity. I had; I knew Anzimee had; wherefore I ordered my life so as to include her and exclude Lolix, whereby I did both them, myself and my conception of God (which is but a redundant expression, for no one finite can injure Infinity) a fearful injustice. But karma lay in wait for the evil of my life, demanded payment—and got it, every jot; no words can paint the suffering of the expiation. I scarcely propose to try and shall rest content if a realization of some part of it shall deter others from sin through the certitude that there is no vicarious expiation for evil done, and no escape from its penalty.

The Law of the ONE reads: "Except a man overcometh, he shall not inherit of My life; I will not be his God, neither shall he be My son." There can be but one way to such over-coming—the ever recurrent plungings into material incarnation, until the errors of the personal will are at-oned to the Divine Will. There can be no vicarious undoing,* and soon will I show why. Another can not do thy breathing for thee. Reincarnation, the ever recurrent prisoning of the soul in fleshly bodies, is but expiatory, is but penalty. If in His Name ye are become free; if in that Way ye have overcome, and in place of being slaves to, are masters over desire, ye have un-done sin. Then is there no more incarnation for you in the prison of this death, miscalled life. There is no other Way; the Great Master pointed none.

In expiation of my dark past I must needs return into the world—thy world of sin, sorrow, sickness and pain, and disap-pointed longings for the peace that passeth understanding. Is not my twelve thousand and more years of further wanderings in the far land of this world, far from my Father's house, and feeding on the husks called joy; suffering the fevers, pains and

---

*NOTE.—See foot note on page 88.

disappointment of hopes, enough of expiation? Yet for a little while longer I must, and, impelled by love, willingly do serve Him. Some souls shall have even more than I, if they turn not. Which will ye? Will is the sole Way to esoteric, or occult Christian knowledge. Whosoever will, shall have Eternal Life. But the will to overcome must replace our will of desire, as the fresh air replaces the exhalations of our lungs. As the atmosphere is around about us, and, inhaled, becomes our breath, so Will of the Spirit is around us, and, entering into the heart that hath determined to strangle into submission the serpent, suffers us not to know defeat. But I and Lolix, refused this Breath, and unwilling, turned away. Oh! the horror, the pain, of those lost ages, lost with her! But refound by us both, in—overcoming. I am sorry to admit that such moral obliquity could ever have warped my character, even twelve thousand years ago! Will is the only Way to Christ.

Is it not an appalling contemplatin, to think that having determined to put Lolix away, and to install Anzimee in her place by honorably wedding her before mankind, I was able to calculate upon my knowledge of Lolix, and to depend upon her acquiescence in keeping my secret because of her unselfish love for me? Monstrous! I knew that Lolix did nothing by halves. Having given herself to me, she would not expose my iniquity, even though I rejected her for another; society had no reproach for a woman betrayed.

In pursuance of my plan I proposed to obtain the spoken affirmation of the love that had long been confessed by the demeanor of Anzimee. Then I would tell Lolix all, reserving nothing, and throw myself on her mercy. Even after these many, many centuries, when—Laus Deo!—reparation is at last complete, I look at the record of this part of my life when I was Zailm, and wonder that the very confession does not scorch holes in the paper upon which it is written. Moral turpitude is a fearful thing, for, though conscious of its being sinful, I was but dimly aware of the hideous blackness of my action.

Canst thou dissociate, reader, thy horror at the one action sufficiently to take interest in the recital of my profession of love made to Anzimee, after I had hidden from my own sight the evil of my life? It may be almost futile to try; yet it is possible to forget anything out of sight, at least to such a degree:—

"That one may smile, and smile, and be a villain."

More especially is it easy to smile when the evil is in such a far, far past tense, is atoned, and the villain is one no longer. Thou wilt pardon me if I hint the Way of at-onement. Of all my thousands of years of my many lives, to which in this history I can but briefly allude, I draw for thee one lesson that the weary pilgrimage hath taught me, and in my soul I pray thee heed it. For I am longing for my release, when I may go out into the blessed realms that mine eyes have seen, mine ears heard, and myself been amidst, with Him who openeth, and no man shutteth, and shutteth, no man openeth. So this know, and these things—so long as any that read my words turn aside, and will not to know and do His Way, so long do ye **keep me out of my part in the Great Peace, until His spirit shall cease to strive with thee, or hinder thee.** I am working and sacrificing that ye may know that Way, and tread it. Yet some of you will, even at the finality, be of them that denying Him, are by Him denied. Out of all the glorious systems of worlds, only Earth denieth, for acknowledging Him by words, and crying: "Lord, Lord," they yet hate one another in their serpent dominated hearts. Think not that I use any figure of speech when I say "serpent;" microscopists know better. "He that soweth to the flesh shall of the flesh reap corruption; but he that soweth to the Spirit shall of the Spirit have Life everlasting." They that are alive have crucified the flesh with its affections. Some will close the eye and the ear to my message I have of Him. By that shall the seed of Eternal Life be closed out of their souls, and they shall die.* But so

*NOTE.—In this connection read the last page of this book, which closes the history given of a Life redeemed upon His Cross.—Ed.

many as in all things turn unto the Way shall in no wise be cast out. He said it who is true. Keep thy lamps trimmed, and be wise, not foolish virgins.

――――――

CHAPTER XXII.

ZAILM PROPOSES.

My mind was filled with the question which I made paramount—how to phrase my proposal of marriage to Anzimee. Such occupation of thought is common to all lovers, of every race and nation, where match-making is not conducted by the parents.

Having set my time for the momentous inquiry, I sought Anzimee. The information that she was absent at Roxoi palace —one of the three set apart for the Rai, but seldom used by him—was rather perturbing. Lolix resided at Roxoi, and had done so ever since the time when I secured her transference from Menaxithlon. But I was not altered in my purpose of seeing Anzimee; so, while journeying across the city, forty miles to Roxoi, I pondered the new situation. I knew that the two girls were friends, and this fact seemed likely to complicate matters.

Arrived at Roxoi, I found Anzimee in the gardens, seated near a cascade that tumbled over a fairy-like cliff into a mammoth dewdrop of a lake. She was alone. As I came near she inquired, in a surprised tone:

"Where is Lolix?"

"Where?" I repeated. "I know not. I was told that she was with thee."

"And 'twas truth. But she took my vailx and went away, saying that she would go and get thee, that we three might have a little outing together."

I thought rapidly. To Menaxithlon was forty miles across the city due south. The vailx must therefore take nearly or quite as many minutes going in that direction, and the same returning. Eighty minutes. That would be long enough. Seating myself beside Anzimee, I took her hand in mine. I had often done the same before, and even clasped her about with my arm, but in a distinctly brotherly way. Now the simple touch of the fingers was electric in effect, and she could at once detect the intensity of excitement which possessed me. The fine language I had intended to use was lost, and instead of trying to regain it, I said merely:

"Anzimee, would words deepen thy certainty of my love for thee? I can not command them; but I ask thee, little girl, to be my wife!"

And for reply she answered in phrase as brief:

"Zailm, be it so!"

What followed the reader may imagine; thine own fancy will please thee best, for surely the picture is not hard to draw.

When Lolix returned, I had departed, nor this hastily, for she had been delayed in coming back, so that three hours had elapsed since her departure.

I knew that few things were more certain than that Anzimee would confide her joy to Lolix. But I had no misgivings, for I felt every confidence that Lolix would not betray our secret, however terrible the blow might be for her to bear. As I anticipated, Anzimee told the story of my avowal, and of her acceptance of me. When the whole was related, Anzimee said that her friend looked at her a moment, then fell fainting to the floor. When she had been revived, she seemed so calm that even Anzimee did not question her statement that the swoon was due to nervousness. This was at the eventide. Anzimee, filled with happy feelings, saw her friend in bed, dismissed the attendants, soothed her to sleep, and came home. These facts I did not learn until next day. I thought it best to have an interview with Lolix at once, and so experience all the pain, and have done with the anguish of it. Deluded mortal!

I went to Roxoi, and going into the Xanatithlon, awaited Lolix, to whom I had sent word that I desired to see her there. She came. Fully ten years seemed to have passed over her

since I saw her last. Worn and pale, with great dark rings
under her glorious blue eyes, into which the tears flooded as she
caught my quick gaze. Poor girl! But what could I do?—
that was my thought. I was even a little conscience smitten,
but very little, for the scales of sin were thick and very numbing to the soul.

She spoke first:

"Oh, my love, my love! Why hast thou done this? Thinkest thou I shall live? I have for long known that no law existed to bar our union, and have waited for thee to do what
was right—confident that the day would soon come when thou
wouldst ask me to share thy proud name. But—O Incal! my
God! my God!" she exclaimed, bursting into a flood of tears,
that were as quickly repressed. Then in a calmer voice, full
of piteous heartache, she went on:

"Zailm, I love thee too well, even now, to chide thee! I am
thine to do with as thou wilt. I gave thee my life long ago.
I gave thee my babe, and thou didst place it in a home where
no man might suspect its parentage. Zailm, I have done more
also—there was another that—that—O Incal, forgive me! I
sent it in to Navazzamin, that it might not accuse thee, Zailm!
And now, I, whom thou hast called thy 'Blue-eyed darling,' I,
who love thee more than I do life, me hast thou put aside! O
God! Why am I made to suffer thus? Why thus stricken?"

She broke into a storm of agonized weeping, and I sought
not to stay the flood, knowing that sometimes tears are a
blessed relief. Had she loved me thus? Fool! not to have
known it from her actions, which spoke louder than words
possibly could. My heart smote me now indeed, and I prayed,
prayed to God for forgiveness, and I prayed to her. Too late!
Conscience came forth at last, born to smite, sprung like
Minerva, full-armed for the combat.

When Lolix had recovered calmness, she said, in such heart-
broken tones as had never fallen on my ears before:

"Zailm, I forgive thee. Not even now will I betray thee,
since whom I once love I will love till death; afterwards, also,
if love survive the grave. If thou art come to say the parting

word, so be it! But leave me now, for I am almost crazed! Yet remember, my darling, that if thy new life be not happy— though I pray Incal it may be:—that there once beat a heart for thee warmer, more loving, perchance truer, than I fancy thou'lt find that of thy new love. I shall not live long to be a shadow over thy peace. Kiss me once as thou wouldst if I were thine own wife in the sight of the world, as I am in that of Incal, and having died, thou wert about to confide my clay to the Unfed Light.''

With these words she stopped, having arisen and come before where I sat, and placed her arms around me, drawing me into a convulsive embrace. A moment thus, then her lips—chill as those of one who keepeth company with Death, met mine in one long, sobbing kiss! She released her clasp, stood an instant, and was gone. So she left me. Long I sat in the midst of the flowers in the great conservatory at Roxoi.

> "The blossoms blushed bright—but a worm was below,
> The moonlight shone fair—there was blight in the beam;
> Sweet whispered the breeze—but it whispered of woe,
> And bitterness flowed in the soft flowing stream.''

KARMA DISPOSES.

That night the banns of my coming marriage with Anzimee would be announced by the Incaliz Mainin in the great temple, for in cases of high social rank it was customary thus to add extra formality to the publication. If, during the ceremony, a death was to occur within the Incalithlon, custom decree that one entire year must elapse before consummation of the marriage rites. In any event one month must pass after the banns, which were, in consequence declared immediately following the engagement. For reasons of his own, Mainin the Incaliz desired that Anzimee should not wed any one; but as he had no authority over, and but little acquaintance with her, he kept silent respecting his wishes.

At the proper hour, Anzimee and myself stood before Mainin the Incaliz, within the Holy Seat. By our side was Rai Gwauxln and Menax, the five of us being the cynosure of the eyes of a great audience.

In a clear, slow voice, the Incaliz began an invocation to Incal. But in the midst of this service, a woman glided quickly across the triangle of the Place of Life, in the center of which was the Maxin. It was Lolix. She was as faultlessly attired as it was her pride always to be. Apart from the awful blaze in her eyes I saw nothing extraordinary in her appearance. But to have stepped into the Place of Life was an impermissible thing, and the act centered all eyes upon her. It meant an appeal to the authority of the Rai.

"What wouldst thou?" asked Gwauxln.

"Zo Rai, in Salda, my native land, it was the custom to allow either sex to woo the other in marriage. I wooed this man, the Astika Zailm, ignorant that he loved my friend—how could I know? And now, I pray thee, deny the banns, as thou hast a right to do."

"Woman, I am sorry for thee! But the customs of Salda are not those of Poseid. I grant not thy prayer."

I had felt a numbing terror lest at last my crime was to be revealed. But the fear faded as the slender, graceful figure of Lolix turned and was swallowed up in the audience. Then the interrupted banns were renewed. When Mainin said to Anzimee:

"Thou dost declare it thy wish to wed this man?"—she replied:

"I do."

"And thou, dost thou declare it to be thy wish to wed this woman?" To which I said: "Even so, Incal not preventing." As I made answer the proceedings were the second time interrupted by Lolix, who again came into the Place of Life, but this time as hurriedly as if pursued. Opposite the Unfed Light she stopped, and said:

"Incal will prevent! See, I come to wed thee now, Zailm, and here! The God of departed souls shall be our Incaliz— this dagger our wedding proclamation, banns and all!"

I ought to have prefaced the narration of the questions put to Anzimee and myself by explaining that after the invocation by Mainin, that person, Anzimee and myself, and the Rai with

Menax, had left the Holy Seat and had gone into the Place of
Life, so that Lolix now stood close beside me. As she spoke
of the dagger her words were calm, but rapidly uttered—it was
the calmness of insanity! Crazed by the course I had followed,
Lolix stood there, her glorious blue eyes filled with the light
of madness. With her last words still upon her lips, she struck
at my breast with the keen weapon. I warded the blow with
my arm, which was pierced through by the forceful stroke. As
she drew it out with a wrench, blood spurted over the granite
floor. At sight of this she uttered a frightful shriek, saying:

"Mad! Mad!! MAD!!!"

—and with one bound sprang to the center of the Place of
Life, where she stood by the cube of the Maxin.

Anzimee swooned; Menax stood as if petrified, gazing at my
flowing blood, while Gwauxln, pale but calm, spoke to a guardsman near:

"Arrest the maniac!"

The order of the Rai attracted the attention of Lolix, who
said to the approaching soldier:

"No, no, arrest not me. I was mad, but I am not. Whosoever shall touch me, him will I curse, and then die in the
Maxin."

Being superstitious, the guardsman paused, for he dared not
touch her, neither disobey the Rai. In his terror he turned to
the latter and began to make excuse.

"Silence!" thundered Gwauxln. Then in gentle tones he
said to Lolix: "Woman, come to me."

"Not so, Zo Rai! At this place beside the Maxin no one
under the law may offer me violence. Here, then, I stay!"

Speaking thus, Lolix rearranged her slightly disordered turban, folded her arms, and then leaning back against the Maxin-
cube, gazed calmly at the Rai. He made no motion, but looked
first at her, then at me. Lolix, though still near to the Maxin,
had assumed an erect position, no longer touching the cube.

Incaliz Mainin had stood quietly by during the excitement.
He now said:

"Aye, Astiku from Salda, there thou shalt stay, indeed, even longer than thou thinkest!"

He had spoken very calmly, even softly, gazing the while at the unhappy girl. When he turned towards the Rai, he saw a look of horror on his face, and hurriedly looked away again, finishing the reading of the banns. I scarcely heard him, being engaged partly with my bleeding arm, and partly with Anzimee, who, but partially recovered, and still half fainting; leaned against me for support. When the ceremony was completed, Rai Gwauxln, placing a hand on each of our heads, said:

"Not only a year must elapse ere ye may wed, but much longer! Zailm, I do forgive thee thy sins so far as it is mine to forgive—the human laws thou hast broken. As for thy partner in wrong, never mind."

Then turning to Mainin, the Incaliz, he sternly said:

"Because of thine accursed deed, thou and I are forevermore strangers! Now I know thee for what, alas, thou art."

Having spoken in this, to his hearers, enigmatical and startling language, Gwauxln left the Incalithlon.   Mainin also left. Menax, become curious regarding the unhappy cause of all this trouble, spoke to her as she stood by the Unfed Light. She neither answered nor moved. I approached near to her and said gently:

"Lolix?"

Still no answer nor movement. I touched her silken bodice, but received a shock which startled me like an unexpected blow! Her corsage was as rigid as stone. I touched her hand; it, too, was cold and stiff. Her face, even her wavy brown tresses, were alike rigid. Not only was she dead, but actual rock! Like one in a dream, too much stunned to be horrified, but still possessed of a strange curiosity, I rapped with my knuckles on the various thin edges presented by folds in her robe, and heard them sound with a metallic clink. I grasped a finger: it broke off, and then in a sudden wave of awful, living horror, I dropped it upon the stone floor; it broke into fragments like any fragile bit of rock. Still were the golden tresses, with which I had so often caressingly played, of the old lovely color. Her complexion, her blue eyes, even, were of the same natural hue they had been in life, but for all that her body was stone, and her soul was forever fled! Her pretty foot, showing from beneath the hem of her robe, was not only as the rest—stone—but it was petrified fast to the stone pavement on which she stood. At last I realized all. This hideous deed was the work of Mainin in that instant he looked at Lolix in speaking to her. He had prostituted his occult wisdom, and for this had Gwauxln cursed him. Lolix's flesh and blood and raiment had been transmuted into solid stone. This petrification was all that remained of poor, wronged, forsaken Lolix—a perfect statue which, if suffered by man to remain, might stand during the many centuries, till even stone at last crumbled to dust.

The awful meaning of it all came home to me at last. Was I primarily responsible for it? In that moment I knew that I was—knew that the murder was on my soul, as well as on that of Mainin, who had never found that opportunity, at least, except by me.

Even in her temporary insanity Lolix had been true to me. Not one word had she spoken to involve me. If Gwauxln knew —and I was aware that he did—he gave me free pardon so far as human law was concerned. For the broken laws of Incal he could not extend pardon—that was become karma, and lay—a weary width of desert sands of sin to scorch my feet in the passage I must make across them ere ever I could tread the narrow way of attainment—the long atonement was before me. I gazed on the mute form of the girl I had so fondly loved, and loved yet, until Menax, who had become aware of the awful occurrence while I stood stupefied, but on whom the main effect was a desire to leave as soon as possible, pulled me by the sleeve:

"Come, Zailm; let us go home."

Giving one last remorseful look, I obeyed. Lovely Lolix. Her voice was still in death, and that through me! As remorse surged over my soul, I thought that I would now be glad to ask Anzimee to release me, confess all to her, and with her consent make Lolix my honored wife—but it was forever too late in that life thus to make reparation. No more could the tender glance of love flash on me from those starry eyes of blue! No more would my weary head nestle down on her shoulder, while with gentle caress she chased away my darker musings with a mild and gentle sympathy. Ah, ye gods! what had I lost? My life, that had seemed complete, and as a sphere like unto the full moon, was come, like that orb when it rises late at night, to seem torn, and but half of itself, wrecked and ragged, careening through the night time of existence.

Anzimee knew nothing of the awful reality; she had been too much stunned by the sudden knowledge of her friend's insanity. She must not know, if it were possible to prevent her learning of it, We went to our carriage and, solemn the one, stunned the other, and wildly remorseful the third, got in one went home to Menaxithlon. Home! I felt that the peace of home was no more mine! Life had become a desert, over which stalked the skeletons of despair, regret and sorrow; overhead a moonless sky, underfoot in the night a howling waste of sand, blown hither and thither by curbless winds. Lolix was gone, Anzimee would never be mine, as I felt in prophetic forecast of soul, and so, with bowed head, I sat in the midst of the desert of my days and let the phantoms dance about and mock me, unheeded.

———————

CHAPTER XXIII.

A WITNESS BEFORE THE CRIMINAL.

States of mind, of feeling and of intuition are the only real things that exist. Jesus, although the Son of God, and John and Paul were all Sons of the Solitude; Hegel, Berkeley, Sterling, Evans; all real theosophists and all real Christians—are becoming Sons, and are in accord with those peerless nature-students of old when they say:—"Spirit alone is real; all else is illusion."

If a man think himself ill, he will become so; if, per contra, he is cheerful under even the most adverse circumstances, he will not see that the world about is full of gloom; nor is it. 'Tis only in himself, and he can change the world all into gall and bitterness for himself, although it be all a song for others.

For weary weeks I wandered about, stupidly a leaden load of grief weighing on my soul, a feeling of dull despair which would have crazed a less well-balanced temperament. Had Lolix felt thus for even a little while? If so—and I knew she felt worse, if that were possible—God pity the bright, sweet and beautiful girl who had so suffered through me! I was tempted to sucide, tempted to sneak out of the back door of life, and I often felt of the edge of the razor-keen knife given me by the Incalian mining superintendent—how long before? Four years, really; four years? Four centuries, for aught I knew by my feelings. I stood by the Maxin in the long afternoons when I was alone in the temple. Or did I but dream that I did this? Aye, it was a dream of tortured sleep, for no one had admittance to the Incalithlon (except the Incala) on any other occasion than on days of worship, or of special ceremonies; and then the edifice was always thronged. Anzimee crossed my desert at times, but though she spoke, and caressed me, and strove to arouse me, it was in vain; all her efforts fell like a ray of sunlight on the inky, lustreless pools sometimes seen in deep forests. Left all alone with my remorse—for their unavailing efforts seemed to my friends more productive of harm than of good, and therefore they ceased them—I took my private vailx, and, to shut off all possible communication with the world, removed from it the naim. Then, no one witting my intentions, I slipped away in the night-time. I wandered then through the realms of the air, sometimes so high above the earth as to be in almost entire darkness, where the Nepthian Ring was visible, and where even the air generators and heat furnishing apparatus were scarcely able to keep the air in the vailx dense and warm enough to support my miserable life. Or, equally alone, equally in darkness, I made my vailx seek the depths of the sea where phosphorescent fish would have mistaken my craft for a larger brother, had I ever cared to light up. But my soul was dark, and of what avail was it to illuminate the vailx, when, with eyes to see, I saw not? So bitterly keen was my horrible anguish of soul that at last the body of clay lost its power to hold Me, and I arose above time and earth, and remained in that state for what seemed an endless period. No light appeared to be in the awful blackness, neither any warmth, but a darkness as of death, a coldness as of the grave. No person crossed my path; no sound was heard, save dull, muttering groans. But at length flashes of red flame leaped athwart my vision, then went out, leaving the gloom more wholly black than before. Horrid hisses, as of giant serpents, assailed my ears now; awful pain seemed dissolving my very soul. At last my nerves failed to respond to the racking agony, and sensation failed. Numbness seized upon me, and I exclaimed:—"Is this death?" But only echo answered. The hisses had ceased; all was silent. Suddenly I felt a deep dread of the horrible solitude, so dark and cold, yet in which, somewhere, I could see a little light, that but seemed to render the intense darkness more smothering. I called aloud; reverberating echoes alone answered. I shouted and shrieked in wild terror. But in all the vast glooms around no sound save my own replying, reflected tones came again. The knowledge that my confines were limited came to me from the fact that my voice was sounded back to me, after what seemed ages between utterance and return. With this knowledge came the sense that I was free to go, and I arose from the place whereon I stood, as if I was endowed with wings, and I fled faster than thought. Tall cliffs I found in the glooms, and ever and anon peaks shone out in the glare from some flaming pit, but no creature was anywhere to be found; I was in a very universe of solitude. Alone, oh, alone! The awful, horrible despair that then seized upon me caused me to wail in more than mortal pain. My eyes were dry and my soul as if crushed. Despair so frightful held me for its own that I longed to perish. Vain wish. Then I remembered that I had an earthly body; to find even that would be some solace. On lightning lines I sped to it, to find it cold and lifeless save for a small glow of magnetic light in the plexus of the heart nerves, and another in the medulla oblongata. But beside it I found, O, Incal! I found Lolix, weeping, praying to our God to restore—me. She did not seem aware that I had come, but sought me in the cold body of earth. Then I knew that I had been reminded of my corporeal self by that fond woman's soul pleadings. Such pleading, such anguish, I could no longer endure. I stood beside her, I touched her. Then she looked up and saw me. She looked long at me; then at my body. And then:—"Zailm, is it thou? My love, my love. Oh, clasp me, ere I fall!''

She fell forward upon my breast, and in that time the body of me disappeared, and also all things, save the sandy waste where we then found ourselves together. * * * Then, before our horror-stricken gaze came a little babe, so tender in age it seemed just born. It was able to come to us, however, and it could utter wailing speech, which smote our ears like cries of mortal agony! It was dripping with blood, and its eyes were as those of a dead infant. With an awful shriek of anguish Lolix cried:—

"O Incal, my God, my God! Have I not suffered enough but that my dead, my murdered babe should come to smite my soul! Zailm! Zailm! See! See! See our baby girl, murdered by me, for thy sake!''

My heart seemed to stop beating in its fearful woe, and I stood paralyzed, gazing at the little one as it stretched its hands, gory with the blood of untimely birth, and raised its glazed eyes—to me! Then I stooped and took it into my arms, holding it close, trying to warm its poor, cold little body, and I wept—aye, at last I wept great tears of real value, because shed for another. With a voice choked with anguish, I said:—"Lolix, thy sin is on my head, because done for me! Let Incal have mercy on me, if He will!''

Then a glorious radiance broke over the scene, and the Cross Bearer was beside us as we stood, clasping each other and our child. He whom I had seen by the moonlit fountain, years before, stood by us again. On His breast shone a Cross of Fire, which leapt or fell again in waves of undulating, living Light. He spoke:—

"Lo! Thou hast called upon the Most High for mercy. Because unto that little child thou hast shewn mercy, thou shalt receive it. Thou hast come unto Me, and I will give thee— rest. Yet, it shall not abide with thee until the day of the Great Peace entereth into thy overcoming heart. Therefore, in a far day, thou shalt garner a sorrowful harvest of woe, and repay all thou art indebted. When thou art come again, also she with thee, and again are ready to go into Navazzamin, ye will find yourselves free of earth forever. Then, having received, thou shalt give. He that causeth another to sin causeth that other's and his own feet to slip, and to turn from My way. He must at-one his heart to Me first, then go again into the field of woe, yet not in a body of flesh, but of spirit. And he must find his victims, and struggle with them, till he turn them back from whence he led them. Thus taketh he on his own back their burden he made them to place there. Then shall he carry it for them until they, following his spirit-counsels to their souls, are come unto Me. And I will take that burden, that shadow, and it shall cease, for I am the Sun of Truth. Can a shade exist in sunlight? Can any pile shadows on the sun? Neither can any pile sins upon Me, and burden Me. That little one I will take unto Me; thou hast offended it, and it shall be as a millstone on thy neck, casting thee into the sea of earthly woe; yet ye shall escape, for thou hast thy name in the Book of Life. But now, rest! And My daughter, rest!"

I found myself in my body, unable to recall anything I had passed through. But I was aweary and I slept. Nature came to the rescue of my tired soul, and for days I was in fever, which passed into a coma, and from that I awoke, weak, but well. Still, I was in a waking dream. And I dreamed that I was in the Incalithlon at Caiphul.

"O, the agony! O, sin's bitter cost!"

But at last I went back to Caiphul, after weary weeks in which I was lost to my people—aye, months, three of them. Back to my home. As I passed through the palace I met officers and ladies of the court, and attendants, to all of whom I had been a friend, and who so regarded me. They now gazed blankly at me, but spoke no word of greeting. Was my life known at last to a horrified world? No. This was not the reason of the strange demeanor of the people. I was unexpected, was supposed to be dead. During the hundred days of my absence, Menax, with Anzimee, had concluded that I was dead, had perhaps taken my own life. It were happier for me had they thought aright as to the first part of the matter.

Now I was come home, resolved to be open and frank in my relations with those whom I loved best on earth. I would confess my evil ways to them, and implore forgiveness. Once again—too late! Menax, long a sufferer from an affection of the heart, thinking me dead because I had not come to him, nor to Anzimee, had not survived the shock which this belief caused him. I was told that for some weeks he was gone to Navazzamin. I dreaded to ask after Anzimee, lest here, too, some terrible news awaited me.

In my misery I wandered about the city, and ere long found myself by the great temple. A little door stood open, and no one was near, so I entered by it, careless that admittance was denied all but Incali. I hoped to find in this sacred shade some relief. No one seemed to be within, and I wandered about until I stood in the triangle of the Place of Life. There, forgetful for the moment, I gazed reverently on the Unfed Light. Then I passed around to the other side of the quartz cube and— O God! there stood Lolix, still and cold! My very brain reeled. I went to her, and found her the same as when I looked last on her dear form, stone, only stone! How many years was it since then? A whole life may crowd into a day's length and cen-

turies pass in a few weeks. O Lolix, Lolix, my accuser! In
blank numbness of mind I laid my hand on her cold form, and
shuddered at the chill, yet bent and looked into the eyes which
saw me not, and kissed the dumb lips which made no response.

"Yet she would not speak, though he kissed in the old place
the quiet cheek."

In her hand was a roll of red parchment; I ventured to
remove it and look at its contents, if indeed it had any writing
upon it. It had, and I read:

"Because this statue is record of a despicable crime, I,
Gwauxln, Rai of Poseid, do forbid its removal until I grant
permission. Let it stand a silent witness before the criminal."

With a shudder I replaced the roll in the stony grasp, and
almost fainted at the hollow rattle which it made as I did so.
Was I that criminal? Not the one. But I felt as if I was. I
would go to Agacoe and ask permission of the Rai to remove
her of whom he knew I was fondest, but had lacked the courage
or decision to say so to the world. Aye, circumstances made
her more precious to Zailm than Anzimee was. I turned to
leave that I might go to Agacoe. But I was startled when,
on turning, I found myself facing Rai Gwauxln, gazing sorrow-
fully upon me. Startled only, for nothing surprised me any
more, nor ever gave me real terror. Ere I had spoken he said:

"Yes, thou hast my consent to remove her."

I felt no wonder at his anticipation of my request, although
I noted the fact; indeed, it was deep gratitude which I experienced instead. I was muscular, and at once acted upon the
permit. I took one long, last look into the deep blue eyes, and
at the face, which seemed almost to smile as I bestowed a sobbing kiss upon the calm lips. Then I lifted her from the granite floor. The one foot that was exposed to view beneath the
hem of her stony robe broke off at the ankle, just above the
straps of her dainty sandal, as I lifted the slight, but now
heavy body. Then I raised her higher, and yet higher, to the
top of the cube of the Maxin, and let her drop forward against
the Quenchless Light.

"Kiss her and leave her; thy love is clay."

As she touched the Maxin-Light she instantaneously disappeared, with no more disturbance of the tall taper than comes from the flight of darkness when the morning sun lights up the valleys. Calmly the Quenchless Light stood, unchanged as ever. As I turned away I saw the little foot, whereon sparkled the sapphires and diamonds of the sandal strap-buckle— my gift! I succeeded in detaching the little remnant unbroken, but instead of putting it also in the Maxin-Light, I wrapped it in my mantle, glad that I had a token, even if it was only a stone foot.

I could not bring my courage to the point of asking my sovereign about Anzimee. No, I feared his possible, and not unreasonable scorn. I would seek her, and find if she also were dead, like Menax. If so, I resolved to take the first opportunity —the morrow might favor me, as it was the beginning of an Incalon or Sun-day of general worship—and return to the temple, where I would bathe away my physical self in the unwavering flame of the Unfed Light.

Anzimee was not dead, however, but had not yet learned of my return. I found her, the sign of her great sorrow in her fine gray eyes, which, as we met, rested on me in a bewildered stare. Then, with one long sob, she fell into my outstretched arms in an unconscious condition. Poor little girl! I held her, I clasped her close to my heart, and while I kissed her pale lips, her black-ringed eyes, her sunken cheeks, my tears fell on her face like rain—the first tears my fevered physical eyes had shed through all my agony of soul. At last she awoke from her faintness only to experience a long sickness, in which her pure spirit came near bursting its earthly casket, and after several weary weeks, finally left her to consciousness. When she was again moving about in her old quiet way, and although frail, was able to endure the recital, I sat down in the Xanatithlon in the seat where Menax and I had sat so long before. Then I drew the slight form down upon my knees, and with my arm about her, told her all the sad story of Lolix, and the miserable flight from Caiphul which I had made to escape the memory of it—alas! how unsuccessfully! No one can run away from self. Then after the unrestrained confession, I asked her to forgive me. For some time she said nothing, but her arm stole around me, so that we clasped each other. At last she spoke:

"Zailm, I do forgive thee—from the depths of my soul I do! Thou art but mortal. If thou hast sinned, do so no more. I do not wonder that thou shouldst have loved that sweet woman."

At this I drew forth the memento of Lolix, which I had carried with me, despite its weight, and without a word handed it to her.

"This is her foot? O Lolix! I loved thee, also! Zailm, give me this. I would keep it in memory of my friend."

Then I spoke:—"Anzimee, my wife, for thou art to be mine; the world knoweth it—thou hast forgiven me. So hath thine uncle, our Rai. But it is yet some months ere we may wed till death. Hence I will go forth into Umaur, in the region where men are not, even in the south part, for in Aixa are certainly mines, and in the sandy deserts there will I find gold. Not that I want gold, for I have millions, aye, three million teki, and much other wealth; but all that the earth will yield it is good for Poseid to have. I go, because I fear I can not be in Caiphul and refrain from being always with thee. In Umaur I can see thee, and hear thee, and love thee, dear, for I shall not this time remove the naim, so that it will be much as if I were here. Therefore, kiss me, sweet one, a fond farewell, and I will be gone when the evening falls. Incal be with thee, and His peace overshadow thee!"

It was two thousand miles from Caiphul to that part of the Umaur coast nearest which I desired to go inland. But, thinking of Anzimee, the distance was passed unheeded until we lay above the region where now the geographies mark the great nitre-bearing desert of Atacama. It was desert then as now. We found on prospecting its deepest sands, near to the base of the Andes, that these were rich enough in gold to justify myself and men in setting up the electric generator of water. This was an instrument containing several hundred square yards of metal plate surface arranged in banks like the gills of a fish, the whole encased in a tight metal box. An air current entering at one end of the case had to traverse every inch on both sides of the plate ere it touched the farther end. As each plate was made and maintained very cool by Navaz forces, the result was rapid deposition of moisture from the atmosphere. In the example cited the generator was of the largest portable size, and the flow of water condensed by it was about a quart every minute—quite enough with which to do a considerable amount of mining in the economical way in which our mining machinery used water.

I had brought a horse from Poseid, and after mining arrangements were attended to, and the men placed at work, I had the animal made ready, and taking a case of mineral locators—light instruments operated by something similar to what would nowadays be called a pile la clanche—hence not Night-Side electricity—instruments used for determining the location of mineral deposits on the principle of the electrometer—and with food enough for several days, I set out to prospect for valuable minerals. I also took a small, easily portable naim, so as to maintain communication with the rest of the world. I soon left this latter instrument in a cache, intending to get it when I came back, for I had not gone above five miles ere discovering that the instrument had been rendered useless by the loss of its vibrator. Where I had lost this essential I did not know, but I concluded not to go back after it. The loss, though no small annoyance, was a relief to my horse, for it reduced his burden by a number of pounds—no small matter, considering that I had a rifle, which I will not now describe, different though its principle from any modern weapon, in that its propulsive force was electricity—my mining tools, my packages of dates and nuts for food, my polar compass, pocket photographic apparatus, and a small generator, with, lastly, my bedding and my own weight.

That night I was far away, and the next evening found me over a hundred miles from the camp. As the sun sank low I found myself riding along the bottom of a deep arroyo.* At a

*NOTE.—A deep, narrow ravine.

little distance I saw the mouth of what appeared to be a small cavern. This might do nicely to camp in over night, and provide shelter. My horse was well trained, and would stay for hours within whistling distance of the place where I left him. So I dismounted, and bidding him remain near, I went into the cavern. It seemed like a long tunnel, and without going further, I returned to my steed and took off his saddle. Then I laid under it the food I had brought for myself; for the animal there was abundance of grass growing about. The tools I also put under the saddle, and taking my electric rifle, was about to return to the investigation of the cave, when my horse pleaded for water, and as the ravine was a dry creek, I proceeded to give him drink and save some myself. The creek bed was of smooth, cement-like rock, with numerous depressions shaped much like buckets. Beside one of these I set the generator, and soon the hole was full of water, cool and refreshing. I watered my grateful animal at this, and drank from the spout of the instrument myself. How good the fluid seemed! As I placed the generator, still running, back beside the hole, I little thought how I would need it soon, and be unable to get it.

I found the bottom of the cavern to be of the same rocky character as the bed of the arroyo. I knew it was not mineral bearing, but my curiosity was aroused, and I concluded to go to the end of the tunnel. In my pocket I had a small lighting battery and incandescent bulb, and when it grew dark in the cave by reason of my distance from the entrance, I used this to illumine my pathway. For fully half a mile I found the cave to open on before me. At that point I stopped, overcome by surprise. In all that region I had not seen a sign of human presence, recent or ancient, until now. But before me, only partially exposed, stood a house, presenting its corner and part of two heavy walls of basalt. I dropped my lumen in my surprise, and it broke on the rocky floor, extinguishing the light. But it was not altogether dark about me, for daylight filtered in from some source.

Long I stood there in that gloomy cavern, gazing upon the

ruined house. Whence had come its builders, and in what forgotten age? Where had they gone? Was this but a solitary
building, or were there others hidden in the sands of the plain
near by, but not uncovered? Conjecture had here full play,
for in all the annals of Poseid, covering decades of centuries
with concisely written records, no mention was made of any
people, civilized, or even savage, having had inhabitants in this
"No Man's Land." The only tenable conclusion was that I
now gazed upon the relic of some people so ancient as to ante-
date even Poseid's forty centuries. At length I crossed the
cave's short width in order to more closely examine this remnant of the dim past—a past forgotten even when Poseid was
young. In the side of the building nearest to me was a doorway through the smooth, finely chiseled basalt blocks forming
the wall. Partly ajar swung a door, apparently formed of a
single slab of basalt about six inches thick by the proper pro-
portions otherwise. Impelled by curiosity, I stepped into the
room, which was easily done without disturbing the door from
the position it had so long occupied. My reason greatly disliked the admission that even a stone structure should so long
have withstood the effects of time; but it was only thus explain-
able, so I dismissed conjecture for the time.

I found the three dimensions of the interior apparently
equal, and about sixteen feet every way. There was but the
single door to give entrance. Excepting two parallel openings
in the roof, formed by placing a stone of less width by a span
on either side of the opening it would otherwise have filled,
there was no break in the solid masonry. The floor, which was
thinly covered by sand, I found to be made of granite, the
jointure of which was as perfect as that of the walls—not a
sheet of paper could have been slipped between any two blocks.
After exploring thus far, I leaned against the wall, near enough
to the door to touch it without change of place, and letting my
gaze rest on the barred grating in the ceiling, gave myself to
reflection. How cold and gloomy it seemed in that lonely room,
relic of a bygone age, forgotten by even so old a race as ours.
The solid construction, the simple severity of its plan, all forci-

bly brought to mind the descriptions given of prisons in Poseid in ante-Maxin days. Was it the solitary example of building skill of its constructors in which I now stood, or was it one of a collection forming a buried city? How this particular building came to be clear of sand in its interior was easy to see. The rain waters had percolated through the shallow soil above, and had run through the crack which I have mentioned as giving light to the cavern. A part of the flow had gone outside, thus exposing two sides of the corner of the house; the rest of the water, running on the flat roof, had entered through the grating. Seeping thence through the sand in the room it had carried it out of the door standing open at the side.

Satisfied with my reflective study, I began to think of returning to the open air, and to my horse. As I turned to pass out, curiosity impelled me to swing the ponderous door on its hinges, if I had strength. Expecting that much effort would be required, I gave force to the action. Alas, for my superficial examination of the slab. I had observed no sign of a lock of any sort, and did not imagine any existed. Hardly any effort was needed to swing the deceitful door, and it went to with such quickness that I lost my balance and fell against the wall, striking my head so severely as to render me unconscious. When I recovered I found the door shut and securely locked. In my cursory notice of it I had seen that instead of a simple slab it was made of two plates of stone, separated at the edges by a segment of a third plate, forming thus a hollow space between the outer surfaces. In that space there was concealed an arrangement of bolts and bars of stone, working on the gravity-drop principle, and releasing the locking-bolts when the door shut tight to place. The ends of these, four in number, then shot into recesses in the wall, and the door was securely locked.

Being of a calm disposition, given to reliance on my scientific knowledge, the discovery that I was imprisoned did not discompose me in any great degree. Instead, I sought for some means of withdrawing the bolts. But none existed. I now thought in dismay that I had not a single tool with me with

which to dig out of this gloomy prison. I then sat down to
reflect on the situation. The longer I pondered, the more terrifying the aspect of things became. First, not a soul knew of
my whereabouts. As I had no naim, my place could not be
determined except by tracking me; this would prove impossible, because I had followed the beds of watercourses, long
stretches of which were bare rock. I would not be missed
for three days yet, as I had said that I expected to be gone
for a period twice as long, and three days more than I had
already been absent, ere I proposed to return. No; there was
no hope of escape, and now I realized how true were the
words of Rai Ernon of Suern when he told me that a Poseid
depended for his very life on his being surrounded by the
creations of his knowledge in the realm of natural physics.

The food which I had brought with me was with my horse
and outfit, as far beyond my reach as the stars. It might be
that they would finally search for me, and find my horse.
But no, he would not be apt to remain three or four days
alone in that awful wilderness; he would wander, perhaps
go back to the vailx. But he would leave no trail to give a
clue to my prison, for he would go as he came, over an unyielding, rocky stream bed. Hunger pangs again suggested
that I had no food; not even had I any water. Hope still
remained, for was not Incal my protecting Father? How futile
this, my hope! God, Incal, Brahm—call the Eternal Spirit
what thou wilt—verily doth heed the needs of His children,
but those needs which to the child seem to be uppermost, are
not always so adjudged by the Eternal One. He operates
through His children, whether human or angelic ones, making
each one interdependent with all others, and thus men or
angels may have for helpers each other, or perhaps only some
animal brother. God noteth a drowning mariner, but unless
some brother be there to rescue, he may physically perish.
He tempereth the wind to the shorn lamb, but generally only
through the fact that self interest, or it may be some higher
emotion, as pity, is aroused in the mind of beholding man.
Nay, it is only through the mainsprings of character, by our

Heavenly Father implanted in the souls of His children, that
He ever helps or saves. And this is mostly true:—that the
physical body must pray with muscular action if it would get
an answer to its needs in physical form; the mind must pray
through mental processes, and its answer will be in mental
results, while the Spirit shall pray through its spiritual nature,
and receive those values which are not perceptible to the natural mind. All this; but although the mind prayeth forever,
and the body doeth no work, the results—save a brother act-
eth—shall not be for the body. And though the Spirit pray,
yet if the mind pray not also, knowledge will not come to the
brain. How shall the mind pray? By being in harmony with
the Spirit. And how shall it have this harmony? By control
through the will of the animal body, that it infringe not the
laws of that wholeness which is health.

When I sat in the cave house and prayed to Incal with my
whole mind, yet, as I could not pray with my muscles, no
release would come for the body, neither food nor drink. I
might, on the mental plane, have influenced Rai Gwauxln
to understand my predicament; this, to him, would have been
clairvoyance; but this I could not while the enemy who had
aroused my curiosity to work my ruin intercepted all such
clairvoyant messages; more especially I could not, being ignorant of the proper method. It would have been mere chance
that Gwauxln would have been influenced by my mental tension of distress undirected by my knowledge. Meanwhile,
unaware of how to use such powers, I dismissed thoughts of
any possibility of escape in that direction. But I would pray
to Incal. So I knelt on the cold, cruel floor, and prepared to
invoke His aid. As I uttered His name I heard a musical
laugh, albeit mocking—a sound which thrilled me with that
dread terror which every man and woman has sometime felt,
either in childhood days or in later life—that chill which
shivers the senses when listening to some weird tale of horror, told by the fire's open grate, while the Storm King rocks
the very foundations of the ground.

Turning, and arising from my knees, I beheld the Incaliz of the Great Temple in Caiphul.

"Wherefore didst thou start at beholding me, as if thou hadst looked on a demon?"

To this question I could vouchsafe but one reply—that my sudden fright must have been from beholding him in that manner, since I was not accustomed to seeing men go about like ghosts, disembodied, yet not seeming to be so.

I felt a great joy at his coming, for I then believed that Incal nad answered my yet unspoken petition for mercy by sending Mainin to my aid. And yet, why should I still be possessed by that unaccountable fear, the fear which overcame me upon first seeing him? I knew in the moment after its utterance that it did not arise from the cause attributed—his method of advent to my prison, because I knew that as a Son of the Solitude he possessed the power to lay aside the gross body of earth as one would an overcoat, and project himself to any desired place. I knew as I looked upon him that his corporeal self was in a trance sleep, thousands of miles away in Poseid. I had no such power to project myself, else it had been easy for me to let Rai Gwauxln know of my danger; at least, unknowing of Mainin's interference, I thought so. But as Incal had sent the Incaliz to me all was surely well.

The priest doubtless read my thoughts, for he said that he had become aware of my unpleasant predicament through Incal, and had come to assist me to escape. He must, however, leave me until he could get aid to me by dispatching a vailx from Caiphul. It would not take long, and meanwhile I must be of good cheer. And then he disappeared as he had come, and I was again alone, awaiting his promised return with a feverish anxiety not to be expressed in words. Hours passed, and he came not, nor any other. Hours grew into days, three days, and he came not, neither came any succor. The pangs of hunger, terrible as they had become, were as nothing compared to my thirst. Once more the daylight ceased to filter through the grating overhead and the crevice leading to the upper ground. I had worn the ends of my fingers to rawness trying to release the bolts of the door; had sounded every inch to see if it did not contain a secret spring that would let loose some part of the prison wall. But fate had no such kindness in store for me. Seven times the light had gone out above me, marking seven nights since Mainin's visit.

Several times my torture of hunger and thirst had rendered me wildly delirious, with lucid intervals. In one of these lucid moments of comparative calm, as I lay moaning on the sandy floor, feebly calling on Incal for help, I heard the same low laugh that had heralded Mainin's first appearance. The sound fired me with temporary strength, and I sat up. I would have cursed the Incaliz for his long absence, which had meant so much suffering for me, had I not feared that in his anger he would leave me there to die. I no more felt for him the reverence I had ever felt, for I was certain now that he was not what men thought him. And I would have therefore cursed him, because of my inward sense that great as was his esoteric knowledge, and the fact of his being recognized as a Son, that none the less he was black hearted, and an abomination in the sight of Incal, and that in him the Sons of the Solitude were deceived as the very elect. That I did not denounce him to his face was due to the fast vanishing hope that he might still be induced to help me escape.

This time he came with changed manner. Now when he spoke, his first words were in mockery of my appeals to the great Father of Life.

"Ha! Much good may it do thee to cry unto Incal or any helper. God! There is no God.* Bah! how blind men are to pray to such empty ideals as their fancies name 'God!' Men of Poseid say Incal is God; men of Suernis say Yeovah, and they of Necropan say Osiris. What madness and idiocy!"

Here I sat more erectly, and regarded him a moment before asking, "If he were not afraid so to blaspheme Incal and to deny his Maker?"

"Thinkest thou, Zailm, son of Menax, that I should do as I have if I thought any God existed? Is it news—aye, it is

---

*Psalms lxiii. 1.

news to thee that I should desire to achieve the ruin of her
called Anzimee—that I came from a former life on earth—aye!
many of them—filled with hatred of her who always heretofore hath caused me to be exposed to the laws of man? She
can not now, for in the Book of Fate I do not find it so written, so that either it is not there, or else I have lost my power
to read fate, a thing I think not likely. But I will, through
thee, wring her heart to the depths, so that she shall cry out
in anguish of soul! What hath Anzimee done to me? Not
as Anzimee, but as a powerful woman and seeres, ere she was
born in the earth as Anzimee. I follow her in vengeance. To
wring her soul in agony I compassed the death of Menax,
against whom personally I had no cause; I have almost done
the same for thee, yet have I naught against thee. I it was
that did work upon thy curiosity that thou here mightest find
thy death. I had hoped to hinder thy confession of thy life-
sin with Lolix unto Anzimee. Then, after thou shouldst have
met thy death, and then been found by me, I would have
gotten so much the greater misery for her out of the public
exposure of thine iniquity, for I had all the proofs well in
hand. But that scheme is foiled; I care not overmuch—thy
death will occasion her much torture. For that purpose also
was Lolix led to do as she did, and thou also with her, so long
ago—for I lay my plans long ahead, being gifted with vast
power of forepiercing the future. For that same end shall the
Rai be brought low, and at the last she who is the object of
my chiefest wrath shall not know good from evil, so that her
name shall be a scorn in the mouths of the people. Revenge
is sweet, Zailm, sweet!''

My horror and my weakness together made it impossible
for me to do aught but sit and stare in silent helplessness,
even had any corporeal body been before he upon which to
act.

"Thou art aghast at my iniquity? I am too old to fear
failure, and am beyond the reach of the laws of men, at last.
No man, nor all the men on earth, could deprive me of life
or liberty. I have long known a secret which prolongs life

many times the common length—'tis a secret won from the deeper Night-Side of Nature. One day shall come when all Poseid shall know these secrets. 'Twill be a sad day for it, I rejoice to think! I was old, old, when Gwauxln of Poseid thought me a boy with himself; so also thought the Sons of Solitude, for I was cunning in concealment. So think they yet. I—yes, I will tell thee, for thou art even now as one who is dead. I have worked for three centuries in this present body. Said I not that I am old? I have counteracted the good done by Ernon of Suern, so that he died of a despairing heart. I do thus that I may, if possible, wither all the hopes of humankind, turn them down from the infinite path—down to demonhood, death and destruction. Ernon worked to the exaltation of mankind; I to its depression; so we came in conflict, and I won. And why knew he not my hand? Because I have ever worked in the dark, kept my own counsel, and obtained mastery over the evil hosts which are not human, never were, and never will be. And against workers in the dark can no Son of Light prevail, for both work on the animal nature of man, which, having no light of guidance, taketh the first offered support, thus favoring Workers in the Dark. But enough. So much would I not tell thee were it not that thou wouldst not have much power thereby over me—ME, understand—wert thou alive instead of practically dead. Thinkest thou now I can have belief in a God? Bah! If God exists, I fear not; yet let Him punish!''*

And now a fearful, glorious and wonderful sight appeared. The night had come while Mainin thus confessed to me and gloried in his apical crimes, and called upon Incal to punish if He existed. In the total darkness of the prison, which, being physical gloom, could not veil the form of Mainin, there appeared that which struck terror to both our hearts, albeit terror of different sorts. A human form, which yet was not of earth, surrounded by a blinding white light, stood before us. Was this Incal? Had He of a verity accepted the rash challenge of the criminal priest? Upon His countenance rested a

NOTE.—"The fool hath said in his heart, 'There is no God.' "

calm but awful expression, though not of anger or any human emotion. For an instant the wondrous eyes gazed upon me, then turned to Mainin. He then spoke, calmly, musically, and while I listened all my pain left me, though the words were of fearful import:

"To feel
The perfect calm o'er the agony steal."

The voice was like my conception of the tones of Incal, as He said:

"I shall not, O Mainin, enumerate thy crimes—thou knowest them every one. Thou hast been fellow with the Sons, and they taught thee all they knew, and of Me thou learnedst more than they could teach—aye, centuries agone. I knew thy way; I knew its evil, yet interfered not, for thou art thine own master, even as all men are self-masters; few, alas, are faithful! But thine altitude of wisdom, prostituted to selfishness, to sin, to crime, more utterly than any other man hath dared, is thy destruction. Thy name meaneth 'Light,' and great hath thy brilliancy been; but thou hast been as a light adrift on the seas, a lure to death of all them that follow thee, and these have been myriad. Thou hast blasphemed God, and jeered in thy soul, saying, 'Punish!' but thy day was not come. Wherefore thou wert let go unrebuked. It made thee bold, and thou wouldst go on, even now. But lo! Anzimee thou shalt not harm, for she is handmaiden of Christ, even mine own daughter in service. Thou hast well merited the penalty, and because thou hast knowingly dared it, lo! now shall it be dealt out to thee. I would it were avertible. But thine is one out of a myriad of cases, more heinous because thou art wise, not ignorant. But as thou art an ego, a ray from my Father, and now give out no more light, but darkness only, I will cut thee off for a season, for thou shalt neither destroy more of my sheep, nor be let to leave unexpiated the evil thou hast done. It were better for thee couldst thou cease to exist. But this may not be of an ego. I can but suspend thee as a human entity and cast thee into the outer darkness to serve as one of the powers of nature. Get thee behind me!"

The High Priest had stood the picture of an awful terror, numbed beyond thought of escape, which indeed was not possible, for the Judge was Man, and more than Man finite— was MAN INFINITE, even CHRIST.

Now, however, as the Son of Light ceased to speak, Mainin uttered a howl of mingled terror and defiance. At this dread sound the Christ stretched forth His hand, and instantly Mainin was surrounded with a glowing flame which, on disappearing, revealed also the disappearance of the Demon Priest.

Thus had Mainin sinned, perverting his noble wisdom to evil and to sowing the seeds of sin, on and in the hearts of unsuspecting weaklings of humanity. He had sown and Suern was to reap, and through Suern, the world. But for this sowing he himself was blasted from the Book of Life by a curse from the Son of Man.

Even those unfamiliar with any but the material aspect of nature, can find no difficulty in comprehending the destruction of the life of a man whose corporeal body was in far away Caiphul, when they consider that the earthly frame is no more an essential of the real man than the cocoon is a part of the butterfly, although in either case these things are essential to physical life.

Terrified by the awful sight of the blasting, I sank on my face on the floor. From this position I was bidden to arise by the Christ, who said:

"Such is the fate of the wholly selfish man. Fear not for thine own safety, for I blast not thee; neither worship me, but my Father who sendeth me. I am reached unto the perfection of the Seventh Principle and am Man, also the Son of Man, yet more than any man, for I am in the Father, and the Father is in me. But all men who will may follow me and be by me in the Kingdom, for are we not all children of One, our Father? I am He, **Christ**; that which I am, the Spirit of every man is. The penalty visited upon Mainin was not annihilation, which can not be; neither was it the death which is transition, but the death which liveth no more as human life, but is cast for a season into the outer darkness of devildom. Behold, I speak, yet having ears, thou hearest not, neither comprehend. But thy hearing shall come to thee, and thou shalt know, and shalt lead my people. And lo! thou shalt lead them in a day to thee yet afar off. But now thou shalt go no more to Atl to live there, neither be seen of Anzimee any more, until she hath gone from Earth twice and come again, and shall be called Phyris. Lo! I have said that these things should come to pass, and did prophesy unto thee in that city called Caiphul, and thou heardst me, yet heeded not. But now thou wilt heed me, for I speak great words of GOD,—and the world is His. Yet now no man knoweth me; but in a far day I will come again, yea! I will enter in and dwell as a perfect human soul, and make that Man first fruit of them that sleep the sleep which is change, so that by me he shall be exalted above Death. Then shall men get them up, and mock me, being unbelievers, and shall crucify me, yet shall I, that am become Jesus the Christ, not be harmed, but mine earthly house only. And they shall be forgiven, for they will not know what they do.* Peace I give unto thee. Sleep!"

————

CHAPTER XXIV.

DEVACHAN.

Obedient to this command I slept. When I awakened I was yet in the prison, but all the suffering, all the tortures of hunger and thirst that I had endured were gone. Nothing seemed strange to me, not even when I arose and found that behind me, as a shell, remained the poor clay casket which had suffered so keenly under the pangs of starvation. All was as natural in seeming as are things in vivid dreams. I thought of Anzimee, and wondered if she, too, felt as happy as I did at that moment. I prayed that she might. Then I thought of the words of Him who caled Himself the Son of Man, and

*St. Matthew xii, 23.

wondered what manner of being He was. His talk had, for the most part, been unmeaning to me; yet from it I understood that I was dead; that Anzimee would see me no more until after what dimly seemed an eternity, and not then as Anzimee, nor would I then be Zailm; yet I felt no regret over this long prospective separation. And in that time this Son of Man would have come again to the world, and left work for His brethren, the children of our FATHER, who in doing this work would be following after Him, and would become as Himself, in so far as to be disenthralled from time and from earth, and have all things, life and death. Yet, dimly understanding all this, I comprehended not its perfect fullness, for my natural mind was not able to grasp its spiritual meaning.

This, then, was Navazzamin, and I was what men call dead. It was much different from my concepts, as taught me by the priests of Incal—because it apparently differed not at all from earth-life, so far as I had as yet experienced. Perhaps it would if I were now to go and pass through the Maxin-Light. To do this would not be suicide, because I was already dead. No, it would purge away the earthiness which possibly prevented my finding the real Navazzamin which had been taught me. Would Anzimee and all others of my loved ones come hither some day, and should we meet and know each other here? Oh! it must be so, it must be so!

Filled with these reflections I stepped to the door, forgetting that its lock had previously prevented my exit. Only when it opened at my touch did I remember that it had defied every previous effort. Lightly I stepped away down the tunnel until I came to the daylight and to my saddle and tools, and yes, my horse, faithful animal! He was eating of the grasses, and evidently made the overflowing waters at the generator his headquarters. Leave him? Not if I could avoid it! I was free at last! I looked around at the dry washes lying under the open sky, with their eroded monuments of clay, capped with wild pampas plumes. How gracefully these nodded in the light breeze, seeming to say:—"Free now, free!"

Then I went to my horse, to take him, forgetful that being dead I could not need such transportation. But he seemed not to see me, or to know my presence. This was a difficulty. I was used to conquering difficulties, but this was one where I was at a loss what to do. I sat down and looked at the handsome animal. The longer I looked, the more perplexed I became. At last I got up in a sort of exasperation and talked very earnestly to the animal. No effect! Of course not! The more I talked, the more contented the horse became, as if he felt that I was near, and was satisfied. Finally I started away, intending to leave him, since I could in no way influence him. This had great effect! The farther I got the more uneasy he became, as I was able to see, until at last he lifted up his head and neighed loudly. Once, twice, thrice, and then he started after me in a wild gallop! When he reached me he grew easy, but as I went rapidly onwards he followed. He was awake to a sense of my presence, though he could not see, feel or hear me. My mind was wholly occupied in getting this faithful servant to the camp. So, feeling no fatigue, nor hunger, nor thirst, nor any sensation of the physical life, I walked clear into camp, all those miles, with that horse following contentedly after! When we reached the camp the vailx was there, but only two of the men, the others having gone in search of me, since I was now overdue in my arrival, thanks to Mainin. These men, like the horse, could not see me, but unlike him, neither could they sense my nearness. My utmost efforts were entirely unsuccessful, and although I stayed for two days—until the search was over and the men had returned to the vailx, to obtain further orders from Caiphul, I was unsuccessful still. One of the hunters was still out, and when he came back I spoke to him. He could not see me, but my presence affected him strangely. So I spoke again and again, till at last he sat down trembling by my desk in the salon of the vailx. A paper and a pen and ink were on this, and I said to the man:—"Use that pen." To my partial surprise, he used it, but seemed in a deep sleep the while and mechanically wrote:—"Use that pen." An idea occurred to me, and I uttered words which had no conection of meaning, every one of which he wrote just as I spoke it. This was encouraging, so I next said:—"It is I, even Zailm, who say these things; I am dead. Go home to Caiphul." Of my body and its whereabouts I said nothing, feeling that it was properly entombed. But what I spoke in dictation was all written, not that the medium heard, but for the time I was the controlling intelligence of his body. The others took the message and hid it, and when the writer had come out of trance, they asked him what he had written. But he denied having written anything. This seemed to satisfy them, the man was so obviously honest in his denial. So they went and gathered the equipage and animals into the vailx, and prepared to leave for Caiphul. Their action satisfied me, so that I thought no more of them, but began to wish I was at home. I reflected that I had left the disability of the flesh in the cave-house, hence I ought to be able to go here or there, as had Mainin. I would try it. So I said to myself:—"I would be at home, at Agacoe, where is the Rai, and he will be able to see me, and know all things of this matter."

With this utterance all things changed, and I found myself in the palace of Agacoe. But neither Gwauxln nor Anzimee— who was there also—were seemingly able to see me, more than the man in the vailx had been. What was this thing called death? this barrier? Was death indeed the threshold between two conditions, communication to and fro being impossible? as futile to attempt from my side as from the other? I had thought Gwauxln able to penetrate this barrier. But alas! I found myself not more able to obtain his recognition than that of the others. I knew he could see those who put off their fleshy shells in order to travel as Mainin had done, and resume them at will; why then not see me? Death perhaps meant more even than putting aside the body. Long I stood there, wondering at this thing called death. As I stood by Gwauxln's side, having abandoned the attempt to impress him with a knowledge of my presence, a human shape came into the apartment. Shape? It seemed as real as any of the cour-

tiers sitting by the arch of the doorway. None of these latter
appeared aware of the new arrival; except the Rai, no one
beside myself saw him, but continued their talk regarding the
sudden death of the Incaliz Mainin, and disposal of his body
in the Maxin Light on the previous afternoon. I had been
dumfounded at the strange resemblance of the new arrival
to myself, but I was immeasurably amazed to hear the Rai
exclaim:

"What! Zailm dead! Dead!"

An attendant, hearing this exclamation, but seeing only the
sovereign, hastily went to him enquiring his pleasure. As he
approached he passed directly through the form which Gwauxln
had addressed by my name! Neither the human shape nor the
attendant seemed aware of the remarkable occurrence, but
the Form, smiling, in reply said:

"Aye, Zo Rai; I am Zailm, but not dead, except in that I
am free of earthly restraint."

Confused, almost stupefied by these happenings, I sank on a
divan near me. Gwauxln could see what purported to be me
—was indeed a very image of me in looks, speech, memory of
events, in fact really was the psychic counterpart of my life
and self—but he could not see me. Mystery, aye, mystery!
How many had death to reveal to me? I had left in the Umaur
prison a material image of myself—was it possible that there
also existed an intermediate counterpart of both my material
body and myself, which yet retained certain gross forms of
life lost by me, making it visible while I was invisible? But
as Gwauxln was a Son of the Solitude, why was he unable to
perceive both my astral and myself? He was not unable, but
would not allow me to know his ability. The reason—plain to
me now, but not then,—briefly is:—That a person in dying is
separated into psychic elements which, not to be too detailed
in the statement, are three-fold—earthly, psychic and spiritual.
Of these the highest is the I Am—the ego. The others are those
above mentioned as spoken to by Gwauxln, and as left in the
prison. Now, the ego seeks an exalted level—the "shell"
stays in the earthly conditions until the body, finally dissolved,

is "dust to dust." The exalted or egoic state is one of isolation. As spoken in Biblical records,* a medium can go to it,
but the ego, after a little while, cannot return to earth, nor
know anything earthly save those extremely tense mental-
spiritual states of one or many individuals who reach out for
the things of God. And these things are not earthly. This is
real mediumship. The genuine medium rises to the necessary
height, but the ego can not descend to earth; can not deny
the law of progress, except during a limited period after the
transition called death, and then it is not retrogression. A
medium is like an aneroid barometer—able to indicate the
degree of ascension above the ocean of water, or of spirit.
But he must be present on the level—the level cannot descend
to him. Hence it is that one in dying is a traveller to that
bourne whence none return. There is no return of the departed, except through physical rebirth and reincarnation. I
leave thee to find out that this is not transmigration of souls—
for the latter postulates rebirth in lower animal form as a
punishment for sin; such a thing can not be. Retrogression is
impossible, and the whole notion is but a corrupt falsity of
conception, founded upon the misunderstood truth of reincarnation, whose successive rebirths are invariably progressive.

To return to the Rai, and his determination not to see me.
Gwauxln knew that I was not yet come into the proper state,
and feared to interrupt my progress. Hence he would not
allow my "shell" to influence him, so far as I could determine.
Having, however, by the contact of his supersensitive nature
perceived the fact of my demise, he sought further, and though
his actions denied to me that he saw me, yet he put into operation forces to the end that I should presently be ready for
him to come to me. But not until my mundane life was faded
would he do so; not until I was gone forth into the "undiscovered country" of Navazzamin. Then he came, and the
meeting was one of simple joy, of unaffected grace, between
two souls equal before God—not in status of acquired wisdom—
for in that Gwauxln was vastly above me—but in that equal

---

*II Samuel, xii, 23.

brotherhood of the Spirit which I wish now reigned on earth. It shall yet do so, for the Cross Bearer said, "Ye are all Children of one Father!" Behold, it is so!

When Gwauxln was come unto me, the sphere of earth was in nowise brought with him. To have carried earthly conditions with him would have been to remand me to earth, and have rendered me palpable injustice. No ego ever permitted, by the very laws of its being, to go back to earth except a wrong thing is thereby suffered. The self-hood of an initiate may project itself into devachan, but the dweller in devachan (heaven) can not go again to earth till it be born again therein. Indeed! why does the soul leave earth after the grave? It is because in devachan it assimilates the fruits of active earth-life. Right here is the explanation of the written Word of God: "Whatsoever thy hand findeth to do, do it with thy might; for there is no work, no device, nor knowledge, nor wisdom, in the grave, whither thou goest."* True it is that in the grave is nothing done. In the following pages much will seem to indicate my "doings" between the grave and the cradle. But observe that the whole of earth was become a perfect blank to me. The soul can not return save it re-embody in rebirth. To call it back is to cause revulsion of this process, and reassociation with the astral-shell which the ego left behind at the decease of the body. Such reassociation revives the astral, whereupon action and reaction take place between it and the ego, much to the detriment of the latter. All I "experienced" was only the fruits of what I had done; I could do no new thing; think no new thought, experience nothing not in itself the expression of something done ere-I came through the grave. And in this rearrangement and crystallizing of my past earthlife time cut no figure. The realness of it was but the reality of vivid dreaming; time had no part in that which was already done.

It lay in the power of the Rai to recognize me, but he would not, that I might not suffer harm. It similarly lies in the power of all forceful mediumistic natures (generally) belong-

*Eccl. ix, 10.

ing to the sect called "Spiritualists" to do likewise. These media can recall the departed, but at what dread cost to the departed ego, and reacting upon the medium to the latter! I say no process of Nature as ordered by our Heavenly Father may be lightly interrupted; every such act carries penalty proportionate to the understanding of the culprit; never light, and often of fearful weight. Had I remained to see, I would have seen Gwauxln—Son of the Solitude—go forth in his own astral shape, after retiring his corporeal to his secret chamber, that no harm might come to the body while he was away. And the shell-Zailm would I have seen go with him to the Incalithlon, and there should I have seen the Rai cause it to pass into the Unfed Light. But of all men on earth only the trained eyes of a Son could have seen what then happened. The "shell" would not have emerged from the Maxi nevermore. What was this? Why destroy it? So that it might not go forth in the earth and impress sensitives such as the vailx-man whom I had impressed in Umaur, and whom my "shell" might otherwise continue to impress. Thus might have resulted much trouble, for this astral of mine was but faithfully repeating my final words ere I parted company with it, when it said to Gwauxln, there in Agacoe, "I am not dead." It was even then like all other shells, its double composite nature only holding together during the limited period it could draw sustaining magnetism from my recently closed earthly correspondence.

In some cases such sustenance is sufficient for ages, in others, centuries, years, days, or even minutes—according to the earthward-turning, or the spirit-turning sympathies of the decedent. The astral is only vivified force, bearing the image in all respects of its ego, the I AM. Even prophecies made by "returned spirits," prophecies which come true after years, perhaps are but the impressed foresight of the ego at the moment of departure. It for an instant sees into vast future depths of time. And this glimpse is imprinted on its astral-shell. It is psychic force. If the phenomena set in motion by man are of that intensely vital sort created by Moses, Buddha, Zoroaster—then just so long as a believer of any one of these religious systems adheres, that long, but no longer, the "shells" of these prophets will continue their derived existence. It is psychic force which is their controlling lever—formed force. It is this same force which holds the stars to their orbits, and the atoms to theirs. It is vital, and dual, being positive and negative. To separate the force or "fire element" of the ancients (ancients to thee, not to me) was to cause the focus for such an Unfed Fire as the Maxin, and in later ages—in Israel—the power in the Ark of the Covenant—alike with the Maxin, fatal to life. These focus points are portals whereinto the entire concourse of lesser forces of nature are absorbed upon contact. These foci are also the sole residence of the much sought "universal solvent" of the alchemists; needless to say that as some of these alchemists have been Sons of the Solitude, that therefore they have had the wonderful "solvent" to serve them.

Equally apparent must it be why the secret has remained carefully concealed. These foci are very auricles of the heart of the Universe, hence any sort of formed force meets here its Omega. Consequently when Gwauxln caused my astral to pass into the Maxin, he returned to the sum-undivided of cosmic force a quantity no longer of use to the formed world. On a very small scale indeed the medulla oblongata of the brain is such a focus—a maxin-point—where positive and negative meet. Were it not so, life would be impossible; destroy this maxin of the body, even by a needle thrust, and vitality instantly ceases. But enough. Gwauxln came to me, who could not go to him. Those not initiates do often thus rise in their sleep to their friends, but they fail at the point of not knowing how to do so voluntarily.

As one great point of my work is to explain these mysteries, I may spare yet a little space in rendering clear, past all mistake, how it is that those on earth can acquire the power of going to their friends beyond the Divide, but never these last come back to earth.

The barometer on a calm day registers at sea level a definite degree of air pressure, and at one mile above the sea, on the

side of a mountain, let us say, the mercury in the tube has
"fallen" to another definite, but less degree. This is in both
cases due to air pressure. If now, one desire to have the pressure existing at a mile's height, will he go up to it, or will he
bring that altitude down to himself? In storm weather the
barometer "falls" also, the air is less dense, meteorological
changes have taken place which in effect have brought the high
aerial altitudes—i. e.—the conditions prevailing in high altitudes—down to the lower level. But thus has a storm been
created; superior conditions have forced one. So it is that by
the exercise of superior force a medium at a "spiritualistic
seance" can bring back or down a soul which had gone on
through the grave; but it will give rise to a psychic storm,
and these are exceedingly costly occurrences. The Witch of
Endor created such a storm when she forced Samuel down
to earth again. Beware, O ye mediums! If thou art, friend,
a human "spirit barometer," thou mayest rise to thy friends,
but never, as thou valuest soul's peace for thee, or for them,
seek to bring them down to thy "circles."

Those who seek only the exciting part of this history will
do well to omit perusal of the greater part of Book I, and
leave it to the reader who seeks the reason and lesson of my
life record, and how I am able to depict scenes past by more
than twelve thousand years ago.

Through the crime of Mainin the Incaliz, I had been forced
to seek my psychic plane, and because I was I, and am I, that
plane is more or less one of isolation. That is to say, it was
peopled with the children of my fancy, my experiences, my
hopes, longings, aspirations, and my conceptions of persons,
places and things. No two people see in the same way the
same world. To Anzimee, with her knowledge, the world could
not have seemed the same as to Lolix, who saw from another,
and in some ways lower standpoint, while to neither was it
the same as to the wise minister, Menax; and with all three
the view of life was different from that held by Gwauxln.

So also the heaven, the devachan, of one person is filled with his concepts of life, while that of his neighbor on either side—so to speak—is peopled with other peculiar mental properties. Now the state after the grave, and his or her knowledge, aspirations and trusts of life is the condition of harvest, where no one acts, but where the rewards of action in the preceding life are paid; it is the land of Lethe, where is no pain, sorrow sickness or agony—for these earthly conditions begun on earth, and they perforce must be finished on earth. So karma decrees. Heaven is passive, not active, and results of knowledge are there assimilated by the soul; that is, made so that the new birth is like the succeeding page of a business ledger—all of the old lives, with the last added in. I hope I have not been prolix. I have not, if I have given a clear comprehension of what the relation really is between earth and heaven, and that the latter is to the former as the resting time of night is to the activity of the day. Let none suppose that the devachan of one that hath committed earth-binding errors, and must by these bonds again reincarnate, is anything like the great Life wherewith are crowned those who are faithful unto the death of that serpent in the heart, animal lusts. The words can well portray mere devachan, they are powerless to depict that Life. Finite can never compass Infinite. Then let the Infinite into thy hearts.

———————

　　Even as I pondered, in the presence of Gwauxln, Anzimee and the others, who either would not or could not see me, my earthly powers were departing. The power which I had a moment before possessed of seeing persons, places and things of the world seemed fast escaping me, while glorious sights and sounds replaced them—sights and sounds akin to the day dreams of the life just left, except that these were real to my senses, tangible and mutually reactive. Ah, well! if those left on Death's first shore could not see me nor know my presence,

nor I see them nor their presence, why not unresistingly glide
into enjoyment of the peace and the new sights and things
which were come in place of the old? Yea! I would—goodbye,
old life; hail to the new.

———————

As peacefully as a dream the sight of the palace and of
familiar things faded from view, and I seemed to have come
into a beautiful valley, hemmed in by azure hued mountains.
Before me stood a building of unpretentious exterior. Irregular in its outlines, it seemed to have been built in sections,
added as more rooms became necessary. What an altogether
excellent idea that was, I thought. It was formed of slabs of
rock, not quarried, but naturally scaled from the ledge. In
places it was three stories high, in others only two, but mainly
all the rooms were on the ground floor. What sort of people
lived here? Certainly people whose architectural abandon was
after my own heart. I felt, ere seeing them, already friendly.
Assuredly they lacked not the love of beauty, for covering the
quaintly picturesque dwelling ran perennial vines, while all
about lay tasteful gardens. Should I venture to intrude my
presence? As I considered, a man opened a door near me and
came forward. He had a very familiar appearance; where had
I seen him? I had forgotten as completely as if I had never
known the life which I had experienced as Zailm, the son of
Menax. My senses were dominated by the feelings of boyhood, and the thoughts and ideas and simple knowledge of
boyhood in the mountain home by Pitach Rhok. As the familiar looking stranger drew close he said:
"Knowest thou me, thy father—Merin Wuminus?"
While this settled the apprehension that dimly arose in my
consciousness that I was alone, and therefore invisible to people, it only quenched the idea that had rapidly faded as I looked
on the house of slab-rock—the idea that I was dead. I no
longer knew any such experience, and the knowledge of death
had passed away so far as it applied to my own decease. I was

filled with pleasure at the question of the man before me, and I now perceived that he was the father of my childhood's ideal, but not him whom my mother had always presented in disparaging light—she, thou knowest, did not like him. But this thought did not present itself then; I only knew that I looked on him whom I recognized as my father. I was overjoyed, at finding him, and I replied: "Verily, I know thee well!" Then he asked: "Wilt thou rest?"

"Being fatigued, I will do so, and no doubt be much benefited."

Thereupon Merin Numinos led me within the great rambling house to what I must call a den, even though the name may seem inelegant. Den it was, cleanly, but so charmingly, delightfully confused and disorderly; books and specimens of rocks, and all things which a boy loves were scattered about in that inextricable litter which fills the trim housekeeper with despair. My pleasure was unbounded, for I felt that I was a boy, only a boy, and had yet to reach maturity, the unknown possibilities of which seemed to fill my whole being with pleasant anticipation of the future; I was a lad of exuberant spirits let loose in his own realm, and in this room free from fear of the orderly mother who had elsewhere always restrained me. On a bed, roughly smoothed up in one corner of the shaded room, lay a pack of books from the district library, each marked, "Pitach Rhok District 5," in Poseid characters. These were in my way, and I laid them carefully—for books were ever almost sacred objects in my eyes—on the floor, in order that I might rest on the bed. Then I laid me down to sleep upon the rude couch which had always seemed softer and easier to fond memory than any downy cushion in the Caiphalian life. Not that I knew this as I lay down—I only knew that I experienced a state of things just suited to my desires. I had no clear idea of any event of the old life in Poseid—no memory of death, nothing. All had gone like the events of some dream which we strive in vain to recall at breakfast next morning. And yet, when I came across things in the new state similar to those known and loved in the old; when I found things here such as I had been wont to dream of some day carrying to realization, then the new realities, which, after all were not new, seemed wholly satisfactory, with the added charm of achievement, though I could not recall the old.

> "The whole scene which greets mine eyes,
> In some strange mode I recognize
> As one whose ev'ry mystic part
> I feel prefigured in my heart."

Nature here, though presenting some novelties, was different enough to excite special attention.

One day I arose and departed from the scenes of this reproduced boyhood's life. The curtain rose on things derived from the later life after leaving Pitach Rhok for Caiphul, and I found myself now in the midst of acquiring knowledge even to the great degree of a Xio-Incala—a degree greater than even any scientist of the modern world has achieved. But this phase of devachan soon passed, because, not having reached such a degree on earth, nor having even tried to do so, I had no real basis from which to draw devachanic scenes. Thus passed the time around me, sometimes with real egoii of deceased earthly persons who had worked with me intimately on earth, and so had with me to reap the results of the collaboration. At other times I was alone with my concepts, which, however, seemed as real as actual persons—for all seemed absolutely real. Lolix was here in her better aspects; but the sin of our day was held against our return to earth.

It seemed perfectly natural to meet Anzimee one night as I wandered by the shore of a sea adjacent to an artificial wilderness, where all things were arranged in harmony with my ideal solitude to which, in Caiphul's busy whirl, I had one day dreamed of taking her when we should be wed. It was sweet when we met to hear her call me "husband," and the peace after action was all delightful as I had imagined it would be.

But my pen is in advance of its proper place. To return to the den:

Without disrobing, for the air was warm, I lay down and slept. When I awoke I passed down the hallway into the garden. A change had come over. I was older; the landscape was different, and the houses were more like that which my maturer needs had painted as a necessity while I still lived near Pitach Rhok. No longer was a river in the foreground, but a broad sea with only the near shore visible. The change was correspondent with the later desires of my youth. These alterations, though startling, as considered from an earthly, physical standpoint, were not startling, nor even remarkable to me. What sort of life or condition was this which permitted such changes, yet did not present itself as anything extraordinary to me—the beholder? Even truth should not be told in prolix phrase, and all that can be replied now is that it was the life after death, to be slightly paradoxical. But this is not the Great Life with God.

Was time consumed in effecting these changes—or was this an Aladdin's lamp sort of land where a rubbing out of one and an installation of another set of appearances took place instantaneously? I did not even pause to consider, for no such conjecture occurred to me. To me things were real. Is earth real? Spirit, God, is real, and the earth and universe are the fiat, or externalized ideas of God. The things of earth are words of God's great Word, speaking to us. So, too, are the things of devachan or heaven. Both are real, oppositely so, but only real within us, not without us. I sought my father, Merin Numinos, and asked: "How long have I slept?" It was no more anything but a habit of thought to ask this, for I had no other motive. That, in the process of death, habits of mind do not suffer extinction together with life's memories of events, was proven by my action on hearing my father's reply:

"Even several years hast thou slept."

"Years!"—dost thou exclaim? It was no remarkable thing to me to hear this account of a Rip Van Winklian nap. No, but my habit of mind which took pride in neatness of personal attire caused me unwittingly to glance at my raiment to see if it were not the worse for such long wear. The allusion to several years attracted my attention, so that having found my attire presentable, though I still gazed at my clothes, it was in an absent minded way. I said:—

"Thou sayest years; also another thing—'thou has slept ever since thou camest into this country.' Now, I pray thee, have I ever been elsewhere?"

Receiving no reply, I looked up, only to meet a stare like that of a statue from my father. He evidently knew nothing of any previous state, nor, by the very form of my question, did I know more than he.

Death was another thing, never referred to, because in the instant when promoted souls find it no more possible to impress their existence upon those left behind on earth, they recognize that they are in the midst of the change called death, of which they were perhaps apprehensive all their earthly days. As the exoteric religion then—aye, and now, also—taught but one death, the devachanee knew or conjectured no other. Hence, death to the disembodied soul was and is an unknown conception. Well, there is no such thing as death for a fact. Likewise pain and sorrow. Devachan the minor is like devachan the major (Nirvana), a state particularly referred to in Revelation XXI.—4. Now, my friend, I am not postulating an argument; I must refuse to argue, and though it savor of mediaeval methods, yet must I also refuse to reason with thee. It is the purpose of this history to state what I know by experience; I state no theoretical ideas. If thou wilt take any small matters left unexplained into the inner sanctuary of thy soul and there meditate over them, then will they become clear to thee, and be as the water which quencheth all thirst, if so gained. Hast thou ears to hear- Then heed that counsel. I address only those who follow these pages for profit.

As the devanchanee knows of but one change, and as that is so different from what he was religiously taught to fear, therefore many souls entering heaven conceive at the moment of death that no death exists—and that the teachings received on earth from priests were but ecclesiastical fictions. Nor are they so far wrong, for there is no other death than the mere change from objective to subjective states of being, save the second death, spoken of in my final page. To be paradoxical, death is different because not different, so far as they can perceive, from the swift view of the life just closed, a view all souls have, however brief it be. Hence it was that I was unaware of the fiction called death when I asked the father I found there if I had not always been there.

Religion taught in that old age as it now teaches, that with death came the cessation of all earthly sorrow. This is true for a time limited by the length of the soul's sojourn in devachan. These earth born mists do not intrude there for the reason that being earth born they must of necessity have abiding places on earth and influence only those on earth.

"The evil that men do lives after them."

Verily; and in the form of crystallized disposition to do wrong, lies in wait for their return to earth life; it is the wrongly so-called "Adamic" tendency to sin, and while the sinner is free of its power in devachan, the seed, like tares with the wheat, is ready to grow a harvest of sorrow along with the growing life of the new incarnated one; and until some good action shall atone for evil done, this evil will continue to grow. Fortunately, man hath an eternity in which to make repayment,* and though following God's laws and being true to right, what ever its source, the tares are little by little uprooted. A good act is the erasure of a bad, and once performed

---

*Do not confuse "repayment" with "atonement." Jews makes atonement for us with God. We can only begin to repay, when,—having obtained forgiveness through Jesus, we try to Live Him. Until we consecrate ourselves to Christ, we can not have recognized that we are HIS because HE owns us. When we recognize this, then we recognize that HE owns us, and we own HIM. Then, but not until then, can we even begin to repay our karma. And if we "Go and sin no more," then HE will equalize our debt to karma, and we be released unto HIM—released or leased again! Karma closes for one who thus is atoned for, and his opportunity for reparation begins. For such an one no more incarnation is necessary, for hath he not the SON? And that is Eternal life. What mean I by having the Son? And by being consecrated to Christ? Is this, then, only the church postulate? Nay, more, friends. The Divine is eternal, infinite. The Human is finite. When the awakened man comes to know himself, he chooses which way he shall go. This choice is the crossing of the Divine by the Human; it is ownership by the Son, which is within.

is "oft-interred with the bones"—thus completing the philosophy of Hamlet.

All about me were those I loved. As time seemed to lapse, I became conscious of the presence of one and another of my friends. Anzimee, Menax, Gwauxln, Ernon, Lolix without the shadow,—all those and thousands more who have no name to the reader were there. They did not come; no, they were with me, each as I had conceived. These were my concepts, for they were subjective, not objective; they were my ideals, not real people; and they formed my world. It occurred not to me that they were not real. Did it ever occur to thee, reader, that the world of thy senses is the only world thou hast? That if thou hadst no sight, smell, hearing, taste or touch, that thou wouldst have no world even though thy soul were imprisoned in a body thus dead, yet alive in a vegetative way? As the soul of each living man, woman or child, is different from every other soul, so also the world is different to every person—not the same precisely in any two cases. Now it is the record of the soul, made on imperishable mental substance, which constitutes much of the life after the grave—the record merges into a reality, and all seems equally real, just as real as when the combined senses first perceived it; in verity this after life is a reconstituted and inverted earth life—subjective now, instead of objective. My supposed friend may be a real enemy, yet if I die thinking him or her my friend, that concept is the one carried into the afterlife; and vice versa.

Thus, all about me were my friends. The things of my sense record, and the places, were the scenes where all these friends moved. But while I had thus my world about me, a concept of me existed in the imaged world of every friend I had. Not that I was with them, but their concept of me was with them. Thus regarding the reality of all those concepts that were non-involute, simple and easily assimilable upon being remembered from the astral record, or, so to say, memory plates of the soul, of every incident small or great, simple or complex, impulse or even unconscious celebrations. But now mark a feature of vast interest, inasmuch as it affirms what I have seemed to deny—any real asociation of the soul in devachan with other individual souls. Devachan would indeed be a drear heaven if the friends of mundane life were never aught but "dream faces." Dreams they are, if the incidents created in our hopes on earth, and in devachan set forth as real to all seeming, were a simple fact. But if, per contra, it were so complex that to solve its equation required the joint efforts of two souls working in harmony, then also in devachan the results of this complex act affected both these souls, and during the assimilation of its results—that is, during the crystallization of such results into traits of character—both these souls would as actually be together as ever they were on earth. If more than two people were involved on earth, so all these souls would congregate in devachan. When the process was complete, the separation came. So it happened that in one moment of assimilative experience that all my concepts were only phantasms, as the persons of one's nightly dreams; the next moment more complex, as my associates were real egoii like myself. To me all this was unknown—all seemed real, and so, perhaps, was so. But it is pleasant to feel that one works with a loved son, father, daughter, mother, wife or other friend; that the consequences of the more serious events of our daily lives here will bring us again together in the heaven of our hopes; that the wife thou takest to thy heart, and to whom thy confidest loving plans for the weal of thy loved ones, to realize which both thou and she must work nobly, earnestly, will come across the chasm which death spreads for thy bodies, and be with thee or thou with her, there in Navazzamin. Pleasant that thy mother, father or other dear friend shall sometimes really be with thee there; and that together thou shalt garner thy various records, and enjoy in a seeming real that which was not on earth aught but a hope never materialized.

In meeting Anzimee, who yet lived on earth, I met sometimes my conception of her, sometimes her own higher self. How was the latter possible? Because she so longed for me that it developed and enabled her to project her pure soul into my plane. This was not only pleasant and beneficial to her, giving her a hold upon things unseen, of which the apostle Paul speaks, but it was a holy joy to me to meet her thus; she could come to me, but I could not go back to her. There is no retrogression.

In communion with these ideals I had my reward, for nothing occurred contrary to my wish. But in experiencing this reward, I also unconsciously assimilated the value of the previous life on earth. Thus my connection with politics in Poseid had brought me in contact with men and manners, and from this contact were born schemes in which I was to have had a leading part. These schemes were now brought into the subjective state, and as such appeared to me to be in process. From these apparent actions my capacities were developed, and tests of the worth of my conceptions made. All of this resulted in making a concrete deduction which became a part of my mental being; hence in a new incarnation I would come forth to mankind possessed of phrenological organs of increased power in the handling of political and social questions. Perhaps this power would not be actively employed, owing to other tendencies being stronger; none the less the power would be augmented, and ready for use upon demand. The same thing would prove true of all these souls really associated with me, both in previous-earth and after-heaven—the results, values and summings-up of our contemporary devachan would give them new mental traits, or increase the force of their old ones—and reincarnation would re-associate us again on earth. And it has done so, else would I never have written this history for thy profit, dear reader. My education as a geologist at Xioquithlon was tested in this same subjective heaven, and from this came added ability as a geologist; in short, an intuitive knowledge of geology and desire for that study after reincarnation. Books would then serve to educe the geological bent I might manifest. I might go on with other instances of the summing-up and arranging process experienced by those who have both the grave and the cradle between them and earth. But this will suffice to hint to the reader that truths lie here and sweeten the

> "Thoughts of the last bitter hour * * *
> Of stern agony, and shroud and pall."

I hope, my friend, that this effort to render death less terrifying, by relating my own experiences of it, will be fraught with success, and that these words may so sustain thee that thou shalt

> "Approach thy grave
> Like one who wraps the drapery of his couch
> About him, and lies down to pleasant dreams."

Zerah Colburn, the marvelous boy mathematician, did not acquire his knowledge in the schools of this modern age, but brought it, a legacy from the dead centuries, his past lives; his latent power was educed. I will not argue with thee, friend, that if thou hadst had a past life on earth, thou couldst "not have forgotten it, but would have brought memory of it with thee." No, I argue not. I only leave it with thine own intelligence to decide if I be not right, when thou rememberest that habits of life grow from repeated actions of boyhood, the details and every recollection of which are gone. And knowing that this is so, decide, if thou thinkest it not absurd, that actions of a life experienced century times centuries agone would be possibly recollected, more especially when all the interval was spent on a different plane of life, whereon no single memory ever intruded—could not by the laws of God. I know whereof I speak.

———————

At length there came a time when I cared no more for the appearance of action, nor for those concepts of persons, places, or things connected with seeming activity. Chiefly now I cared to remain in some quiet spot and listen to Anzimee— the real, not the concept—as she read to or talked with me. I slept much also. One morning I did not arise; I did not care to. I was not ill—no one ever knew illness in devachan. But

I had lost all desire to see or hear more of anything. I did indeed feel languor, but not weariness. So I turned over again, facing the wall, and slept. It was the last occurrence in the last chapter of a life's long rest, which, though I knew it not, had covered twelve thousand years of the actions of men on earth. Death had never appeared in that home of the soul, for my concepts did not die—they only disappeared from the view of their creator. Even the real souls of men or women did not die. No. But when they came, one after another, to the retributive awakening at the cradle, if their lives in heaven were still associated with mine; if they had not gone elsewhere in devachan, as neighbors on earth separate and put the world between them—then they disappeared, just as my concepts disappeared when I had assimilated their value. They disappeared, because all the deeds of previous earth life had crystalized as traits of character, and they were ready for earth life again. Only myself could be conscious of my own change; I could not be conscious of theirs. I was ready for activity once more. I slept, and in this sleeping, died out of that life of passivity into the waking of earth, a babe in a cradle. Born to see my Master in this life, and enter the Great Rest with him!

NOTE.—But one will come after me who shall tell thee more of the Great Deep of Life than I. Await her words.—Author.

End of Book First.

BOOK SECOND.

APPENDIX.

SEVEN SHASTA SCENES.

By Frederick S. Oliver, Amanuensis.

I.

If there are "sermons in stones and books in the running brooks, then is "Tchastel's" craggy pile a noble library, in veritas. In it the vastness, the grandeur and the solemnity of nature are expressed in mystic numbers carved in the eternal granite. On those stony, stratified pages Nature's students may read the doings of the gnomes, mother earth's treasurers. Here, too, in characters of lava, is writ Pluto's kingly record. Aye! 'tis indeed Nature's own volume, bound between covers of snow and ice; and marking the treasures thereof is a silvery ribbon whose ends hang out of the vast tome—at the north one end, at the south the other—the name of the one "McCloud" river, and of the other the "Sacramento." Again, two lesser markers are in this sublime epic, viz.: "Pitt" and "Shasta" rivers. A volume of poems should bear poetic title; so shall this. Can we bestow one more appropriate than the aboriginal appellation—"Ieka"—a name retained and used by the earliest white men whose eyes gazed on that land, far northern California—land of romance, of gold and of adventure; retained through that intuitive recognition of eternal fitness, which pioneer and trapper have ever, in all lands, exhibited toward existent nomenclature. For years the noble mountain bore, for white as for aborigine, the name it had fetched from out the night of time, as its sister peak far to the north—Mt. Rainier retained its primal christening of "Tacoma." But, alas, for human conceit! Alas, for man's vain discontent, unable to let well enough alone! To the one snowy mount came a Russian trapper, and thereafter "Ieka" was no more on the tongues of men, unless, indeed, it was still lovingly murmured by the dusky Modoc and his savage bride. To the other glittering peak went an egotistic Englishman. His lordship found "Tacoma" "so beastly savage, doncher know," and so over its Indian appellate he tacked his own patronymic. Time evens all things, and "ever is justice done." The patriotic Americanism of the Northern Pacific Railroad topographers reinstated on the company maps musical "Tacoma," tossed to rubbish the imported name, and rebuked one egotist's vanity. That "Shasta Buttes" will ever know a parellel experience is problematical; if not, 'tis perhaps as well, for American gratitude willingly concedes the privilege of nomination of this proud peak to its friend, and, in the '60s, champion of our national autonomy — — — — Russia. So much for a kind of mental view, past and present, of this pride of the crags and peaks.

II.

On the old wagon road which existed ere ever iron rails linked Oregon's greatest city to the metropolis of the Golden West, there still stands, as for thirty years, not many miles from the State line, a station established for stage line uses, and "run" by "Daddy Dollarhyde." A lonely place, hidden amongst towering pines, which make regal raiment for the great "Siskiyou Ridge" of the Coast Range extending in gloomy grandeur not miles, but hundreds of miles—Dollarhyde's appeals to the heart of the traveller as Saharan oasis to the weary caravan. " 'Tis a lodge in some vast wilderness," and in the days of this second "Shasta Scene" (A. D. 1884) was the only footprint of civilization for many a long mile.

Leaving Dollarhyde's the road wound as directly as possible up a two-mile stretch of exceedingly steep mountain. Up this steep, long before aught but painted dawn lit those grand ridges, a youth, on foot and alone, was climbing. A tramp?

Temporarily; down below, at Dollarhyde's, the rest of his party
yet slept. Up, up he toiled, stopping when the love of nature
prompted him to "hold communion with her visible forms,"
and listen to her "various language"; pausing, the better to
enjoy the exhilarating freedom, the beauty of the piney slopes,
the whirr of the early grouse, and the chattering of squirrel
and chipmunk. Once, enchanted by the exquisite charm of a
crystal spring that leapt into and across the road, he staid his
steps; and again, he stood, gazing afar down into the gloom of
a great canyon, which became lost to view "in the dawn's
early light." The summit at last! But still no sun in the sky.
All beneath was yet quietly resting 'neath the sway of Morpheus. Ah! what is that? Away in the south is a huge, dim
mass, dull grey below, but, where its peak holds aloft the sky,
'tis a rosy, glowing pink. As the youth gazes, spellbound, Old
Sol dispels the valley glooms, thrusts aside the night, and the
new day is born. The rose tints are gone, but also the grey,
and in their place appears a giant, pointed cone of purest
white, albeit streaked at its base with black lines—each some
awful gorge. It rises not like other mountain piles—from
ranges rivalling its own height—no, all alone it stands forth
from its high plateau, piercing heaven's blue, from base to
summit, eleven thousand feet, from ocean's plane to apical
peak thirty-five hundred more—Shasta, O, Mt. Shasta.

III.

Of the youth, what? A year later we find him suffering a
violent fever—the "gold-fever," which yet lingers in that
region of once famed mines, lingers, though it be now A. D.
1890. Away up on a mountain's side with pick, pan and
shovel he has camped where a little gold may always be found;
where hope whispers he may find a "pile" some time and—
fortune.

All through that region forest fires have raged many weeks;
all the valleys lie hidden under a pile of smoke. But the miner
on the mountain is above it all, and as he labors looks out over

the undulating surface of the silvery, smoky ocean, down below. He sees a strange sight. No waves disturb this sea, which, nearly a mile deep, extends away beyond scope of vision. Two or three islands dot its expanse; these are all that is left to see of lofty mountain peaks whose bases are hidden. Perchance the words "smoke-ocean" seem figurative. Look heavenward from its bottom down in the valleys; the sun, appearing like a globe of blood, needs no colored glass to shield too sensitive eyes. Now go aloft to the miner on the mountain, looking down on, but seeing not, Yreka (town). With him again gaze at the "islands"; one only of them is not black in hue. It is the largest; sharp-summitted, white—shrouded in eternal snows, Mt. Shasta rises, a noble island in the murky ocean about it—nine thousand feet.

IV.

Night. Otherwise the same scene. Our miner sits in his tent door, meditating on the novel beauty of the scene before, below him. A north breeze has rolled the smoky sea silently away, and left no sign. Beneath the tent outspreads a vast abyss, dark, silent, "the night's Plutonian shore." Our miner's fancy fills it with golden phantoms. Only the stars—"night's tall tapers"—lighten the gloom. But far away east, over ranges of lesser mountains—dim shapes couched in the darkness—far away, miles real as well as seeming, familiar shadowy shape of vast, uncertain size appears to shut from sight vision of some awful conflagration. Look! It grows, it brightens, till on the charmed eyes bursts a sudden, intense spark, then a full flame in Ieka's side—'tis the moon at its roundest! And now Ieka's snows glow in its ray like molten silver, the dark abys before, beneath the tent lightens, the phantoms flee, while over all, sublime, glorious, supreme rises Shasta's argent image.

V.

Traveling, southward, miner no more, the youth bends his course. A year agone the golden phantoms died, the mine

caved in ,and "no man knows that sepulchre" in the wilds of
Siskiyou. Winter wet had extinguished the flames, and laid
the smoky sea. But the succeeding summer saw all aglow
again, matched by the lightnings of heaven. Our traveler is
at the very base of Icka Butte, and he and his steed crawl
along the slopes and vales in the bed of the fireborn ocean
of smoke as do crustacea on the bottoms of aqueous seas. A
flaw of wind decreases the denseness of the clouds, and above
his head he sees an indistinct shape, lit feebly by the smoke-
smothered moon, at its full now, as on that other night, a year
ago. Beautiful through the murky air it is not; but when told
that the point dimly seen overhead is the smoke-free, gleaming
crest of Shasta, fifteen miles away as the crow flies, e'en though
we gaze at it from its own base, we feel an indescribable sense
of awe. And we liken the mount, with the flaming forest
glowing at its feet, and its own muffled form rising in obscure·
grandeur--to a silent sentinel by his watch fire, wrappe·
around with his cloak, and meditating on the trust he has kept
lo! these many ages, still keeps, and forever!

VI.

Returned from the far south, and in camp. In camp at th·
timber line on Tchastel's side, awaiting the nightfall, an·
through the long afternoon gazing out over a wealth of scener·
not in word power to paint. To the north "Goose Nest" moun
tain—its crater ever full of fleecy snow—rears itself aloft eleve·
thousand feet. Down yonder in that gem-like valley is th·
lovely town of Sissons; down, to our traveler, albeit on a plane
seven thousand feet above the ocean. Night. But not in a
tent door. No, on mule-back, he and a companion are toiling
upwards. There is no moon, no wind, no sound, save a few
strange noises arising from the nether regions. No moon; yet
plenty of light, since the snow seems self luminous, so that
objects appear against it in sharp silhouette. How black the
bleak rocks and ledges! And those glimmerings of light afar
in the night—what are they? Lamps; lamps miles away, thou

sands of feet lower, yet in seeming not so far off. It is cold; oh, so frightfully cold, numbing the mind! And still—as the grave. No sounds now arise to the ear; 'tis too high for aught save silence. So cold; and yet mid-day sun heats reflect from the snows as from a mirror, and then the temperature is fearful to feel, yet the snow melts not. Here is a hot, sulphur spring, one thousand feet below the apex. Warm your chilled hands in the hot mud, wipe them quickly, lest they freeze, and climb on. Your eyes, could you see them, congested as they are in the rarified atmosphere, the color of liver, would horrify you. Your breathing pains you; your heart-beats sound like the thuds of a pile driver, your throat is afire from thirst. No matter; here is the top! Two o'clock a. m. in July, 188—. As yet no light, but faint dawn. But ere long the soul is awe-stricken by a weird glow in the east, which lights nothing. The beholders are filled with a strange disquiet; see the waxing light, and—in a fearful wonder, almost terror—see the great sun, scarce heralded by the aerial rarity, spring from beneath the horizon. Yet all below is in "the darkest hour before the dawn." No ridges, no hills appear, no valleys, nothing but "night's deep darkness." We seem to have lost the world, and, for the nonce, are free of time! The planet is swallowed up, leaving the mountain top's half acre sole visible spot of all the Universe, save only the fearful splendor of Helios. Understand now, for you may, the sensations of Campbell's "last man." The world all gone, and self and comrade alone on a small spot in mid-air, whereon the almost rayless sun casts cold beams of strange, weird brightness. Look north. Afar in the night are four cones of light—Mt. Hood, Mt. Adams, Mt. Tacoma, and St. Helen's tall torch, all peers of our Ieka. As the Day King soars higher lesser peaks appear, then long black ridges—ranges of vast extent—begin near by, only to lose themselves in distant darkness.

Now the void of night vanishes, hills stand forth, silvery spots and streaks appear as the dawn lights lakes and rivers, and at last, no fog obscuring, in the distant west, seventy miles away, is seen a great gray plain, the Pacific' broad expanse.

To the south interrupted streaks of silver show where flow
Pitt and Sacramento rivers, while over two hundred miles
away behold an indentation of California's central coast, marking the Golden Gate, and San Francisco's world-famed bay.

VII.

Beside a roaring, dashing mountain torrent—falling in
myriad cascades of foam white as drifted snow, interspersed
with pools of quiet water—deep, trout-filled, blue, reflecting
flowery banks and towering pine-crested ridges, "ribs of the
planet," we pause. The day is hot, but the waters of this
branch of McCloud river are cold as the pristine snows of
Shasta from which they flow to our feet and thence away.

We recline on the brink of a deep blue crystal pool, idly
casting pebbles into and shivering the image of a tall basalt
cliff reflected from the mirror-calm surface.

What secrets perchance are about us! We do not know as
we lie there, our bodies resting, our souls filled with peace,
nor do we know until many years are passed out through the
back door of time that that tall basalt cliff conceals a doorway. We do not suspect this, nor that a long tunnel stretches
away, far into the interior of majestic Shasta. Wholly un-
thought is it that there lie at the tunnel's far end vast apartments—the home of a mystic brotherhood, whose occult arts
hollowed that tunnel and mysterious dwelling:—"Sach" the
name is. Are you incredulous as to these things? Go there, or
suffer yourself to be taken as I was, once! See, as I saw,
not with the vision of flesh, the walls, polished as by jewelers,
though excavated as by giants; floors carpeted with long, fleecy
gray fabric that looked like fur, but was a mineral product;
ledges intersected by the builders, and in their wonderful polish
exhibiting veinings of gold, of silver, of green copper ores, and
maculations of precious stones. Verily, a mystic temple, made
afar from the madding crowd, a refuge whereof those who,
"Seeing, see not," can truly say:

"And no man knows***
"And no man saw it e'er."

Once I was there, friend, casting pebbles in the stream's deep pools; yet it was then hid, for only a few are privileged. And departing, the spot was forgotten, and today, unable as any one who reads this, I cannot tell its place. Curiosity will never unlock that secret. Does it truly exist? Seek and ye shall find; knock and it shall be opened unto you. Shasta is a true guardian and silently towers, giving no sign of that within his breast. But there is a key. The one who first conquers self, Shasta will not deny.

This is the last scene. You have viewed the proud peak both near and far; by day, by night; in the smoke, and in the clear mountain air; seen its interior, and from its apex gazed upon it and the globe stretched away 'neath your feet. 'Tis a sight of God's handiwork, sublime, awful, never-to-be-forgotten; and as thy soul hath sated itself with admiration thereof, in that measure be now filled with His Peace.

———————

CHAPTER I.

"I have called you friends, for all things that
I have of the FATHER I have made known unto you."

With Chapter Twenty-four of Book First closed the last devachanic experience of a personal life history—a history enacted over one hundred and twenty centuries ago. It has its good and its bad phases. Under the social rules and customs of a people whom the modern world regarded as pure myth until after the cruise of the "Challenger" and the "Dolphin," there existed a personality whom those who have followed this history thus far know by the name of "Zailm,"—an Atlantean cognomen not less euphonious than its significance is interesting—viz:—"I live to love."

According to his narration, Zailm's youth was that of an obscure mountaineer. He was possessed of an overmastering ambition to make his name blaze among those of the noble of earth. He succeeded in his ambition—for his name, his wealth,

his social and political position became of the highest of the
aristocracy of a proud and, in myriad ways, marvellous people.
If he failed in one particular—if his moral life became awry,
his record in other respects was most commendable. For the
one failure he paid dearly, and, if you credit his own appre-
hensions, the payment would not be complete for many a long,
long year after you would have lain

> "——down with patriarchs of the infant world—
> With kings, the powerful of earth—the wise, the good,
> Fair forms, and hoary seers of ages past."

You have a view of Zailm, that boy so obscure, that man so
celebrated throughout a land not paralleled to-day, nor ever
matched since old ocean rolled over it, and the sun saw it no
more in all his proud course.

From the perusal of that record I ask you to turn to the
history of another personality—that of Walter Pierson, my
own humble self. If the Poseida Zailm was proud to declare
himself a Poseida, I am equally proud to say, "I am an American citizen!"

————————

While I was still so young as to be unable to understand
anything concerning my parents' death, except the agony of
being left alone, I was orphaned by the fell stroke of an epidemic. I cried in my childishness, and begged to be allowed
to see my papa and mamma, nor could I comprehend the statement—"They are dead and gone."

My orphaned boyhood was passed under circumstances of
such sharp contrast to those years of my babyhood which
knew parental kindness, that my inherent tendency to rove
grew stronger, until at twelve years of age I became a cabin-
boy on board ship, running away to accomplish my ambition.
For many years thereafter I realized that actual hardship was
an unforeseen part of the dream of travel and of sailor life; but
its toil and trouble had to be endured.

My ability, willingness and honesty in service told in my favor so well, that at eighteen years of age I found myself first mate on a splendid British merchantman. With this advantageous position, intervals in which to study such books as the captain, an educated man, had on shipboard, were mine, and I used the opportunity to excellent advantage, reciting my lessons to the captain, who took much interest in me. An invention for which many a seafarer has been grateful, and to which many a man whose life has been spent on the ocean wave has owed continuation of that life, paid me such a handsome sum, in royalties, that ere I was of age I had no small fortune, which by wise investment soon gave me a sum to put in the bank with the assurance of a fair support for life. I did not long continue in marine service after my money began to accumulate, but left sea life to enjoy travel on terra firma. I had seen the chief ports of every land, and now was bent upon seeing the interior of my own country.

In the gold placers of California I added immense sums to my fortune during the years 1865-6, where I drifted after my discharge from the Army of the Cumberland, having served two years in that famous corps during the War of the Secession.

I gloried in the absence of two fingers, lost by a vicious fragment of shell at the battle of Missionary Ridge. I wonder if any reader remembers the morning of the 25th of November, 1863?

"All night the flash of rifles from the outposts had gleamed through the fog; and when day dawned it had not yet been determined whether the enemy had been forced from his almost unassailable position on the mountain. The morning was clear. All eyes in the Union bivouacs were strained towards the summit. Gradually the east purpled with strengthening light, and just as the sun rose, a squad of men walked out on the rock overhanging the precipice. Then, in full view of the watching tens of thousands, they unfurled "Old Glory." Amid thunderous cheers an army of veterans looked long through its tears at the Stars and Stripes—mute announcement of victory.''

At the close of this saddest of wars, because the hands of fathers against sons and of brothers against brothers were raised, I presently found myself in the city of my birth— Washington, D. C.

———————

Two months later I was in far-away California, in one of its most beautiful mountain countries, and formed one of a company of gold miners. So rich were the returns of labor that we soon began to feel the work onerous, and employed men to do it for us. Amongst these was a man from China. I say a man from China because he certainly appeared, from the very first, to be not one of the class sneeringly called "coolies," but a real man. "Coolies" were numerous in the town, some two or three miles from our mine, but Quong had nothing in common and did not associate with them; neither was he privately addicted to their habits of gluttony, gin-drinking or opium-smoking. His dress was that which always distinguishes the Tchin from other nationalities, but his features were not thus significant. Indeed, his high, prominent forehead, well developed sinciput, bold eyebrows and delicate neck marked him as a man of high character, spiritual cast, splendid perceptive abilities and nervous temperament. His eyes—such eyes!—calm, clear, light gray, resting upon one with so kindly, unprejudiced and dispassionate a gaze—charitable, forgiving and strictly upright and conscientious himself, but always ready to overlook faults in others. Such was the appearance of a remarkable man. His speech was intelligible to every one with whom he had dealings, yet it always seemed to me that his broken English, a commingled Chinese and Anglo-Saxon idiom, would have been wholly unintelligible gibberish in the mouth of any other Chinese. I am no Don Quixote, and do not propose to contend that it is not an evil of serious import to the white man of America, Australia and the people of

the Spanish-American republics to be forced to compete with
Chinese laborers or the commercial products of that nation. I
think it a very real evil, and I sympathize with the Caucasian
race. But in all frankness I would ask if the hordes of unskilled, uneducated, almost unassimilable laboring poor of
Europe are not an even greater menace? The immigration of
either is fraught with fearful peril to the free institutions
which I believe in, to the extent of having at the point of the
bayonet risked my life for their preservation. But far be it
from me to urge a spirit of strife—rather I counsel you to
follow Him whose life meant "Peace on earth," and the true
brotherhood of man.

In deference to a correct sentiment these pages will henceforth refer to my one Chinese employee as the "Tchin," or
Quong (his given name), instead of "the Chinese."

After the change of policy which gave the hard work to hired
men, my partners and myself resided in town, although one
or more of us were always at the mine in the capacity of over-
seers. We employed two gangs of workers, that worked on
alternate days, each thus giving but half of the time to labor,
although the wages were not reduced in consequence. These
easy arrangements made the men extra faithful, for they saw
that our object was not to get all the work out of them which
they were able to accomplish, irrespective of their comfort, or
the fact that they were men, not beasts of burden. That white
men treated thus considerately will do more in the way of results than those who are made to work at their highest power
every week-day hour has been my uniform experience. Treat
your fellow men as you would like to be treated, were you in
his place.

None of the men felt the least objection to Quong as a fellow-
worker; most of them were ready to admit, indeed, that he
did not seem like a heathen. They were right, for he was not
one. His demeanor towards all was respectful and manly,
rather reticent, very quiet, but always so full of benevolent
feeling that he won the affection of his fellow workers. They
felt that he was a true man. On one occasion a new man was

hired by the company, and he "didn't like pigtails." But in less than a week he fell ill, and, unasked, the despised "coolie" not only worked all day, but nursed the sick man through the brief but severe fever, sitting up all night, and only taking a few hours rest next day—his "off" day. No more was heard from the shamed objector to coolies, for he was completely won over, so far as Quong was concerned. Thus he, too, was proved a real Man, when the canker of intolerance was healed.

More than once were the Tchin and I companions on his leisure days. Sometimes we went to the town, but more often we turned our horses' heads away into the wilderness of the mountains. Without his guidance I had surely been lost there, amid the vast gorges, with their shade of giant pines lying between the almost interminable ridges, those stern ribs of the planet. But Quong was never lost, never hesitated, though the night was upon us so dark on more than one occasion that I could not see my hand before my face, a fact I never quite comprehended at the time, though it is clear to me now. Once at such a time as this I felt the need of a light, so greatly—it was in a cavern which we had found—that he said:—"Here, I give you light." I heard him break off a fragment of rock from the side of the wall of the cavern; next he put it into my hand, saying:—"Have care now, it must not touch you—like lightning; would kill you." As may be imagined, I touched so little of the rock that Quong directed me to hold it tighter. Then up sprung a brilliant light from the tip of that rock, illuminating all the cave like sunlight! Had this amazing thing occurred a few years later, I should have first pronounced it an electric light, then, bethinking me that no battery was there, nor any dynamo-electric machine, I would have done as I did do—sat down and gazed at the marvellous light, forgetful of where I was. As Quong would give no other explanation than he had already given, I was, perforce, content—only I was not! but his power of keeping his course where not even the track of an animal was not to be discerned, was sufficiently astonishing, and I was often amazed at the man for not losing his way amongst ranges of sierra which stretched away to where the vast snowy peaks defined the horizon, and kept the blue of the sky from blending insensibly with the blue of the mountains.

When we took such trips as these we were accustomed to leave the mine as early after supper as possible; that is, at half past five in the afternoon. If the other men were fatigued, Quong never seemed to share their weariness, although there was not a fellow worker but admitted that he accomplished more than any of them.

If the night was one of Luna's own, it was our habit to ride for several hours, frequently not halting before midnight, when we might be thirty or more miles from the mine.

On one of these occasions, when we and our horses were alone with nature and the night, we stopped in a remote solitude to wait for morning—to sleep or not as we felt most agreeable. Quong sat down on a rock by the edge of a roaring crystal torrent, and gazed in silent enjoyment upon the solitary grandeur of the sombre pines and moonlit peaks. I left him there and wandered up the stream, till, on looking back, I saw that my friend was hidden from view by a sharp turn in the cañon. But heedless of this I wandered on, musing at the scene—"rockribbed; ancient as the sun."

It is not possible for a person alive to the beauties of nature, long to remain insensible to the more serious thoughts evolved by meditation pursued amidst the wilds, untroubled by man's sordid methods. Gradually my thoughts assumed a reflective cast, which, almost unperceived, became tinged with the dead black shadow of materialism. Many a time and oft had grim despair seized upon me while pursuing to philosophical end the mysterious questions of the soul—"Whence" and "Whither?" Unreasoning faith had never held any place in my nature, and yet mine was a deeply religious disposition. "To reason is to be lost," thundered the church of those days, and even yet does it maintain this attitude concerning reason as applied to faith. The queries which haunted others pursued me; but I lacked the Ingersollian desire to propound the question, which madened me, to a world I doubted not had misery enough already. But the despair which arose from the hidden questionings was not less keen because hidden. Eagerly I read scientific works; studied anatomy, physiology, mechanics, the structure of cells, and the essays of Darwin and Huxley, and I came to the same conclusions that have troubled the world so mercilessly in all ages. The gray matter of the brain, and the white cerebral substance; the medulla oblongata and vital magnetism, and the blood—these became so much phosphorised fat, haematin, and magnetic vibration—that same "unconscious cerebration" theory in fact, which even yet disturbs certain philosophers. Thus joy and sorrow, and every other emotion, became a form of vibration, akin to sound waves, heat waves, light waves and undulation in general. I saw, in brief, my joy become a mere vibratory thrill of nerve tissue, similar, but more complex, to the throb of a violin string. My grief became a similar pulsation or wave. But neither were less keen; if my delight were mere pulsation of bundles of fibers proceeding from a cell or nucleus, principally composed of phosphorised fatty substance; if in passing, this delight but gave rise to a magnetic thrill, and a minute quantity of phosphoric acid, while any chance muscular exertion produced, ultimately, only relatively small amounts of carbonic acid and other excretory chemicals—nevertheless, it was keen joy. And my grief over a deceased friend, if it produced exactly the same chemics, having their formulas reducible to the symbols PO_4 and CO_2, etc., etc., was this emotion less agonizing, less painful? None the less, when all queries were finished, when all were reduced to their ultimates, ever and forever faced me a blank wall, insurmountable, and everything ceased short of God. In my despair I cried:—"There is no God, no immortality, and man differs from the oyster only in having a more complex organization. Only because I, believing thus, lack incentive to crime, am I prevented from lust, from murder; what reck if I kill a man and no witness be there? When I, too, die, the clock of life is either

worn out, or broken; both are irreparable, and there will be
never more resuscitation, nor punishment, for death levels all,
equalizes all. Perhaps I myself am only a complex vibration
of atoms, not dyads, but mult-atomic arrangements of matter
acted upon by—what? Force, wave force, moving ether. We
are but puppets, creatures of uncontrollable circumstances.
'Kismet,' says the Arab, and I must say so, too!''

Do hideous, natural causes of fright seek those moments to
appal poor, despairing man when he is already a prey to shapes
of awful oppressiveness to his very soul's life? I have thought
so, and even the next moment thought so; soul in peril, and
body also—for then in my path arose a terror, a huge grizzly
bear, **Ursus horribilis.** "Surely horrible enough," I thought,
as the animal raised himself in frightful posture. I had no
weapon except a clasp knife, and the remembrance emphasized
the reality of my peril. Wildly I looked about for a tree, into
the branches of which to climb for safety. None except giant
pines were near; down the stream towards Quong were cotton-
woods, but to go there was to put my friend, unwitting his
peril, into extreme danger. Yet bruin was rapidly forcing me
to decide on the courses of flight, or remaining to be eaten, so
I turned to run and—stood face to face with the Tchin! Calm
and cool himself, he bade me have no fear.

Stock still I stood, amazed to see him walk slowly up to the
grizzly, which, from its fierce-eyed aspect changed to docility
of looks, got down on all fours, and awaited the man's approach! Was Quong insane? I expected to see him rent in
pieces; instead, he placed his hand on the head of the animal
and said:

"Lie down!"

The order was obeyed at once, and then Quong sat down on
the prostrate animal and fondled its great, stiff ears! Very
gently, the bear licked the human hand, as gently indeed as if
caressing its own cubs. What occult power was here? Was
the Tchin a worker of miracles? Never before had any action

betrayed to me this ability of his.   True, the example of producing the light in the cave was one, but it had not then so
occurred to me, because I knew enough, and at the same time
not enough, to know that the production of electric light was
a possibility, but not possible to any electrician or chemist in
the way the Tchin performed it. It was not possible to ordinary science then, nor is it now any more so. But it would
be possible to them if they would but take the porper occult
method; it is one of the earliest learned and easiest feats performed by the novitiate. But I was not then a novitiate.

After a few moments Quong got up and, speaking to the
conquered ursine, said: "Go!" As obediently as before the
shaggy beast lumbered heavily off up the cañon and was soon
lost to view amongst the rocks and shadows of the night.

Once more the granite boulders shone silvery in the glorious
summer moonlight; the dark pines swayed in the gentle breeze
which, descending from its play with the whispering boughs,
blew the spray of the rushing torrent over the grateful wild
flowers nodding on the banks. And beside the rocks, the crags
and peaks, the torrent and the pines, the moon shone down on
two figures—two men. One stood wrapped in meditation; the
other, not thinking at all, simply regarded the first with eyes
where amazement yet lingered. Neither moved, neither spoke.
But one, at least, though he thought not, yet felt. I felt how
little difference existed between men, so that they were worthy
men. I would have acknowledged the Tchin as my equal before the world; perhaps, indeed, as my superior. In the clearest nights some mists come over and obscure the face of things
So with the soul—in its clearest moments it knows Truth, only
to forget in later moments how Truth seemed. Then, anon,
the fogs clear away again. Sometimes, alas, it is after the
obscured orb has set. So also the soul—death may set its
darkness over it ere the clouds of prejudice have melted, or it
may not.

But there in the moonlight, the sky of my soul was also
clear. But neither man moved, neither spoke.

CHAPTER II.

A SOUL IN PERIL.

Many days I pondered that scene in the mountains, marvel-
ing over the wonderful power possessed by Quong over wild
animals. Did he know how he exerted this control, or was it
simply a feature of his nature, sufficiently astonishing, truly,
but still not understood by its owner? At Bombay, I had seen
snake charmers exercise the same dominion over serpents,
but it was an inherited ability, unexplained even by the operator. To querists they would reply:

"So did my father, and my father's father, and his father.
I know not, except he got it from Brahm."

But perhaps Quong knew the law which governed his phenomena; if he did, and knew one occult law, did he not know
two, or more than two? I determined to ask him when opportunity presented. While in Hindostan I heard that there were
certain men there—not fakirs, but learned men who lived in
the Himalayan solitudes—who wrought magical feats of wonderful variety and power. Had Quong come from these; learned
of them? Was he an occult adept, such as I had heard of?
These were called, so I had been told, Ragi-Yogees, and to the
curious person trying to learn more about them than the
meagre statement of their vast occult or theosophic wisdom,
the native laity proved dumb as the Sphinx of Egypt.

I had an early chance presented to question my friend, who,
well as I knew him, still proved more communicative than I
had hoped.

It pleased me greatly to learn that not one in a hundred
thousand Chinese had any occult wisdom whatever; pleased
me, because I felt that if the degraded, groveling Mongol had
such knowledge, then because it did not lift that benighted
race it could not be of an elevating character. But all through
the Orient, here and there, the magicians were to be found;

the reasons for such secrecy, as they maintained, arose from the fact that ere such knowledge as they were custodians of could be gained, the soul must be calm with that calmness which comes best from life amidst the wilds of nature. Now this may seem strange, but it is a calm which can hardly be maintained in the habitats of those addicted to meat eating, or of persons engrossed in the selfishness of common life. You may imagine that these students could seclude themselves from disturbance; men who wish to study do so seclude themselves, even in cities. Not so the occultist. For, from the social order and communal life of the world emanates an aura, or atmosphere of its own disturbed muddiness—an aura fatal to the absolute peace required by the theosopher. I am impelled to remark at this point that what goes under the name of "theosophy" in the world to-day is an article so far removed from the genuine that the name has even thus early been laid aside by the silent nature student, who, now as ever, is a Son of the Solitude.

But to return to Quong and the question which I asked him. I append his answer verbatim:—

"Yes, in this land of the Starry Flag there are students known as the 'Lothinian Brotherhood.' Their lodges, called 'Saches,' are habited throughout the western hemisphere; there is one Sach near here. No one not privileged could hope to learn where it is, or who are its members. Yet as I have led you, Mr. Pierson, to ask the question you have; as I have done this with consent of the brethren, to every one of whom you, who, however, know none of them, are yourself well known, to what do you ascribe my action?"

I could construe it in only one way; so I told the Tchin that doubtless they knew and favored my deep desire for occult fraternization, a desire ever baffled until that hour; I felt my Sonship; I did not know it.

"It is so; thou art to be taken as a Brother Son by a class of men who seldom allow fraternity even to new affiliates, and never to any other persons whatsoever. But be this clear to thee forever—there is no order of mystic students anywhere, never was and never will be. The Lothins of America, the Yogis of Hindostan, do not combine for study of occult lore. It is not possible so to study. He who attains, grows; he does not study as collegiates study. It is not in books. Each student of God is in himself the plane he dwells on—a radiating center of God-wiseness. The very vows asked of initiates are but tests to determine if in themselves they are that which they seek to affiliate with. The Theo-Christian indeed does live with others as to body—but because similars are mutually attractive only. The Kingdom of God is within thee, or else (for thee) non-existent elsewhere. Be that thou knowest, and then Christos will give it to thee to know and become more, which also do thou become—and thus grow, as the lilies of the field, which toil not, nor spin, but are God thoughts external-ized. "I am the Way, the Truth and the Life," said our Great One. Thou art, Walter Pierson, of right by growth one of the Sach. And this right is because thy life for ages is known to them."

"My what? My life for ages? Am I so old?"—I asked, laughing at the supposed joke.

"You will learn in time, Mr. Pierson; in time," gravely said Quong, in meditative tones. "I am not speaking humorously."

The reason assigned for the interest taken in me made noth-ing clearer, so I fell to studying the question.

"No, you can not guess why, sir," said Quong. "Look at me; you say I seem about thirty years of age. I am more. Multiply that figure by three and add its half, and you will be correct within one year. I have watched over you since your birth, using my pschic powers for the purpose, since until a year ago your present eyes have not beheld me. You are born with powers which you can educe so as to become wiser than I. If it please you we will go to the Sach to-night. You are surprised that I, whom you have heretofore heard speak only in pidgin-English—as it is called—now use such fluent language. I have my reasons, believe me; perchance you find them obvious."

In the afternoon I went to town, telling Quong that I would meet him there, if access to the Sach was as convenient from there as from the mine.

On my way into town I met an acquaintance at whose very popular liquor saloon I had more than once taken refreshment, thinking it no harm, for I drank moderately. When we came near his place, on the main street, he insisted on my tying my horse and coming in to have a social glass with him. But the idea of acceptance jarred, and I felt that it disturbed the calm reflections which had filled my thoughts on parting with the Tchin. Quong never drank liquor, smoked, or was aught but absteminous in his habits. But I entered, resolved not to take any form of spirituous liquor. The scene presented was familiar; men stupid, foolish, or excited from their potations, and public women mingling with the crowd in the place. Previously to the week just passed these sights were viewed by me with indifference. But now they seemed revolting in the extreme. One exemplification of the satanic influence of liquor I saw with different emotions now from those of other days:—a fair, beautiful girl, a moderate user of liquor, not reached to the depths as yet, but a wanton, for all her education, culture and refinement; beginning life in the midst of the influences of school, church and home, in the far Eastern States, but fallen through a man's heartless treachery, and that cruel and equally heartless judgment of society—that whited sepulchre, outwardly stainless, but secretly worse than the victims it stones with its merciless opinions. All the worse is this pharisaical spirit in that it lets the betrayer go free.

"Let him that is without sin cast the first stone." She was already passing her days in the midst of hell. And the original cause was liquor. Liquor? Yes, I knew her history. Her parents saw no harm in the moderate use of wine, and with the taste created in the girl's nature for the use, came that for "fast" society—and then ruin! Only eighteen years old, yet her feet had stepped on the embers of Hades. Was she lost, entirely lost? I hardly thought so. I believed her story, that all the glitter of erroneous ways, wine and fast society had

been embraced in her eastern home because not discouraged
by her parents. She said she had no care for those wild ways,
but rather a disgust. I felt that she spoke the truth, for tears
of genuine sorrow stood in the bright brown eyes, and I knew
the possessor of such eyes had trod the path of sin, not through
preference, but, as she said, "Through it seeming that at home
no one cared what she did, until her disgrace, and then they
had put her out and locked the doors of house and hearts
against her." All this she told me while she sat in her own
home, the finest in the little city, known as the "Retreat."
She was occupying the day in painting, for her skill as an
artist was only equalled by that which she had as a pianist.
Her walls were covered with pictures of her own execution—
such paintings!—so sad and full of pathos. One was an ideal
picture representing a fair maiden, with a feverish light in her
eyes and a look of defiance on her face, sitting under a great
tree on a lawn. Beside her was a young man, and before them
was a serving woman with a tray on which were four glasses
—two full of milk, two of red wine. With a smile of ridicule
the young man placed his hand on the wine, and the girl, with
flushed cheeks and defiant eyes, was reaching for the other
glass of liquor, although it was evident that she preferred the
milk. Behind her, unperceived by any of the three, stood a
shadowy form, a man with a face of divine purity, who was
gently weeping over the girl's error. Behind her companion
was another shadowy form, black, and with a satanic countenance, his hand on the young man's shoulder and a smile of
triumph on his evil features. Below the picture was the title:
"The Defeat of Purity."

After I had studied long over the picture, I turned to its
painter and said:

"That represents your life and its woe, does it not, Lizzie?"

She made no reply other than to break into a storm of tears.
I waited for the cessation of her anguish, and as I sat, she dried
her tears and replied:

"Yes, my woe. Oh, God! that I have fallen so low, and
there is no hope! No hope! If I could, I would leave this

sort of life and go away to begin anew where no one knew anything of me or my past. But I can not, for I can not get away; I have no means of support if I could."

"Your art, Lizzie,"—I suggested, gently.

"Yes, my art, I know; but I fear not, for I have no means adequate to a beginning."

It was from that girl's parlor I had gone forth when, in the evening of the same day, Quong and I went into the mountains, and the grizzly bear episode occurred. That was a week ago now, and to-day I stood in the saloon of Charles Prevost, and saw, engaged in conversation with the barkeeper, over a glass of sherry, Lizzie.

The barkeeper turned away to wait upon another customer, and at the same time I went up behind the girl and bending my head close to her ear, said, almost in a whisper:

"Would you not rather that sherry was milk?"

The hard look died out of the mournfully sweet face and a tear leaped to each eye and trembled there like a dew drop, as she said, oh, so wearily:—"Yes."

"Then come with me; let us go to your house."

We went, followed by the curious, misjudging eyes of the saloon idlers. Having arrived and having entered the parlor, I offered her a chair and took another myself. Then I said, as she looked at me wonderingly:

"Lizzie—let me rather say Elizabeth, for it is more stately, dignified, and so suits you better—you said you would rather it were milk; now, I know what you meant—that your soul yearned for the better life of which we were speaking last Monday. Well, I am rich; no one in the west dreams how rich. To me the loss or mere absence from my control of twenty thousand, or even more than twenty thousand dollars, would be unfelt; the income of a couple of months would replace it. Since we talked here last week I have thought of you many times; to-day I come prepared to—to, well, smother your pride, and accept this check on the First National Bank of Washington, D. C. Will you, Elizabeth, will you take it and go there; flee from the misery of to-day and begin life there anew?"

"But, but—how can I repay it, if I do; or how will you know that I do not waste it and abuse your confidence?"

"My girl, I do not want you to repay it ever, in any way—to me. Use it as I ask; as for me the Savior has said:—"I'e that giveth even a cup of cold water shall in no wise lose h.' reward;" and again He said:—"He that loseth his life for my sake shall find it again." If life, Elizabeth, what of mone/. which is so much less? I trust you. Will you take it from rv as a 'cup of cold water' to save you from perishing?"

"Yes, if you give it in that way, I will, and as God shall he'y me I will be true to promise!"

How she kept her faith, dear reader, you will find by-and-by But, ———— City knew her no more, nor was a trace of her destination known to any one there except myself. All that was known was that her finer pictures were boxed and consigned to a firm of picture dealers in New York City, via San Francisco and the Horn. This was a blind, for while the impression was sought to be conveyed that they were sold to the consignees, such was not the case, for nothing could have induced her to part with them except dire necessity. The l·se valued pictures were sold at an auction, along with her hous and furniture, bringing quite a sum of money. Her own tick·'. I was told a month or so later by a mutual acquaintance a Catholic Sister of Charity—may God bless those siste·s' —who went to San Francisco with her, was purchas·d for the City of Melbourne, Australia. The informati·o surprised even me, and I thought her plans were deep la·d, indeed. The Catholic Sisters gave me a small painting wh·ch Elizabeth had left for me. It was a picture of the Capitol a· Washington, and under it the words in quotation mar·s. "Home, sweet home." The sister had never been in Washi··-ton and did not know what the subject of the picture was, i·r had any other person seen it, so that not a soul but myse'· knew through the picture or in any way else where the fe·i frail, but newly born to a high purpose, artist had gone.

Dismissing further special thought about her whom I believed to be saved, I began to reflect on my next actions. I felt, in thinking of my proposed visit to the Sach, as if I were about to leave the world; joining their order was, according to Quong, virtually, and perhaps in fact, leaving the world of ordinary humanity. As I walked along the streets after writing out the check for Lizzie, a wind-blown sheet of paper fell on my arm and remained until I picked it off. As I was about to let it flutter away, my own name on the paper caught my eye and aroused my curiosity. Then I read the entire note, and will repeat its words for your sake:

"Give not the rest of thy fortune away; so far thou hast given well, but do not rashly throw away the rest of it. Yet, as thy mining days are practically over, as well as thy life in this community, therefore sell thy share in the mine. It is a good mine, and will bring a high figure; yet be not discouraged if thou find not a taker for it now, but wait. Offer it now, for time is an essential.

M————."

Whence came this message? I could not tell, and, strange to say, my usual abundance of natural cautiousness never suggested that the whole thing was an artfully planned scheme to defraud me. So far from such an idea occurring to me, I sought my partners and asked what they would give me for my third share of our joint property. The reply was not immediate. At last, one cautiously asked:

"Pierson, why do you sell? Do you fear the 'pay' is petering out?"

I replied that I did not, but had reasons of a private nature. Then, too, I wanted to go home. They did not know that I meant by the word "home," a figurative rendition; that home was not Washington, the city which they knew I had come from, and that instead, I meant affiliation with an occult brotherhood. They promised me an answer upon the next day. To this I agreed, but "next day" came not for more than a month; when it did, the interim had seen a "strike" at our mine, uncovering what was, in the belief of the company, millions of dollars. In the "pay dirt," lying on the "bed-rock," a lode of gold quartz was found which, according to the assay, ran

into the thousands of dollars per ton. Unconscious of this
coming good fortune, I left my partners engaged in debate
and went out upon the street. At the appointed place and
hour of seven o'clock in the evening, now come, I met the
Tchin. Our meeting place was beyond the town limits, and
night had fallen when I arrived. He sat by a tall pine tree,
and I did not see him until I had been there—supposing myself
first arrived—some five minutes. It was the night of the full
moon of that lunar period, and I sat musing on a rock
by the roadside, thinking of the myth of Morpheus, who with
leaden sceptre wafts the many into the dim land of dreams—
the only respite from woe that weary millions of sufferers
ever find on earth. But Quong was not to usher me into peaceful slumber; he was not come as Morpheus—but he was to
introduce me into a realm which, new to me, was old in the
earth since the first flight of years began back in the aeons
of dead time—a realm that has existed from the time of the
creation, the spiritual, far away land of the soul, where the
vagaries of dreamland are supplanted by verities stranger yet
I was about to enter on the path of Kabala, wherein travel
those whose researches into the occult penetralia come from
an antiquity of hoary seers of ages past. Would I prove
worthy? Then the Tchin broke in upon my reverie with the
bidding

"Let us go."

Strange as it may seem, I was in no wise startled at his
sudden appearance. Soon we were among the rock-ribbed
hills, and the pine forests waved above us, around us, and
adown the slopes beneath our feet. Deer roamed here, despite
the comparative nearness to the habitations of men, and many
a bright flower was faintly visible in the moonlight, peeping
from its shy retreat—wood lilies, tiger lilies, violets. My
thoughts dwelt musingly on these natural beauties and seemed
to say "How fitting that they who, in love of nature, hold
communion with her visible forms should go, from listening

to the tongues of the visible, to take note of the various language wherewith she tells of things unseen." To the thrill of feeling which swept over me at the meditation, my very soul responded.

By the time we were fairly amongst the enforested mountains and the silences of nature, the night was well advanced. The moon's round shield now shone broadly upon us, or again peeped forth between swaying pines. Scarce a cloud floated in the heavens, the air was warm and still, the entire scene seemed a most appropriate introduction to greater beauties which I felt were about to be presented.

Then, as I beheld Quong ahead with his blue Mongolian blouse, and in the act of uncoiling his queue to sool his head, the sight acted upon my deep seated prejudice against the Chinese race and, like a ruffling breeze, swept over my placid soul and marred my enjoyment, my serenity. For a moment I forgot the superiority of manhood in Quong, and there arose within me a repugnance to investigating, in the company of a Chinese, things which impressed me as sacred. My vanity whispered that, because he was a Chinese, he was my inferior; yet for the world I would not have breathed a word of it to him. I almost felt inclined to return to town, nevertheless.

Quong's voice interrupted this disagreeable train of thought —and his words became a mirror to reflect my conceited egotism so faithfully that I was aghast, and wondered that my own sense of justice had allowed such vain ascendancy of meanness. Swept away at last was every vestige of the notion that nationality was of the smallest consequence where real manhood was under consideration. Replacing the narrowness was the conviction that, while one race may have more numerous exemplifications of nobility than another—none the less the individuals of every race may leap the highest social barrier, and stand equal at last—because it is the soul, not the casket, which springs aloft to God.

"What said the Tchin?"—do you ask? This:

"Alas for human vanity! It is more prolific of evil than any other emotion—makes men weak when they should be strong, cringe to prejudice when bravery is meet, and sows the seed of Injustice, which hath the flower Intolerance and the ripe fruit Iniquity.''

He then turned to me direct, saying:

"Brother, ought the penalty earned by the depravity of the Chinese race to be visited upon me, who have no part in their iniquity? Shall the good stone in the pile rejected by the masons of society be also cast aside? Perchance it might become the head of the corner. Oppression of tyranny is rejection, for it denies a man's rights. Behold, then, what a pillar of strength is built of the rejected stones of the nations upon the rock of the American Declaration of Independence! Yet, let it not be built too high, and never of any but choice stone, whatever its source, lest it become of ill proportion and fall in ruin!''

"Indeed, indeed! I knew not that you could so easily fathom my thoughts; nor did I know how illiberal I had grown through my vanity! Forgive me, my friend!''

"Ask not my pardon. I am not offended. But I saw clearly that you were doing yourself an injustice in allowing such play to prejudice. It was to set you right, not to humble you, that I spoke.''

Somehow the beauty of the scene was enhanced in my sight. Like a gladdening rain laying the dust were the words of my friend, and my soul's atmosphere was cleared, so that all things appeared more lovely.

As we walked, a doe and her fawn stepped into the path before us. Their impulse on seeing men was to take flight. But Quong held out his hand and called them as if they were pets familiar with him. The animals stopped, and returned along the path until within reach. He stroked them gently, and as we passed on they followed behind. I was wondering if Quong, in his many solitary walks in the mountains, had not made a few pets, as, for example, these deer, and even the bear, when the idea was put aside by a new occurrence. As we came under an overhanging rock a puma, or "California lion" (Felix concolor), leaped into our midst with the evident intention of having venison for supper—indeed, had not the deer for which he sprang been too nimble, it would have been an instant victim; but it and its companion affrightedly closed about Quong, and the latter turing to the panther, said sternly, but in a calm, low tone:

"Peace!"

And there was peace, for the carnivore slunk down for an instant, like a whipped dog, then resumed a normal cat-like attitude, and, purring, walked with soft, feline tread on one side, with the deer on the other side of the human mediator, and I, lost in amazement, brought up the rear. Verily, the fable of the lion and the lamb was realized in actuality.

"See, my brother, what it is to know the law and to live it—for I myself am a vegetarian, and the perfect peace such food allows renders my soul calm, so that I see the law as in a mirror. Behold proof of the truth in this occurrence!"

As he ceased to speak we halted in front of a huge ledge of basaltic rocks, some hundreds of feet in height. The ledge was broken and twisted as if by some rending convulsion. All about the base lay huge fragments broken off the face of the wall. Against the cliff rested a giant block many tons in weight touching this with his hand, the Tchin said:

"Here is our Sach—our Temple, so to say; this rock is guard at the entrance to a place remarkable, to say the least, if viewed from an occidental standpoint."

I looked in vain for the doorway, or any crevice which might lead into a cavern. Meanwhile Quong laid his hand on the great cat with us and said:

"Go!"

And the lion, pausing not, went leaping along in bounds—for these animals have such a limber spinal column that they can not run or trot like other animals not of the feline tribe—leaps by which it was soon lost to sight. Then Quong said·

"As it will not return here, these gentle deer would best remain; no other spot is so safe for them. Good bye, my little friends!"

Continuing, Quong said to me: "Have you found the door-way? It is not strange that you should fail, for it was con-structed with the special purpose of baffling the curious."

Again he touched the enormous quadrangular block. Im-mediately it tipped on edge and leaned outward over us, caus-ing me to spring away in terror lest it fall on me. "Be not afraid, my brother. See, it is under my control as if on hinges;" and he swung it back on its lower outer ege with won-derful ease, only keeping his own nearest hand firmly upon it. To my amazed query he replied that it worked to his will through magnetism. But I saw no magnet, and said so.

"Truth! In me is the magnet you do not see. Did it ever occur to you that the proceses of all life are carried on by what for our present purpose may be called magnetism? Assimila-tion of food and drink, waste, excretion, all vital processes whatever? The magnet is in the cerebellum or back brain, and in the medullary substance of the corporae straitum—a veritable wound magnet. The force which causes the heart to act, the lungs to act, maintains bodily heat, and so on, is enor-mous; it amounts to many hundreds of thousands of foot pounds per day. He that knows occult law can make nature parallel this magnet, for the universe itself moves only be-cause of the current which flows from positive to negative— from one-half of matter into the other half, continuously. Here, now, is an occult secret:—make a place of separation in this, the Fire of Life, and where the poles come in contact there shall force be in action. This block of stone, the door, is an armature in a natural field of force. Here on the ground is another."

Putting the door stone back in place, Quong drew a circle on the ground about a foot across. Then in this circle a couple of lines in a simple cross, one north and south, the other east and west. As the four ends of the cross were contacted with the circle, a tall, steady flame sprang up, its spear shaped cone trembling within itself, but being wholly ;unfluenced by the wind, which had some time before commenced blowing in vigorous gusts. Then said the Tchin:

"Behold the Vis Mortuus. Of all mankind only an occult
student could bring it forth; only such a one could put it out,
unless by accident. Touch it not; 'twould be fatal, on the
principle that the greater contains all lesser forces, and it
would instantly absorb the force of life, or of wind or wave,
or projectile; it exists visibly here because on a thaumaturgic
symbol. You think that symbol might as well be of any other
form? So think those who comprehend not. See that moth
darting about the flame of the light; it will enter, but not be
burnt; no, quicker—see! it touches, and disappears, and leaves
no sign—yet the light is not hot, no, not even warm. I will put
it out."

Suiting his action to the word, he drew a stick through
beneath the dust on which the circle was described, and the
light in that instant was gone. Then another circle made he,
drew but one line across it, north and south, then stepped
into the figure, one of his feet on each semi-circle. Immediately his whole person was covered with a brilliant flame, so
that he appeared on fire. I was exceedingly terrified.

"Do not fear for me! It is well with me. The other flame
was negative odicity, and would have instantly been fatal to
whatever motion touched it and have disintegrated its form;
yea, a rock thrown into it would at once have disintegrated, or
a cannon ball discharged from the muzzle of the piece would
have fared the same. But this is a positive flaming of the Vis
Naturae, and preserves life. I might stand here till the centuries mounted and be not weary, nor hungry, nor sick; eat not,
nor drink, yet live; for this keeps all things untouched by
time, as when they enter it. No difference in symbolic figures,
think you now? Indeed, yes. But my soul will not progress;
so that ease of living though its use offers, I care not to
employ its aid, except that when weary it gives me rest; ill,
it restores health."

He broke the circle with his foot, and coming away, swung
back the door-stone again and stepped within the tunnel dis-
closed behind it.* I followed, the door was replaced, and I

NOTE.—This was in one of the walls of one of the vast canyons
which seam the sides of Mount Shasta, in Northern California.—Author.

found that the passage led into the mountain. I was still thinking of the biblical legend of the rolling away of the stone from
the mouth of the sepulchre of Jesus the Christ, and paralleling
it with this act of the Tchin—aware now that neither were
miracles, but manifestations of higher natural law—when we
began to walk along the hall of the tunnel I followed closely
in the rear of my guide, whom I could hear but not see, for
since the closing of the door-stone the blackness was apalling
in its intensity. Mistrusting this blind guidance, I approached
the wall, that I might feel my way, when suddenly all about
me shone a marvellous white light. It was not emanent from
any point, but all the air was luminous, for I observed that
nothing cast a shadow, either below, above or on any side.
'Twas the same marvellous light I had once before seen in the
cavern we had found together. After going about two hundred feet we came to a door made apparently of bronze covered
with artistic cameo and intaglio figures of men and animals
ranged about a double triangle inside of a circle. This door
gave entrance to a large circular chamber not less than sixty
feet across, with dome-like ceiling ten or a dozen feet high at
its junction with the wall, but over twenty feet in the center.
The same wonderful illumination was omnipresent in this great
apartment as in the hall outside. But I asked no questions—
I deemed observation the better way. Here it was that Quong
temporarily left me, going into another room through a narrow doorway closed by a portiere. I devoted the time to looking about me, examining the surroundings. I found that the
chamber, like its approach, was hallowed from the living rock,
only that while the beginning of the hallway was in a basalt
cliff, the room was in a differe t formation, being in mineral
bearing rock. The central pa. of the walls and ceiling cut
across a wide vein of gold-bearing gray quartz of hard texture.
This lode, fully twenty-five feet wide, had on one side a granite
ledge, and on the other red prophyry of the variety chiefly
found in the quarries of upper Egypt. Beyond the granite
was another lode of metalliferous rock, and in this one side of
the room was reached without cutting into other veins. The

prophyry almost completed its side of the chamber, but not quite, as a second body of gold quartz was intersected, but not cut through. Now imagine the extreme beauty of such walls as these when polished like glass, thus enhancing the veinings of the clouded rock and brilliant beauty of silver and gold—both native and in their ores—and not a few other metals and minerals.

The makers of the wonderful room had "builded like giants and finished like jewellers." But how had such an enormous task been accomplished, and when? A town of many hundreds of people lay but a few miles distant; but the inhabitants knew nothing of all this. It did not occur to me in explanation that its builders were of the Lothinian Brotherhood, and had formed their temple by the disintegrating force of the Vis Mortuus, into which I had seen Queng cast a stone and had witnessed its instantaneous disappearance. It was long afterwards ere I, musing o'er memory's pages, thought of this solution to the puzzle of the existence of the Sach, or Sagum. But when I did, I knew it for the truth; knew that neither pick nor drill, nor any tool of human kind had been used, and that what I had thought the result of years of patient toil was but the work of a short time. Yet this was the fact, my friends!

On the floor was a carpet of oriental variety. The fabric was of long fibres woven together at one end, but loose like hair at the other; in color a quiet gray. A foot-fall upon it gave no sound whatever, any more than would a carpet of eider down. Around the sides of the Sagum extended a wide divan, continuous except at the three entrances. Covering it and depending from its edges was the same silky fabric as lay upon the floor. The one article of movable furniture in sight was a singular looking stand made of brass, which stood in the middle of the apartment. Its top indicated that it was used as a brazier. I would have made sure of its real use, but refrained from asking, not desiring to appear curious.

"Indeed, ask questions if you wish," said Quong, who had just returned. "Have no fear of seeming inquisitive. That is, as you suppose, a censer; its use will appear."

I was again astonished at my friend's occult powers, for
his answer proved a clear case of mind reading. I now felt
an unconquerable sense of fatigue and sleepiness, and without saying anything, or asking permit as I might more courteously have done, and would but for my being so sleepily stupid,
sat down on the divan, and then reclined at full length; but this
act seemed to arouse me so that I could not sleep. I tried very
determinedly to do so ere finally admitting to myself that it
seemed impossible.

"So you can't sleep? I will aid you."
Again the Tchin had fathomed my wish, for I had hoped as a
last resort that he would offer to put me to sleep, having
myself no doubt of his power to do so. He leaned over me, and
touched a knob in the wall; a small door flew open, disclosing
a number of shelves. From one of these Quong took a peculiar
looking flute of reed pipe. Placing it to his lips he began playing an air which had a very familiar sound. Like some sweet,
half-forgotten memory floating back from "Lang Syne," bringing an exquisite sense of pleasure and pathetic pain—so the
wild, sweet notes brought to my mind a faint, indistinct recollection of some former delight. In trying to remember where—
what—remember when—ah, me—sleep had overtaken my
senses.

It matters little how long I slumbered, whether minutes or
hours; yet it must have been hours.

——————

CHAPTER III.

TAKE THEREFORE NO THOUGHT FOR THE MORROW.

When I awoke, rich, delicate perfumes, and the low hum of
voices greeted my still slumberous senses. On opening my
eyes, I found that Quong was by my side, having either remained while I slept, or returned before I roused. In the center of the room, sitting on the floor, I saw about a dozen people,

each clad in a long gray robe. Quong had one of these robes on his person, and to my astonishment, I found myself attired in like manner. A high caste Thibetan, two Hindoo pundits and Egyptian were, excepting Quong, the only foreign brethren, the remaining persons being American and English. The Egyptian was to the Sakaza what the Grand Master is to a Masonic fraternity. Understand that he was not a teacher in the sense that a professor in a college is an instructor. He was in himself more of the Way, more of the Truth, more of the Life of God than any other present. And hence, as in himself the highest plane, he stood before the rest as a pinnacle each might study, and rise unto. This man alone was standing.

Perceiving that I had awakened, Quong said:

"Let us seat ourselves in the circle, brother, that the ceremonies of the evening may commence."

When seated we formed two in a circle of ten persons, arranged in a ring in the center of the chamber, our hands clasped on either side by our neighbors, and so around the circle. In its center stood the brazen censer, and beside it the Grand Master. Presently this person began to speak in the best of English, giving a clear, concise statement of the wisdom-religion of the Lothinians. He disclaimed the idea that anything which was performed under occult law could be a miracle, and declared that no miracle had ever yet taken place in the world, because a miracle would be a contravention of law—and what was a violation of law but evil? It being evil, Jesus the Christ would have been the last ever to have worked one. Not a man or woman, it was asserted—and it is true—comprehends how these laws operate, or understands anything of their nature, unless such man or woman is an occult student. The world of science is more ignorant of these mysterious forces of Nature than even the sect styled "Spiritualists," for these do comprehend a little, but so very, very little as to expose them to fearful dangers, handling as they do forces so terrible when abused, that their field of operation might well give pause to the wisest ere they trod therein. Yet science soon shall know, following the Cross-Bearer.

Beyond admitting me to free hearing of what was said and
done, no notice other than salutatory courtesy was paid me;
that is, I was not invested with any membership degrees; no
degrees can be conferred, for each is in self the degree represented. But the Adept, as I clearly perceivd, had spoken
so personally direct, that I knew he addressed me. This was
when he said:

"There is within this sacred place of meeting one who hath
studied deeply; studied as scientific modernism contemplates
all life, and ever hath the study filled him with melancholy,
yea, even despair. He hath questioned of the stars, 'What art
thou?' and no reply hath been given beyond that which astron-
omy ever returns—'Worlds, suns, blazing orbs, mighty beyond
power of mentality to conceive.' And of the grass, and it
hath said, 'I am of cells aggregated and vitalized by the spirit
of nature.' The animal hath replied, but in Darwinian terms:
'I am a form evolutionized, and come up from protoplasm.'
Man has he seen to be at the apex of animal life, and so he
says of himself: 'Lo! there is naught but at one end the simple
cell; at the other a complexity of cells aggregated. But to
me the world and all its forms speak of action, and eternity;
but of the immortality of man, of a soul or a spirit, or of God—
nay, no word! Death ends all!' O my brother! speaketh not
this joy, these griefs of thine, to thee of aught but mgnetic
vibration? Art thou blind to the message of God that the
'vibratory' joy or grief or 'unconscious cerebral action,'
whereby thou comest to a given knowledge, is but the method
of thy life? And the animal, saith it not: 'Lo! I am a soul, and
this animal body is fit tool for my soul powers, which, if they
increase beyond the power of the tool to express, force me
(the ego controlling) to cast it aside and seek a fitter tool in a
body suited to my progress.' And saith not man to thee:
'O brother in darkness, I am at the apex of animal life, truly;
in my admirably adapted physical body is a fit tool to prose-
cute to the utmost any and all material processes. It brings
me to the wall of all physical life, and behold! it enables me,
the ego, to reach the top of this wall, and find that I am a

spirit, not a vital stone. And because of my sight, I will leave behind the pursuit of materiality for that of spirituality, and go even unto my Father's house, where are many mansions (conditions) of spirit, but where matter breaketh not in to corrupt nor steal the treasures.' Who hath asked, let him hear me. I have spoken. May peace be with thee."

I thought my friend Quong was speaking in a humorous vein when he said that the Adept, whose name was Mendocus, had not so much as opened his lips, or used his vocal organs at all. Not so, however; I was mistaken. Quong read my thought, and said:

"Nay, my brother, not in jest! Each of us has heard Mendocus, and to each it seemed that his national tongue was used; to me, my own; to you and five others, Anglo-Saxon; to the Hindoo pundits, their tongue. Because Mendocus spoke from his soul unto ours is the reason of this seeming paradox.

I thought at once of my Bible, which was a treasure to me above all other books, and of the passage wherein it is written:

"Now when this was noised abroad, the multitude came together and were confounded, because that every man heard them speak in his own language."

In answer to the unspoken thought, Mendocus, the Adept, turned to me and said:

"Verily, they spoke unto the souls of that multitude; it was no miracle, but law. The Bible is sound occult doctrine so far as the matter in it has escaped the revisers, and worse than revisers—the Roman Catholic interpolaters and twisters of its truths. Thou doest well to read it; I have read it through eighty-seven times."

Here another brother joined with the remark: "The hearers and the speakers were to each other as a perfectly attuned violin to its bow—every string ready to respond to the least master-touch."

To this Mendocus added:

"They heard the speakers as thou heardst me, not with ears, for no aerial connection is needed between souls in sympathy, but the consciousness of what was said existed as does the con-thoughts that thine ears may convey to thy consciousness what sciousness of one's own thoughts; thou needst not speak thy thoughts thou thinkest. Neither are thine ears of more use in comprehending me. Yet because the thoughts did not originate in thy brain, but in mine, and so were external to thine inner consciousness, therefore thou didst suppose that thou heardst me with thine ears, when it was thy soul which understood, for my voice I used not.''

I now understood, in the light of the mind-reading power which these students had revealed, why no question had been put to me concerning my life, my thoughts or will in regard to affiliation with themselves; they knew these things, through this ability, without asking.

Mendocus, Master, now requested attention from all present, and then made an invocation to God and to all occult initiates in this world and elsewhere in the universe. At the conclusion of this petition, he slowly raised his right hand, whence, after half a minute, he dropped it to his side and bowed his head. The wonderful light commenced to wane and, simultaneously with its disappearance, a blinding flash of light seemed to dart from the ceiling overhead, striking the censer by his side. Then succeeded that inky blackness which follows the midnight flashing of the lightning of heaven; but it was not destined to last very long. Soon in the deep darkness there was a noticeable lightening which continued to increase until the whole interior of the Sagum was illumined by a lurid glow which rendered every object clearly visible. Like the other, it seemed not to emanate from any particular point, but as if the entire atmosphere were like red-hot iron—self luminous. The next instant I observed that the faces of the Lothins had assumed an exceedingly ghastly hue, bloodless in appearance as are the countenances of dead men. Their pallor was soon explained, however, when my eyes fell on the brazen censer standing in our midst. The gaze of every brother was fixed with unwavering intensity upon a small globe of blue fire which rested on the fire-pan. I noticed also that the self-luminosity of the atmosphere was gone, and that the light from the blue globe cast shadows. Although in size it was not larger than a filbert, yet its intensity counteracted the luridness of the air. It was beautiful in the extreme, but not dazzling. On the contrary it was cool and calm, resting the eyes. Evidently the light was the same as the positive flaming of the Vis Naturae with which I had seen the Tchin envelop himself. It trembled and quivered like a globule of molten, boiling metal.

Such absolute silence reigned, not even a sound of breathing being audible—that I turned a quick glance on my friends. Except for the glitter in their eyes as they gazed on the blue light, every one would have seemed only a perfect but non-vital semblance of a human being. Then my gaze reverted to the object which centered the common attention. It had been growing, and, now of a size of half a dozen inches, was gloriously beautiful. Although I had seen no human agency concerned in its creation, yet I felt that it was produced by the occult knowledge of which I had witnessed so many other manifestations. Mind over matter. Marvellous, novel—all this to me, but I knew it was not miracle, although magical. "What is magic?"—do you ask? Magic is the comprehension of laws not ordinarily possible to grasp by means of physical experiment, because their phenomena in general lie higher than the physical realm; just a little lower than mental or psychic operations, and partaking of the last to a major extent.

As I watched the blue globe, I gradually became en rapport with the mental condition of the Lothins about me. Instead of wondering what were to be the perfected dimensions, and what the object of this glowing ball, I contentedly watched it, with a sense of perfect knowledge of its ultimate size and use. But this intuition aroused in my mind no train of disturbing conjecture. I thought of nothing, absolutely nothing, taking no thought for the morrow, or the next moment. My intelligent friend, try this once; try to think of nothing; to have no thought, not even the one that you are not thinking. I doubt your success in the attainment of such a state of mind; but if you are, happily, successful, you will remember to the end of your allotted years on earth how great was the sense of rest, of peace, of perfect joy, felt—not thought of—in that moment. Could you attain and then retain such a mental state for half an hour, you would become clairvoyant and clairaudient during that time, and both see and hear across the leagues of earth; aye! and be conscious of futurity, so that a prophecy then made by you would be found to come true in every detail, though its scope was over years mounting to centuries. You must perceive, then, what a beautiful condition the Lothins enjoy:—the whole present, and each way, from the present almost to eternity, is theirs to know. These states of mind are protracted with them, and in the quiescence which is theirs at such times, they find themselves en rapport with the architect of the world, and know His ways. Like Job are they then:— hearing of Him by the hearing of the ear, their eyes also behold Him.* Some few of God's works they can do, many more of them they can understand, laying the line on the foundations of the earth; entering the springs of the sea, knowing where light hath its way, and the place of darkness and the bounds thereof; yea, in this still time of their souls God opens to them even the gates of death, through which they go and return. But though they know all this—and so, friend, might you, too—yet it is because the Creator shows them the paths unto the place thereof; and He will show you if you enter the occult door through which Christ has gone unto the Father. Follow Him, and greater things than these shall ye do.

Mendocus, Master, now perceived that the lurid glow of the atmosphere had been neutralized by the light of the blue sphere, which, full twelve inches through, rested motionless in completion, its glorious, radiant center of entrancing loveliness. He raised his hand slightly, as if giving an unspoken command. Upon this the sphere of light rose to a height of perhaps eight feet from the floor, where it hung without visible means of support. Again the hand waved in command, and the sphere moved horizontally over our heads to a point about fifteen feet from the center of the chamber. Here it

*Job xlii—5.

was permitted to remain. Although every one present was intuitively aware of all that was about to occur, I will describe every incident for the benefit of my readers. Following the pure blue light came a sphere of intense indigo color upon the brazier, its process the same as that of its predecessor, and when complete it was assigned position thirteen feet from its neighbor, on the same eight-foot plane. Next came a sphere of violet, of equally intense brilliancy, differing only in color, not size. Then followed a globe of pure red, then one of orange, another of pure yellow, and lastly one of glorious green. Every one was at the same height from the floor, and equidistant, approximately, from its neighbors. Any attempt at describing the extreme beauty of these iris-hued spheres would indeed be futile, as they hung, motionless, above our heads.

Once again the Master gave silent order, and the spheres began to move horizontally around their common center. Slowly at first, gradually the speed increased until persistence of vision presented them to the sight as a great circle of light ninety feet in circumference; nevertheless the orbital revolution did not in any degree merge the colors into becoming white light. And now an additional feature of beauty was presented:—as the seeming ring sped around, from each of its compound globes a shaft colored like its parent was simultaneously projected horizontally to the center, when, from the junction a perpendicular column of light of purest white went forth, upward and downward, the one to the great quartz crystal in the ceiling overhead, the other to the carpet of gray below, for the censer had been removed from underneath. Thus was presented the spectacle of an enormous wheel, axle, spokes and rim, revolving at great speed, and all formed of imponderable light. Though it rested on the carpet, there was no scorching, for this was but Viviant Fire—positive, not the negative Vis Mortuus. Buddhism symbolizes the latter element as "Siva"—the destroyer; it is the Fire of Death, the one wherein I had seen the moth perish and the stone disappear. There is an esoteric Buddhism as well as an exoteric, or religion of the masses, and the names of Siva and Vishnu, which to the exoterist are names of personal Gods—of the Destroyer and the Preserver respectively—are to the esoterist merely the terms distinguishing the obverse and reverse aspects of Nature, that is, growth and statiety, change and destruction.

Would power like this of the Lothins ever be mine? It seemed to me that if Mendocus, Master, had come to such wisdom, he, being but a man, could not do more than I—we were both souls. The wondrous temple in the heart of the mountain; the lighting of the darkness; the lifting of the great stone at the entrance; the Vis Viva and the Vis Mortuus—all this that I had seen and was to see, was only the work of men who had, in their calmness of soul and purity of heart and body, done these things because the Christ-Spirit, in the pure of heart, is perfect human and extends unto the Father. Could I not hope to attain the power of doing likewise? I asked myself, and knew that I could, for I was then in the peace of clairvoyance. Yet I saw not all that must intervene—not all the events of the nearer future, nothing of them, in fact, but only the more distant perspective of my soul's destiny.

"Verily," said Mendocus, "but not now; not until a time of trial be past. To thee, as to all other occult neophytes, will come moments of darkest doubt, and thy very soul will weep in the agony of despair. No, thou will not doubt the truth of hermetic wisdom at any time, but thine ability to acquire it only. Study, then, the principles of truth, not its phenomena only. For its own sake it is more to be desired than its works, and though usually less attractive to neophytes. Thy doubts will be born of an imperfect conception of thine own self—a want of perception of symmetry; giving undue proportion to certain facts, and upon finding these of less importance than thy conception of them originally painted, thy heart will fail thee, for in themselves they are great, and if comparison declares them small, what power shall grasp the greater? Then will it be that thou wilt fear thou art but finite, and these things infinite, and thou wilt say to thy soul: "My weakness is to these things as packthread wherewith to draw leviathan.'' But this is not so, for no creature is more than the Creator, and thou art of the Father and joint Creator with Him. What shall prevail? Only Faith like that of the Spirit that over lighteth Jesus and all them that triumph over time. Woe unto thee if thou shall faint while buffeting the billows of doubt. Miserably indeed is the lot of such a one, for, debarred from the society of the Brothers because of his faint heart, he is yet possessed of a knowledge of something purer, better, higher than the ordinary ambitions of humanity. After his glimpse into the greater possibilities of his being, he disdains to resume his former sense-relations with the world. He can not descend to the world's level, nor raise his fellow man to his own height. So through the rest of his life on earth he is alone. My friend. there is no solitude so drear as he hath who is in the world, but not of it. Wilt thou venture onwards, braving this peril? At this point there is yet a chance of return without incurring the danger which follows when further advanced. Set not thy hand to the plow if thou canst not go to the end of the furrow; it is long and difficult to follow. The world hath not so hard a task as this to impose in all its power. I offer thee option.''

Mendocus now watched me as I pondered the proposition. I felt that I could not in any event resume the old life; within me the fire was already alight, and the Sword of the Lord had cut off the old from the new, so that I felt it was between me and the past. No; ''Onward, Christian Soldier,'' must be my song leading to victory. I was decided in my mind, though I had not as yet said so; but I had no need to utter aloud my decision, although, forgetting this fact, I was about to do so, when Mendocus said:

''Thou hast, then, decided to go onward. I am sorrowful because of it. For though thou shalt come forth at last as gold burned in the fire, yet the ordeal confronting thee is fierce. But I will not allow that thy feet go alone; for that were unwise. I will so do for thee that the step be not irretrievable, lest it perchance be as I fear. O, Brother! I fear me woe is thine!''

After this decision I was required to take vows of secrecy, whereby I was bound not to reveal any part of what I should learn in any manner which might give the hearer of my words practical use of what I told him. I might drop a hint which might be followed as a clue to the Voiceless Silences to where blooms the Flower of Life; but, beyond a hint, my friend, I can tell you nothing. Of hints I have given many. Nor, were I to disregard my word, and divulge secrets of immediate working value, would you thank me. No, rather would you curse me. Why? Suppose we wit an instance: Suppose I were to reveal the secret of the Vis Mortuus, would you thank me? It is, I remember, that force which may be projected in all its fatal strength to any distance and which is personified in the famous poem, "The Destruction of Sennacherib"—in the line:

"The Angel of Death spread his wings on the blast."

Suppose I revealed that secret? How long would it be ere the world would find that the unscrupulous amongst men were using it to work undetectable murder? And its uses are many besides—for it is the principle in nature which governs transmutation, disintegration, decay, destruction, death. All these but never does it build anew—it is Siva, the Destroyer. Used aright, it is a beneficent force, for without it there would be no progress in nature, because no change could occur—there could not even be retrogression, but utter stagnation. Its sign is ⊕ Much as that means to me, it can be but a hint to you. Study it if you will, and one day it shall be revealed to you. In reason you can no longer ask why occult matters are so imperatively secret, for it must be evident that this fair earth would be made by the unscrupulous into a very hell of misery and crime, were they not thus secret. For a time those who chose to subvert their knowledge would seem to thrive and prosper, even though the world about them suffered. But subversion of the law is violation, and the penalty at last visited is in tenfold

degree upon those who went astray in their blindness and sin.
It would cause them to curse the giver of such wisdom. Nine-
tenths of the people of this world are unable to govern themselves well; they cannot in saneness expect to be made sharers
of such awful knowledge as Siva represents. Men and women
are really not following the Christ until every part of their
own nature is held in an iron grasp of merciless subjection to
high principles. But study, my friends, study. Christianize
the money power of this world, so that capital shall not work
harm to men but good, and from good thus born the karma of
the world will lead to the goodness of heart which gives calmness of soul; in that calmness your study will bear fruit, and
then it will not be a mockery, in seeming, of your hopes for me
to say "Study!" I rejoice in those earnest workers whose
motto is:—"Look up, not down; look out, not in; look forward, and not back, and lend a hand." Only this: the occult
student gazes in, and not out! But these are not esoterists.
Their name shall one day be great in the world, and though
you who desire to study and know occult truths now may not
see your hopes fruit in your present incarnation, yet in coming
lives you will grasp these truths which elude you at present.
Follow Him.

Before me, Mendocus, Master, had opened a view of life
so radically different from the old, restless existence, that
my heart grew warm, regardless of his prophecy that bitter
woe was perhaps to be my portion ere I could enter the haven
of my desires. The fact was that my optimistic nature deceived me with a hope that somehow I could manage to avoid
the threatened sorrow, and, having escaped its menace, could
go happily onward. Alas, poor me! I knew nothing of karma,
and in that day knew nothing of Zailm of Poseid. Else, had I
known, I would have trembled when the Master expressed his
fears for my sake. I saw before me a great ocean of wisdom,
flashing in the light of truth, its horizon defined only by the
voyager's temporary inability to go farther, its depth measur-
able only by that of the Universe. Free from the dogmatism of
cramping creeds, and of superstition, that ocean reaches out

into the eternity which enshrouds the stars as well as the dust in mystery—that mystery which veils the Creator from the created—veils it from the joint Creator, man, too, just so long as his soul shall lean to creation instead of to the Creator, his Father. Veils it until the aeons of time shall be swallowed up in eternity—beyond the stars, Earth, Venus, and Mars, when man shall cease to be man in becoming more than man, and Life the Less be gathered into Nirvana, sum of all the parts. I repeat it—sum of all the parts—for it is not in any wise that horrible cesation of being which Sanscrit scholars have interpreted the word "Nirvana" to mean. They have misconceived the facts; it is not the end of life, except Life the Less— any more than the statement "God is nothing" (that is, not one thing, but the sum of all things) should be construed as a denial of the being of God, the Eternal Father of Life.

A change had come over the Master. Up to the present his attention had been that of one controlling a process. Now, with his back to the shaft of the wheel of light, he stood beside the censer, looking upward, his gaze like that of one beholding a sight pleasing, yet absorbing. At last he bowed his head and said:

"Welcome Mol Lang, friend and brother!"

I saw no one, but was aware that the person addressed could not be one of the Sach. Mendocus, Master, turned to the brazier by his elbow and struck it lightly with his outspread fingers, whereupon the fire pan became red hot. Then he thrust his hand into a pouch depending from his waist and drew it out filled with a white powder, which he cast on the fire plate, producing a dense white smoke. I regarded this as a mere ceremonial offering of incense, and thought it savored of superstition, for I had now lost my intuitive perceptive power, and could only depend on conjecture. This idea was scarcely formed ere abandoned, for the cloud of smoke rapidly took the human form, into which the solid appearance of genuine personality was introduced as the incense consumed, until upon the glowing stand stood a man of commanding presence.

Some men seem to be not of any distinctive nationality, but very citizens of the world, or, even more largely, representatives of the race, and one feels that they might be of this world or of any other capable of supporting human life. Such was the man before us. He was addressed by Mendocus as, Mol Lang, of Pertoz;—and though I knew no such country, I unquestioningly accepted this appellation.

His deep-set eyes, under massive brows, and a head of similar contour to that of the philosopher Socrates; his snowy hair and long, white beard, together with a soldierly erectness of person, made Mol Lang, the Pertozian, the very personification of occult wisdom, from my point of view; nor was I far wrong. His turban, which in fact was blue, mottled with brown, seemed, chameleon like, to assume different colors as the vari-colored spokes of the wheel of light passed by, not through him, but he through them. He wore a long, gray robe, depending from the shoulders and belted at the waist. On his feet, of goodly, delicate shape, were sandals.

The Pertozian stooped and put his hand on the shoulder of the Master, making some remark, the import of which I did not catch, then stepped to the floor with a light bound, and with Mendocus went to the divan and sat down, engaging in an earnest conversation, which they held secret from the knowledge of the others. Do you ask where our clairaudient, mind reading ability was, that this converse should have been unknown to any of us? Unless one who knows that mind readers present are apt to exercise their ability, desires to have them share his thoughts, they can not. He preserves as an almost unconscious habit the mental desire of having his thoughts remain impenetrable, and to such a will no human power can pierce the barrier it sets.

At length they returned to our circle, and Mendocus seated himself with us. The visitor then said:

"Though the men of Lothus have known others of my fellow Pertozians, few heretofore have known me; none, indeed, but thy Master. I am come to induct one of thy number into the land of the departed, while another I take home with myself.

To you, Lothins, I need not say that the body is like unto a coat, to be put off or on at pleasure—by those who know how. I say this only for him known in the world as Walter Pierson—but unto me as Phylos. And some day the world will hear of him as Phylos the Thibetan, yet shall he not reside in Thibet in Asia, but shall be so called because he shall for a time live on the soul plane of the occult Adepts of Thibet. Unto thee, then, Phylos, I say when thou shalt be free of thy mundane body, then if thou wouldst go to any sphere of heaven, unto Neptune, or any planet or star, thou hast but to desire such transference of thyself, and it is accomplished. Wilt thou go with me this night, which is now nearly morning?"

Where was this I was asked to go? I knew not clearly whether he meant the soul realm, or in fact just where he did mean to go. But my faith was strong, and I replied:

"Whither thou goest, I go also, for I have faith in thee that thou wilt do me no hurt."

The faith inspired in that hour by the gentle dignity and kindly love I saw beaming from those deep-set, calm gray eyes, has known in all these subsequent years no cause for regret; nor for the action which my faith then inspired me to make, has this heart any but a feeling of supreme thankfulness that the Christ-Spirit then put it into my soul to have that faith. I fancy I hear some reader, timid at the prospect of trying the unknown—which might for all I knew at the moment include my corporeal death—saying: "How came it that you felt so sure of Mol Lang; did you not fear he was a devil?" No, I did not, for I was under the protection of goodly men, into whose midst no demon could enter more than night can reign beneath the noon-day sun. At least one of my protectors (Mendocus) had arrived at a finality so far as earth's present cyclic age can teach; the physical nature had no secrets from him; but the illimitable realms of the Father hold many "mansions" besides the universe of matter and the house of light, or the dwelling place of darkness. In this mansion of the material universe nothing remained for Mendocus to gain; he stayed but to give. Death had no power over him; he was supra-mundane, and until himself otherwise elected, he must live; only the word of God (the true Logos) by himself invoged could "loose the silver cord." Would you, protected by such an one, fear demoniacal influences? One other query of the multitude you may desire to ask, I will answer. You enquire how these highly favored ones of God can be certain of the truth of their intuitive perceptions—and I answer: the man who lives in his spiritual nature does not believe, but knows that his being is one with God the Father—the Great Parent. And his spirit speaks by the voice of intuition, informing him by a single flash of that which otherwise he would be long years in learning by external methods of investigation, if, indeed, externality could ever impart the knowledge. His spirit gives him from its own source—the Father—an effortless, instantaneous perception of facts, principles and things. I am reminded of the words of Mol Lang to me in this connection: "Phylos, some day thou wilt comprehend this:—Earth is a letter in a seven-fold alphabet; the stellar universe is but one book; its pages truly are myriad, its chapters legion, yet, besides this book, the library of the Creator is of endless number."

It occurred to me that we were the ones who should thank our visitor, and he not thank us at the conclusion of his remarks, for it seemed to me a lecture of wonderful power. A few minutes later he turned to me and said:

"Phylos, art thou ready to go with me now?"

I replied affirmatively, as did Quong, whom the visitor called Semla, when the same question was put to him.

Gravely the Brethren arose and took the hands of the Tchin in their own, as one by one they said to him,—as to one going into a far country to return not for years, and perhaps not forever—"Semla, may the peace of God attend thee evermore; fare thee well." Then Mendocus, Master, said:—"Semla, my peace I give unto thee."

I noted the difference in valedictory, and at another time asked of Mol Lang and received the explanation that while the Brethren could not give peace, not yet themselves perfectly possessing it, Mendocus, Master, having it himself could give it, especially to one who, like Semla, was so near its attainment. To all these Semla said, quietly:

"Peace do I wish thee."

To me no such farewells were accorded, for they said "We shall see thee here again." This to me was unpleasant, in the frame of mind I was in, but I concealed my feelings as well as I was able, and replied as kindly as they spoke. Then Mol Lang said "Come."

He started forward to the door of the Sagum, and I should have followed without looking back, had it not seemed as if some one touched me. Imagining that some Brother wished to speak with me and had thus called my attention, I turned and saw that which will never fade from the tablets of memory! Lying on the long, soft silk of the carpet was a human form. Looking more closely I saw that this was my own physical form—my body, my materiality, in short. In the act of raising it from the recumbent position were four of the brethren—two on each side. Others were doing a similar act for the corporeal shell of Semla. It was my consciousness that something was being done to my earthly body which I had mistaken for a touch. It had not occurred to me that I was divested of my mortal casket, so easy had been my disembodiment.

"Death is, after the agony of illness for those long sick, as easy and pleasant an experience," said Mol Lang, in answer to my mental reflection. "If thou wert not to re-enter thy corporeal body again, this would be death for thee,"—he added.

I was so greatly amazed at this last phenomenon that I stood still, saying nothing as I watched the bodies being removed from the main apartment and laid on couches in a smaller room. Mol Lang then remarked:

"Essentially this is death. Behold then, body death is but a casting aside of the grosser forms of life, which have served their purpose. As thou wilt return, this is not absolutely death for thee. Semla will not return. His body is therefore dead. When real death takes place, the gross body

is cast off, and the sword of the Lord ⚔ cuts it off, and Siva
⊕ takes possession of it and distributes it to the elements,
in order that Vishnu ⊘ may receive it for new uses from
Brahm ○ the Creator.   Then the soul is free for a great
length of time, compared to that spent on earth.   Though the
astral shell can come into spiritualistic circles and manifest
through mediums, yet the I AM comes not into any earthly
condition until it returns for reincarnation; and then always
on a higher, never on a lower plane of progress, still exists a
penalty of sin, or, what is the same thing:—incomplete sever-
ance of one's self from desires for earthly experiences.   Will ye
prefer Earth to Life?

"We go not immediately to mine own home, but into that
realm where those go who have died from earth into devachan—
that is, heaven, or the Summerland' of the 'Spiritualists,' or the
'Land of the Obb River,' or, again, to 'that bourne from whence
no traveller returns.'   Phylos, the sect known as 'Spiritualists'
are in error when they speak of 'spirit communion,' and regard it as they do, for no ego returns out of devachan except
it be forced, and this is harmful and vastly unjust to the ego*
The astral soul and animal principle may thus return, but the
I AM never.   To the latter there is no past earth state—mind,
I do not say for it, but to it.   That is, it has no consciousness
of anything earthly or of anything occurring on the earth.
We can go to them, but they can not come to us.   Let us,
then, go."

The mind works quickly, and ere we had reached the bronze
door, my consciousness had mastered the truth that death is
not in itself agony; that it brings no startling changes, and
does not invest the soul born into the hereafter with any wonderful power of foresight.   In fact, there is but freedom given
from the earthly body, and a few concomitant powers bestowed; nothing remarkable, considering that earth has no
more hold on the soul.   I speak of those who in mundane de-
cession seek disenthralment from earth, having but little love
for its conditions, though much love for its children.   Such as

---

*I Samuel xxviii, 14-15.

these have worked for their brethren and accumulated a good and high karma which takes them away from the prisoning conditions of earth.

Mol Lang here interrupted my reflections, saying

"One thing else; let us leave thy second self, that part of thee which perceives earthly things and preserves earthly memories. This in order that no disturbing comparisons may arise between that state into which thou goest and the earth behind thee, which thou shalt not see more than they can who really die. But between thee and earth will I preserve a vital link formed of thy second natural principle, so that it shall not be death to thee."

Then he said: "I believe I have no further use for this transient form."

Had an uninitiated observer then been present, the astonishing, not to say terrible, spectacle would have been presented to him or her of a man dissolving into smoke, for Mol Lang liberated the bonds of his smoke-form and it floated away in formless cloud.

Mol Lang laid his hand on my head, and as he took it away I no more remembered anything of the world. I dimly saw before me the bronze door of the Sagum; I knew that Mol Lang opened it, and that we three stepped forth, not into the long hall of the temple, but into an open expanse of green, sunlit meadow or prairie land. But it was no surprise, for I remembered nothing of any special features of earth life—I only knew that I was I, and that I was in a pleasant land—it was much like a vivid dream; no one in viewing a dream landscape is conscious of any other belonging to and seen only in waking hours; the faces in dreams are natural, not novel, not strange, and when seen are not compared with those known during wakefulness, for knowledge of the latter state is blotted out during sleep.

Mol Lang spoke:

"Thou hast come through the portal; lo! physical nature and laws do not reign here; they reign in the objective world, but not here, for this is the subjective world, in no sense physical or

existent, nor perceptible to senses belonging to matter. Yet
it is real, for Spirit is real, and subjective states, no less than
objective ones, are born of the Spirit of the Father. This is
another of the Mansions in His House. It is farther from the
earth than the farthest star of the sky, because in no wise of
material nature. Things of earth to the inhabitants of this
world are but dreams, and vice versa. To either, the other
seems unreal. This we are in is the 'Far away home of the
soul.' ''

I listened to Mol Lang and had ears to hear, so that I understood. Earth, of which he spoke, was vague, and knowledge
of it as an almost forgotten dream. And the vagueness was
because that principle of my terrene nature—which was the
seat of earthly sensing and of memories of things perceived
—was left with the body. This principle might visit a spiritist
medium and it would be called me. Yet it would not be me,
but my shell, my link of connection between my spirit and my
corporeal body. Friend, you will agree that an author is reflected in his autobiography; but that book is not the author.
No more is that which has its "actions, passions, beings, use
and end" in the body the MAN.   Yet that book may live and
guide men to action. So may the astral shell of a man or
woman who is dead. And the vitality of the medium may
galvanize that shell so long as its influence governs any living
earthly man or woman. Hence we see the phenomena of the
"circles" of believers in spirit communion. There is no return
of the ego (the I AM) to circles, neither communion from their
plane down, though sometimes from your plane up to theirs.
And yet you persist, my spiritist friends, in saying that I am in
error. You say that what I call "shells" can not be such because they tell of events after death. Yes; they do, I admit.
And they do because they are but records of the ego which
for a few brief moments at death is sometimes highly prophetic,
and sees forward over every detail—frequently for coming
centuries. Or again, the departing soul catches a glimpse of
its own self-conceived devachan, and the record of this is imparted to the shell, which carries such views to the spiritist

medium. Witness the often absurd description given of the character of the "spirit-world," and that through honest mediums, too. They give none of CHRIST, save where two or three are gathered in His name.

Mediumship is true; its ordinary explanation is false. The medium goes into a trance, his or her vital force is transferred to the "control" which is but a shell, and not the true spirit or ego. Then the hearers enjoy a "communication." Like a reader of a book of record is that medium; events of the past are retold, and more or less accurate prophecies made; the shell lives for the nonce a galvanic life; just as Poe lives anew in the person of an elocutionist rendering "The Raven," from the rostrum. Just so long as the "Commentaries" influence mankind, just that long will the "spirit" of Caesar control mediums; and while the Book of Mormon retains its hold on the deluded masses of Utah, so long will the "Prophet Joseph Smith" influence sensitives. But I grow prolix. Let us therefore turn to the world of effects, and see what it presented to our psychic perceptions. Will you come with us and see what we three saw as we went forth across the plain which confronted us at the door of the Sagum?

CHAPTER IV.

PAYING LIFE'S REWARDS.

"Phylos,"—said Mol Lang—"thou shalt now presently behold a man, all in a world of his own. He may not come to us, but we will go to him, and enter into perception of those things which he sees, and because we enter into his perception, therefore we shall be fellow spirits with him, not mere images of his conceptions. Then shall his environment seem as real to us as it does to him; nevertheless his world is (except for such visitors as ourselves, and those few, or perhaps many other souls who are on his identical plane) merely a world of his own conception; it exists not for him who is his neighbor, who will be, as we shall see, on a different psychic plane. Both persons will be existent in the Mansion of the Father, who thus giveth His beloved rest.

"Let us enter into the state of that man; he is an inventor from the world of cause, and all about him shall we find evidences of his inventive dreams—which here seem to be real to him. On earth, he in imagination beheld multitudes of his fellow beings using his adaptations of mechanical and natural forces. He had motor railways which were free to the public; none indisposed to pay were obliged to do so. And he had designs of coin, which the mint (owned by himself, as he had desired while on earth, so that he might correct abuses) minted free for use by the people. So also with all other things which he had hoped to see realized on earth. Yet he died without it, and coming to the world of effects, finds it all (to him only) a fact. We will walk across this plain to the grove yonder, a mile."

For some time after this we walked in silence, each content to note the beauty of the scenery. Gurgling brooks meandered through flowery meadows, groves dotted the perspective, while far away on the horizon was a line of blue hills. When we came to the grove designated by Mol Lang I saw that we were at a station, where cars of strange appearance stood on a net work of tracke. People were coming and going past this central point in all directions. The cars had immense spidery wheels, many yards across. A light flight of metal stairs led to the top of a tower; the tower was also an elevator, so that while some people walked up, others were hoisted to the top, where, several rods from the ground, they stepped into the body of the car; then an engineer on the car manipulated certain machinery, and the immense wheels began to revolve, swifter, swifter, and yet swifter; until the great, light vehicle could be seen moving at an amazing speed across the country, up and down hill or around curves with equal facility.

"Let us take a ride"—quoth Semla. So we walked up the spiral stairs, and there found a pleasant man in uniform, who asked if we would pay or not.

"Yes," said Mol Lang—"I will, but my friends will not." Thereupon he produced a coin of gold, and while the official was making the entry in his book, Mol Lang handed the coin to me to look at, and I saw that it bore a face of a man, and around the edge the superscription:

"MERTON FOWLER, THE PEOPLES' FRIEND."

"What conceit!" thought I, whereupon Mol Lang smiled slightly, took the coin from me and paid it over. The official asked where we would go, and for answer Mol Lang said:— "To the Falls." The official knew of no such place, but said that he would put us on a car, the engineer of which would know. He conducted us to a car on the other side of his platform, and having entered, we were soon speeding away like an arrow for swiftness. The stops which we made were numerous, all for the purpose, so the engineer explained, of complying with Merton Fowler's rule that all who rode on his cars must inspect his many inventions. The variety of these was bewildering to me, and so many of them seemed to be in operation solely for the purpose of demonstrating peculiar mechanical principles, that I will not consume space for description. At length, after travelling across half a world as it seemed, though not taking a tedious amount of time, we arrived at a splendid group of buildings. Then the engineer confessed that he knew nothing of the Falls, except that he had heard his master speak of them as existing. He would go to him. Accordingly the car ran up before an edifice which looked like an office, and there he put us in charge of another person with directions to take us to Merton Fowler.

That gentleman we found in a palatial environment, where things were of great beauty, but where all seemed to be mechanical contrivances, and to exist for that great underlying principle of the designer—the systematization of his knowledge, and the putting of it to more or less utilitarian uses. It was a very paradise for a machinist, but I was not a machinist, and it fatigued me. The number of people was amazing. Moi Lang said that not all of these were mere ideals of that prolific mind, Fowler, but that on the contrary, many of them were real personifications, a few of whom were media like ourselves, but the majority "dead"—that is, disembodied souls who were on the same plane of invention and realization as the real mind in control—Merton Fowler. He was the chief here, the others similars. I asked where the Falls were situated, and the inventor, Fowler, replied that a certain author of his acquaintance lived there, and had the pleasure of listening to a mammoth pipe organ made for him by the inventor—"By myself! All men whatever," said this egotist, "are beneficiaries of mine, and recognize me as the chiefest of human kind, and greatest of all living people!"

I turned away in contempt of such mammoth conceit and vanity, and as we left, Mol Lang said:

"That man is arranging his concepts of a Christless life as gained on earth. When all is assimilated, he will recarnify on earth, and from his early childhood self conceit and self admiration will be his ruling characteristics. In his last life on earth he sowed the seeds of the one to come. Here, he enjoys the growth of those seeds. Here, too, will the harvest mature, and when all gathered, he will take it to earth again to replant. Thou mightest ask what good cometh of perpetuating such vanity. I would reply: "First, 'tis the law of God. Secondly, out of his future egotism will arise self confidence. His spirituality of temperament is large, his animal qualities well balanced and strong, and the good of all his conceit will manifest itself next as a governor of those forces which will lead men forward. Ere he died on earth he was a retiring man, timid, feeling himself never appreciated. When he next appears there will be a strong soul, and a leader of men to higher levels of life."

"Truly,"—I said—"all things under the hand of God work together for good!"

The Falls were in the devachanic realm of an author, who, while on earth, was a very pleasing writer, albeit extravagantly

hopeful in his imaginative excursions and thought plays. This
was, indeed, doubtless the reason of his popularity as an
author. His mind dwelt on the sublime in nature, and on the
good, the true, and the beautiful. Here in his heaven he lived
his books, and found all about him the characters, the emotions,
the delicate imagery and the sublime beauty which made his
pages seem real to their readers, and over which tears of sympathy were shed by most perusers. To him also, these things—
figments of his imagination when penned, were here become
what his desire had always painted, realties, and he enjoyed
the seeming actuality, nor knew it but as a dream of his life's
night time. "Of what use, since it was only a dream?" I
answer—these glorious creations of the imagination all make
for that high spirituality, that keen sympathy of soul which
shall soon bring about the universal Brotherhood of Mankind—
it shall dawn with the dawning of the new century, creedless,
boundless, asking nothing of any affiliate except high, unfaltering aspiration and action. And this author, who has been in
his soul-home these many centuries, shall be one of its prophets,
recarnified.

We found the Falls in a vast gorge, deep as the Royal Gorge
of the Arkansas river. It connected two great lakes of rare
loveliness, not the Scottish lakes, or Lake Champlain are more
beautiful, though either were as great as Nyanza. Over a cliff
half a mile high, and, in the form of a double horse-shoe, each
more than a mile wide, were two magnificent falls of the river,
separated in the center where the middle points of the two
curves met, by an island. From this cliff rose three tall conical
needles of rock, up, up, up into the air, over a thousand feet
each one. Around each was a spiral stairway chiseled in the
enduring granite of the stream, and from top to top of each
swung a suspension bridge. From the one overhanging the
falls ran two suspension bridges swung on great cables, miles
long, reaching as they did the shores on either side of the river
by a diagonal course. I felt sure that the inventor—Merton
Fowler—would have conceived no such bridge, because his
mechanical training would have told him such lengthy bridge-

cables would break from their own weight. But this author, who was no engineer, saw no such difficulty, and consequently his concept found no bar to execution in his imagination. As it was not objective, but subjective, it existed for him, and as we were temporarily on his plane, and perceiving through his senses, we also saw them and found them real; and to all on his plane they were real—subjectively real. But earthly eyes could not have seen them, for they see nothing except objective realties. And both states are real, but to those on the respective planes only. If the things of the spiritual are foolishness to the natural man, so are the things of the natural world to the devachanee. But I digress. The myriads of people, creations of the author's mind, used his bridge; they lived in a Utopia of his creation, and the whole was a very heaven. It all nurtured his spirituality, his reverence for God, his constructive sense even, as well as his sense of sublimity. His soul has almost assimilated the whole of these "steps toward God" and it is almost ready to recarnify as one of the deeply artistic, constructive, reverential souls of earth; one of the nobly beautiful, Godward turning leaders of the race. Is he not a worker for the Father? "By their works ye shall know them." And while and because he leads, he himself will draw nearer with every passing hour to God; nearer to Nirvana, that glorious resting time of all the lives, out of which the spirit of man shall awake to find itself more than Man, find itself one of these sublime World-Spirits whose glittering forms fill the skies of night! Or servers of the Father in some other untellable way.

———————

The fact must be sufficiently obvious that the life between the grave and the cradle—life in the world of effects—is a life of assimilation of results due to causes set in operation while on earth—the world of casuality. It is the character forming realm, where effects are so arranged as to present them as causes in the succeeding earth life; not in the shape of segregate influences, but as traits of character, giving rise to well defined policies in life on the part of individuals. Like attracts like, and if parents have certain influences governing their lives at critical times, the soul in devachan, which is perforce seeking re-birth on earth, will seize the opportunity presented of finding its similars—similars at that time, though perhaps at that time only, like itself, but never so before, possibly never to be so again; suffice it if there be a concordant trinity at the time. There is no accident, no chance, in the Universe; all is immutable law, cause and effect. Zerah Colburn, whose precocity in mathematics while he was yet a little boy amazed the world, did not inherit his powers of calculation. Mozart did not inherit what neither of his parents possessed, though it is true that the maternal mind did provide attractive mental similarity by her own love for music, prenatally experienced. Atavism has been invoked to explain these cases of infantile precocity when it has been well known that neither parent had the traits which seem to have been passed to the offspring. But atavism will not wholly suffice. The question of heredity is a deep one; parents are moved by special influences, and children of that time are souls attracted from devachan to their mental similars. Such was the young Zerah Colburn; such the infant prodigy, Mozart. Zailm Numinos might have told you that Colburn was a noted Atlantean mathematician had he not neglected it in his history of Atl. And Mozart was Alcman, the poet and lyrist of Spartan Greece.

———————

Night seemed to be coming on; the air was pleasantly cool, and we found ourselves, after a long sail on a lovely body of water, standing on a shore whose sands and pebbles were of agate. Bamboo fringed the lake margin, and many graceful houses in quiet nooks dotted the varied landscape. The country bore some resemblance to the land of Japan, and indeed we found that we were in the concepts of an American who had resided for many years in Japan ere his entrance to devachan.

We went into a spacious veranda of a house of fine appearance, which in architectural style was a general combination of things, most comfortable. Contrary to Japanese customs, we found easy chairs instead of mats or rugs, and in these chairs we took seats, Mol Lang saying we would be welcome to do so. Ere long a servitor in Japanese costume appeared, and placed a table before us, and upon it laid covers for five persons. Presently a handsome, elderly man, with a young girl, who, I judged, was his daughter, came out of the residence, and exchanged salutations with us, after the manner of true gentlefolk. This was, as Mol Lang afterward explained, the real ego about whose imagery all things in this place clustered. The lake, the tropical vegetation, the remodeled Japanese people whom we met—in short, all effects here, were arranged in accord with this man's ideals. In them he saw realized his dreams of a quiet, care-free, hospitable life, and because he saw them, we also saw them, for Mol Lang had insinuated our perceptions into this man's soul plane. With him we partook of a generous supper. Liquors were not on his table, nor could any have been found in all that soul land, for the man was a total abstainer. Of course, the people whom he believed he saw, and who, for him, resided in this, his country, used no liquors more than he, for they were either his imagination's concepts, or, if real individuals, were in sympathy with the master mind— else they had not been there with him. But all this he knew not any more than one who in slumber dreams, knows at the time that the vivid dream personages and places exist solely for himself. Sometimes, truly, a night dreamer really goes away with another harmonious soul, the two being real souls on a psychic journey, it being no dream, but a fact.

This man, in all of his princely extravagance, his artistically beautiful buildings, the richness of raiment of the people whom he conceived, the statues, fountains, groves, all things—was but quaffing imagined joys, wholly unconscious the while that they were subjective creations. They were all conceived for a single purpose, pursuit of which formed his chief joy—that of caring for the happiness of his daughter. She was his idol, his joy, his reason for being, he would have said. And she was a pretty girl, though not to my mind beautiful. She was engaging, witty, well educated, and accomplished. But I have seen many such, and thought of her as only one of hundreds I had known. We were invited to stay indefinitely in this home, and, upon Mol Langs' suggestion, accepted the offer. Days passed rapidly in this paradise, of which our host's home was the central attraction. He had great parks, and gave splendid entertainments to scores of happy people. His house was a palace in itself. The libraries, the art gallery, with thousands of fine paintings, all this, and more, made life so pleasant that several months had elapsed ere our party of three bade him adieu. In it all we saw that the gay life was for the sake of the daughter, and held little pleasure for the father. The art gallery, too, was added to his home for her sake. The libraries were for both, and, as he said, he thought he took more pleasure in books than she did; to him books were sacred treasures. But it was in music that his soul found ecstatic rest. Such divine melodies and such exquisite technique and feeling as he exhibited in his rendition of fine music I had never even dreamed of, much excellent music as I had heard. It was as the fable of Orpheus come true. Hour after hour he played for me, while Semla was away with Mol Lang, and my soul responded in a thrill which swept it with sublime joy, until it seemed as if my being had become a personless, throbbing, sobbing stress of harmony, that could flee on the winds and set the souls of men pulsing, beating in unison! I knew that the player was a companion to me in it all. We were two souls on the same plane, reaping identical experiences.

At last a day came when Mol Lang said:—"My friends, let us go hence, for other things claim our attention. A few hours here must suffice us. We will go where the daughter of this man really is."

My friend had, I thought, spoken of the months of our tarrying in this paradise in a figurative sense when he said "a few hours." But he had not; it was really only a few hours as the people on earth had counted the safe interval through which we had so recently passed. Time is, after all, only a measure of so much done by or to him who experiences its lapse,— myriads of people have lived a whole century during ten minutes of other people's time. Mol Lang's remark about our being ready to go where the daughter really was I could not comprehend at the time, nor did I know for years—all because my own astral had been left behind in the Sakaza on earth; I had no means of comparison of ideas. The place I was in was the only place existent for me—that is, it and the country of the author and that of the inventor, Fowler. These I know of, and for them a memory shell had been formed by me as I went through them; not that I was conscious of such a process of creation; I was only aware of the memories which were retained for me, and which seemed part of myself. But Mol Lang explained only that the American really had not his daughter with him, but only his ideal of her ever before him.

On our departure we went down to the lake and got into a boat, and as we traveled, somehow it seemed as if, without my knowing just how or when, we had left the boat and the lake, and were in a garden, walking amidst a profusion of flowers. It was unaccountable, but did not particularly surprise me, nor long occupy my attention. No one is ever astonished at anything in the psychic realm.

It was a city garden, and, situated on an eminence, the residence of the owner commanded the view of a great city, extending in all directions. The house was evidently the home of a person of refinement, and while evidences of wealth were numerous, these seemed to be adjuncts of comfort, instead of a display of riches. No person could long be amidst the influences of that home, to which Mol Lang admitted us, without feeling that the owner believed herself to have a great and sacred mission in life.

"This is the daughter," said Mol Lang. "The girl whom we saw in the other home was the daughter, as the father imagined her to be when he died, leaving her at that age. See how different is the woman from his conception of her. I bring thee here that thou mayst see what difference exists between the devachanic conceps of the soul and the objects conceived of. It illustrates the saying that 'heaven is what we make it.'

At that moment a lady entered the room, evidently on business; her manner was full of power. She seemed not to perceive us, and after a little I coughed slightly to attract her attention. Mol Lang smiled in amusement, as he said:

"Phylos, thou mightest cough long, and she would not know of thy presence. Why? Because we are temporarily on the earth, and I have given thee power to see earthly conditions—that is, while we are on the earth—for it might be all about us, yet if we were in a different psychic condition, the earth would not be near, but vastly remote from us. This lady has not yet come to the change called death. She is one who labors to place woman on the proud basis of independence—proud, because rightfully hers. But woman will never attain to it until she does so by self-effort; nothing is won worth the having except by self-effort. When she so wins it, she will be by the side of man, not above him, for woman is not man's superior; neither below him, for she is not his inferior; but beside him, for man and woman are equal in all things. It will be a blessed day for humanity when this time comes. This lady and her sister workers are now guiding those dwellers of the earth who have not such clear understanding of the needs of the times; and they will succeed, more or less, during this century, but not brilliantly, since no great reform, nor anything greatly good, can succeed in any century, decade or year nominated by the number nine. Hence, human hopes will wax or wane, will seem to go forth to victory, but will meet only failure until the new century. Darkest of all the years will that be which is just before the dawn. This brave leader we see here will see Hope set in that last year like a star in the west, and she will die then, despairing, though hoping, with prophetic Mackay, that 'Ever the truth comes uppermost, and ever is justice done.' "

For a considerable time after this we were silent, for Mol Lang seldom spoke without definite cause, and it now served his purpose better to be silent. I spoke next:

"What good can it be, what good can be achieved through such bitter disappointment? Such heartache?"

"That which cometh ever from all things. "Man never is, but always to be blest,' is wholly true. And it is not form the hopes we are able to bring to realization in earth life that our devachan, our heaven, is made; but from those hopes, longings, aspirations and determinations which through life are our dearest desires because we have never been able to satisfy them. They have the most happy heaven whose high-soaring souls have ever been forced to be content with the mere view of Caanan from their mountain lookouts. Let no poor, disappointed soul on earth mourn because of life's unsatisfied longings, for we do not know to-day whether we are busy or idle. In times when we have thought ourselves indolent, we have afterward discovered that much was accomplished and much was begun in us. These beginnings are fruitful, indeed, for they bestow upon us our longed-for aspirations, 'over there' if we will, in His way."

During this discourse of Mol Lang I had glimpses of the whole—both of earth and of heaven. A thing which struck me with a feeling of peculiar anguish was that that gentle soul who thought he lived for his daughter, really had not that daughter with him, but only his self-created image of her. I had not thought of the fact that even on earth we do not have our friends, but only our concepts of them; that our supposed friend may really be our secret enemy, but if we know it not, we remain happy in our ignorance. Mol Lang observed the feeling on my part, and said, as he turned and placed an arm around me as we walked onwards:

"Phylos, beloved son, feel not so! When the day cometh when this lady shall enter the devachanic life, then whenever and wherever she has ideals and concepts like those of her father, or he like hers, then will they two be really together, 'two souls with but a single thought.' It is the same on earth; only identity of thought makes nearness of souls. As the grand march of souls following after Christ draws nearer unto God, those planes where all souls are together in the thought and concept will be the planes mainly occupied by humanity, till at the glorious last, none shall be apart from any other, or from the Father.''

———————

The room and its earnest worker had faded from view. Instead of it we found that in front of us was a monastic edifice, set on a lofty mountain peak which arose from a lake. Dim vistas of water, of wooded shores and silvery, shadowy isles were in perspective. Over the tower which rose from the monastery was a flashing crescent of purple light. I asked what place we were now come to. The answer was:

"The Lunar Temple,—a part of devachan, but having nothing to do with the moon. Here, where many occult students come after laying aside the earthly body, is a holy place of rest. Here are many theosophic adepts and neophytes; they saw them with eyes of spirit, hence had then, as now, much the same concepts of life; devachan to them is not, therefore, on the same plane as with other mortals, any more than their objective life was. Here Semla takes leave of us, to appear no more on earth until after fifty centuries of mundane time. He will then incarnate, not as a Tchin, but as a member of the American Nation of that far distant day, because his life has been mostly spent in that land this time. But now he enters into rest he has earned; this is his devachan.''

There, under the flashing purple light from the monastic tower, Semla took his leave, invoking upon us the peace of the Father.

Through ability conferred by Mol Lang, I had seen the nature of the life after death. For a few moments my soul was able to compare the newly gained knowledge with my old time ideals of nature. I thought—"If all this is but a dream, what is a dream? If this which seems real matter is not such—''

"Nay, my son,''—interjected Mol Lang, as I thought upon the nature of matter—"this is real matter. Why, what is matter, dost thou think? Matter is a One Substantially, having not a single quality which any human sense can cognize. But

force also is one of the creations of the Father. And force hath
two polarities—the positive and the negative—absolute oppo-
sites. Now man on earth hath certain senses; seven are these
senses—sight, hearing, feeling, smelling, tasting, intuition, and
one innominate. These last are not yet evolved, for the fullness of days is not come; the Fifth Day is; but the Sixth and
the Seventh are not. With the last, man becometh greater than
he hath ever been. Only they that have ears that hear shall
solve this saying. Five senses cognize the positive dynamic
affections of matter by Force—and behold, man senseth the
earth and some of the stellar bodies. But all these are of the
positive, and hence are in the Father's Mansion of Cause.
These five senses are what the Apostle Paul called the 'Natural
mind.' But 'In my Father's house are many mansions.' And
this—which is the briefer life after the grave, is His Mansion
of effects, and it is the result of matter affected by negative
force. Here the first five senses call all things pertaining to
devachan 'mere dreams;' even wise Hamlet asks, 'What dreams
may come?' But I say unto thee—both earth (cause) and devachan (effect) are material; both due in their every phenomena
to force—but either state is cognizable only by senses special
to it. Man in one hath five special senses, and these know the
earth, but call heaven a dream; and Man in the other hath
other seven special senses, and these know of devachan, but
call earth a dream. Yet both states are really material, and
similarly, both are unreal, except to the Father. So Man is
constantly dying from the one state and being born in the
other, back and forth, and only that state where he is, is real
to him at any time. Myriad times does he repeat the process,
incarnifying and discarnifying, and each time of rebirth on the
earth finds him ever on a higher plane, until at last the concrete
condition miscalled life is over, and the conditionless 'long
devachan' (Nirvana) is attained. Then man and his Father
are together and at-one. Man came from God; unto Him must
he go. But only a few have done this as yet, and of these Jesus
Christ of Beth-le-hem is so far the only One who can truly
say, 'I and my Father are one.' "

Mol Lang had no desire that I should continuously retain the memories of the experiences just passed through; the separate facts were to become quite as unknown as if never observed. All was solely for the purpose of surrounding my soul with influences calculated to force me upward and onward, out of earth life, or desire for it, until at last I would come to realize that I had known something higher, and must return to the plane of the spiritual nature. Yes, the word is MUST.

After leaving Semla, with the new life open to him, Mol Lang and myself sought the lake, and after taking our seats on a bit of sandy shore, I asked questions as to the appearance of the scheme of creation to occult perceptions. It seemed to me that life must have a wider significance to him than to me.

"Phylos, it hath. Grand as the vision of life seemeth to the ordinary man, made up, as it is, of his few years on earth, supposedly followed by unending existence in heaven, to me it is infinitely more sublime than even earth's loftiest vision can present it! Man's ideas are full of error; they involve the childishness of admitting that in the life on earth the multitudes who 'make in their dwellings a transient abode' are in the course of such a finite time, able to set in motion infinite causes which shall be carried out in psychic effects eternally. Only through the Great Master are any so able.

"I have so willed, my son, that the features of this visit to devachan shall be withdrawn from thee, and thou wilt remember them only as a vague, delightful dream, which shall have influence in leading thee to the pinnacles of the Father, and the summits of the soul. It is easy to erase these memories; I have but to disassociate the astral body here formed by thine experiences, and thou wilt thereafter know this state only when that astral shall control thee as its medium. I will take thee to mine own home in Hesper, and there thou wilt come to know my son, whose name is Sohma, and my daughter Phyris. Yet that knowledge also will I dissociate, after the time of it, and thou wilt forget it all; yea, even me wilt thou forget, and know only through the same mediumship, because thy karma orders for thee long years yet to come on earth, and atonement for evil works which have cried unto God for redress, lo! a century of centuries, and longer. Christ hath said:—'One jot or one tittle shall in no wise pass from the law till all be fulfilled.' Save thou be re-leased to Him.

"But thou hast asked a question. Hear the answer:—I sow a seed, and it shall grow, and blossom and fruit, and though the sower be forgotten, the plant will not be. Thou wilt remember my words forever, nor forget them for one hour, for such is my will—yet for get me wholly.

"Besides the heavenly world, there are many more which are imperceptible to men. Yet matter and force compose them all. Many of them are worlds of Cause, but no merely human being is in them, nor can any earthly sense cognize them, or know of them. They are peopled, but by beings of whom some are good, and some are evil; in the sight of the Eternal Cause, relatively good or evil. That which exists under laws inimical to man is evil to man, though not in itself evil. But these 'mansions' are set apart from one another that they may not interfere. There is that which is astray, but in itself not evil, for in all the creation there is no evil eternal, for God is perfect.

"The worlds of human life are seven in number; yet four of them are invisible, unknowable to earthly senses, and this not because of remoteness, but the kind of force-affection of their constituent matter. Mankind occupies but one planet at a time, for like its present dwelling place (earth) the human race is but a letter in the Divine Library of Being. To be exact, the more advanced, occult souls do inhabit Venus, which I have called Hesper, and which was by the ancients of the Earth termed 'The Garden of the Hesperides.'

"Yes, Phylos, life does mean more to me than to thee. I look at its stately march, and I see the battalion of being wherein I am but a corporal, progressing around its appointed seven spheres, whereof only Mars, the Earth and Venus are matters which terrene perception can know; I see the human race progressively incarnating on each of its peculiar planets as it goes, every individual ego about eight hundred times, approximately, on each world each time the race comes to it, which is seven times also, making forty-nine world-carnate epochs. Each ego thus hath incarnation and discarnation periods to the number, more or less, of forty thousand. It is in these, that beginning as an irresponsible creation, far from human, as thou wouldst define the word 'human,' and ending as a Perfect Man entering into Nirvanic rest—that the scheme of the Eternal Uncreated Father is perfected. Yea, verily, man sins, but as his incarnations progress, he atones for every jot, every tittle. Karma is penalty for evil doing, and it is the law of God; it knows no abatement of payment, accepts no vicarious price, but is faithful gaoler over that prison which is life-action; whoso is cast therein shall not come out till every farthing is paid. Beware, then, of doing wrong, for thou must bear the penalty, only thou. Verily, life is long enough to make payment; 'tis better to have none to make!*

"We go now to a view of the truth that the spirit came from the Father, and returneth to Him after it hath fulfilled the law and the prophets; it liveth in the worlds of cause a short span, but in those of effect a long span, for passivity is to activity as about eighty to one, and the lives are many, strung like beads on the one cord of the individual ego.

"Lastly, the ego coming from the Father hath no sex; it is not man, neither woman, but sexless. When it entereth upon life it becometh double, so that in the earth there is a man, and there is a woman, and though the bodies and the animal souls and the human souls be different in the twain, yet behold, their spirit is one and the same. Now sometimes the two, being of one spirit, are also husband and wife. Yet more often, they are not, for the age of harmony is not yet at hand. But it is of such singleness of spirit that the Bible saith, 'What God hath joined, let no man put asunder.' There is no man who could, if he would, so sunder. But that saying is not of the carnal marriage, but of the spirit unit only. And the latter hath no lust. But when the twain shall, after the millions of years which lie between the non-esoteric Christian and Nirvana, come to know all the law of life, then will the union be as it was be-fore the separation. Thou canst not really comprehend the truth now, but when thou shalt at last be done with earth life, thou wilt then recall it and know. And knowing it, thou wilt then tell the world of it. But not now. Now is this true—Mates in the Lord can not know each other as such, until they both will to live after the rule of His Highway. And the lat-ter hath nothing carnal. 'Straight is the Gate and narrow is the Way that leadeth unto Life, and few there be that find it.' Until they find it they find not each other; neither release from incarnation in the flesh.''

Mol Lang arose after this long discourse, wherein he had briefly described the works of God. He said:

"I have answered thee. Come, let us go hence, and thou shalt know my son, and my daughter, and my home.''

He laid his hand upon my brow, and I seemed to sleep; when I was again conscious we were in an immense garden, and before us I saw a house which at once impressed me as being a real home. This I say because somehow occult study had seemed foreign to home life and influences. How entirely com-patible the two are will appear nearer the end of this history.

I found on acquaintance with it that it bore out my first impressions perfectly, for it was the most genuine home that could well exist, and typified all human life in this world of Cause—Hesper. It was a home of human glorified beings, of occult students incarnate in exalted casual life.

Do you ask me how any portion of the human race came to be so far in the van as the Hesperian contingent? The answer is that their septune natures had been so far perfected by the trials to which the study of occult adeptism subjects its initi-ates, that they had become enlightened, responsible beings; they had drank of the cup concerning which Jesus inquired of the children of Zebedee if they had the ability to drink it. And in consequence there had come to them the keys to that realm of spirit which no natural mind can understand. They had learned the seven-fold character of their natures—that man is a composite being, having seven principles, viz:—the I AM, or ego; the body of the spirit, or spirit-body; the human soul; the animal soul; the astral reflection of the two lowest princi ples—by name, vital force and the earthly body thereby animated. Thus far, I regret to say, the mass of mankind is not developed much beyond its animal soul; a minority have the human soul shining forth; but only occult adepts have the Sixth or spirit-body developed, while none of whom the world knows except Jesus and Buddha are perfect in the Spirit of the Father.

With Mol Lang I stood, looking upon his home in Venus, the world to which Terre's children will come, leaving it deserted until another round shall return them, although on a higher plane—that of perfect love. "The greatest thing in the world." But now Hesper is the planet of this Christ-like love, its home in the course of nature and man's development. Ye will not all come, alas!

"Phylos,"—said Mol Lang—"my son is of nearly thine own number of years; my daughter Phyris is of the same age as thyself. Both will tell thee of occult truths, as I have done, yet they nor I, nor aught but the intuitions from thine own God-given Spirit can teach thee. If a soul hath not in itself perception of God and His works, no man can teach it, for having ears to hear and eyes to see, he heareth and seeth, but comprehendeth not. To me it is given of God to show thee and tell thee of those things which many prophets and righteous men have desired to see and to hear, but have not. Blessed are thine eyes, for they see, and thine ears, for they hear. Yet, nevertheless, thou wilt go again to earth, and wilt forget, and restlessly long for a better state, yet shalt not find it again for long years. O Phylos, my son, would that thou couldst even now know! But karma pursueth thee, seeking repayment. And karma shalt have its dues, and thou wilt then go free. Let us pray unto God now, for I speak no more of these things; I have spoken already. Here- after Phyris shall tell thee and show thee in my place."

Then, in that Hesperian garden, we knelt together, and Mol Lang repeated that eloquent voice of the ages, so old, yet ever new—the prayer of our Savior. I think tears were in our eyes when we arose. Turning, I beheld a lovely woman.

"Phyris, my child, he is come! Phylos, this is my daughter, of whom I told thee."

It had so surprised me to hear a man who had so much of what untaught fancy calls God-like power speak of his children that Mol Lang had said to me, in comment:

"Phylos, thinkest thou that because I have wisdom which thou hast conceived only God to possess, that I am not human? My son, I am more wholly and truly human because thus near unto God. But the mass of people on earth are not fully developed even yet in the human principle—their lives, actions, passions, are centered in the Fourth or animal soul, and only the more exalted are come to the development of the human within them. When mankind shall come fully into its humanity, then Earth can no more be its planet; they must come here. Bear in mind ever, that all thou seest in Hesper is but human, and so thou wilt know more of what Man is, how glorious a being he is. Man is only partially human, and not filled with the Father, nor come into his Spirit body, and he must therefore marry and live in marriage, else the race would cease to reincarnate. Each ego must pay its debts. But many will die debtors to Him.

We three, father, daughter, and myself, went into one of the wide porticos of the brown Parthenon like mansion, and sat down, being where we could see over the profusion of flowers in the great gardens. So beautiful was the scene, both near and far, that I was content thus to remain, unmoving. Here was no devachan, no scene of effects, but an active life in a world of cause.

This life differed from that upon earth in being broader, more perfect, more glorious than terrene conditions can produce in the present round. Ordinary life in Hesperus is all that the highest form of life can be on earth; and thus has all the wonderful development which exists in the midst of the secret occult brotherhoods of Earth. It is impossible to express adequately what perfection of physical life exists in Hesperus. But it is a perfection of the physical nature, amid ideal surroundings, all of which prepare the animal man to work for the human man, and he for the Spirit man —the I AM, or ego. Thus does the ego progress through matter. Is it not a sublime thought that reincarnation does not mean transmigration of souls? The first leads man ever up; the other—which is false, even in theory, merely a perverted notion of the first—might mean progress, but more often would mean retrogression, and in all this Universe there is no retrogression. Reincarnation is but a chance to expiate the errors of life, chiefest of which is not overcoming and containing self, Will ye not pay? Then are ye doomed!

CHAPTER V.

HUMAN LIFE ON VENUS.

"It is good to be at home again,"—said Mol Lang,—"I love my home because here are my friends, and here is the congenial atmosphere of spirtuality. I see about me the environs of my last objective incarnation—this present. For me there is no more birth, and no death of the body except through transition of the Logos. Here I passed the ordeal of the crisis and am become androgynous, for in me now are the feminine and the masculine; I am whole, not half, and I and my egoic mate are one individual. We twin are one, and have come unto the Spirit in the sense uttered by the Saviour when He said, 'Be ye therefore perfect, even as thy Father is perfect.' And thou, my son Phylos, wilt surely come into this same glory, for by thy karma it is so fixed. Yes,"—said he, reverting to his first thought,—"it is good to be at home."

The old man arose from his seat and paced with stately erectness up and down the veranda. "Old?" Yes, as earth counts age, for Pertoz he was just in early prime, not yet come to his two hundredth year by some forty-eight months And age could never affect him more, for he was come to deathlessness; to bodily immortality. Of him, as of many, are the words of the beloved apostle, John.* At that moment he was in his astral form, his physical body being in his sleeping room, where he left it, in order to cross interplanetary space for me. Curious thought! An inhabitant of Venus able to visit earth at will! Yet it is not really difficult. It merely involves the leaving of the physical body and plane at one point, and entrance to the astral, or psychic plane. From this latter it is as easy to return to the state of cause at any point—be it Alcyone, chief of the "Pleiads, glittering in their eternal depths," or even further, beyond ken of the telescope —as it is to return to the place departed from. The whole difficulty is in leaving the physical plane at all, and for the advanced esoterist this is as nothing, because the normal state of his soul is always in the astral or psychic, instead of the physical. The difficulty with a student is in the repugnance he feels to the thought of returning to an inferior state of being, like life on earth. But the Life of Love is: "I serve." So we return.

That we were in the astral, disembodied state was no hindrance to Phyris' perception of us, for like all Hesperians she had the sight of the soul as you have ordinary sight—a mere commonplace power. Her eyes, as indeed those of all souls on this high plane of being, have psychic clairvoyance as a normal possession, though not the less endowed with ordinary physical vision on this account. As in the long ago of Earth, her eyes were still the same clear, calm gray—the kind possessed by Jesus of Nazareth. They were windows for her pure soul, which seemed to be just behind them, gazing out. This slender, graceful girl was no devachanic ideal, although not gross enough to be visible to eyes used only to perception of objective, earthly states of matter; her sweet, grave demeanor, her light laugh at something said by Mol Lang, her perfection of physical life—all breathed the fact

NOTE.—Kindly see St. John xvii. 21-26.

of her objective being, and bore evidence to the truth that
her rule of life was obedience to the law. And yet I doubt
if your eyes, my friends, could have seen her at all. No telescope will ever reveal human life on Venus; not that it is not
there, but its forms are of the One Substance effected by a
range of force rendering them imperceptible to earthly eyes.
You will not think the air any less material, or electricity any
less real, because your eyes cannot perceive them. Your eyes
are very limited in their visual range; if the One Substance
vibrates more or less rapidly than an exceedingly small length
of time, producing correspondingly minute force wave-
lengths, your eyes cannot cognize such vibrations. It is the
same with your ears and hearing. If your eyes and ears were
not thus limited, you would see every sound and hear every
sunbeam. Every rainbow would be vocal, while heat, which
now you only feel, would furnish amazing wealth of sound
and vision. So it is with the Hesperian people—their persons you could not see, their voices you could not hear, yet
they would not be similarly limited in regard to your persons
and voices. But so long as you fancy that because you have
eyes you can see all that there is to be seen, and that your
ears hear all that is worth hearing, so long will you depend on
these organs, and gain that sort of false ideas of the Universe
which must arise from entire ignorance of all except the tiny
bit of creation you occupy. So long, too, will you depend on
the telescope to reveal truths about other worlds; you will
hunt for evidences of human life on the nearer planets, but
you will never find any until you cease to expect that matter
will reveal soul; it can not do it, for the finite can not reveal
infinity. Turn it about; ask of the soul revealment of itself
and of matter also, and all worlds will draw near to you,
show their teeming vitality of life, and all nature will uncover such treasures as the hungry soul of science has never
found before.

Phyris was able to look over all my past—over the other
lives which I had yet to attain the power of re-collecting.
She knew every deed, thought and motive of it all. Had she

cared to examine this history? No fear existed in my mind, for I did not know of such a past myself, and my ignorance preserved my peace of mind. I did not try to analyze the reason for my eager desire to win this maiden's good opinion. If I had, I should have railed at myself for a presumptuous fool. As it was, I was happy in the knowledge of my purity of purpose.

Though dissociated from earth life, my soul development was but little more than before. Therefore, to me, Phyris seemed a sort of goddess; and to have estimated only as perfect human, herself and her wondrous occult powers, would have been an impossibility with me. To have found that I was in love with her would have frightened me. I am glad that I was then prevented that thought. But deep in my soul it was true, nevertheless, and the leaven was working. Closer knowledge was not to have the effect of detracting from her exalted position; but it to raise me to the understanding that these psychic powers were attributes of human nature, for in itself human nature is essentially God-like.

By the way, what is the mundane idea of God? You say that God is omnipotent, omnipresent, eternal. Very good. But the earthly idea of these things is very narrow. Conceptions can never rise higher than their source, hence God is, although a noble ideal, not nearly so great to the world as He is to Hesperus. Do you say that I am inconsistent, denying my own high claims for Man, and that I am virtually negativing the statement that conceptions can rise to the level of their source? I reply that the Father limits the height of the source. "What do I mean?" I mean that He speaks to the but partially developed human soul on the earth plane from the level of human principle in Himself, but from no higher plane. Hence, the terrene conception of Him is that of a perfect Person, all-powerful, ubiquitous, eternal, but a person; whereas He is impersonal. But to the Hesperian, God speaks of Himself and His works from the level of Spirit, which is above soul—it is the level of the Over-Soul of Emerson. I hope you will study that statement, for nothing I have said means more, is more important in all this book.

I have said that the earthly conceptions of omnipotence, omnipresence and eternity are narrow. It is true. The first means only the most extravagant exercise or suspension of known laws, but scouts the existence of fearful, wonderful, unknown laws. Omnipresence means to the non-occult mind a variety of vague, impracticable ideas, only the few recognizing it as immanency and constant self insertion and creation. Finally, eternity; the mind readily agrees to unlimited, endless time, yet is aghast at a mere decillion, almost refusing credence. Yet one is to the other as all to nothing.

At the time I first met Phyris my ideas of God were similarly limited, and when I saw her exercise powers which no terrestrial man ever dreamed that even God could possess, I was truly aghast. Love her? Not then. Respect her, adore her, as a Hindoo does an image of his God—yes. But the seed was sown; it groweth sure.

Mol Lang left me in the large parlor of his home, whither we three had gone, and when only Phyris was here besides myself, I immediately was constrained by a diffident fear of my gentle hostess. Although she soon dispelled this feeling I nevertheless felt relieved when a young man entered and she introduced me to—

"My brother, Sohma."

As I looked upon the two, and remembered Mol Lang's appearance, I thought:—"What splendid physique these people have—how graceful and perfect every line; it is as if the body were moulded upon the soul, and perfect in its every physical contact."

"Yes, thou art right in thy thoughts," said Sohma. He had replied to my thought, as Mol Lang and Phyris had: "Thou art right. We make our physical lives correspond to our rigid adherence to law, though that adherence is to us a second nature, not onerous, nor even in its exercise consciously applied. Excesses, intemperance, indulgence of that nature so pleasant to the animal senses—these have no attraction, but instead are utterly repugnant. Vegetarians strictly, never taking life for any selfish purpose—is it wonderful that our material frames conform to our soul shapes?"

"Truly not"—I replied—"but in my case how could conformity to law change the appearance of an unhandsome maturity? My body is already grown, completed in obedience to laws not wisely nor very closely kept. I see you possessed of occult wisdom, but I am not, and find it hard to remember what I have heard of it; as for making the knowledge practical—impossible!"

"Phylos, my brother, the occult adept, is born, not made. His or her knowledge is from within, not from without. Unto thee shall be given the key of the Spirit, and behold, the All Knowing will enter into thy soul, and though no man shall teach thee, neither any book, yet shalt thou become aware of all things, for all things are of our Father, and that is the Spirit.* But ere the Spirit come in, the house must be swept, and, my brother Phylos, I would that thou wert not destined to endure this ordeal. Yet the occult that knoweth all things is born of many lives, and in these has been evil. Thou art so born; it is karma."

Mol Lang had now returned clothed in his material body, and I alone was in the astral, yet not solitary in the sense of loneliness, for my friends were not separated from me as a result of our diverse physical conditions. True, I could not array myself in material form, for I was in Venus, and my body was in a distant planet. This condition was the reverse of disabilty, however, for in going from place to place I had but to desire to be in the more distant, and I was there, though this power enabled me to have such freedom only in Hesper, and a sense of restriction consequently arose. Discontent was growing in my soul; I felt already a stranger on this high soul plane whereto my friends were born. Though I knew nothing of earth because my earthly self was in the Sach in the care of Mendocus, yet I had most uncomfortable feeling

---

*St. John xvi. 13.

of foreignness; a feeling that some other and previous condition, somewhere, was not strange, and I had longing to be
again in its familiar environment. Poor me!

————————

CHAPTER VI.

AN INDIRECT ANSWER.

An eminent author has said that "literary themes are necessarily limited; that authors can not create as a fiction that
which has no counterpart in fact." And this is absolutely
true. Literature is restricted to ringing the changes on love,
hatred, hope, despair, greed, indifference, envy—the gamut of
our human emotions, in short. When these are presented in
their threefold aspects—tragedy, comedy, or serio-comic—the
scale is run, and the only further variations possible are the
lights or shadows of faintness or intensity of emotion.

Perhaps the thought arises that in this history some new
phase will appear, that Theo-Christianity has some new phases
to present. Such an idea is doomed to disappointment. Indeed, the occult will be found to exclude even certain potent
earthly factors of literature—all those of the lower animal
nature, because these have no place in human life. Envy,
greed, hatred, have no place in a nature which is close
kin to that soul of love—Jesus. Indifference, sloth,
despair, these can have no room in a soul which scans so
absorbing a vista as that open to Mol Lang, yet so loving a
soul that—like Jesus and Gauama—perfect willingness existed
to turn from such sublime reward in order that they might
lead their least brethren thither also. You may say that such
love as this is not animal, when I say it is not human. Right.
But it is spiritual; it is that love which only those know
who have begun to tread the Path, knowing within the soul
the advent of the Spirit. If any of you come to feel that
you will not shrink, though karma demand you also to show

that "Greater love hath no man" than that he "give up his life for a friend"—then brother, sister, you have known the birth of the Spirit within you. Blessed are you then.

No one can rightfully expect that by the relation of weird things I shall give him a half hour's amusement; such is not my aim. This book is a work of love, done for a sacred purpose. The second coming of Christ is upon the world, not only as a time simultaneously arriving for all, but also unto each human soul as it becomes ready to receive Him in the heart, and do His work.* He is at hand now in the sense that if you will open your soul to receive His spirit, He is there to enter in. Truly, of the moment He comes to His own no man can tell the day or the hour; yet I say, tarry not for Him as a man or an external spirit, but as the Christ Spirit entering into your very being. And He shall not wait to come as a man, but come as the Spirit of Divine Love, just so soon as you are ready to make that your rule of life; and as the Christ and Father are One, so therefore shall you that hear and attend be glorified, and presently arise, depart from this world, and go unto the Life. Who hath ears to hear, let him hear. Likewise He shall come as a person at the last.**

I certainly have strange things to relate, but nothing, weird, unreal or sensational. That which I say is from my Father, and can lead the earnest hearer into the Path whither the Cross Bearer led the way. What I say concerns a larger measure of life—Hesper, the planet of Divine Love. I hope to reveal some further idea than I have hitherto of the extent, kind and duration of occult life. Heretofore I have given only rules—now I give the result of faithfulness to them. I hope to show what a glorious being man becomes through heeding occult law, the law of the Spirit whereof I testify—upward through all the ages, with never any descent, Man pursues still the glorious march which shall eventuate in making him one with the Father—more than Man finite—Man infinite! Angelic!

*Luke xxi, 34, 35. 36.
**St. Mark xiii, 26.

But my pen is years ahead of my visit to Hesper. I must return to that time lest my words become merely words, erected like modern buildings—fourteen stories high.

My desire to investigate the occult truth did not diminish, because of the rapid growth of my desire for a life more familiar. Yet ever and again I caught myself studying whether psychic truth might not be pursued where,—ah!—amidst— well, some set of conditions less rigorous to the animal instincts struggling within me, and setting me so far below my friends. As well hope to mix oil and water as to study the occult amidst unspiritual, earthly influence!

As preceptor, Sohma contented himself with telling me of principles, and not of marvels—lest in pursuing wonders I should lose sight of causes; the fruit of a tree is apt always to be more attractive to the ignorant than is the tree itself. Here is a chief truth in guidance to occult study—pay small heed to the marvels, or to magic, and all heed to laws, for the laws are the tree. The marvel worker is the least of the brethren, understanding not the laws of the Father to any profitable extent. Know the law, know the marvels incident; know not the law, but only the marvel, and you are not following Him, nor shall you inherit His kingdom, though you could do more magic than the Tchin, Mendocus, or even Mol Lang. It was their possession of least value; may you regard it likewise.

During a stroll in the garden, I asked Sohma concerning his remark that though I should be given the key to occult wisdom, I should not be taught details. "Sohma, you say details are omitted, and effects also, and only general laws are to be taught me. Now, my nature seems incapable of learning much in that way. I seem to feel a different method necessary, a method born of—of—" here I passed my hand across my brow in perplexity, for earth memories were not supporting me. "Well, I know not exactly what; I seem to have some vague idea of a past life, somewhere, in which other methods of learning were in use. I do not know now, brother. I am lost."

"No, not lost, Phylos; misplaced—ahead of thy common place in life. But thou makest reference to the analytical philosophy, which reasons from effects back to a common cause. It is not a sure process, as witness the status of chemical science in that vaguely remembered life of thine. Chemistry is a proud science, though handicapped by clumsy analytical processes. It cannot tell what a grain of sand is."

Suddenly my chemical learning returned to me, in obedience to Sohma's will, although the environing circumstances of its acquirement were prevented. But with the return of the knowledge itself I became immediately argumentative, and I replied to Sohma:—

"Pardon me, but chemistry can tell that. Sand is silica—silicic acid, and it is composed of the element silicon and the oxygen of the air, in the proportion of two of the latter to one of the former."

Precisely. But thou hast not really told anything; thou art as far from a finality as before. Thou sayest sand is composed of two primary elements?"

"Certainly."

"And being primary, cannot be reduced farther?"

"No, they cannot,"— I said, yet, remembering certain wonderful things I had already witnessed, I was beginning to be nervous.

"No! Art thou sure?"—he queried, persistently, and I, both from a feeling of stubbornness which his manner aroused, and a determination to be true to my science at all hazards, replied:

"Assuredly!"

"Phylos, if it were not that thy stubbornness were tempered with an admirable fidelity to principle, I should say that wisdom will die with thee. But, my friend, thy system of chemistry, with its sixty odd 'primal elements' and its 'monads, dyads, triads' and so on; its simples, binaries, tertiaries and the like numerous compounds, is nothing but a fine working hypothesis—well adapted to producing the result it has produced, but because it is not the whole chemical

truth, not capable of ever attaining that wholeness of results which marks the sublime constitution of nature. So
far from conducting to the truth these theories have just the
opposite effect; they teach the multiformity of matter,
whereas its unity is the truth. As I said, though, the chemists of the earth have a good working hypothesis, one which
will do until the better method of truth is found.''

Sohma paused, whereupon I asked what the better method
was. He did not answer me in direct words, but instead he
put before my mental vision a workshop, wherein were many
kinds of instruments and machines in states either of completion or approaching completion, lying upon tables and
benches. I saw here a clock, there watches, there again an
old style typewriter; there were time locks and combination
tools, besides many intricate mechanisms that even the sight
of suggested no use for. At a little distance upon a table lay
a confused mass of parts of machinery not put together. He
said:

"Phylos, canst thou put these things together? In this
pile are portions of clocks, typewriters, locks and so forth.
Thou sayest thou art not a machinist, hence cannot deal
with these things. These things are not unfamiliar to me,
who am a machinist. With all the parts before thee thou
couldst not construct a clock or other mechanism. But suppose thou shouldst take carefully apart a clock now in running order, and study carefully all its relations, and do so by
not one only, but by several of these instruments, then the
whole would become familiar to thee, and while merely taking
one clock apart would not be apt to teach thee, doing so by
many would enable thee to put them all together again as
they were. That is the process of analysis, deduction and syn-
thesis; it is the same, practically, in physics, or in mechanics or chemics.''

"But my friend,"—I said in dismay, "I cannot do these
acts, not having opportunity to thus experiment.''

"That is my point, Phylos. I will show thee the better
method of which I spoke. Here before us is an invention of

my own; practically I am its creator, and therefore do I understand it. Here also is another identical machine, but it is in separate state; its parts are a confused pile. Now thou knowest nothing of constructive mechanics; I do, and I will point out to thee the principal parts of the machine, which is in running order. Observe!"

Sohma went up to the machine—which stood, a marvel of mechanical beauty, its burnished brass and silver wheels, springs, cogs, chain belts, etc., showing through the quadrangular glass case. He spoke into the mouthpiece, explaining the machine to me the while. He said that he would remain near the mouthpiece, so that his words should be reported and printed and bound in book form. As he spoke he loosened a set screw. Then he said:

"A microphonic diaphragm sets strong currents of electricity in operation. These act only as my tones impinge on that vocal diaphragm, whereby, as thou seest, carbon discs close other circuits, and operate levers carrying type upon their extremities. Observe that this vocal diaphragm is made of sonant steel cords, like those of a piano, and there are of these just as many as experience has demonstrated that there are vocal tones and octaves. Hence there is in one alphabet just that number of letters, and our written language consists in the proper sequential arrangement of these letters, either type, if printed, or symbolic chirography, if written. Along with our spoken tones, then, if near such an instrument as this, we can 'utter' a printed volume. The congregate tones affect each its own chord; this in vibration compresses the carbon discs, sets going the instant electric current, the type lever does its work, the paper is carried a space forward and the next type strikes, and so on till the voice ceases utterance. The spacing between words even, is automatically done, for, so long as one is talking connectedly there is a utilization made of the return of the carbon disc from its compressed active state, whereby a spring moves the paper carriage one space for every minor pause in the voice, and two for periods, but it is not sufficient for more than a double spacing motion. I am done speaking, nearly, and will move this lever up, thus releasing the stored force which arose from the motion of the parts—especially of the heavy balance wheel. No more printing will be done, but the reserve force will fold, cut and bind my speech, and when this is done, the last of the force stored—equal in all cases to the special work—is exhausted entirely by the ringing of a bell which signifies the end.

Though Sohma ceased to speak, the instrument still worked, and almost quicker than this sentence will be put in type, the bell rang and behold! Sohma's words in boök form dropped into a little box at the end of the case. The instrument stood motionless in its case, and for the first time its compactness struck me—it was but eighteen inches high, by two feet in width and three in length, yet it had done all that marvelous work.

"Couldst thou take apart this instrument and put it together properly again?"—was the startling question, startling because I thought he intended me to do it! "No, my brother; but as its creator, knowing all its most obscure points, my comprehension of it and of other machinery, and of truths not mechanical as well, but scientific physics, is a veritable spirit of knowledge, and observe—this spirit I will to enter into thy mind, at least so far as concerns this mechanism. Behold it and know it."

Strange to relate, I, who previously knew almost nothing of such things, seemed on the instant to understand the whole of the delicate apparatus, as a watchmaker does a watch. Sohma, perceiving this, said:

"Such, Phylos, is that key to all wisdom whereof I spoke. God, creator of all things whatever, shall one day enter into thee. Then thy spirit, which is a ray of His Spirit, shed into the darkness of life by Him, shall reunite with Him. And because He creates by constant Logos all things and states of Being, and is immanent in it all, knowing it all, so when He entereth thy soul, thou shalt know all things likewise, and, in less measure, truly, create also. Thou shalt know that, in chemical sense, only one element exists, operated upon by Force. Then all "elements," as thou knowest them, shall be seen to be but different speeds of the molecular formation of the One Element by varying degrees of the One Force—and light, heat, sound and all solid, liquid and gaseous substances will be seen to be different not in material, but in speed only.

"That knowledge underlies all life—physics, chemics, sonants, calorics, chromatics, electrics and all and every possible aspect of nature. Such is the supreme law of God, and He is nature, though Nature is not conversely God. Another law is that of compensation; may I tell thee of it?"

I replied that I should be but too glad to listen, for his words revealed God in all things, whether high or low. So he continued:

"This law, then, not only governs all matter, but that of which matter is the reflection—Spirit, and the soul realm. I need state but a single brief instance in material nature—the screw plane. As the plane of a screw is greater or less in its inclination, so will its action be either rapid or powerful, but never both at once. If the thread be slight in pitch, the screw bar will progress through its nut very slowly, but—as exerted in a screw press—the crushing force will be enormous. Vice versa; if the pitch be steep, the screw bar will progress rapidly, as to-wit: The screw nail, which may be driven into wood with a hammer, and revolve as it goes in.

"Now, in the soul realm, if a human being is content with the gradual, easy pitch of the God-ward ascending plane of pure daily life, daily temptations to work in error, and too often fall, progress upward will be slow, but very sure. But, on the contrary, if eager to learn rapidly, it must meet in a few hours all the crushing force of temptations to err and to sin which the ordinary man meets distributed through many, many incarnations, covering ages, aye, aeonian time. In the one case the Father giveth sufficient of the daily bread of strength unto men to enable them to progress very slowly, but with certitude. In the other, all the splendid reserve of resistant force of a very God is needed, for all the power of Lucifer—that high nature spirit who was incarnate in the planet which disrupted into the solar asteroidal belt, upon the lapse, the failure of its Soul—all of his glorious power sufficed not to carry him to victory, so he fell. GOD-CHRIST in thee can alone win this struggle. Truly, no mere human, so long as he remains Man, can have such a temptation; not thyself, not Mol Lang, my father, hardly Gautama were subjected to such a severe test as was that sublime world soul, Lucifer, except relatively. I say relatively, for consider this: that if a fly or an ant be subjected to all it can endure, then its pain at that point is as severe as that of a man at his breaking strain. But as Jesus and Gautama were tempted to the utmost and did not fail, therefore their victory was greater than Lucifer's failure, and when thou shalt come to a trial like his, thou'lt doubtless succeed; though, again, thou mayest fail. There is but **one** Guide; **follow** and win; follow not, and fail.* It is a new conception to thee to learn there is an animating ego, a world spirit, inmateriated in each star, each planet, every stellar body, just as there is an individual soul in each human, animal or plant body. Yet this is true. True also it is that the spirits of men will progress; will face the supreme ordeal, and, if they pass victorious, will enter that long rest, heaven, devachan—call it as thou wilt—Nirvana. But that is not the end, for life had a beginning—it hath also an end. And the perfect human ego emerging eventually from Nirvana, that long devachan of all the incarnations, emerges not as Man; it does not live, but It Is, and Its post-viviant existence is a state of Being which no human mind could understand, except inferentially it do so through the knowledge that that state is to Life as the senior to the junior. But ere then is the **trial of transfiguration;** to it my father hath come, I have not. If we fail, then that is the second death**, but meet it we must, humanity must. But it is long ere then, for it cometh not until the essaying soul be perfect, and be ready to leave the pupaceous state of Human Life,

*John xvi. 13.
**Rev. xx, 13-15.

to be judged according to (its) works for Him who made all. Do I weary thee, Phylos?"

I replied that he did not, though it did seem that I grasped his meaning only to lose it again. None the less I was eager to have him go on, fancying I understood, just as every person you or I know is fond of thinking his or her comprehension of abstruse subjects perfect. Sohma smiled and said in reply that, when he was done, all that I would have gained would be the psychic bent favoring my progress, for I was destined to forget the very ideas I fancied I was gaining. But he continued, observing that a favorable prejudice was a worthy thing, calling for his best effort for me.

"I wish thee to observe also this: that if thou thinkest the judgment day, when according to its works thy soul is arraigned by thy spirit, which is God in thee, if thou thinkest that because that day may be in remote aeons ere it come, and therefore thou hast ample time to lag, to err, I counsel thee it is a fatal mistake. For if at the great trial any man fail it is because, day by day, as the lives were run, he neglected his chances, either by omission or commission. Then shall such suffer the second death, be cast into the 'lake of fire'—in other words, their Spirit will depart from the soul and go unto the Father, while the soul will be gathered into the sum of force— the 'Fire' element—that which is sum of all lesser force forms, out of which springeth life, heat and vibration. But this will not be until the erring one hath passed from his soul into his spirit. So the 'second death'* is not of the sinner; it is the cutting off of all his, or her, spoiled work, and a chance to begin again, to build better; our Father damneth not His child, but only the imperfect work, the sinning soul. In our library thou canst see a book brought here to Hesper from the Earth, a book which speaketh of the order of the Rosicrux, wherein this supreme Fire is written of. 'Tis also that Fire once called in the Earth the Maxin.

*Rev. xx, 13-15.

"Phylos, thou wilt suffer the ordeal of the Crisis before other men; whether thou shalt succeed or fail no man knoweth save those who have passed heretofore."

When Sohma ceased speaking, I looked around me, and found that while the clocks and typewriters, and locks and various instruments, were gone, the vocal printer was not gone; it was an actuality—the rest only concepts which Sohma had willed me to see. My mind was not trained sufficiently well to continue on a special line of thought so long, and while I fancied that I possessed a clear idea of all my companion had said, and was pleased by the notion, yet had I tried at that moment to recollect his meanings, I should have been chagrined to find that I had nothing beyonl vague ideas. Still, I did not try the experiment, but, content with the supposition of possession, my mind wandered to a new theme, and I asked Sohma if Hesperians had not found aerial vessels possible among so many triumphs. He turned toward me and looking behind me, smiled as he answered:

"I will leave Phyris to tell thee that; I must go elsewhere."

I was pleased at this new event, yet shyness at once asserted itself, and though vexed at this fact, my vexation seemed only to increase my diffidence. Taking, as I supposed, no notice of this diffidence, she said:

"We rarely go, except we go astrally. We care but seldom to avail ourselves of our aerial vessels; but we have them. It may be that thou—or shall I say 'you' to lessen thy—your—shyness of me?"—and Phyris bent a pair of laughing eyes upon me, a gaze that, while it gave most delicious pleasure, effectually confused me, past recovery, I feared.

"Perhaps"—she continued, after gently laughing at my piteous abashment—"perhaps you think we Hesperians can transport our physical bodies here and there by some occult process, or other. For instance, as all forms of matter are but divine ideas clothed in the One Substance, it is possible to disintegrate the material form, but preserve the psychic idea and transport that as other thoughts move, by effort of will, then rehabilitate it in matter. Thus it is, articles can be brought

from the earth here to us. But if you think we can do this by
our own bodies you err, for ourselves are the ideas embodied.
Truly we can emerge from these bodies, and travel in one brief
instant from one to any other star. But we can not have two
corporeal bodies at once. If we leave the one we have, we can,
by putting it in a cataleptic trance, leave it in fit state to re-
occupy upon our return. But if we leave it and make around
ourselves a new one, like in all respects to the other, and abide
in it, the deserted temple will perish. We could do it; but we
have no need to, and consequently do not. All about you is
matter—every breath is matter, differing only from iron in
its molecular speed. The air is matter; electricity is matter. I
will show you. See, I wish a plate, several plates, cups, saucers,
knives and forks, so I image them—(imagio—I create) in the
mental or psychic form. Do you see them? Eyes of Earth
could not; thou hast for a time Hesperian vision.''

Before me was a pile of delicate table ware, with the pattern
upon each piece of a different kind.

''These articles are really only thought forms; no eye unable
to preceive a thought could see them. But now look, I gather
to myself the higher rate of speed, the extra force which makes
air of the One Substance, and the force which I leave is just
that of the various minerals of which I desire my ware to be
'made'—observe that one plate is a ruby, the real crystal aluminum; and another is a pearl—others are of various gem stones
—as that cup and saucer—crystal carbon, diamond each one.
On the Earth those dishes would be valued into the millions
of dollars, yet here they are valued for their uses and their
beauty only. Do you see, Phylos—I know the terms of your
language and what ideas are conveyed by your words. But
now I, like Sohma, must go, for I have a dinner to get, a use
for my plates, cups and saucers, which I have made, as well
as more yet to make. Quite like an ordinary mortal, you say?
Indeed, and why not? Do you think an occultist is always
rapt in abstruse speculations? You err, Phylos, you err, indeed. You may go into the library, where you may find something to interest you.''

To the library, therefore, I went, and if you will, you may go with me, in a mental way, and see something of it. Do not object that these Hesperian objects were unreal, just because I have said that no one with ordinary terrestrial eyes could see any evidences of life on Venus. Reality does not necessarily imply terrene solidity.

At least forty thousand volumes lined the shelves; many of them were plainly, but some richly bound. On my first introduction to this apartment I had found that the books on the shelves were all in the phonetic print of Hesper. But I saw on a table one whose cover bore in Anglo-Saxon in gilt letters the title and name of the publishers, and as I looked, for a brief time the memory power of Earth returned. The inscription was:

"A THOUSAND MILES UP THE NILE."
By Miss A. B. Edwards.
Published by
Longmans & Co.
1876.

That volume had been brought all the many millions of miles across inter-planetary space along the "currents"—just as Phyris had done when she "made" the tableware, only in the case of this book she had not created the thoughts in the book, but had disintegrated the matter, preserving the astral—the only reality about an object—and after bringing it from Earth to Hesper, had reclothed it in matter after its journey. I looked about, and found other volumes—one entitled:

"THE ROSICRUCIANS."
By
Hargrave Jennings.

I found copies of Milton's works, of Tennyson's earlier poems, of Moore, and a pile several feet high of other standard works; on top of all lay the "Essay of Emerson"—upon which, as I gazed, appeared a piece of white paper, and as I looked, the words seemed to form as if precipitated from the air:

"Phylos, these books I have brought for you from the distant earth. I did so that you might contrast them with our Hesperian works. Finally, consider this: that we who are illumined by the Spirit of the Creator do little with books or such crude methods of learning, caring only for them as specimens of the work of souls on certain planes. To read them we have no need, no desire—they serve only as texts, for when we would learn, we retire within our souls and listen to the All Knowing Spirit."

That message was signed by Phyris. It was written in English. Written? No, precipitated, and as soon as I had read it, it disappeared as it had appeared—with no hand to remove it, no person save myself in the room. With its disappearance I also ceased to retain memories of the world whence I came. As I stood, considering what next to do, Phyris came in and said:

"Here is an invention by Sohma which will render thy delight greater; I know it is always great where books abound."

She picked up a book from Earth—Shakespeare—and placed it in an instrument which turned the pages automatically, and a strong electric light being cast on the visible pages, its beams reflected upon a metallic plate. Unseen wheels revolved within a case, and a voice issued from a funnel shaped mouthpiece. To my pleasure I heard the reading of page after page of the great English literary gem, in appropriate tones for the various characters. While I listened, absorbed, Phyris withdrew, and it was some time ere I noticed her absence. I think I should then have gone in search of her, or of Sohma—Mol Lang had gone to a distance, on duty bent, leaving his body asleep in his room—but as I was about to go out of the library, a hand—a woman's hand—reached over my shoulder, and a soft voice said:

"Put these over your eyes."

It was Phyris, who gave me a seeming pair of spectacles. They were indeed spectacles which all the fortunes of earth could not obtain. How thoughtful she was of my pleasure! As I put them on, all the shelves of books disappeared, and a book being placed in my hand—as I know from retrospection,

for I did not know then—I found myself seemingly amid scenes
of most familiar aspect. All the mental pictures conjured up
by vivid perusal of Scott's famous poem, "The Lady of the
Lake"—all the voices of its characters became seen and heard,
as if I were on the spot where all was said to have transpired.
For the time I was transported by means of those magical eye
pieces into the mental world of Walter Scott, which, while he
wrote,—

> "Lay around him like a cloud,
> A world he could not see."

—except with the vision of the creative imagination.

The whole was presented in a few moments, for thought is
swifter than the senses, and when the King threw his golden
fetters over Malcolm's neck and laid the chain in fair Ellen's
hand—without waiting for the rest, Phyris withdrew the wonderful spectacles from my eyes, and said:

"These would banish material surroundings, and let the
reader directly into the author's realms of imagery, whatever
the book, but not whoever the reader—for only fine, developing human senses, none that are controlled by the animal, can
enjoy the use of them. And this because they are a species
of sensitive magnet, linking psychic facts, but not material
things. But there, I do not know much more about them, and
you must ask father of them if you would learn more. I am
only a girl, and must learn to be more ere I can assume to teach.
And I should dislike to fail in offering you an explanation.
Your good opinion of me would lessen, and that would be mor-
tifying, for I treasure it—I, well, never mind,"—she said, as
a delicate flush spread over her face—"come with me; I think
it is well not to be too long a time amidst any one set of influences—as literary environs."

Much, aye, most that I saw in Hesper had been unfamiliar.
But that delicate blush—it set me thinking—my own ideas
meantime in a confused, ecstatic whirl. What did it mean?
Did it denote reciprocal affection?

"It does in truth,"—she said, in reply to my unspoken query.
"Bu. the significance of it is beyond thy knowledge. Thou—

nay, you!—see me a maid of not many years. Your love shall behold me a woman. Do I speak a riddle? Only time can solve it. You are with me, and I with you, and our ages differ not greatly. You have little understanding; I have more; both are imperfect, yet the Spirit shall make us whole. If I asked you now, 'What is will power?' you could not answer it truly. Yet I tell you, and my words shall sink deep, and guide you to me. I said erroneously that you are with me, and behold, you are so only in the sight of our Father in the beginning, but not now. Yet one day shall come, and when I shall ask, 'What is will?' you shall say of your own knowledge:—'Will is the fiat of consciousness.' If it be will of the animal soul, its result will be only a subjective thought which shall energize muscles to do an objective reality conforming to the subjective plan. If it be of the human soul, it will be of greater intensity, and nobler, but still the brain, and through it the muscles, must render its fiat into material form. But if the will be the fiat of our Spirits, and trained, we shall say to any material force, 'Obey me,' and it shall obey. Because our Spirits are of our Father and one with Him, and the Will of the Spirit shall need no mediate brain nor muscle, but shall find every natural power its direct servant, and this is the faith whereof Jesus spoke. So, Phylos, my own, I have told you, and yet you, hearing, hear not. Why not? Because our Father is not yet manifest in you. But when you, having heard, understand, then shall we twain be one, for it is so written in the Book of Life.

As she ceased speaking we came into a plot of ground wherein grew the fruits for table use. Of these she gathered some, but of others desired, none were growing. Stooping, she drew on the soil a figure which looked familiar, although I could not tell where I had seen it previously. It was this ⊘; and the reader will remember that it is the same that I described the Tchin as making when he caused the Vita Mundi to flame as he stood within it. It was also creative fire in Phyris hands, though it had not been so as exhibited by Quong. In the space Phyris planted seeds, and then, completing the symbol, the flames rose above the area sown.

"Behold, Phylos! If I have but the seed, the herb shall come forth after its kind.* But if I have not the seed, my poor, human soul wisdom could not make that herb grow. Mol Lang could, being transfigured. Having seed, I can bring Gods Viviant Fire to aid its germination—see! it sprouts; and again watch it—it grows visibly."

I was astonished to see, mounting up as fast as evening shadows lengthen—green tendrils, and buds unfolding even, as the flowers of primula spring forth, flowers, blossoming, blossomed; seed scarps forming, formed; and the matured fruit hanging in clusters in the radiant flame of the Vita Mundi, as high as my head from the ground, where erst there had been but vacant soil. And this girl, who declared herself not a grown woman, exercising such magic as this and thinking it only ordinary! This was an inherent power of the Human Principle, my friends, and will be common to you also when you become developed in the Human. Earthly man is yet only in the initial of his humanity in a few favored cases, but is very largely in his animality. Most of mankind is merely animal, not human, save by courtesy. Yet the dawn of the glorious new era is at hand, and in its fullness of days Christ shall come again to it and enter into the hearts of his own; and it shall be the Father that shall enter, and by Messiah. Be yet then prepared for the coming of the Spirit, for no man knoweth the day nor hour thereof.

CHAPTER VII.

"THE DESERT IS BEFORE THY FEET."

So the days passed. It was over two weeks of the local time that I had been in Hesperian environs. And during this interval the longing for the past life grew; the few occasions when

---
*Genesis 1, 12.

Mol Lang, Sohma or Phyris had recalled the vivid memories of Earth had been seized upon by my Pertozian astral, and thus each such event renewed the certitude of my having had a past in which all my surroundings had been familiar. It saddened Phyris to know that every time I was left alone my thoughts yearned with increased longing for that past. At times a strong effort of my own will would successfully bring it before me—bring, in fact, my earthly astral from Earth to me —that astral which was the sum of my experiences and memories of Earth. Then, being in Venus, I yet knew myself a man of Earth, and a stranger, and my yearning grew strong for America, my "ain countree." That was home to me, oh! so much more home, although I had no relatives living—all gone to devachan's rest—and no friends comparable to those I had so strangely found in Hesper. My friend, it is the soul that is chained, not the body of man. Unchain thy souls, oh, brethren, and seek to know the things of heaven, of the high life with God, and all things else shall be added unto you—yea, even to the ability to explore the stars in person. Mine was bound to Earth by love of home and native land. Then these moments of knowledge of Earth would cease, because my will power was not strong enough to hold the astral summoned, and it gravitated to its own level, which was the world. Again I would be left unconscious of the Earth life, and brooding over the puzzle, until some of the family banished the mental state producing it! No, I was a soul not at home except on Earth; I was here on a higher plane; I might be born after devachan into the level of the Hesperian, but the fact ever obtruded with increased emphasis that as yet I had not been so born.

It was a pleasure to me to sit at table when my friends took their simple repasts, for though I could not eat, nor indeed did I need food, it was agreeable to be with them when they collected thus together.

The next day after I had seen Phyris grow the fruits to eat, I was at supper with the family when Mol Lang, speaking to his son, said:

"Sohma, is it wise to tell our guest so much philosophy as thou and sister have done and contemplate doing?"

"Wherefore keep secret the truth, my father?"

"Because, son, Phylos must return to Earth; it is so fated. He can not know these things, for hearing is not knowing, nor is seeing. He hath no faculties developed whereby to know them, and thou nor I can not permanently enter our knowledge into his soul. Jesus of Nazareth, except He entered into the souls of His hearers as into a temple, could tell them nothing. Caiaphas, the High Priest, and all the Israelites heard the Savior with their ears and saw His doings, yet were blind and deaf and comprehended not. But unto those who were His disciples and followers, He entered, and they saw and heard and profited. That was the Spirit which the Master awakened in them and they followed the Word, even as Jesus followed it. But the world has had to read the printed Word for these many centuries, and though many have believed, yet none, no, not one, has been illuminated by the Spirit like unto Paul. What thou wouldst say to Phylos will come to him in astral form when he begins to yearn for Hesperus, even as his astral of Earth now comes to him as he yearns for Earth. And, having forgotten Pertoz—forgotten us—he yet will utter these bits of occult lore, and will suffer therefor. Suffer, because some hearers will be mystified, others scornful, and none, himself included, able to explain or understand."

"Yea, my parent, thou speakest wisely. Yet let me say—he will utter truth. Truth is mighty and will prevail. If, at the time, it be misunderstood, not less must it cause some act in both speaker and hearer. I need not say thoughts are things, for all things are thoughts. Even a stone is a thought concept of the Eternal Spirit, and the stone seen by ordinary eyes is but the externalization of the idea. If, then, Phylos shall think, and his hearers think on his utterances, that is an action, making the actor responsible. If a small thought, then a small act; it will doubtless finish its karma in the life of its utterance. But if a great thought, or deed, it will make its doer his or her own legatte, and then? I speak to thee also now, Phylos

—the inheritor of his own actions shall find the deed become part of the great karma of the human race, and himself responsible for its fruition, because, Till heaven and earth pass, one jot or one tittle shall in no wise pass from the law till all be fulfilled.'* Only thus can Phylos ever come to us again."

"Well spoken, my son!"—was Mol Lang's sole comment.

Sohma then said to me:—"Phylos, my brother, there is no man or woman but hath in some past as well as present life done grievous evil to one or more fellowbeings—man or animal. Whatsoever a man soweth, that shall he reap. And our Father hath ordained that in life, subsequent to the one witnessing the greater sins, he that did them must also requite them. Must do so by setting against the evil counter-balancing good. Not else shall any one come into the Kingdom. This is the law of karma."

On leaving the table I went with Sohma into his own rooms to see a painting which adorned his wall. Its size was three and a half feet by six feet, and it was framed with rubies, sapphires, diamonds, pearls and other gems set in cement— precious stones which on Earth would be each valued into three period of figures. Not so in Hesperus, for they were produced as Phyris produced the jewel-dishes. But the picture exceeded the frame—a production of art magic which all the wealth of the world could not buy.

I saw a view of a boundless ocean, the billows lashed in tempestuous fury, sea-birds skimming the crests or flitting through the air above. It seemed a sunset on the great waters, for the red beams shone through breaking clouds, lighting the aftermath of the storm with a great glory. Close at hand— so close that one could see the anxious intensity of mingling emotions on their faces—two men and a boy clung to a floating spar. One of the men was held by his mates as he wildly waved his arms to a ship that lay—an acute silhouette against the monstrous disc—right in the very middle of the vermillion sun.

*Matthew v, 18.

"Such a scene could not be worth so great a sum as I named?"

Truly, it were idle to attach a figure to what no money could buy. But what think you when I say that the pictured billows rose and fell as does real water? And the wind scudding along caught the combing, breaking billows and hurled spray and spume for what seemed hundreds of feet. The petrels and gulls dipping their feet in the water left a momentary ripple as they rose again. Clouds flitted across the horizon, and coming athwart the great sun, were lit by its crimson, while, even as I looked, the blazing orb sank its lower edge beneath the waters. The tall ship had sailed to the edge of the shield and, looking, I saw a flag raised and lowered as if in answer to the men on the spar. Then a boat, a mere dot at the distance, was launched. But the castaways were too near the level to see these things, and as the sun sank wholly from view, one of them raised his arms in wild despair, and slipped from the spar to his grave in the depths. After a time the light of the full moon replaced that of the set sun, the clouds cleared away, and in the pale, silvery light I saw the approaching boat, seeking the castaways. I saw them, now floated to one side of the canvas, but the searchers at first did not. They rowed here and there, and finally were successful. Lifting the perishing man and the boy into the boat, they pulled away to where the lights of their ship gleamed in the night. Then the watery waste was left lifeless as the boat disappeared in the gloom towards the ship, which, as I looked, sailed out at one side of the picture, as if the whole scene was one beheld through an open window, and the vessel had sailed behind the window casement. The canvas slowly whitened, and presently was perfectly blank of color or figures.

While I yet gazed, out from the side on the right of the frame appeared a black point, coming slowly into view, and tossing up and down. Waves grew in green sullenness across the whole canvas, and Sohma said:

"See, it is about to repeat itself. By watching thou shalt see the whole again. It is a scene of a shipwreck on the Atlantic Ocean, on the distant Earth. As often as it is all completed it turns white, and then is repeated. It is another example of the power of an occult mind over matter; the artist's will changes the speed of the color, and either reduces or raises it so that the vibrations making red are increased and range up through all degrees of color-force—always exactly in harmony with the astral image put on the canvas by the creative power of the occult artist. 'Who painted this? dost thou ask?' Phyris. She painted it ere thou camest to Hesperus—when thou didst rescue a woman from a life of shame. This scene is prophetic. It is that of a time coming on Earth—when that rescued woman shall be lost at sea, years hence. But look at the picture."

I looked, and saw that though the storm was yet only a menace, it was surely coming and would overtake the proud vessel that now had appeared in full perspective, half a mile over the waters from me, as it seemed. At the mainmast floated the Stars and Stripes—Flag of the Union. The sight brought my astral to me, and memories of Earth and homeland filled my eyes with tears. But Sohma put away the sad feeling, leaving me but partially conscious of the past. I could see a sailor go to the ship's bell and ring "eight bells"— see, but of course not hear—four o'clock in the afternoon. The sailor had hardly struck the time ere a man came on deck and seemed to give orders to "close reef." The men swarmed into the rigging and obeyed—it was from their actions that I knew what the orders had been. Then coming back on deck, they battened down the hatches and put all safe for storm. Not a moment too soon. First a cloud overcast the sun; then a black pall in the north, obscuring the view—I could dimly see that things on shipboard began to flap in the wind, and soon the noble vessel careened far over to starboard under the white-topped rush of frightful billows. Then the fugitive craft, with its mainmast hanging over the side, began to flee before the demon of the storm. I could see it as it rose and sank in the maddened swirl, while it seemed as if the vessel was in rapid motion, giving the effect of flight. Presently a squad of seamen made a rush across the decks for the pumps, at which they worked with the energy of despair. A woman came from the one hatch left open for passage below decks, and winding the cordags of the stump of the mainmast about her slight form, cheered the men in their desperate toil. The foremast now snapped, and was cut adrift. The vessel was filling faster than the men could pump out the leakage, and a jump for the boats was made. One by one these were lost—swamped as they touched the water, till only one remained. Into this the captain ordered his men. Two more men than there was possible room for in the boat; and the captain and his mate, and the woman whom the mate held in his arms, stayed. The boat was not seemingly a hundred feet distant when the gallant ship pitched forward, prow first, and went down. A spar floating by the lone boat was the salvation of some of those in the frail shell, which I saw overturned by the heavy waves—a moment I saw white faces, for the boat was near in the foreground—I saw the woman's face as she sank, and she was near enough so that I saw, not terror, but a peaceful smile depicted on her features. Then I saw two men and a boy, clinging to a spar, and the scene was come to the repetition, for on that spar, when two days had elapsed (in seeming) I saw them as at the beginning of this description. "In seeming?" Yes, because the canvas depicted that night's blackness, the next day's sombre light, another night and the second day. The whole scene took about two actual hours for its rendition.

Sohma said no more concerning occult wisdom. He knew that my mind, ignorant of the philosophy of this higher life, was not in touch with its significance, and that I wearied of it as a child does of studies at school; abstruse occupations presenting to its limited comprehension no actual connection with the facts of its little world.

Mol Lang taught me yet one thing more there in Hesper, saying it was for my guidance, and that I would not forget it at any time. We were beside the great river which flowed past his abode at a few hundred yards distant. I sat on the gravel of the shore, Mol Lang sat above me on the bank, close enough to touch me. He planted a seed, and over it held his hands, palms downward. It grew fast, and soon stood mature at the height of his head. Banana-like fruit hung amongst its broad leaves. He plucked some of the fruit and ate it.

"See, Phylos—such is plant life. Thou hast said: 'Why not take animal life to nourish our bodies,' and 'If it be wrong to take life of animals is it not wrong to take that of vegetable growths'. My son, where any form—mineral, plant or animal—exists, there also is an entity created by the Spirit; the matter-form is nothing but clothing to the astral, and this to the soul. Now there are plant souls, animal souls, human souls, all children of our Father, but not evolutionable one into the other in any given period of planetary activity; but all progress towards the Creator as plants draw sunward. No man can make even a plant soul exist; but if he know the law, he can find a plant soul and give it a body of plant shape, if the body be a higher type than it had before. He can—I can incarnate such a plant soul. It is a simple experience; it begins by sprouting of seed, by growth of the young plant body, by maturity, budding, flowering, fruiting and ripening more seeds—seven simple actions. I can hasten these, and crowd them all into a few minutes. Then have I given the plant soul its little experience. Left alone it would have no others, but would die—the last experience in its incarnation. Very well; I take its body, but cut off no needed process. It is as virtually my body as my own flesh, for I made it and loaned it to the plant soul. Out of me went strength to do it. Reverse the process, eat the plant, into me returns my strength. But no man could foresee the experiences which each day, hour and minute bring to an animal soul—each and every one necessary, for it is growing toward the Eternal, and each experience is a responsible link, making it a karma which shall bring its animal soul into a next incarnate life. Kill it, and thou canst not compensate it for its opportunities; but to a plant thou mayest. Compensation is God's law. If thou doest a thing and can not compensate for it—that is sin; but if thou art able to make proper balance, it is no sin. Hence the Master of Nazareth did no sin in the matter of filling the fisherman's net; but thou wouldst have sinned in doing likewise, for in thee the manifest Spirit is not made One with thee. As thou canst not compensate an animal soul for its bodily life, thou sinnest in killing. And the flesh is accursed by reason of that sin. Behold, I say truly, if thou shalt do such sin, thou shalt reap the penalty; no butcher can see God in His Kingdom; he must cease to be a butcher ere he can have hope of knowing the occult realm which is His Kingdom."

Mol Lang arose, and I did also. He put his arm about me and said:

"My son, the desert is before thy feet. Its hot sands will scorch their soles, yet heed thine own intuition* which reveals God unto thy soul, and thou shalt come out of that desert, Be thou faithful unto death, and thou shalt have a crown of life from our Father. God be with thee and keep thee; I, also, will guard thee."

————————

My friends, years elapsed ere I again saw Mol Lang—weary years of sorrow and trial. He left me there by the river, and there Phyris found me not long after.

Soon gathered about us other people, mostly young persons, even some children. In Hesper, the Seventh Principle has a fair beginning of growth, while as for their physical perfection, any Hesperian has an almost God-like beauty and grace. But to illustrate how great is the height of that plane above anything earthly, and how many seemingly miraculous powers have there become characteristic of humanity, so as to be common inheritance of every ego thereon incarnate, instance this:—A little child, only four years of age, but very mature in demeanor, while essentially child-like in many things, came and stood beside me. Though the little one laughed and chatted with me, if I had at first been disposed to think her babyish, I soon regarded her differently. Young as she was, and of course unacquainted with any deep occult laws, yet as

—————
St. John, xvi, 13.

child of a branch of humanity advanced to the perfect human plane, and upon the threshold of the spiritual, she herself was fitted to be there by untold previous incarnations. As heritage of these many lives the little maid possessed astonishing powers which earthly men and women must acquire by the slow process of study through years.

Study first to conquer the animal nature, then meditate on the principles which, for those who have the will to know, are in these pages. Do only as they teach. Follow the Way. One shall guide all who earnestly ask Him, even before the Day of Man.

Apparently satisfied regarding my appearance—remember that I should have been invisible to non-clairvoyant eyes, but was not so to her inherited psychic sight—the little one remarked in sweet confidence:

"My father hath often told me of a numerous branch of the human race, compared to which we Pertozians are as the leaves of a single tree to those of a forest. He hath pointed out the planet where these dwell; I have never seen any of these lower human beings until now I see thee. Is it not strange? And they tell me, too, that neither thou, nor the mass of people are yet come to have knowledge of the karma, nor other occult powers—do foolishly scoff at it, indeed. It is strange. Still thou, and they also, will grow in knowledge. God demands it. Then thy personal appearance will become more pleasing." (!)

I was wholly abashed. To hear a mere child talk thus, and conclude with the remark that I would grow, well, grow to grace, was most astonishing. It was pleasing, too, for though it exhibited the vast gap between the Earthly man and the spirituality of Hesper, yet it showed the vista of human possibilities with a clearness which nothing else had done. Man needs comparisons to enable him to judge of relative values. St. Peter's Church at Rome is the greatest building the world now knows. But these vast buildings must be set about with others—themselves large—to enable the human mind to comprehend how vast they are. So with spiritual truths—until this little child revealed it, I had not had anything but a vague conception of the exalted truths I had heard. Mol Lang's marvelous actions; those of Sohma and Phyris even, had impressed me as acts of a superior being, whose side I could never gain as an equal. Truly, Mol Lang said he came there by study, and, further, faith in the Father. But my eyes saw not his progress—they but saw his attainment; neither had I seen this child acquire her position, but my soul could recognize the fact of her growth being still in progress. In place of vague desires, I began to feel the thrill of hope, and a knowledge that I also might grow. Until that moment I had accepted the statements of my friends that I could grow up to them. Faith was now replaced by knowledge. Through this little one my life was lifted, and linked to the higher life of Pertoz,—that of man perfect. I was ready to say in earnestness,—"Of such is the kingdom of heaven."

The dozen or more friends present asked me to tell my life story, in order that hearing the living voice, they might study me as I spoke. I complied. At last I finished. I had told of my hopes in life, and they were lofty, noble hopes, like those which throng the breast, subduing the animal nature, when one listens to music whose chords thrill the soul to do and dare for the high reward of hearing Him say:—"Well done, thou good and faithful servant."

To me then spoke Phyris, slowly, but how sweetly only one can know who puts away all that sullies the human soul. I noted that she no longer used the ordinary personal pronouns, but in this last conversation reverted to the solemn style though using the familiar English language.

"Phylos, thou hast related of thy life all that thou knowest. I know much more, and I will tell thee also, though thou goest to Earth, forgetting us, forgetting me."

"Phyris, say not so—I can never forget you!" I said sadly.

"Yea, Phylos, thou wilt forget me, because only thy Hesperian memory knoweth me, and it must yield to thine Earthly astral when thou hast returned thither. Yet it will but sleep, not perish, until the time again cometh for it to govern thy

life. When the years of karma are flown, thou wilt once
more come hither, and then thou wilt no more yearn for Earth,
as now. My twin, I fain would keep thee here; I can not, for
karma is set against me, and karma is the Christ law, saying—
'Whatsoever a man soweth, that shall he also reap.' Though
forgetting Hesper, yet thou shalt have an astral record, and it
will at times come to thee, even as thine earthly record cometh
here, disturbing thee, and it will be a strange thing, for it
will seem as thyself, yet thou shalt not recognize its words
as thine own history, so it shall seem also some one else.

"Thou hast told thy life so far as thou knowest it; but back
of it thou hast heard that thou hast had myriad other lives.
And in these I have been involved. Naturally so, for my spirit
is also thy spirit—though our souls are not now near together
as they have been in other times. I could tell thee much concerning this eternity past, which thou hast had and known,
but forgotten page by page as the Angel of Death turned the
leaves of thy book of life. But I will not tell thee, Phylos,
though I could remember it from that living, eternal record
of cause and effect, of the mutual action and reaction of the
forms of life and of matter; 'tis the astral record, the Father's
'Book of Life.' Memory is but the power of the soul to read
this great astral record. I have that power, thou hast it not,
but I will not tell thee, but leave thee to find all this thyself;
to know this past from thine own coming wisdom. Then thou
shalt know me as one with thyself. And I will in that time
write the long history of our lives from the remote days when
thou and I lived in old Lemuria, days ere the Earth had known
the continent of Atlantis, or the glacial epoch of geologists—
'twas the golden age. But we will know farther back than
that, even to the time when Earth did not exist, nor Venus
nor Mars, neither the sun nor any star. But of this I will not
try to tell the world all, not that it might not be told, but no
reader could comprehend that state wherein Man that is, was
a race not become Man as yet. When I say Man I say also all
associate animals, for every sort of being that lives on the
Earth is Man—there being men and animals—lesser men. No,

they who heard the words could in nowise comprehend beings neither animal, plant nor mineral, which nevertheless lived. I will therefore deal solely with the later time which came ere the last glacial epoch, and still later with the time of Zailm, and when of him, of thyself—for my Phylos is but Zailm reincarnate, returned from devachan.''

I raised my head, which I had kept bowed while Phyris talked. We were alone, the others of our party having withdrawn. Phyris continued:

''I will write of Anzimee, and so of myself; and I will write of others also. But now I speak of ourselves.

''When Man was born into the earth from Mars, as he is eventually to be born from the Earth into Hesper—that was the basis of the allegory of Adam and Eve, but back of them came all their lesser brethren—the animals of land, sea and air. And back of the Race birth were the Race lives on Mars, and ere then lives on two other planets, neither of which are of matter which the Earthly eye could perceive. There is in them now no life process—for these world souls are resting, and so also is Mars. Thus have I spoken of four of the seven planets to which the human race makes cyclic visits, going from One to Two, to Three, to Four (which is the Earth), to Five (Hesper), to the one to which Man will go after his years on Hesper, and thence to the Seventh or Sabbatic world. These two last, like the two first, are imperceptible to the eyes of man on Earth. Seven are the worlds, and seven times the race of Man circles them—three times aleady hath Man circled the series and arrived en masse at the fourth of the number in this, his fourth round. So, Phylos, I speak of all these many Race-lives; of Earth, of Hesper, of Mars, and all other human planets, after the ordinary sense. But whosoever wills may go with our Great Master, escaping the Rounds, and of that Life, no words can tell. But such will is rare, and few there be that find that Way. Yet here are some of the signs along that Path; hear them, heed, and thus find—me. Use all things as abusing none. Drugs, as drugs; food, as not gluttonously; drinks, as not bibulously; society, as a study; marriage* as a Way, but continency as His Highway. The most of our race must go by the lower path, for the Cliff-brow Way is too dizzy; none can walk it, save He holds their hands, and few there be that will to let Him, for desires tempt them. But they that refuse that Life now, how shall they find it again? They will not, and so shall cease with the world. Then will have come true that which is written—'There shall be time, and times and half a time.' Alas that it should be so. A message of this judgment shalt thou render in a day not afar off. Begin in the middle of its sojourn upon the Earth, the race is half through an experience of life that hath engaged it for a period of time too vast for thy real comprehension."

"Will you not tell me?"—I inquired. "I am curious."

"Tell thee? Yes, and in words thou canst understand, yet the figures can convey but vaguely to thee, who know not what all the period hath seen transpire. These are the figures" —and Phyris solemnly counted a period of time which my mind confronted as one helpless, lost in thought. "But see thou convey to none other this knowledge, until our atonement hath recurred. Such is the lapse of Time since the Universe was without form and void, and darkness was upon the face of the deep. Each man we see, except those who have been transfigured, is but a semi-ego, and each woman the same—two of these having one spirit. When the perfection time cometh, all the halves shall unite, each with its own— and lo! this is the marriage made in heaven. But first comes the Trial—the Crisis of Transfiguration."

"And if"—I asked—"if a soul pass not, why not, and what will happen, and if one half, one mate, shall fall, shall the other also?"

"Oh, my twin! If a soul pass not, it will be because the waywardness of its many lives hath clipped the wings of its strength so that it can not fly above the concentrated temptations of that trial. Such a fate is the portion of all failures

*I Cor. vii, 1 to 9; also 29, 31, 32, 36, 37 and 38.

in this supremest trial. And lastly, personally, if thou dost
fail?—Thy soul shall go into the Second Death, and because
of that, so also shall mine, for we, and all egoic mates fight
this last fight with our combined strength. On me thy eternal
life depends; on thee my hope rests; but upon the Spirit rests
all our hope. And we can not find It if we follow not the
Path shown us by Christ; if we seek It not, It will not seek us.
Save Christ is ours and in us we must fail in that fearful trial.
But come, Phylos, and see the Earth as it was in the days of
Zailm and Anzimee, and seeing that time, behold it now."

Thus speaking, she arose and touched me, and I perceived
for the first time that she, like myself, was in astral form. I
seemed to sleep momentarily, yet was conscious of motion, the
sort of motion that one experiences when passing from deep
sleep to full wakefulness at once. This was the passage from
Hesperus to Earth. The sensation was due to the fact that
my present astral was in some sort material; as I had not even
an astral when coming from the Earth, and so nothing material,
therefore I could not be conscious of that transition. The
sleeping unconsciousness was now due to Phyris—who wished
to draw my attention from her words and—herself.

———————

Once more all the scenes of Earth appeared. I saw the broad
waters of the Atlantic. Phyris said:

"Names are appropriate; see here is the Atlantic Ocean
where was the Atlantean Continent. And now we descend
into it; above are its waters, and around us. They harm us
not, for our psychicality is superior to their psychicality. Behold the psychic record of the past, the concrete history of the
world, imperishable until Time shall be no more. Wouldst
thou read of a first destruction of Poseid? Seek it in thy
Bible, and find it as the Noachian deluge. This was before
the age of Zailm, or of history which they knew, many thousands of years. Wouldst learn of the destruction of Lemorous,
that great people who were in the Earth before the Age of Ice,
when the world knew no cold, nor snow, nor frost; who ante-
dated Poseid by countless ages? Turn to the Book of Job and

read of how the 'deep boiled like a pot'—and reading, thou
shalt learn that Lemuria perished of fire from out the inter-
planetary depths. So one cycle of mankind dieth of fire, and
the next of water. And again, the next dieth of fire. The
races of Earth to-day shall come—afar off as is yet that day—
to perish of fire, and the Earth be blasted and rolled together as
a scroll—find thou its prophesy in the second Book of Peter
III-10. Yet knowledge of all this is not from my telling. I
have spoken. And now, my other self, I take thee yet awhile
to fulfill the law and the prophets and thy karma. And I will
abide thy coming again unto me; we part—see, here is the
Sagum, there Mendocus. Aye, beloved, we part, but it is for
a little while, and then for eternity we shall be one together.
Let some dim perception of me awaken in thy mind, and
sweeten thy life, and lead thee ever upward. My peace, so
much as it is such, be with thee, and keep thee!''

She put her arms about me, and held me long, while our
eyes looked into each others souls. Then her lips met mine in
one ecstatic throb, and—she was gone!

———————

CHAPTER VIII.

OLD TEACHERS TAUGHT OF GOD.

I awoke. The place was in one of the smallest rooms of the
Sagum; it seemed not unfamiliar, although I had theretofore
been only in the greater apartment. Mendocus sat by my side.
There was a sense of having lost something; I knew not what,
but the loss made me inexpressibly sad. I felt hampered, as
if my freedom had contracted. Otherwise, too, I felt weak, as if
long ill. But Mendocus put his hand over my eyes, and I
slept.

The next conscious moment came, and the weariness was
gone, but not wholly so the sense of loss—of restricted
freedom. It was one thing to lose prehension of memory and

events; to have entirely forgotten Hesperus and Phyris, and Mol Lang and Sohma, as I had done; but it was a wholly different and impossible thing to forget or in any wise put away the growth of my soul during my five weeks of absence from the Earth. Yes, five weeks, for despite the seeming months in devachan, and the time in Pertoz, all but one part in a thousand of my time of absence had been spent in Hesperus. Five weeks of Earth time.

It would have been impossible for me to have remained in Pertoz and been happy. It would be impossible for you, my friends. Why? Because it was a plane of soul life so exalted above our familiar Earth, that only growth can introduce the soul there—long, slow, oft times painful—but growth. To me, then, or to you now, irrevocable transference to such a high plane of life would be fearful punishment; all our ordinary powers of life, all our present selves put away, and an entirely different set of sensibilities and a new, unknown, untried self in their place—knowledge in the use of all which, amidst wholly strange phenomena and unlearned laws—the misplaced soul would have to acquire through long, unhappy years. It is a divine blessing to humanity that sudden transition from one plane to a higher is as impossible as is any real retrogression.

I sat up, and then stood up, Mendocus assisting me—for I was weak and dizzy. I remained at the Sach until several days had elapsed, learning of various occurrences and making various decisions and resolutions. Asking for Quong, I was told he was dead, and knowing now nothing of the past five weeks, I accepted the news with keen regret.

Mendocus told me that I was a man yet possessed of earthly appetites and passions, although I had lately been where humanity was of the heavenly order, as measured by terrestrial standards—where no sensuality ever invaded, although the people were not austere, nor was life there devoid of pleasure. I assented for the sake of courtesy, without knowing anything of whom or what he spoke, more than an untravelled commoner of a great city knows of interior Africa. He saw my ignorance and became silent.

His remarks about social sin I felt inapplicable to myself, for although I mingled with the people of this world, I did not sin in the meaning of the term as he applied it. Perhaps from environment, I was not free, but free of these errors I was, and without any pharisaical self-praise.

Speaking of the fallen, however, where was the really sweet, noble girl I had tried to raise, and who, seconding my efforts, had gone to Melbourne? Life interests were again claiming me. The animal soul was reasserting itself, and warring as strongly as its feeble self-hood allowed with the human soul and the stirring spirit which cannot sin nor err, because it is one with the Over Soul, and so ever draws the human soul upward, whilst the animal pulls it downward.

Then said Mendocus to me.

"Mr. Pierson, the sins thou dost condemn in thy fellow-creatures were once thine, and, if thou shalt condemn the doer, may become thine again. That thou judgest, thou art not past danger of committing.

"Judge not, lest thou be judged. But in thine inner soul these past five weeks have placed a light—a lamp from God. Hide it not, but let it so shine that it give light to the sinful who have no light. Pity them, deplore their error, but if thou condemn them thou wilt not follow Him who said 'neither do I condemn thee; go and sin no more.'"

Mol Lang had set a proper estimate on my powers in refusing to make irrevocable my ascent to the Hesperian plane. I had stood ready with the torch of desire to fire my earthly ships. If I could have known of my escape I would have felt thankful. As it was, Hesper was become an unmeaning name, and the ships were not burned. Pleased as a child I had gone to the devachanic plane, where all things that the child in experience desired, although it wished never so foolishly, seemed to occur. Now the child having confronted the sober fact that inexorable laws govern all the reign of being, had become stricken, broken-hearted at his failure; had returned to his own sphere, and—blessed mercy—was enabled to forget it all until such time as the five weeks' leaven had leavened the whole, and return was possible in the circumstances of one coming to his own. Friend, never assume the attitude of childishness toward the sublime—you may not escape as lightly as I did. Count the cost, or else plod along with the common-place masses. Both roads lead to the goal, one short but inexpressibly severe, the other long, and, alas! quite severe enough. It is no paradox to say that the shortest road is the longest; life is not always measured by years—some lives are but a few short years—but oh: the bitterness and not impossibly, sweets, too, crowded in them would require a thousand years of other and less marked lives to essay.

Before I left the Sagum, Mendocus laid down esoteric rules for my guidance in the days to come, days when sole dependence must be stayed on my knowledge of these rules, since no esoterist would be near to counsel me.

"Mr. Pierson"—said the grand old sage—"I have here a Bible. Lo! I have read it, the Old Testament, eighty-seven times; the New, even more times. Yet I see ever new beauties in the Book. I have here the Books of Manu, and also the Vedas. All are authored by the Christ-Spirit, under different human names, truly, and in different ages. All are more or less allegorical; all require His Light to interpret; without it, serious errors may arise as they have arisen heretofore in the world with sad frequency and fearfully long lived persistency.

"I will therefore declare unto thee a guidance from them. Knock, and it shall be opened unto thee. But see thou knockest with the will of the Spirit, for although the mind knock forever, the Way shall not be opened.

"Ask, and it shall be given. But although the animal man ask ever, no answer shall be given, for this meaneth also except the request be made by the Spirit in thee for the Truths of God, and not for earthly things; these last follow as shade the sun.

"Whatsoever is asked of the Father in the Christ's name, that shall He grant. But consider that asking in the name of the Christ is asking for the things of His Kingdom. With the gift of these things all lesser things shall be added—food, raiment and all else the body hath need for. This is hard for the natural mind to comprehend. He will not let thee perish though thou die of hunger.

"Whatsoever a man soweth, that shall he also reap. This is karma and the law, and every jot of it must be fulfilled. Man is a creature of many incarnations, each earth life one personality, strung on the unbreakable string of his egoic individuality, which reacheth from everlasting to everlasting, from the East unto the West.

"No demand of karma may be ignored—all must be paid in the course of the lives.

"Then 'do unto others as thou wouldst be done by,' and remember, as thou doest unto the least of thy fellow creatures, in that manner and measure is it done unto our Savior, and unto the Father, and shall be done unto thee again.

"Keep all the commandments; thou shalt so come to everlasting, where is all wisdom."

That evening I went out of the sacred precincts and back to the town.

There I learned of things various. My mining partners were now willing to buy my share without further parley. From that sale I received approaching three hundred thousand dollars, paid in installments—seven quarterly payments of nearly forty-three thousands dollars gold coin, each one.

The arrangement having been made for depositing these sums, as they fell due, with my bankers in Washington, D. C., I was overcome with a desire to travel; this and my ability to gratify it took me to nearly every civilized land. Yet no object except unrest prompted this nomadism.

———————

Almost two years had passed since I left ———— City, the scene of my esoteric experiences. I was in Norway, away from the wide, wide world, in a little hamlet close to a celebrated fjord, where I had arrived the previous day. My guide and general utility man spoke English sufficiently well to make himself readily intelligible. He proved to have been a sailor on the ship in which I took my first voyage, and had returned to his native land to minister to the wants of travelers, in which service his knowledge of Anglo-Saxon did him good stead. He was delighted to see me, a feeling which I reciprocated. His name? Certainly—Hans Christison.

Hans said that four or five other summer travelers were staying in the village—"One ish ein young leddy; she haf a crazy for paint und brushes—ish ein nardist, I think so."

A week elapsed before I met this "purty leddy"—and meantime Hans guided me, equipped with gun and fish rod, he rowing our light skiff. One afternoon I took the skiff and went off alone to a rock jutting out of the fjord, whereon grew several birch trees of graceful beauty. I tied the skiff, and then climbed out and sat down to read the letters forwarded to me from New York.

While reading these I heard a little sound behind me as of some person else on the tiny island. Turning my head I saw a woman, and then I laid down my paper and sprang to my feet. I was too much surprised to raise my cap or even to speak, and she seemed equally astonished. Then I said the one word:

"Lizzie!"

"Mr. Pierson!"—she replied.

"How came you here?"—was our next exchange. I told her of my aimless wanderings, and she related her life since we parted in ———— City. From Melbourne she had gone to New York, and thence to Washington. There she bought a residence and established an art studio, assuming the name of Harland. People were told little and learned less of her antecedents, and were allowed to suppose that she was a young Australian widow of moderate wealth. Each of the two summers after her advent to life at the Capital had been spent abroad, and this, the third summer, she was spending in Norway. Her pictures had sold well, and she had made up the entire sum which she had used from what she called my "loan." This she insisted on giving back to me, but I laughed, and tentatively agreed, saying, "Before I leave, if you insist." I staid four weeks there; staid until I learned from a chance remark that she was going away in a few days for a little stay among the Scottish lakes. Then without saying anything to Mrs. Harland, I bade Hans take me by night to the steamer which visited the little port once a fortnight, and was then due, and going on board, paid Hans, adding a douceur. As the ropes were being cast off, I said:

"Hans, let the 'young leddy' know that I am gone; tell her—if she asks—I am going to St. Petersburg. Good bye, Hans."

To the Capital of the Czar I went, and was there a week. Then back to Paris, then to London, and in another week I sailed for New York, thence to Washington.

A year passed. One afternoon as I strolled up Pennsylvania Avenue, I came face to face with Elizabeth Harland. We stopped, spoke, and then I turned and walked with her. The old memories surged over us; I remembered the days in California; then more tenderly, the peaceful month in Norway, when I had come to really believe I loved this girl, not only for her radiant beauty and sedately sweet womanhood, but for her tremendous effort to triumph over error, and her success, wherefore she was come forth from the fire, pure gold.

Before we parted I learned her address, and resolved to call as soon as an opportunity offered.

Next evening a bank messenger came to my apartments, and left a packet. It held two hundred bank notes of the value of one hundred dollars each, and a letter. This I opened hastily and read:

Sept. 3rd, 1869.

"Mr. Walter Pierson:—

"Enclosed find the sum of my indebtedness to you, and accept my heartfelt gratitude for the same. And we will be friends; you are ever welcome to come to the home of
                    Your sincere friend,
                            Elizabeth Harland."

I pondered the situation, and when the moment of decision came, made up my mind very suddenly. The money which she had returned I put into my pocketbook, took my hat and being in proper attire, I went down the street until I found a cab. Entering this, I gave directions to the driver to take me to No. —, ——— Street.

It was a pretty place. When I rang the bell it was answered by Mrs. Harland herself. Her manner was cordial, but I fancied somewhat constrained.

On the wall of the parlor hung a picture of rare merit. A man whose face and mien was as expressive of divinity as it lies in the power of paint and brush to depict, stood looking on a woman whose face was hidden by her hands. In the dust at his feet were characters written. The environment was that of the architecture of the Holy Land. Under the painting, which was half life size, were the words, "St. John, VIII—11."

I sat down in a proffered chair, and for a moment silence reigned. My hostess broke this, saying:

"You received the money, Mr. Pierson?"

"Yes." I drew it out of my pocket and following my resolve, and waiving all prefatory remarks, I said:

"Except you give me yourself with this money, I will not take it out of the house. Will you be my wife, Elizabeth?"— I asked as I knelt by her side.

Her eyes gazed into mine a moment, and she said:

"For myself, because you love me, and veil the past with the success of the present?"—tears in her eyes, tears in her voice as she spoke.

"Yes, darling!"

With a convulsive sob she rested in my arms, and cried as if her heart would break. At length she said, tremulously:

"All the world is less worth than this true love."

Our wedding was quiet, and after it we went for a brief trip abroad, going only to England, and in a short time returned home.

CHAPTER IX.

THEY WHO HEED HAVE PEACE.

Once during the wanderings before my marriage, and while I was in Hindostan, I met an old man of unprepossessing figure, whose faded eyes no sooner rested on me than he said:

"You are he of whom Mendocus told me, and charged me concerning, saying 'tell him certain things for me.' This I will do. Young man, your life shall be sad and bitter on Earth, but sweet after that. Things will transpire because of which your animal soul shall embrace itself and say, 'This is joy.' But immediately the still voice of the human soul in you shall say, 'This joy is but a Sodom apple,' and in that moment you will know that it is so. Hence you will have ever a war between your animal soul, which is innate depravity, and your spirit, which is of God, Brahma, the One. See in it the allegory of Adam and original sin; it pulls your human soul down to death; the other, the Spirit, draws the human upward. Attend then its sayings; I will render them for you:

"Before your eyes can see God they must be incapable of shedding tears for any suffering of your own. Before your ears can hear, they must have lost sensitiveness. Your voice may not speak eternal wisdom until it has no power to wound. Before your self can stand in the presence of the Eternal, its feet must have been bathed in the blood of suffering, penance, restitution. Then kill the ambition to excel in the poor paths of Fame. Cease to regard this life as your best possession.

"Then work for God as earnestly as others work for Mammon; and respect thy life as those respect life who treasure it most, and be happy as those who live for happiness. In the hearts of all is the source of all error, in disciple as well as in the man of desire. Study a plant of mustard—witness it grow and bud. But if thou shalt hew it down so that it never beareth seed, behold a strange thing—it will sprout again and grow through the years, if it never beareth. And this although it is only a material form. Now, therefore, if a human soul shall not be cut down, yet shall not enter into life as a creator by reason that it wills not, then the Spirit of life everlasting shall go into it, and it shall contain itself, and therefore live forever. Study the truth of mustard life. Only the strong in God can act upon this teaching and hold the lower nature. The weak must wait its maturity and then will come their struggle. It will strive to keep the feet from the Path; and may succeed. But if once all its power be wiped out; if once thou doest the will of the Father earnestly, as His obedient child—that is the atonement, for it shall give strength to do every work of the Creator of Being. It will seem to take the very life. That is because it takes the animal soul and throttles it. But the human soul will recover, and the Spirit come into it. This is the time of the Silence of the Soul. Then it shall be clear to you how dark are the lives of those who are around you and have no goal of union with the Spirit towards which to race. And you will see and know karma. Also you will see that because of your past incarnations your karma is inextricably interwoven with the karma of the world. This is that saying which the Nazarene answered when it was asked of Him 'Who is my neighbor?' If, Walter Pierson, you shall once be able to know the Peace of Silence, you shall then learn of all things about you, for the Earth is Brahm's, and all in it teaches His works.''

I was surprised at being called by name, and also of being told of Mendocus. The old man said further:—

"If your soul once knows this Peace, no storm of sin or of sorrow can ever more ward you far aside from the Path, for its knowledge is an abiding wisdom. Heed also the words of Mendocus, read your Bible, read the Vedas, read Manu; and study. It shall all be a staff to your hand and a lamp to your feet. Peace be with you.''

"And to you, peace.''—I replied as he turned and walked away into the crowd—for we had stood by a public drinking fountain.

Now that Elizabeth was found and was my wife, I pondered deeply these things I had heard of the occult lore. Not that she had connection with it. But because, as the years went by, I found she knew and cared little about these abstruse studies, which I did. So our lives drew apart. But she was oblivious of this fact, and I was glad because she was. She had her churchwork and I aided her in all her sweet charities. To us came two lovely little daughters—the greatest treasures of our lives, and oh, so carefully taught regarding life and shielded from its dangers. So long as these little ones were with us, I was content. And yet I felt, in an ill-defined sorrow, that Earth's experiences were but Sodom apples.

Sometimes I found my lonelier hours disturbed by a strange voice which whispered to my inner consciousness. As time passed it grew stronger, and one day it appeared before my sight as a wraith. The Shape talked. What it said made me eager to hear more, so I cultivated it. It became thenceforth a regular visitor, and from that to being always present when I was otherwise alone was but a step. It spoke of having been on a distant planet which it called "Pertoz," sometimes "Hesperus," again "Venus." It spoke of persons whose names were strange, calling one "Mol Lang"; another "Sohma" and a third "Phyris." Then it described these people, and I listened eagerly. Who were they, and what human soul was this which had gone to Venus? The ghost looked marvelously like myself. But my slumbers at night were as sound as if it visited me not.

I called it my ghost. How unconsciously true It told of everything related to my being with Mol Lang, and in Venus; it drew my mind's eye to the psychic scene in the bed of the Atlantic. It told of a visit to the sun with Sohma—of which I neglected mention in sequence. Briefly, Sohma went with me to the sun, and showed me that it was a vibrant body of less size than astronomers believe, but of enormous density. I saw its oceans—they were heavier than Mercury. But it had no life forms which I took as such. Yet life of some sort there is everywhere. Perhaps, indeed, not animal, nor vegetable, but from the high standpoint of those who know much of the works of the All-Father, forms that no earthly man would call life, are such, nevertheless. But the sun is force of such fearful vibrative pulsing that even my subtle astral body was not unaffected. Sohma said of it:

"See the immediate center of our solar system. Thou wouldst call it a dynamo, the great dynamo of the system. Right wouldst thou be, and wrong also. The attempt to define the sun as an analogue to a dynamo-electric machine has much to support it. But to define it as identical is erroneous. The trouble with that theory is the trouble which lies at the root of and weakens all other theories to account for sun-heat and sun-light. It is that science does not assign a sufficiently high value to the sun. The combustion theory is invalid; the solar mass contraction theory is but partially tenable and meteoric showers do not account better than the first two. Neither does the electric-dynamo theory. Truly, the latter explains how sun-heat and sun-light may coexist and not be inharmonious with the awful degree of cold between earth, the planets and the sun. It explains that which denies the simple combustion theory so completely—viz.—that the farther one goes from the earth center, either in a balloon or on a high mountain, the colder and darker the air gets—so that inter-stellar space is several hundred degrees below zero, and black as midnight, with the sun a luminous disc, without rays. But the dynamo theory does not explain the solar spectrum, nor the bands of spectra, nor coronal 'flames,' nor 'sun spots,' nor solar nor lunar eclipses."

The above statements were made by Sohma, as will be remembered by the reader, while I was still in the Hesperian astral state and for the time was unconscious of a previous terrene existence. I had therefore no memory of the mundane knowledge and was unbiased in my judgment of the remarks of my friend. He had ceased to speak after uttering the word "eclipses." I waited for him to continue, but as he did not, I finally interrogated—"Well, what does explain all? What is the truth?" Thus questioned, he resumed:

"I have said that the value accorded by astronomers is too small. Seeing a fire, they would seek to explain by its means the sun. Finding this untenable, and aware that a contracting mass gives off heat, they next essay explanation on that hypothesis. But this will not do, nor will meteoric showers, nor any hypothesis based on facts now known—all are too low in aim; the Infinite cannot be explained by the finite, nor will less explain greater; fire is energy, and electricity is energy, and God is energy. But fire will not solve the query, 'What is electricity?' nor will electricity answer 'What is God?' but God will explain both the others, for the sum of the parts is equal to the whole. But as man does not know the full number of the parts, the partial sum he does know will not explain God."

Sohma ceased again. But I, filled with some vagrant earth memory, allowed no time of pause; I was too eager to wait, and I said

"But this does not tell me what the solar puzzle is."

"Thou art impatient, my brother; know then, what was at one time known upon the earth, but is now for ages forgotten; that Nature has a dual aspect—is double—is positive and negative— that the great positive side is the side known to mundane science, while the other or negative, or 'Night Side,' or, as it was once known in the earth by the men of Atla, 'Navaz,' is a side all unknown, and scarcely guessed in the most exceeding flights of speculation, left unbroached, secretly kept by a few, who know not that they entertain an angel,—an angelic wisdom that in a century more—yea, less time!—shall overturn much of the face of terrene things—shall bestow aerial vessels, and all else once known to those men of Atl of whom I spoke. Thou dost not yet understand?"

I said that I did not; that I thought he referred to some domain of the physical forces not yet known; but what had this to do with the sun?

"This: the suns of systems are centers of forces of the Night Side of Nature whereof I spoke—and are force, and matter of a higher value than are planets and satellites—just as water above a cataract is water, truly, but being above and mobile, flows over and down, developing energy. In other words, out of the cold, dark, negative side, or 'night side,' force emerges, drawn to the positive polarity which constitutes in its outgoing flow that termed Nature, and develops in its fall, magnetism, electricity, light, color, heat and sound, in order of descent, and lastly solid matter, for this latter is a child of energy, not its parent. When the Navaz forces drop to light, if the light waves enter a spectroscope, they will emerge as colors; these correspond to the various spectrum bands, and will, as the descent progresses, give the noted lines of the solar spectrum—as the great 'B' line of oxygen, the conspicuous 1474' line, and the brilliant 'H' and 'K' violet bands."

I thought I now saw the truth; but I saw only a part; a grand vista was yet to open. I saw it when my companion resumed:

"Thus the evidence of flames, and metals on fire, and all that leads astronomers to think sun and stars flaming hells. But their 'fires' will not decrease—for the Father is immanent, and the forces of 'Navaz' are perpetually fed by Him. The graphic picture of a 'burned-out sun' is a dream, never to be fulfilled. A day will come again in the earth when instruments will be made which Atlantis once well knew—when the prismatic rays from a spectroscope will be found to be a source of heat, and of sound, so that the so-called 'flames' of the sun, and of the stars will produce music, harmonies divine.[*] Yea, further—for going on down, the dark green solar spectrum of iron will be made to yield iron for use in the arts, and so with the other bands and lines—the intense greens, blues, and blue-greens give copper, lead, antimony and so on. It is by these Navaz currents that the circulation in the universe is kept up, as blood in a man's arteries. The suns are the systemic hearts. But thou art tired, my brother, or I would

---

[*]Job xxxviii, 7.

explain yet more—that the planets which receive all these currents, must return their equivalent. And thus would an other vast field open before thy sight. This last would explain that which so worries science on earth—the molten terrene interior. That also is something of an error. All the phenomena which seem to declare the earth to be in a melted condition inside do not prove it so in truth; all point to the return currents—the positive; all exhibit the venous currents of our universe, back to its hearts."

Sohma concluded with an apostrophe to the leading minds of the Earth which was beautiful indeed:

"O Science of Earth—in thee is the hope of the world, when thou shalt become handmaiden of God. Look up, value His works highly, and thou shalt read clearly many things which now puzzle thee sadly. Thou art the Joseph, and Religion the Mary, and ye twain shall show forth the Light of Life. Blessed art thou."

When my "ghost" retold me this conversation I seized my hat and went out to look sunwards and marvel if all were true, and astounded, reflect again, "Who is this Sohma?"

The puzzle grew, and my discontent with life grew—the lump was becoming leavened. The more I studied the truth of the mustard plant, the clearer grew my perceptions, and I knew that never in my present body, could I attain much progress, for in our union Elizabeth and I had passed by the mustard unheeding, writing another karmic chapter.

For a time my "ghost" was amenable to my will as regarded its comings and goings; but it now seemed to have entered in and coalesced with me. I no longer heard or saw it, but instead was often one with it, and saw and heard its visions and perceptions as if they were my own; and indeed, as you know, this was a fact. It was in verity the record of my visit to Pertoz, and was a true cast in all ways of my life there.

Ofttimes my soul was torn by steadfastness to the duty of life as pointed out by Mendocus. And then my only escape from trouble was to allow myself to rest in the Hesperian astral to the exclusion of that of Earth. At such times I was

living again the life with Phyris and the loved ones of Pertoz.
Elizabeth sorrowed over this aberration, as she thought it;
and my blessed little daughters grew to regard "papa" as
"funny" and I was held in awe. Not a pleasant experience,
my friends. My wife would look at me sadly and I know she
wept when alone because I often absently called her "Phyris."
Indeed, Elizabeth was my closest realization of the Phyris of
whom I knew but could not find on Earth. Under all this I
grew thin and pale, and aimlessly wandered about possessed
of a huge disgust for worldly interests or amusements; filled
with sorrow for the sorrow I saw the world held, and yearning
for the high plane which I at last knew was not a fantasy, and
where Phyris was, and Sohma, and Mol Lang. But I could
not get there; and they came not to me, therefore I studied
the rules of the Path, because torn with crazed regret when
the lower nature triumphed and I fell in sinful error, but
although I fell, I rose again. Then the effect this had on my
sweet, loving wife came home to me. Was this doing as I
would be done by? No. So I set my will in firm resolve and
subdued my own sorrows, and made my nature a tool for my
soul, not a master over me.

Then once again I smiled, and the color and flesh came
back to me. So Elizabeth was happy once more; and I? I
had found the true Path at last. Service. I no longer wept
for myself; my ears were no more sensitive, my tongue no
longer wounded any one with its morose utterances—chiefest
triumph of all, my feet were bathed in the life blood of the
animal nature, so that I lived unselfishly, my whole being bent
on doing my best, living as happily as if solely for happiness,
as earnestly as if for ambitious motives. Then it was that the
Peace of the Silence came, and I waited for the Savior to take
me and fight in me and do His work with my hands. The
Paraclete was come into my life.

It was a sad blow when my little daughters died of epidemic
scarlatina in the year 1878. Thereafter I used my life to comfort the sweet woman whose vital breath nearly died in that
cruel loss. I think Elizabeth never cared for anything in life

after that, except my loving devotion. And I gave it, for I knew Phyris would have me do so, and I waited on Earth now only to make it tolerable for the woman I had sworn to cherish. She waited in anticipation of rejoining her children in heaven, and meanwhile devoted all her time and energy, with feverish application, to doing all the good she could—using our unlimited money for the purpose. How exultant I was that the money was drawn from the gravel of the mines, and not come to me from harrassed debtors.

It was less than two years after Dora and Maydie—our two little girls—had gone to the Summerland, ere Elizabeth followed after them.

I felt the need of a radical change in living methods for the sake of my health, and so, under an assumed name, secured a situation as mate on an American sailer—a splendid vessel. My purpose was to expose myself to the toil of a sea life for a season in the idea of recuperation coming from active duty.

Nothing would satisfy Elizabeth, except going as a passenger on the same vessel—she refused to leave me out of her care. The captain knew her relation to me, so did the crew, so that her being a passenger was natural.

Near the Bermudas a terrible storm came up, and I ordered the sails close reefed, then the squall struck, the mainmast went over, the vessel sprang a leak, the pumps were inadequate, and the boats were swamped—all but one—as fast as they were lowered. Into that went the crew, and I would have put Elizabeth in, but the men, seeing the boat full, pushed off and left her, Captain Washburne and me to our fate. Hardly five minutes elapsed when our noble vessel pitched bows on under the engulfing waves, carrying us with it.

I had lashed myself to the deck cleats to avoid being washed overboard. So now I was doomed to die—and was glad. As the waters swept overhead, I called out in my soul:—"Phyris! at last! at last I come!" I saw Mendocus as I lost consciousness, and when I next came to knowledge, I found myself in the Sagum in California. Yet my body drowned off Bermuda's coast! Here was Phyris, and—yes! Mol Lang. It was not long

ere I again bade Mendocus farewell, and with Phyris and Mol
Lang went home to Pertoz—home now—my own attained
plane, and "Earth with its dark and dreadful ills" left behind forever, but not Earth with its mighty secrets of life.
Yes, Terre is, if insignificant, a point whence the Human soul
reaches out into the boundless sidereal universe and formulates
its laws, knows them, and is greater than all. I was come to
leave the Earth where so many incarnations had known me.

> " 'Twas a time
> For memory and for tears. Within the deep
> Still chambers of the heart a spectre dim,
> Whose voice was like the wizard tones of Time
> Heard from the Tomb of Ages, points its cold
> And solemn finger to the beautiful
> And holy visions that have passed away,
> And left no shadow of their loveliness
> On the dead waste of life. That spectre lifts
> The coffin lid of Hope and Joy and Love."

O Earth! point in the heavens, yet type of all the stellar universe.

Shall I descend a moment to figures? Shall I speak numbers
almost inconceivable? I will. Just for a moment think of
what we have come to know in the schools of Earth—think of
our human civilization that permits us new comprehensions—
see the parallel of how we measure time and distance compared
to the Indian who measures one by "moons" and the other by
"looks"—one being the interval between one full, or new
moon and the next; the other being how far he can look and
distinguish a man. Civilized man measures by years and by
miles, and science by "light-years." How much is a light-
year? In the time of one second light travels one hundred and
ninety-two thousand miles, approximately. In one year there
are thirty-one million, five hundred and fifty-six thousand, nine
hundred and twenty-nine seconds—hence the distance of a
light-year is the multiplied product of one figure by the other
—briefly, the inconceivable distance of sixty trillion, five hundred and fifty-three billion, ten hundred and fifty thousand
miles. All that, and yet we see a star in the northern heavens
said to be one hundred and eighty-one light-years distant from

the earth around which our own sun revolves, one of its satellites, as the moon is satellite to the earth. Such is the material universe, an infinitude, one of God's Works, but only one, and yet it is a comprehensible mechanism, not, from the material point of view, comparable to the value of one soul of Man. Why do I thus digress? Friends, to let you know what proud place Man occupies. Think of all that nearly interminable distance to Arcturus, and then reflect that that bright member of the constellation Bootes is only a little way out in the boundless universe! That vast bulk of matter, capable of being seen nearly one hundred and twenty million times farther than the distance between the earth and the sun. How great is that bulk? Estimated by comparison it is more than half a thousand million times larger than the combined mass of the Earth, Venus, Mars, Saturn, Neptune and Mercury. And yet the human mind reaches into this almost infinite thing called the universe and grapples understandingly with its problems of matter, force, time, space, eternity, infinity! Laus Deo! Thus Arcturus is our yard-stick in the siderial universe, which in itself is in the House of our Father only one mansion! Besides it are "many mansions" and, friends, there is one mansion of the many to which I have called your attention—that of the Soul. The Soul is not material, and one loved one who shall go away out of your home into the "Unknown Country" is farther away from you than Arcturus, for it is in another condition of being. Wondrous privilege—you stand on the threshold—for you are embodied children of the Creator. You can learn His Ways, and go unto the loved ones gone before; or you can leave matter behind and go into the psychic mansion, and re-enter matter wheresoever you will; be in the World one instant, in the astral the next, and in Arcturus the next,—I speak no idle tales—who hath ears to hear, let him hear.

————————

Now I had left the world for a new life—a new vantage point. So far I had lived a life purely one of sacrifice to duty, and that duty one to Elizabeth, all the later while knowing

myself, through my other astral, to be far from home and
Phyris and knowledge. And now the release had come; my
sacrifice to Elizabeth was completed, my charity had covered
a multitude of sins—oh! many more than I knew at the time
of the completed sacrifice. And yet, I had not quite atoned
for all the weary errors of past incarnations. Almost free,
however, almost free!

While yet living with Elizabeth, my obedience to the rules
of which I have spoken and others of which I have not spoken
—all from Mol Lang and Mendocus—had given me insight
into somewhat of the past. Thus I had learned a little of the
dead personality known to the reader as Zailm of Poseid. I
knew that Zailm's spirit, human soul—his individuality—were
also mine—that I, Pierson, had been Zailm. I was able to
form a fair remembering of Zailm's life; and of its events
and his friends. I knew that the acts he did and the sins he
committed, were my inheritance, and that I was responsible
for them—because though his personality was not my personality, his individuality was, and is, mine. Although I
knew not who Lolix was, or that she lived, yet, for Zailm's
(my) sin with her and for her tragic death, I must atone. To
whom? Anybody in the Earth whom I could serve as CHRIST
had said in declaring, "Even unto the least of these." I served
with the sacrifice of my living happiness the duty I contracted
to Elizabeth, by living for her, and dying on my ship that she
might have the chance to escape. I had rescued her from a
nameless sin of life in ——— City, and brought her to saving
faith in JESUS, THE CHRIST. If as Zailm, I—the Me—had
tripped with Lolix,—I, as Walter Pierson, had arisen with
another (?) soul to salvation. So karma balanced there.
Karma—self made fate—binds the soul to make reparation in
some life or lives for its sins in others. It bound me; I paid
the debt. It binds you for debts contracted sometime, somewhere, and will you not follow the Path, and after paying the
debt, be with the free forever more? Charity is great: its

least worthy aspect alms giving, for although I give all my goods to feed the poor, and have not (that) charity (which is love) it profiteth me nothing.''

——————

I have said that my wife, Elizabeth, cared little for my esoteric studies. But to infer that she cared nothing would be wrong. She once found me in my library, using an occult needle. This was a steel bar seven inches long, square, and one-third of an inch thick, pointed quadrimidally, with gold tips. It swung in a glass case suspended by a hair, over the symbol.

Could you have been gifted with clairvoyant sight, and have looked upon me as Elizabeth found me, you would have seen that needle hanging motionless, and all about it a golden light or aura. From either end went a beam of this odic luminosity —one to me, and one to a distance. Looking along the latter you could have seen at its end a man, standing beside a dining room sideboard; in his hand a glass of brandy. That man was a dear friend of mine, with but one grave fault—inebriety. As he poised the cup to drink, I said firmly:

"No! 'Touch not, taste not, handle not!' Neither now nor henceforth! Heed my voice, or you shall not enter the King-dom of Heaven.''

Willis Murchison, the would be drinker, let the glass fall to the floor, where it broke to fragments. A day or so later I met him, and he related that he had had a vision, and heard a voice from God, saying that he should no more drink lest he lose his chance of heaven. He never did touch liquor again. He heard the mysterious voice and heeded; yet he had not heeded his friends. By the occult secret of that aurant tipped needle whose power enlisted the service of spirits ᴜot human, I held mesmeric power over him. Herein is the peril of letting the masses know these things,—for had I been unscrupulous, lawless, a sorcerer, I could as easily have moved Murchison to any crime.

Elizabeth asked what I was doing there in the dark. Having achieved my purpose with my friend, I said to my wife—"Let me tell you certain things." I told her of the law of karma, and much besides. When nearly through, I willed the gold pointed needle to connect her mind psychically with mine. Between us the line of light was established. I whispered then:

"Look! See your past life on earth, and know it. Then tell me, nor forget what you learn."

She was silent for a few moments, then her breath came as in sleep. Presently she said:

"A noble, wonderful man is guiding me. I see him seemingly uncover a remote age of the world; it is the day of a mighty nation, who sail the air in what they call 'Vailx.' A splendid city is about me. Now I am in a vast temple; the interior of it is ornamented with real stalactites. I stand by a large cube of crystal quartz, and on this is a strange flame which burns without fuel. I see a young couple whom a grave, priestly man is uniting in marriage. Ah, it seems as if I loved the one to be wed better than I love life! I implore the one in the assemblage who seems to be a ruler of the nation to prohibit the wedding. Then the priest turns to me—now he looks at me, and—oh! my God!—his look chills me in death! I seem to rise above the scene and yet my body still stands in a stony, petrified rigidity.———Now it seems some time elapses, and I see the young man who was to be wed. I see the Monarch, too, and they are both in the temple. Now the young man lifts the —my body of stone,—and lets it drop into the Light on the great quartz cube, and it disappears instantly. But a foot was broken off, and this the young man hides in his mantle and. carries away. It seems all this was due to some evil done by him, and by me through love of him. I——ah h h!"

Elizabeth sighed and then awoke to her surroundings. I lighted the study-lamp, and she watched me curiously. Suddenly she said:

"Why, husband, that young man I saw was—was you! Oh, I believe now in all these things you have told, but which I never believed till now I have seen this."

This experience had a great effect on her, so that she looked more and more into the strange learning, and as a result, redoubled her efforts to do good in the world. Thus did she observe the Scripture,—"Be ye doers of the word, not hearers only" for strange though this learning seemeth, it is not so to Christian Esoterists, but only to mere hearers, and in a less measure, to doers on the exterior plane of Christian service. Thus had I, who led Lolix astray, led Elizabeth back into His deeper Path. But I first had to travel in it somewhat myself, ere I could guide her. This occurred only a few months before her last voyage with me—the Bermuda trip. But she had learned enough to know we were both doomed on the occasion of the wreck, and when I would have placed her in the boat, she said:

"Husband! Walter! I will not go into that boat, for out of the past I know that now we change. I have come to know that in esoterically doing His word, and not hearing it only, is there alone Life. Now I see again into a past age. And you and I are together, and a little babe is before us, wailing to us. You take it bleeding, into your arms, and me also you clasp. Then you ask God for mercy. Generously you took all the blame; yet I, too, having broken the law, had to share the penalty. Then said One who was verily the Christ, although then we knew it not—Therefore in a far day thou shalt gather a sorrowful harvest of woe, and repay all thou art indebted. When thou art come again, also she with thee, and again are ready to go into Navazzamin, thou wilt find thyselves free of Earth forever. My dear, dear friend, it must be that we both die now; I fear not, for we will of necessity meet again. Farewell, my love, till then; kiss me. Is not my karma paid in full, so far as Lolix's error is? More even, possibly? And Christ,—shall He not receive me now?"

And I said: "Yes, dear wife, it must be! Good bye, and God bless you, for we will truly meet again, beyond the great deep River, with Him." And so in death I held her close.

Do you longer marvel at her contented smile in the photographically true picture of the death scene executed by

Phyris? And I, friend? Was not the special crime of Zailm atoned for, in that I brought her to know God's law, karma, and in making my life a living sacrifice for, and at the last dying in an effort to save her to happiness and enlightenment, was that score not requited, fulfilled, and Jesus the Christ obeyed? Sins, evil deeds, lies, thefts, adulteries, murders even, are in themselves only the shadows of lives turned to face away from God into outer darkness; they are weak places in the chain of character; unsymmetrical places in what Christ our Lord would have perfect, even as He is perfect. For in Him, the Perfect One, are none of these things, nor shadow of turning. He beseeches us, saying, "Be ye likewise perfect." "Come unto Me, all ye weary, and I will give you rest." So, in His divine love He proposes Himself to take all these (to Him) shadows that to us are so horribly real. Of ourselves we can do nothing, for as we undo through the lapse of ages, we also do fresh evil. Not shadows to us. But He is the Light of the world. So the glooms we see while we look from His way, will cease to be if we turn to His following. If we have kept all the laws from youth upwards, yet, that is but doing no sin of commission, behind is an unrequited eternity. And, brethren, friends, the time is short: (Cor. vii-29.) He will take these sins, and it shall be to us as if we took a boxful of shadow from a cellar and opened it out in the noontide rays of the sun. But while the sins are all by Him atoned; while when the days mount to years, the one robbed or lied about, or otherwise injured, finds the Father's laws have made it all up to him, if he only also knows that Father too, still, we have a work. Jesus, the Great Master, took all when we, a weary, asked him. But—we, while doing these crimes, walked in darkness. The tree of our lives could grow nothing but sickly growths, pale leaves, dwarfed buds, blighted fruits, in that darkness of the soul. We may have ever seemed righteous to others; may have even cried, "Lord, Lord"—with our lips. But if our deeds knew Him not we were growing our life-tree with fair bark, but decayed wood. So, after He has taken on Himself our sins, and they are ceased, yet with our faces to Himwards, we see our tree of character, pale, sickly, with few leaves, and no fruit, standing in God's karmic light. Will we work to make green leaves, and fruit in plenty? If we follow Him, yes. For He always said in language unmistakable to those having ears to hear, that only those who obeyed the Father's law, God's Will, could hope to win salvation. He will remove our burdens; will mediate and atone, but we must undo the errors with the strength He gives; we must take each our cross and follow Him, and He, the Good Shepherd, will lead us Home, to the immortal heights, where is no more death, nor sin, nor suffering, neither parting. In Him we have, all of us, time, strength, opportunity to undo, after He has atoned and shown us the way. He is that Way. And we, letting Him dwell in us, make our life the Path. There can be no homegoing till, in Him, we become our own Path. If there was another way, I would tell you. For I am come before His second coming. It is near. Beware, lest night find you idle. Say not I knew Him not, either as Zailm, or as Pierson. To know Him by lip service is one, to know Him by life lived as He bade us, is another. Having lived, now I speak. Be ye doers of the Word, not hearers only.

CHAPTER X.

AFTER THE YEARS, RETURN.

Sparing details, what was the appearance of Phyris after the flight of the years? When I left she was a bright, beautiful maiden, in the budding days of womanhood, having the divine, spiritual glory which characterizes the higher race of the perfect Human grade. How looked she now? Different only in the maturity of rounded womanhood, the prime which in Venus withers not with age, because there the animal is subdued, and there are no excesses, indulgences, nor any of that feverish grasping after unattainable things which stamps the "children of a larger growth" who dwell in the human-animal plane of Earth today. Phyris, the dark-haired, starry-eyed girl, who was yet more than a girl, was a woman divinely fair, was again before me. Again I beheld the sweetly natural, dignified mien that reminded me of the first time I ever saw Mol Lang—that air of quiet, but marvelous power. Enhanced by this appearance, as is a gem by its setting, her sweet, pure selfhood shone forth—that sweet spirit which in Phyris was divine, yet had lost none of the human characteristics which have rendered Jesus so dear to mankind. The spirit was there—the perfect human, also, but the animal, the nature of Man on Earth, was reduced to its place of servitude. When I met the fair, beautiful **woman** I was abashed. At that moment the tide of the years overflowed my soul, and awed me. Sometimes I had known of Phyris when the Hesperian astral controlled me. But far oftener of later years—the years of duty—this astral did not come, and then I knew Phyris only as an ideal, and with the attributes of that ideal I tried to endue Elizabeth, and the failure was agony to me.

Wonderingly, wholly delighted, I looked on Phyris now, nor deemed it lack of propriety that she should kiss me and whisper, "Home again"—her eyes lighted with the peaceful joy reflected from my gaze.

No passion was in me, no prompting to be sentimental—no, that was gone with Earth's feverish dream.

How familiar all things appeared when at last I was come home. For six Hesperian months* I did nothing but wander in my psychic form in this Elysium—this stellar garden of the Hesperides. In the other time most of my visit was spent in the company of Sohma or Mol Lang. But now Sohma was otherwise engaged. Mol Lang, too, was occupied in the work that attracted him—that of guiding, teaching and helping mankind, en masse, as well as individually; that portion of our race yet on Earth. Unconscious of his agency, or of how, with others equally great, Mol Lang was influencing the affairs of men—these men on Earth went on with their doings, fondly

---

*About 112 terrestrial days. The solar year of Venus is 224.7 earthly days.

thinking that themselves were doing all. How little humanity on Earth knows that it is thus guided. Yet our Father gives it to His occult children to lead their lesser brethren, just as He gave it to Jesus,—one of the Sons of Light, higher than any other, who was an incarnation of the Christ. Perhaps human acts were not, are not, guided individually, as a rule, although exceptions exist. But just as shot, running in grooves, is checked by the leaden pellets before and behind, so the acts of one man depend on the acts of others; these on others still, until finally it appears that the mass is influenced in the whole, and every individual in the mass has his or her acts unconsciously controlled by what are termed circumstances — fates — adverse or propitious — inexorable — the grooves in which they run. That is to say humanity is ordered in its action by what may be named the Universal Karma. So long as men grope in the dark, ignorant of occult laws, so long must they produce this inexorable karma. It is fate, self-made, running from life to life, incarnation after incarnation, unavoidable, for it is born of the infraction of the laws of the Creator. Even Mol Lang, before he passed and triumphed at the Crisis, to which I was soon to come, and which he experienced a century ago, was controlled by the great, Universal Karma. But in passing that ordeal he passed from finite life to everlasting, and became a law unto himself. And then, free of karma, he returned to minister to those bound by circumstances. Mol Lang was become more than man. He had taken of the Tree of Knowledge, also of the Tree of Life.[*] Such as he utilize the elementals—those non-human, non-embodied powers of the air. They find in mankind the tendency to sin, and use it, so that the erring ones mount the ladder on rungs, each of which is a conquered fault. The great religious movements, wars, and the fields of commerce, all furnish experiences for mankind. Do some seem cruel, evil?—yet each is a part of the scheme of the Creator, each is a tool in the hands of His ministers, and all teach that except a man, as part of the Eternal Whole, works for that Whole, subduing the

---

[*] Revelations xxii, 14.

selfish animal in himself, he can in no wise come to the Father.
"Except by My Path," says the Savior.

If Sohma and Mol Lang could no longer be with me as companions, who then could? Phyris. She became my tutor, my
guide, and led me farther on towards the point where soon I
must take the Key and enter alone on the dread struggle,
with only my faith in God to sustain me.

One day Mol Lang said—"Phylos, come with me."

I went to his special apartments. There he said:

"Hitherto thou hast but an astral body, but now thou needest
a physical body as a base of action, for now must thou learn
of thine own self. Sleep, that I may gather material atoms
about thine astral."

I immediately slept, as I lay on the couch where he had bidden me recline. When I awoke he was regarding me, and, for
a moment forgetful, I sat up.

"Arise,"—said Mol Lang. I obeyed, and found myself
clothed in flesh. Thus I became a Hesperite. I was now of the
same apparent age as Phyris, and was thereby seemingly dis-
possessed of some twenty-five years. Before any lengthy period
there came to shine in me somewhat of the Spirit-nature, and
as the same ego shone in Phyris, so therefore we grew into
similitude of each other. Because of this indwelling Spirit,
Nature was become an open book, and occult wisdom addressed
me from all sides. Soon I could leave the body at will. Other
steps succeeded, and I grew with marvelous rapidity to know
many of the minor things reserved by our Father for His
aspiring children.

With me now was abiding a Voice,* and as it demanded
of me, I answered and knew. It said:

"What is heredity?"

And I answered from my spirit, knowing this thing:

"Heredity is the sum of experience which the souls of men
carry from one life through devachan into reincarnation. It
is in nowise transmitted from parent to child, but its leading
trait is attracted by the like trait in the parents. The lesser

---

*St. John xvi, 13.

traits are educed by cultivation, or else lie dormant, according to environment.''

Again the Voice said:

''It is not well; thou who hast reaped, must now sow. I am the Eternal Spirit in thee; obey me. Thou art now able to stand in my presence; able to see; able to hear; able to speak; conqueror of desire, attainer of self-knowledge. Thou hast seen thy soul in its bloom, heard the voice of Peace. Go thou and read my writing in the Hall of Learning, which is My Works. Read:

''To stand—is to have confidence. To hear—is to have opened the door of thy soul. To see—is to have attained perception of My Works. To speak—is to have gotten the power of helping others. To have conquered desire is to have acquired control of self. To have self-knowledge—is to have come unto Me, whence thou art able to impartially view the personal man that was thyself. To have seen thy soul in its bloom—is to have had a momentary glimpse of that transfiguration which shall eventually make thee more than Man.

''Stand aside in the coming battle, and though thou fightest, be not thou the warrior. Look for Me, and let Me fight in thee. Obey My orders for battle. Obey Me as if I were thyself. My orders thy desires—for I am thyself, yet infinitely more than thee. Look for Me, lest in the fever of battle thou pass Me. I will not know thee if thou knowest not Me. If thy cry come to Me, lo! I will fight in thee and will fill the void in thee. Then shalt thou be unwearied. Without Me thou shalt fall; with Me thou canst not fall, for I am the Spirit.

''Listen now to the song of life in thy heart. Say not 'It is not there.' Listen deeper. This song is in every breast; it may be obscure, yet it is there. Not the most wretched outcast but it is in him, for all are children of the Father, which is I. Listen to My Song, for while thou art yet but man, I shall not speak continually, and thy strength must sometimes be in memory of Me. Inquire now of the Earth-matter; of the air, of the water, the wind, and seek the treasures of the snow. My Peace I give unto thee.''

At last I saw; I heard; and, my friend who readeth this,—I speak. My words go to the multiplication by types, and then by myriad copies through the world, to be known by those that "seeing, see and comprehend.'' And with each copy shall go my love and greater, mine eye shall note each hungered seeker for the truth, and, be it in the palace or cottage, there, too, will I be, not figuratively, but my Spirit.

I had gone into a lonely mountain spot to hear this Voice, and now as I walked, a Being not Man joined me. Its presence was one of light and glory and goodness. With it came Mol Lang, saying:

"This is one of the Beings of Good. Behold, Phylos, our Father's House hath many Mansions, and in these are Beings created by Him, and endowed with volition like as Man, yet they are not human, never were, nor ever will be. Man shall be perfect when the Spirit of the Father entereth him. Then shall he know all things, and be perfect. What is perfection? Absolute harmony with His Infinite Creation. So there may be perfect men; also perfect Beings which are not Men, as this one with us. This is a Good Being. But there is an opposite in the Things of the Creation. There are perfect Evil Beings, which likewise are not, never were, nor ever will be human. What are these? They are in perfect harmony with the laws of their existence, but those laws and their conditions are absolutely opposed to ours, and to good. Hence such are inimical to our life and so—evil. Yet this sort seek us not, nor we them. In the scheme of Creation evil and good are evenly balanced. What disturbs harmony with us, therefore, disturbs them by disadjustment of balance. Hence they seek not our harm. But Satan, know ye him? He was an Angel of Light, fallen, and come to so much the greater fall in that his height was so lofty.* He is a rebel, and out of harmony.

"Life, Phylos, is limited, for it is but the action in the Mansion of Human environment. But existence is not limited.

*St. Luke, xii, 48.

Hence this Good Being with us is not Life, but of Existence. See, It goes. This is Its symbol, and the name of Its Mansion △. And when thy trials are thickest, draw about thee on the ground that figure and stand in it; go not out, but call on the Father. He will send His △ Beings to aid thee. Peace go with thee."

Mol Lang disappeared, and I was alone.

Men dread most those insiduous diseases, which attack not openly, but the weakest, most unguarded point. So, in the last, final Trial of the Crisis, I should be likewise insiduously attacked by the Satanic hosts. Earth has tried me during many lives; now was to come a trial greater than Earth. The attacks of mere human error differ from that of the well organized, intelligent assault of those to whom evil has become natural—to Lucifer and his fellow-rebels.

Of what nature is this Trial of the Crisis?* It is the deciding whether in the long series of incarnate lives the soul has improved its opportunities for good; if it, in the main, followed the Path which Jesus pointed. If so, it has or will have strength to cope with the best efforts of the Satanic foe. If not, it must fall and die the second death.** His incarnate life made the soul forgiving of all wrongs, forgetful of selfish interests, helpful to those having less light, more gloom, misery and sin to encounter—a self-contained nature? Has it become like the Man of Sorrows—full of faith, hope and charity? Then it hath heard the Voice, and will not fail. But if the soul is not like that, then, although it have the prophetic sight, and knoweth all things, though it have faith to removing mountains, yet shall it be only the more like Satan, and the worse its fate.

"Go into the Holy Place."***

And I, knowing obedience, went into a room built of stone, apart from the house. Then was I in the Presence where I had been as Zailm when Priest Mainin was blasted. It was the Presence of the living Christ. It was Man, yet more, for it was the Spirit; as much more than Man as the sun is more than a glow worm. Then a wondrous Voice said:

---

*St. Luke, xx. 35-36.　　**Rev. xx. 15.　　***St. Luke, iv. 2.

"Be not afraid; it is I."

Around that Holy Place were forms of fire. Ink and paper can give little idea of the semblance. Yet look at the picture and try, with my aid, to see. The bolt blazed as a thing of flame, so also the Great Star and all the lesser ones. The Leaf was as life, and the cross the open Way, to the House thereof, while the Ring, I knew, symbolized the Eternal One—endless, beginningless. The Book was the Word, and it blazed with scintillant crimson flame. But over all—a Personified Presence —was the Eye, the Eternal, sleepless, omnipotent, omniscient Supervisor. So stood I in the presence of the Father, made manifest for me. As I remained, I knew all things of His Works, for the Spirit entered in. But not to abide, for as yet the Trial was not come to pass.

For weeks I staid in the Holy Place, and came not out to eat nor drink, for I was wholly sustained by the Spirit. At the day of the Great Peace this Spirit must enter in and I be in It and It be in me forever more. But no guide could exist, no law for the Trial, except my strength of ages. Even the Spirit would be veiled in that ordeal.

CHAPTER XI.

TEXT: ST. MATTHEW IV.

"To be, or not to be: that is the question."
—HAMLET.

That was indeed the question when I arose one morning, and knew that the event of the Crisis would that day decide whether or not I had Eternal Life—whether I was for the Spirit, or the Second Death.

I arose and went forth into the wilderness of the mountains, accompanied only by a pet animal, somewhat resembling a fawn, which went with me everywhere. In a woodland moun-

tain meadow I traced with my staff the symbol △, and it instantly became crimson fire, which leaped and rose and fell,
unbroken, continuously. I was inside, the pet animal grazed
on the meadow. After making the symbol △, the Good
Being introduced to my knowledge by Mol Lang was with me,
and it spake much to me, and I to It. It said:

"Lo! Thy time cometh when I △ must leave thee, although I △ would do for thee, but it is so that no being
can endure for another the fierce Trial, neither help them in
its midst. Yet I △ say unto thee, I △ believe thou wilt
win, for have I not known thee, lo! many ages? But now is
that Trial come for thee, when thy past, in all days and lives
thou hast ever had, shall rise up and thou shalt be judged
thereby, whether thou shalt become perfect, and thy name
be Phylos ✳, or whether thou shalt fail, and have again all the
bitterness of life to go through during ages to come. The
Father saith through the Spirit 'Every idle word that men
speak, they shall give an account thereof'—how much more
then of their actions?"

I listened mutely, for what record was against me? It might
be evil, or good, or, worse, that lukewarmness which the
Spirit will not entertain, but rather heat or coldness of nature.

"Fear not,"—said Ovias △ "for not in vain hast thou
lived. Neither expect a record written concerning thee. For
know this—that the principles inculcated by the Christ-Spirit
which overshone Buddha and all the mightiest of the Earth,
incarnating in each, and Itself being Son of God, not they, until
by union of It they became Sons of God—know that if thou
hast made these principles both warp and woof of thy character, thou hast no need to fear. For this sort of fabric is
strong, and was that which Jesus meant when He said, and
says ever—Timeless One that He is—"Lo, I am with you
always even until the end of the world." Not one individual
act shall be brought forth to accuse thee, but each, all and
every greatest thought, and least, and word or deed, in all thy
many incarnations—these have formed thy character. Is

that character, then, woven of the woof provided by Christ, and shown forth in the Divine personality of Jesus, and illuminating Buddha, and Zoroaster, Moses, Manu and other Salvators? If that be the cloth, then indeed shalt thou prevail, though no one sustain thine arm. But if not that weaving, lo! thou shalt fail, and not even I Δ could save thee. I Δ go. Be thou brave, and may the Comforter be in thee. Peace."

All that day I stood there, and was not weary. Night came. About the midnight hour my pet cried out in terror, and came leaping toward me. As it came I warded it from the Δ flame, and it stood outside, trembling. But I saw nothing to alarm it, save Mol Lang, approaching over the level around me. He hesitated not, but seemed about to cross the line of fire, as he could, but mindful of my perilous position I said:

"Stop! If thou art Mol Lang, then come. But if only a tempting shape, woe unto thee if thou shalt cross that line, for Δ It shall punish thee as only an immortal can punish."

He came not; instead he ceased to appear as Mol Lang, and was another sort. This tempter said

"If thou art proof against me, who so seemed thy loved preceptor that thou really knew not, then thou art conqueror over death and sin. I have no power over thee, and thou art free to enter eternal life, wherein shall no more incarnations occur. I go."

This Shape withdrew, but the Voice in my soul whispered:

"Beware yet awhile."

I stayed on unmolested until I caught myself napping, and knowing this to be the fatigue of the flesh, I regretted that I had not met the Trial in astral form.

"Not so,"—whispered the Voice—"all thine elements, both physical and psychic, must attend thee here."

But again I dozed, and quickly aroused myself, for the scene all about me was changed. The mountain meadow was gone, and in place of night seemed day. I gazed, seemingly, on a scene where all the races of men and immortals were gathered under the sweep of my prescient eye. I seemed to be taken over this realm, and a fair, god-like being in appearance was my guide. Yet in caution, I sheathed myself from head to foot in the $\triangle$ flame as in an armor, at which my guide smiled, but said nothing. He took me with the speed of thought, so that we seemed to go from star to star, now crossing vast interstellar spaces, now come on fresh realms. All these realms were inhabited by creatures of human shape, or at least they had human attributes. Before me they all bowed and worshipped, for my guide said to them:—"See thy master." Otherwise they were all engaged in pursuit of pleasure. The multiplex passions of man on Earth were indulged without fear of penalty. My fair guide said:

"These are souls in whom I created certain passions and appetites, and shall I punish them for indulging, without stint, traits I have given? Now, tell me, why should all creation not have free license to get pleasure as it may? My creatures do. There is no sort of restraint placed by me on their free pursuit of carnal things, lusts, appetites. See, they are happy! For a time I am giving thee control of them. Through indulgence of their passions they beget a sort of vital magnetism, and as their present ruler, it thrills thee like new wine."

As my guide said, the sight and sensing of all this license did thrill me ecstatically, and was affecting me with a delirious, carnal joy. I put it away and refused to feel. Whereat the beautiful Being said

"Oh! thou art blind! Behold, thou shalt have these realms for thine, and have absolute authority, so thy word shall be life or death to these people, if thou wilt. Here, too, into this eternal joy, thou mayest bring Phyris, and lo! forever thou shalt with her do thy will, and hers, and no penalty be exacted. Wilt thou take this gift of supremacy? It is free; I ask no return for it all. Only take it."

Oh! where was my knowledge, gained from the many lives, and from the Voice? Gone! Gone, else I had known at once not to accept the alluring gift. I was offered all this free, thereby violating the divine law, which never allows something for nothing. But I gathered my $\triangle$ armor about me, lest this Being, who seemed so fair and good, were not so, and if not good, its touch might be fatal. Then I said:

"It must be that thou art arrayed in the livery of heaven to serve Satan better. Demon, thou offerest that which subordinates all other beings in these realms to my will. This realm is governed by pleasure, passion, appetite, lust—all selfish; and no penalty set upon wild license. These carnalities would conquer me, too, if I accepted—me, who am otherwise about to be become immortal—more than Man, karmaless. These are selfish. Pleasure so gotten is the essence of selfishness. Truly, thou must be creator of it all, since it is selfish. It is thine. It could be mine? Yea, but only because over me thou wouldst reign. I am not now thy subject; nor will I be. Only the Unknown God is my Master. Get thee hence, behind me!"

The scene slowly faded, like mist in the sunlight. There came a lull, and I hoped the battle was over, for I was weary. But I stood on the meadow again, with the △ fire leaping, quivering in crimson pulses around the lines. Nothing could break that guardian flame, for it was a symbol of the perfect state of being of another, but non-human, race. Only perfection could avail against it. Perfection of good might; so, too, perfection of evil might; but the latter had not yet come against it. I even doubted the existence of any perfection of evil. What offer, after all, had been made but of the things which were mine by reason of the divine Sonship? God giveth his children control over each other for good, and for evil also, through mental influence. What more absolute sovereignity is there than love, exercised as He hath ordained. None. While I reflected, a soft and lovely vision came, and lo, Phyris stood before me.

"Art thou Phyris?" I asked.

"Could any but Phyris disregard the △ flame about thee?" she replied, penetrating the barrier, and sinking by my side. This seemed truth, for Ovias △ was perfect being of Its own condition. Only perfection can stand with perfection.

At last I heard her sigh softly, sadly. Her eyes brimmed with tears.

"Why this sorrow, Phyris?"

"Phylos, thou enquirest? I reply. Because of my confession to make. I, too, am on trial as thyself. A sad story of sin is mine. Woe is me if thou shouldst spurn me for it." She hesitated.

"Speak," I answered, apprehensively.

"This, then. In a far Poseid day, when I had a personality called Anzimee, and thou hadst one called Zailm—thou knowst the day? Aye, and with sorrow e'en yet! When thou hadst gone in thy vailx, fugitive from memory of Lolix, I sorrowed intensely. And I knew not thine abode then. When thou returned not, crazed, I went to Mainin the Incalix. He marvelled at my frenzy; then said:

" 'Lovest thou Zailm, Rainu?'

" 'As my own soul, Incalix.'

" 'I marvel thereat. But never mind. Aid thee to find him? What if I love thee—I who am a vowed celibate? What if, in my ability, I say Zailm shall no more come back?'

"Then, Phylos, I begged for thee as for my own life! I implored his mercy. At last the stern lines of his face relaxed, and he kindly said: 'I would not keep thee apart; I was but testing thy love for him. Yet my aid must receive compensation. Not money, nor jewels, nor power—these have I in abundance. One only thing in thy gift will I have; listen: in other days, when I came to knowledge of Nature's deeper secrets, I was curious to experiment, and I sought the aid—all confident of my power to subdue my servant—of the host of Satan, one demon. But my power I overestimated, and I was subdued, a victim. So one day coming my soul is forfeit to Lucifer to pay my debt and its ever growing size. One only way can I avert this—by delivering another, although less experienced soul, in place of mine. Ere this night a maiden and her lover will seek me at the hour of worship, that I may solemnize their marriage already long published. But I shall be gone, purposely. Thou wilt be there, and except thee, only those two. Now. they are weak, but have never sinned.

"Their natures incline to error. All I ask of thee is that when they ask for me, tell thou them I am gone, but say, 'Thou art come to be wed?'—then smile and say, again, 'Only the simple folk publish their matings; the wise are never wedded, yet are wedded in verity.' Say no more. If they take that mild hint, they will sin, and lose their souls, but I, the great Incalix, shall be saved. I will in any event bring thee Zailm again, for perchance thy hint will not be acted upon.'

"Mainin ceased speaking. I recoiled in horror. Yet even as I was about to refuse, he said, 'Remember, only thou canst save Zailm.'

"I thought him a fiend. Then I thought—it is but natural for him to wish to save his own soul, even at another's cost. And oh! I so desired the return of my Zailm! Tearfully sobbing, my soul whispering the wrong of it, but my heart pleading me to be blind for that once to wrong or right, I yielded and said, 'Even as thou requirest, so will I do.'

"I did so. But false to Incal, Mainin was false to me, and he brought not Zailm back. When Rai Gwauxln told me of Zailm's death, I, too, died of shame and a broken heart. The man and woman took my hint, and died after years of well concealed, direful crime. But I, Phylos? In my consent to Mainin's will, I sold my soul to the Arch Fiend, Mainin's master. So my life is forfeit unless I can be helped. Forfeit, much though I know, and hard as I have striven to do right and atone—all in vain! Yet, my twin soul, thou art able to save me. If thou savest me not, then shall the Eternal Law cause me to die the second death. My soul will be annihilated, my Spirit, which was unable to unite with my soul, shall go back to the Source—our Father. And then, being a soul, but thy Spirit also my Spirit, thou must also perish. Save thyself then as well as me."

"How?"—I queried, soul-sick to the depths, and suffering such intensity of misery as almost of itself to cut off my life. Sick, because I felt Phyris, my other self, my pure angel, to be in mortal danger, herself in a fatal mire, and threatened with soul death. And because she was, I was also, for our Spirit was the same.

"How?"—I again queried, whispered.

"Thus! The man whom, as Anzimee, I led astray, hath incarnated several times since then, each time worse and worse, until now, a man on Earth, he is about to confront a temptation which, if he fall, will aim his course ever henceforth for evil, and final death of his soul. If he yield not now, he may or may not at last escape—but the delay will put him beyond use to us, and we shall surely die, whether he does or not. Aye! we shall if thou actest not now. If his soul is now made forfeit, we shall surely escape; so saith Mainin, who is blasted and in outer darkness, yet owneth me; 'tis an only, though slender hope. O Phylos, think! think!! On the one hand eternal life, brightness, and a chance to atone for all our sins—perhaps even rescue this man at last—but on the other, death, blasting into outer darkness and eternal demonhood.' '

In the calm night she stood before me and besought me to act for her, her hands clapsed, her eyes streaming, her agony fearful to see. Act for her whom I loved better than life, and for myself; save our lives that all might be well. How? By using my occult power to whisper to a man, already sin-sodden, —on a distant planet—a man who might not conquer his temper even though I withheld my influence. Do what? Influence him to sign his name as Governor of a great state to a denial of pardon to two men about to die for murder. Yet they were innocent. I knew it; the Governor knew it, because he had already sinned horribly in using his office, money and power to weave a net of circumstantial evidence which would hang his two enemies for a murder committed by his own hand. He would, in an hour more, sign or not sign the fateful paper, for at the last his courage was faltering. All I needed to do was to occultly encourage him. Already so sinful, was it likely he ever would turn from evil ways to good? Barely possible. But I was to psychologize him to pass this opportunity and complete his double murder, in order to save Phyris, whom I so loved, whose Spirit was my Spirit, whose soul's destruction meant my soul's destruction also. It was so easy to do!

All crimes are easy. But while the agony of despair numbed me, a ray of hope came, and the question arose—would this act not save us? Had not God said—"Thou shalt not kill";—and would not the double murder be on me as much as on the Governor. Then I arose, and said, calmly,—Oh! how frightfully, despairingly calm!—

"Lo, then. If we shall both die into outer darkness, yet will I never do this thing. Thou, who art more precious than mine own life, must not ask this! Saith not our Father: 'Whoso shall do evil, of him will be exacted the penalty, of some thirty, some sixty, some an hundred fold?' And if I—we—shall consign a soul to darkness, thinkest thou, oh! my spirit mate, we shall not the more surely go thither ourselves? Then, although these words seal thy death—and mine—yet will I refuse to sin. I will not do thy will. I have not erred so but that I can put forth my hand and, by the aid of the Christ-Spirit, cut off the progress of thy sin, and thou mayest go back to the time, place, where thy soul was ere thine error, and recarnify on Earth so often as needful to expunge and atone this sinful act. And I will await thee where my soul is now progressed, during the years, though they be tens of thousands, until pure, thou mayest rejoin me. I will guide thee, so that thou wilt sin no more during expiation. Aye, except that I must stay to so guide, I would go again into the life of Earth with thee; but I must stay that my light be clear. All this will I do, or if vicarious atonement were a possibility in the Universe, I would go for thee, and let thee stay. But condemn the man on Earth, and ourselves with him, no! I can not so sin."

With a convulsive shudder, and a despair in her starry eyes that smote me so that I cried aloud to God in my agony, Phyris said in a mournful wail, as of a lost soul:

"O Phylos, think well; for it might be that thou art hedged about with that sort of righteousness that maketh the Angels to weep and the Fiend to smile!"

"Phyris, beloved, I have spoken! I alter not."

She moved away with her hands covering her agonized face, sobbing in her intensity of despair. When she came to the ⌣ fire she said:

"Phylos, I could enter. My power is fled, and I can not go out; put it aside."

I looked from where I lay almost dying in my pain of an immortal hurt, and found that I too was too weak to lower the barrier. Then I looked within my being, and I saw that no more was the Light of the Spirit within me, but gone forth. And then I knew what that awful appeal of Jesus of Nazareth meant—that He, too, in the fearful strain of his Human trial of the Crisis had beheld the Spirit in Him wane—when He cried out:—"Eloi, Eloi, Lama Sabacthani." Like Him I cried out to the Father, and in that instant the Light returned, and with a roll as of mighty thunder the darkness broke, and the night which had been around me fled, so I saw that the sun was high in the heavens, and I alone had been in a local gloom. The △ flame paled, and "Phyris" knelt before me and implored mercy. Then I knew that Phyris had not been near. I knew that God the Father was entered in me to dwell forever, and that the perfection of evil had failed in its last, most subtle, horrible and isidious attack, its last attempt to open the door to downwardness for me. My strength out of all the lives had withstood, and, all fainting, I was come unto Christ. All the weary way of woe I had journeyed, atoning as I came. And now my karma I had blotted out, and in me was Life Everlasting. Gloria in Excelsis! Laus Deo! The song I heard was the song of the starry hosts of God.

Then the Voice spoke: "Thy trial is over; I am well pleased. It is written in sacred Scripture, 'Ye must be born again, of water and of the Spirit.' Even so hast thou been born now. Of water, which is the world of matter. And of the Spirit, which is I entered in. But the death of the carnal body, and rebirth in the new, is but night after day, and day after night. To these successive days and nights of the soul, that Scripture refers not. Thou hast been born in the Earth many times, and each time thy carnal body hath died. But the rebirth was not that rebirth of the waters and of me. Those incarnations did but prepare thee out of the waters of materiality for Me. But now thou art born of that and of Me, and become a Son of Light, and at one with the All—Father—and like unto the Nazarene. Carry thou My Word unto all men, that all may come likewise unto Me who will, even as thou, following the first Man who came unto Me, have thyself also come.''

Now when I saw Phyris come, I knew that it was she in verity. She, too, had had her Trial, and equal temptations had been offered her, and been withstood, ninety centuries of years before, however. How say ye: ''I thought twin souls must fight the final fight together, and now you say nine thousand years were between?'' Behold, friend, time is but measure of energy exerted. We wrought the same work, so were together. Is Paul more saved than the latest regenerated soul? Yet Paul knew Jesus Christ near two thousand years earlier. It had seemed to us both that the Great Crisis had occupied centuries. Unto us, as we stood clasping each other, came a glorious vision, and the Voice spoke, saying:

''Behold. Look back over the mighty past. And when thou hast so done, look on Earth, and see how there to effect the work of giving the people of Earth thy life history. That shall take but a moment for thee, but that moment shall seem years to thine agents on Earth. Then again, look; I am thy Voice and thy Spirit. Thy souls shall unite. Behold, thou shalt presently hereafter have no more two bodies, but one only, and it thy Spirit body. Mine, for without Me thou art nothing. Peace is thine forevermore.''

Friend, thou mayest have trouble in understanding this strange union. Yet, ponder it deeply, for it is to be thy experience some day if thou art true to thy Savior and follow Him, drinking of the cup which He drank, and triumphing at the Critical Ordeal.

End of Book Second.

BOOK THE THIRD.

CHAPTER I.

YE SHALL REAP AS YE HAVE SOWN.—THE PERCEPTION.

Suppose the struggle had proven me wanting, and the verdict had been, "Mene Mene Tekel Vpharsin"?   Then my—our fate would have been that of Mainin of Caiphul. To me who know the dread meaning of this fate, it is more utterly frightful to contemplate than it can be to thee. It means being a brother to devils, and subjection to Satan who could so cunningly, awfully tempt as we were tempted. and when successful, make a servant of the victim, ever to pile up fresh karma. And such karma as Satan's service makes is worse in a moment than the wickedest man could pile up in a long lifetime. It means such servitude until—when? Forever? Until the end of material things. Then, when the heavens are rolled as a scroll and melt in fervent heat, Satan (Lucifer) shall, with his minions, be cast into that lake of fire which is the second death:—which meaneth that the force, the energy of the rebels, that which has made them distinct, potent souls through all the past, shall become depersonalized, and disindividualized, cast into the sum of the Fire of Elements, which form the forces of Nature—the winds, odic and magnetic and electric forces. But annihilation there is not, death there is not, though there be such a change as constitutes the destruction of the union between soul and Spirit, the return of the first to the great impersonal Vis Natura, the return of the other to Him who created life. Then, after millions of years the Father will gather the fervid elements into nebulae, star-plasm, worlds, suns, systems, and a "new heaven and a new earth" shall come forth. Then will the depersonalized rebel host begin to rein-

carnate in protoplasmic life, and thence evolutionize up, up, up
along the myriad incarnations, until after an eternity of matter, they come once more to human conditions, to another Crisis,
to win or fail, and either, like Sisyphus, run again the weary
course, or else inherit hard-won entrance to unconditional
being. There is, nor can be, any death of the Spirit, but of the
individuality only. Study this well, my friend, for such is the
fate of evil doers who sell to Satan, because such is Satan's
portion. Our Father hath provided a Way. It is the sharp,
knife-edge Path, whereon all things so evenly balance that
there is turning neither to the right nor left, but steady, even
pursuit of the Path, wherein all who travel that way, contain
themselves in all things, in eating and drinking, in sleeping and
all those things which cause the cares of this world. Those
who shall be accounted worthy, without further incarnation,
to obtain the resurrection from the body of materiality neither
marry nor are given in marriage, but must receive the Kingdom of God even as if still little children. Yet whoso doeth not
so, it shall not be eternally counted against them, but only
till another incarnation. It must be that the things of sensation which are an offense unto the Spirit occur, but karmic
woe will attend the offender, until he finds the Path and travels
therein. Hear, if hearing and understanding be in thee, for
these are the words of the Master.

--- ---

CHAPTER II.

JOB XXXVIII-7.

Contemplating the victory in us of the Father, we chanted
a song in answer to that of the Sons of God who were our
fellows. Perfect at last, in rapport with all the law fulfilled—
karmaless, immortal, beside Jesus, no more need to incarnate,
Life was ended, but Being just commenced. Paradoxical? In
all the aeons of time we had Life, but Being, which hath no

beginning, neither end, and is not under the dominion of Time, every ego hath ever from the Father. But Life hath beginning, so also it must have end; it hath end. If its conditions are strong enough to enchain for aye, then the soul is diverted from its ego to the tracks of Life, and is then heritor of death. Only if a soul forfeit not to Life its hold on Being—on its ego—shall it not die. Sin is the error of turning from Being unto Life, whereof the shadow is death. The soul that sinneth and turneth not away from finite life and the conditions thereof, it shall die.

Down all the realms of light echoed the paeans of praise, as when the "Morning stars sang together and the Sons of God shouted for joy."

———————

CHAPTER III.

"Fair forms and hoary seers of ages past, all in one mighty sepulchre."

For a little while yet Phyris and I were not wholly one entity. But we were come to retrospection. With arms clasping each other, we walked slowly onward, till by the banks of the babbling brook we seated ourselves. Then I said:

"My twin, let us scan the past; let us draw aside the curtain of bygone ages, and see the record of the Book of Life—mirror of all events, sights, sounds, shapes, all things. We can do this, because we are karmaless, deathless, and are at one with the Father of Being, seeing, knowing as He knows, because He is in us."

We pondered the scenes of our Atlantean life—lives—and I saw ill-fated, sweet Princess Lolix, to whom I had been her ideal. Where had her sad soul gone when Mainin petrified its clay? In the imperishable record we saw where her life-line crossed ours. In her Poseid devachan she had found her dream of life seem realized. Reborn into activity, again her life-line crossed mine—her heritage pursued her—and she conquered it, for Lolix's individuality was Elizabeth's (my wife). Her crime in Poseid was expiated, and so, too, was mine. Karma was fulfilled there.

Man's course upward to God is so blind, so untaught—instinctively like the sunward turning vine. I had so confidently, in the Sagum, taken a step irrevocable, except for Mendocus; and then had fallen again into blind darkness, despair, but instinctively true to law and to Elizabeth, the object of my efforts—so upward, till at last I had gained the immortal heights. So had my alter ego—Phyris. Down below were the deserts of life, and fair appearing fruits,—apples of Sodom. These ashes are good, for they cause the soul to essay the heights.

Poseid, and all the lives, had meted us a large share of gall fruit, but our errors required it, and Karma is a sure pay master.

Sin begot karma and karma had exacted pay. Thus had I—for I am not relating Phyris' history—given up hopes, happiness, as one gives his open veins in the Sahara to quench the thirst of his friend. By this abdication I had lost my life and found it again. Karma, as the long record showed, was not always requiring pay; for every good act I had ever done I saw that I had been fully paid in kind my every jot. These were providences and benefices of life. There is no accident in life; allow that a man may die "by accident" and no man could be sure whether the ensuing night might not find the earth dropping into, or else away from the sun; or, seeing the sun set, could feel sure it would rise again. All things, small or great, are ordered. Not always from any pre-existent incarnation; sometimes from one's last year's, or yesterday's action the fruit springs. In short, I—we—saw that the lesson of life was "whatsoever a man soweth, that shall he also reap"—cause and effect. There are those who will make cavilling argument, contend that "accident does exist, and all is not order." I argue not, for "they that have ears to hear" will understand. One cannot see over a mountain range save he stand on a taller peak. To the greater vision accident is but an arc of design, and disorder is but an arc of order.

CHAPTER IV.

THE FALL OF ATLANTIS.

Again we looked over Atlantis, and saw many things else. The Zailm time possessed a peculiar interest. I saw that dim, distant past, a past old in the earth and ancient when Earth was yet a babe in the cradle of time. Atl, chiefest of the pre-historic races, numbering at home in Poseid, and abroad in the colonies, almost three hundred millions of souls; Atl, known through the olden earth as Atlan, Queen of the Seas," and her people as "Children of Incal—i. e. "Of the Sun," and as the "Sons of God." How are the mighty fallen! For now I behold her ancient site as part of the bed of the restless sea, covered with ocean ooze and slime, and to be known as the haunt of man only through the clear vision of the perfected eyes which scan astral records. Again the scene was presented so that we saw it as the eyes of my poor, weak, and pitifully mortal personality of Zailm had seen it. There was stately Caiphul, the Royal; and there, far away, and not so stately, Morzeus—its towers and turrets and chimney-stacks and lofty buildings marking where had stood the great-est of Atlan manufacturing centers—where the machine shops and the mills had been which supplied Poseid with valix, and naims, and all sorts of machines and instruments; with the products of the- looms, the cereals and endless articles of use, and of art. Over a million artisans there by day, but by night scarce fifty thousand—all gone by car or vailx to their homes anywhere from fifty to a hundred miles away—a few minutes' ride. And all this to perish because of man's iniquity, a few short hundreds of years later. Here and there I caught glimpses of canals, distributing either natural rivers or streams, or the product of aqua-aerial generators, such as Zailm had a small model of in his last days in Umaur.

We saw the world as Zailm saw it—Suern, with its millions of people; Necropan, with its ninety odd millions; Europe, then a barbarian land, only about one-sixth its present area; and Asia, not so large in extent then as now, but containing over a half million of souls. But the sparkling, brilliant civilization which was more than peer of even proud today—that was glorious Atl! Eleven hundred millions of people, civilized or but semi-civilized; and as many more scattered over the continent and islands of the seas who were utter barbarians— such was the world of Zailm, generally viewed. The numbers of the human race, and especially their increase during several generations, has appalled the pessimists. But the greatest of pessimists, Malthus, need have felt no alarm had he but known. Because:

"The world goes up, and the world goes down,
And the sunshine follows the rain."

There are a varying number of people always in the world; now more, now less—for as a soul comes to Earth (having been in devachan) a soul passes from Earth into devachan. But now two come while one goes, or two go while one comes—relatively. Wherefore the world is apparently encroaching upon the sources of supply, or again the supply of all things exceeds demand. But only a fixed number of Human Rays went forth from the Father, and only so many have Life, or ever will have. But these come and go as the tides ebb and flow, now on Earth, now in Heaven. Malthusians need not fear.

Zailm had been my personality.

Thirty centuries later, approximately, we saw again this land. But how changed. Now had Caiphul lost something. Not the tangible matter visible to earthly men—no, this was not gone. But the men we saw were not the high, lofty, noble souled men known to Zailm and to Anzimee. And when manhood suffers decadence, degradation, all nature with which he has to do also sensibly alters for the worse. Marzeus, the city of manufacturing arts, was no more; it had gone down before corruption. Art had not suffered so much as had science. But the science which drew upon the mysterious forces of nature--

the "navaz"—this had so far disappeared that air ships were forgotten, or at most were semi-mythical history. So were many other instruments which Zailm had known—the naima, those wonderful, wireless combined telephonic and photographic image transmitters. And the vocaligrapha, the caloriveyant instruments and the water-generators—all were lost in the night of time. But the men of the twentieth century shall find them all again. Twenty-eight decades of centuries hath Day now here continued, and soon it shall be proclaimed, "The evening and the morning are the seventh day." Ye who hear all my message are the men and the women of this new day, and shall inherit all things from our Father forever. And the full even-tide of that day which cometh shall behold you caught up "into the heavens" to escape the end of all things, when the earth also, and the works that are therein, shall be burned up.*

But I should deal with the past, not with the future. The seeds of corruption sown in the hearts of men by the Evil One, master over Mainin, germinated and throve, and then began, some centuries after the time of Gwauxln and Zailm, a long, steadily downward course which weakened the self-respect, manhood and womanhood of Poseid—a loss revealed in countless ways, culminating in national depravity and ruin.

It was upon one of these phases of ruin that we next gazed. We saw a woman upon whose face rested a light almost divine in the power of its transfiguring beauty. Her slight figure seemed not so much of Earth as of Heaven. The loose robe of gray which she wore fluttered in the breeze, the long tresses of brown hair, unrestrained, swept back from the glorious face, on which sat pity and despair, yet mingled with a wonderful radiance of appealing, entreating, agonized hope that some might hear and turn away from the course they were following. Her appeal assumed that most perilous form—for the champion—which an appeal can assume, that of sharp denunciation. She denounced the hideous system of blood-sacrifice in religion as being at diametrical opposition to right to God, to man, and as responsible for the corruption of the people. At this, the priests among the crowd uttered hoarse cries of rage. In a voice, the astral record of which rings yet, and forever, for those who have ears to hear such psychic tones, she cried, from her high place on the pedestal of the monument, twenty feet from the ground and the upturned faces below:

"Oh, ye! Think ye that Incal will accept the blood of innocent animals for your crimes? Whoso sayeth this doth lie! Incal, God, will never take blood of anything, nor symbol of any sort which placeth an innocent in a guilty one's stead! And the Incalithlon, and the Holy Seat, and the Maxin Light are dishonored whenever a priest layeth an animal on the Teo Stone, and striketh a knife to its heart, tears it out and tosses it as sacrifice into the Unfed Light. Yea, the Unfed Light doth truly destroy it instantly. But think ye because of this that merciful Incal is pleased? O ye brood of vipers, ye priests that are charlatans and sorcerers!"

An angry Incali stooped as she uttered this, and picked up a jagged bit of stoneware. In front of him was a litter borne by sad-visaged slaves. On this, reclining amidst soft silken cushions, was a woman of languorous beauty—the very impersonation of shameless abandon. In the warm, tropical atmosphere she lay, innocent of any covering, except that the heavy waves of the hair of her beautiful, if wicked, head partially concealed her nakedness. The shameless sight did not attract notice because of its shamelessness; the only attention bestowed by the dense and wrathful crowd around her was that of sensual admiration from one or another. Such sights were all too common in these last days of Atl. Seeing the priest pick up the sherd, this woman said:

"What wouldst thou with it?"

"Naught," answered the priest.

"Naught, forsooth! I know thou wouldst throw it at yon blasphemer, if thou hadst courage!"

"Courage, I lack not," was the sullen reply.

A voice in the surging crowd now called out that the blasphemer of religion ought to be sacrificed on the Teo Stone, and her heart given to the Maxin.

"Listen to that! The people and the Incali would be with thee," said the wanton. "Throw the piece, and see if perchance thou mightest not reach the game."

The ecclesiastic raised his hand back, and poised the missile, while the crowd nearest him gazed with eager eyes. Then the cruel bit of pottery hurtled through the air towards the fair speaker overhead. Her temple was presented, and the missile she might have avoided had she noted its coming, struck full on the dainty mark. With a cry of pain she threw up her hands, reeled, and then fell outwards, downwards, the twenty feet to the hard pavement below. The crowd, which had hushed an instant, now uttered fierce growls, and those nearest ran to the victim of the coward-priest. Several of the sacerdotal caste picked the poor body up, and carrying it by the feet, arms and hair, quite as if the assault had been preconcerted, instead of being the work of one miserable fiend, started off to the Incalithlon, whose vast pyramid loomed not far away.

"See!" said Phyris, "the first human sacrifice in Caiphul! Me, even me, they slew, for trying to stem the tide of depravity and ecclesiastical criminality. I repeated to them the prophecy of the Maxin, and they heeded not, but slew me. For that woman was my personality when I re-incarnated, three thousand years after thou, as Zailm, did leave me, as Anzimee."

With a strange ecstacy of crime, the priests, scarce an instant pausing, placed the still unconscious victim on the Teo. Then the chief priest, still called the Incalix, stepped from the Holy Seat, as it once had truly been. By the side of the victim he stopped and profaned not God, but Man, by a prayer to God; for no man can injure God except through injuring Man. Then he threw open the gray robe and bared the white breast. Swiftly he raised aloft the keen-edged knife, then smote. A shudder shook the reviving victim, who was about recovering consciousness. The murderer then tore out the quivering heart and cast it into the Unfed Light, where it disappeared and made no sign. Then the flesh was divided piecemeal amongst the murderous crowd, together with the blood-stained garments. But the most of the blood had run into a depression in the Teo, made for sacrificial blood. To this the priests added liquor, and in maddened frenzy quaffed the mixture from golden goblets. The scene was sickening, and I felt my very being revolt! And that poor murdered woman, a virgin— who had given her life to rescue her nation from sin—that was she, who had long centuries before been Anzimee, and now was Phyris, part of myself, and I part of her being, for our Spirit was one, re-united. I could forgive the crime I looked back upon, for the criminals knew not what they did. And they have suffered for it, and yet shall suffer, for it is their karma. When Death, the conqueror of all mortals, garnered his harvest in Atl, these souls, which had sown sin, and grown tares, were reaped by the Great Reaper, and the tares were sown with the good wheat when next those souls re-incarnated. And they have had to glean and uproot as they could, and so must continue to tear up the evil weeds till every one be uprooted. Then will they have atoned unto God. There is time enough, lives enough, but O friends, none to waste!

After this human sacrifice the thirst for blood which the people manifested became unappeasable. They demanded the life of the priest who struck down the woman—for they were not yet accustomed to the rights the Incali had so newly arrogated —those of human sacrifice. They claimed that he had really murdered the woman—that they were unprepared to go so far, that therefore he who threw the missile must die. The tumult became so violent, and insurrection seemed so imminent, that the wretched priest was dragged out and offered by his fellows as the woman had been. But now came the denouement. When the high priest turned to cast the heart of the last victim into the Maxin, he staggered as if struck, his hand fell by his side, the heart dropped on the pavement, and the stricken man fell forward unconscious! The tall taper of the Unfed Light was gone—the Maxin book was gone! In its place stood a human form—that of a Son of the Solitude. In his left hand was a sword, in his right a pen.

"Behold, the day of destruction is at hand which was foretold ages ago! Atlan shall soon be no more beheld by the sun in his whole course, for the sea shall swallow you all! Attend ye!"

Then the dread apparition vanished. But the Unfed Light came not again. The people fled, shrieking, leaving the priest who had fainted lying on the floor. It was as well, for when venturesome ones came into the Incalithlon many days later he still lay as he fell—for he was dead. In his greater knowledge, for wicked as he was he yet was chief, and knew, sorcerer that he was, that there really was a power of right which was destined to bring the corruption of Poseid low, and uproot the hideous mockery of sin enslaving the nation. And in his knowledge his soul had gone forth from his body in desperate fear, to return no more.

But the stupid sensualism of the masses, finding that after a few years nothing terrible occurred, gradually lapsed till worse than before—for human sacrifices became common, lust, gluttony and drunkenness ran riot, and the moral night's deep darkness closed in yet more blackly.

One man and his family who lived apart partook not of the general wickedness. True, he and his mate, like the ordinary people about him, were not married, save as the higher animals monogamize. Nor were his sons and their wives any better. But blood sacrifice he nor they would do. And when the monarch proclaimed that all must worship according to the new standard, and sacrifice babes and women, these men, giants in stature, and far superior, any one of them, to a dozen of the corrupt slaves of the Rai, refused to obey the mandate. Fruits and treasure they offered, but not blood. In his seclusion the father, Nepth, had a revelation. It came from the Sons of the Solitude, who were nowise altered from the ancient high standard, but Nepth thought it direct from God. The revelation was but a repetition of the prophecy of doom, but the knowledge of that prophecy having been centuries neglected, bore to Nepth all the force of a new revelation. So he came to know of the coming destruction of Atl—he and his sons. And they considered how to escape. Vailx were unknown. Nepth and his sons were unskilled builders. But they received instruc-

tions from the befriending Sons of the Solitude, who came to
them in astral shape. And so these better men of Atlantis
began to build a great vessel.. It was clumsy, but secure, and
had room to receive several of all kinds of useful animals found
in Atl, and to simple, ignorant Nepth these constituted every
animal on earth, for he knew nothing of other lands across
seas—scarce knew of the provinces in Incalia or Umaur, for in
these last days communication was not closely kept up. His
neighbors and friends jeered and reviled him as a blasphemer,
and he and his sons as men crazed. But the years lapsed, and
the great ark of refuge grew, until one day it was complete.
Then Nepth and his sons provided it with ample stores, and
they took the animals from the pens wherein they had placed
them as they captured them in .years past. Indeed, most of
these animals had been born in captivity, and were tame, so
long had Nepth carried on all works together, not knowing
just when the dread prophecy was to be fulfilled. The final
preparations were none too soon completed. Only a few days
elapsed ere the earth shook and trembled in a frightful manner. Rivers left their beds, or sank through vast crevices in
the earth; mountains shook till they were left as hills, and

> "Bowed their tall heads to the plain."

A crevice opened close by the vessel of refuge, and the river
which, half a mile wide, had flowed past to the ocean, fifty
miles away, now poured with a mighty roar into the opening.
For three days this awful turmoil continued. A man
came, beseeching for admittance. But Nepth said:
"Nay, thou wouldst never believe in other days. I told thee
then this land should sink under the seas, and thou didst revile
me. Now go thy ways and tell all thou dost meet that 'Nepth
spake truly.' "

Three days of horror, and three nights. Death stalked
through the land, for the mountains fell on the plains, and
floods swept unrestrained. But the worst was to come. On the
morning of the fourth day it seemed as if the rains of heaven
would drown all, yet the thundering and turmoil was not les-

sened. The gates of heaven and of the great deep were yet to be broken, and the continent, yea, much also of the world to be drowned. The people not yet destroyed were myriad, and were gathered in the high places. Suddenly it seemed as if the foundations of the world were withdrawn, for by one frightful, universal motion the lands left unflooded began to sink. With never a pause to the hideous, sickening sensation, all things sank, down, down, down—one, two, a dozen feet! Then a period of rest. The rains, which came in sheets, instead of drops; the wild blasts of furious wind; the sinking motion—all ceased while men might count a score. One score, two, three, yet no resumption. The wretched people, hidden in such poor shelter as they could find and dared avail themselves of, began to breathe easier—perhaps the fearful ruin was at last stayed! But, no! A slight tremble, scarcely noticeable after the mad three days—and then with one swift leap down to death the great continent of Atlantis sank as a stone sinks in water! Not a paltry dozen feet, nor even a hundred, but almost a mile it sunk at one horrible bound!

Nepth! In the middle of the third day his vessel of refuge had floated to the ocean on an outgoing rush of the floods, and there the winds had carried him until, when Atl sped down to death, he and his storm-beaten ark were a couple of hundred miles away. A very few other people had been similarly forced seawards, and these, after weary weeks, at last came around the southern promontory of Africa, and drifted northeasterly, to land on the west coast of Umaur. Here, too, the destruction had left but a few miserable survivors. But the few hundreds thus left founded the race which—repopulating that land—was found by Pizarro after many centuries upon centuries had elapsed. And a few thus became many. They would not permit blood sacrifice, but yet, like Nepth, offered fruits to Incal, and retained the name, slightly modified, so as to be Inca, a name bestowed upon their rulers. A few survivors landed further north, and repopulated the land conquered by Cortez, the Spaniard, a few short centuries ago. But these heeded not the lesson, for no sooner were they landed on the desolated shores than they slew a woman as a thanksgiving for their escape. But Nepth? For many days his vessel drifted over the silent seas, with only the ceaseless roar of rain upon the roof to break the stillness. At last the vessel grounded. He knew not where he was, for he was an ignorant man. But the aspect of things was changed wholly. When at last he descended, and let loose his living freight, though he knew it not, he was in Asia. This land had not suffered as other lands, but yet floods had covered all the western part of Asia. The eastern portions, and what there was of Europe and America, had not remained inundated after the quick subsidence of the enormous tidal-wave, which, thirteen hundred feet in height, swept outward from Atlantis' site upon the recoil of the engulfing ocean. Thus closed the scene for us; the great deluge was over.

Then Phyris and I turned to other phases of the mysterious past. These, though not less interesting, may not enter these pages. Rai Gwauxln was come to be Mendocus, while Rai Ernon of Suern was with us now—Mol Lang. Sohma was that Son of the Solitude whom I took on my vailr, when I was Zailm, away from Suern. So we saw the interweaving of the life lines. Then we saw the course of the lost soul, Mainin, from remote ages when Atlantis was not known in the earth, a sin-laden man then, until we found him, serving Satan, an outcast from human ranks, blasted thence by that Son of God—"first fruit of them that [had re-incarnated] slept."

Looking, we saw that early Rai of Poseid—him of the Maxin Stone and the Unfed Light—the Law-giver. We knew him for the Christ, illumining man then, and later as Buddha, and again overshining that greater than Buddha, the Nazarene. "Before Abraham was, I am." Whosoever the Christ-Spirit entereth into and abideth in, becometh a Son of God, and equal with Gautama; but into no one will it enter who doth not travel the Path. That mighty One blasted Mainin. Yet we saw that because Mainin had crossed our life then, I was thereby made the instrument of mercy to him by Christ, and that occasion was yet to come.

Back to the time of Zailm we gazed upon a scene on the great continent of Lemuria, or Lemorus. We saw a great house built of stone, standing on a grassy sward, a plain, over which roamed herds of cattle, and queer little horses, having three toes to each foot and high shoulders. Far to the east was a blue mountain range, beyond that a great ocean. But between the manse and mountains flashed a silvery lake. Within the house were many people, servitors all to two people—a woman and her son. Gloom overspread all faces—the gloom of blood. To a chief among subordinates the son gave orders. This slave, grim, ferocious, a very incarnation of cruelty, attracted my notice. His brown skin was swarthy, his hands talon-like. Only a breech-cloth apparelled him. Receiving his orders, he disappeared, but soon came again, pushing two manacled people, plainly of a different race from any there. One was a youth, lithe, erect, rather haughty of mien, his hair brown, his features symmetrical—that individuality of twenty-three thousand years ago is now Sohma. The other captive was a fair girl, sister to the youth, it seemed. Her beauty was delicate—but voluptuous. The fierce, cruel eyes, gleaming like live coals from under the shaggy brows of the master of the house, lighted with admiration as he saw the girl. His heavy-set figure, his coarse jaw, thick neck, and round, shaven head—all fitted him to be master of the brutish crowd around him. This man extended his hand as if to touch the captive maiden. She shrank away, and drew her figure erect in a queenly scorn.

"Ha! Unyielding as ever!" quoth the master. "We shall see."

He nodded to the chief slave, who threw the captive boy on a sort of altar beside him. He bound him. But the victim said firmly: "Sister, yield not; die first." Her eyes shone with an awful light of horror.

"Stop his voice," exclaimed the master, and the slave, nothing loath, cut out the poor boy's tongue!

"Beast!" hissed the girl to the master.

"Ha!" he replied, "I will prove that true," and he struck the bared breast of the tongueless lad with his own dagger, and tearing out the heart, threw it at the sister's feet. A goblet of the blood was caught and the master's mother, a priestess, who stood by the block, took it and gazed into it. Then she said:

"The gods say that the girl also must die."

"Say they so? By all the powers I will not obey," shouted the master. "Not though my troops of war fail, and the King fails!"

"My son," said the priestess, "thou mayst not avoid this sacrifice and live, say the gods."

"No? Then the gods be served. Give me that knife. He felt its keen edge, and then asked, without taking his eyes from the weapon, "Say the gods yet so?"

"Even yet," said the priestess.

"Bind the maid," and his orders were obeyed, though the girl had fainted. The executioner laid his ear to her breast; a faint smile relaxed his features, and he said in his soul, "She is dead"; he laid his hand on her breast, stood erect and said:

"Accept, ye gods, this sacrifice."

An instant the knife glittered overhead, the next he had buried it in his own heart. So had the heart that knew no mercy yielded to love; the stern warrior was dead. The gods must have blood, he thought, but he gave his own. What personality was he—was the girl, dead from horror? Myself!—and Phyris!

CHAPTER V.

"MAN'S INHUMANITY TO MAN."

Again the dead past revealed another scene. I saw myself in the person of an ill-fed, ill-treated slave—ever hungry, wretched, too much so to feel resentment. I died hungry, and then had a devachan of seeming realization of my wants. Then again re-birth, and through a karma not here to be explained, the new man had ease, wealth, plenty. But a physical karma

pursued, and he was ever hungry in the midst of plentitude,
and lazy when action was necessary. This state begot disease,
and the product of—[in his previous life]—"man's inhumanity
to man"—was afflicted with cancer of the stomach. This
killed the ferocious appetite, and the sybarite, free of this, set
to work to cure himself. Finding he must fail, he sought comfort in religion, and went forth to the wilderness to become a
religious hermit. Now, a hermit's life is one of uselessness to
mankind. In that lone state my individuality lost opportunities to cultivate moral strength by worldly contact, and behold
me after death come again to life as Zailm, weak enough to sin
with Lolix, and beget then a karma that lasted, with newly got
vigor, till only a few years ago, punishing me more bitterly
than death, as thou, friend, knowest. If Zailm had sorrow, thou
knowest he had also joy. So every life-karma is made up of
sunshine and shadow. "A tooth for a tooth?" Yea! But
also "for a kiss a kiss."

CHAPTER VI.

WHY ATLANTIS PERISHED.

Looking along the line of life's yesterdays the reason became
apparent why all the wondrous attainments of Poseid had
ceased and left no sign—why Atla, which metaphorically
held aloft the world into the light of science—had sunk beneath the waters and gone down into deep, mysterious caverns,
to be hidden in an ignorance greater than that which shadowed
Pompeii and Herculaneum from subsequent centuries.

Natural decadence tells the story. As the centuries succeeding the time of the great Rai Gwauxln lapsed, ten, fifteen,
twenty and more, the nation came to a greater glory of mechanics, of science, and of physical condition than even Gwauxln's
time had known. One by one the scholars found that those
things which had always been possible only through mechanical

contrivance, were more easily accomplished by purely psychic means; they learned it was possible to divest themselves of the flesh, and in astral body go whither they would and appear, instant as the electric current, at any distance. They learned that they could perform material actions when they had thus projected themselves. Then it was that the cruder methods—vailx and naim, and all else similar, was suffered to lapse into that semi-forgetfulness of the Suerni—and exactly as they, so the mass of Poseidi depended on the priesthood for all these things. For only the few exalted minds could thus reach out into the deeper night-side of Nature—the many must remain in the lesser places. Inevitably then came corruption of power; the few were masters, and the many had no recourse, because the master of psychics is invulnerable to the laws of physicality when wielded by men less than he.

Then, indeed, was the day come when ripeness was on the land and on the people. The ripe pear can not keep perfect, but at the heart begins a decay that spreads from core to cortex, and lo, the end. So in Poseid, at the core began the outward-spreading rot. That core was the education of the people. Whenever earth's nations shall cease to educate the coming generation, decay shall begin for the people. In Poseid the few had attained such exalted knowledge of natural forces that the many could not hope to overtake them. Then, discontented with the comparatively poor education themselves had, they suffered all its marvels to wane. Thus, ere thirty centuries after Gwauxln the Poseid race was as Suern, but more corrupt, and lust, appetite, passion and power had laid fatal grasp on the proudest people the earth has ever known. How little dost thou realize when thou readest in Hebrew Scriptures of the destruction of the cities of the Plain it is the account of the doom of Marzens and Terna, destroyed by the Naraz forces they had forgotten how to control. That destruction heralded that of the continent, nine centuries later. Aye! Poseid arose to an altitude which the wildest dreams of science have not predicted for the modern world; arose, flourished and decayed, in the fullness of cyclic times. And America is Poseid come again, reincarnated, and shall see its scientific people repeat, but on a higher plane, the attainments of Atla. As the centuries pass it shall see the successive enfleshment of those souls which in Atla made that land proud, prouder, proudest. But it shall do more, for America hath developed that soul-element which, when her people were Poseidi, was first faintly traced. So, though repeating, it shall do more—it shall have all Atla's marvels wedded to the glorious soul foreseen for mankind by Him of Nazareth. It shall flourish so, and then, in the fullness of its time, decay. But that shall not be for four and a half centurial decades.

––––––––

CHAPTER VII.

THE TRANSFIGURATION.

I might give many more life scenes. Let these suffice. Turn now to our present.

The reunion of the semi-egoii is one in which, after the mighty ordeal of the Great Crisis, the souls of the feminine and masculine elements become on the same plane; both are perfect. This is the marriage made in heaven. Become so that each thinks, wills and expresses itself the same in all ways simultaneously, the two alter egoii are then one, having a feminine—negative, and a masculine—positive—aspect. Then these two potentials unite and receive the Spirit, or I AM., which was always undivided, and which illumined each soul of its pair equally. So is this last union. Thus Phyris is me, living, being, immanent, and speaks this message with me—is I, and yet, mysterious truth, is herself! Likewise I am her and yet again, myself. I speak, and it is she; she speaks and it is I—for we are one being, one spirit, androgyne, perfect. Yet not perfect as our Father is, for He is perfect as Conditionless Being, but our perfection is that of a part, because we are all of God, but not He of any one of us. Indeed, were this not true, then our attainment of perfection, Jesus attainment of it, or any child of the Father, would find in its realization annihilation. But only the soul that sins is cast into the second death, fated to the Sisyphic round till it does succeed. Perfection may be conditionless in all respects save that it is not that of the whole. And because we each are parts, therefore are we forever attracted to the Father, who is sum of all parts, and this attraction is to onward Being. And we are ever attracted to the other parts, both those which are peer and those which are less. It is because the part is forever drawn to the sum that there is no death, save in defying and abandoning all hold on the Whole. Perfection of a part but draws it nearer to the Whole, and perfection of the Whole compels It to depend on each of Its parts. There may be change, there is no death. And there may be extinction of personality, the erring soul may perish, and itself and deeds be annihilated, but the Spirit from the Father dieth not. If for thy soul thou wouldst have eternal life; if thou wouldst not see thy soul, that product of untold ages of time, lost in the second Death, and thyself, oh Spirit, child of our Father, doomed to recreate another soul to lay as acceptable offering before our Lord, then subdue it, subdue thy soul, at-one it to God through Jesus Christ our Lord, by recognizing that it is His, given Him by God, made by thee to serve the Creator. If thou make thy soul serve thee in His service, thou hast it eternally. But if thou serve it thou shalt lose it and have to make another during coming aeons.

Wilt thou follow the Path, even as I have pointed out to thee that it leadeth to the Kingdom? Be sure of thyself ere thou dost embrace occult learning, lest it prove a veritable Bridge of Mirzah, full of fatal pitfalls for thy feet. Better shun the Secret Wisdom than fail, for strait is the gate and narrow is the way that leadeth unto Being, and few there be that find it.

Knowest thou me? A good tree cannot bring forth evil fruit, but a corrupt tree. Wilt thou hew me down and cast me into the fire, who testifieth concerning the Spirit? "Not every one that sayeth Lord, Lord, shall enter into Heaven, but he that doeth the will of my Father in Heaven. The time is brief.

I have spoken. Peace be with thee.

The End.

NOTE BY THE AUTHOR.

Friends, thirteen years have become past time since the words of this book were dictated; purposely hath publication been delayed unto the end that statements then made might acquire weight through the coming to pass of many of the predictions to be found within these covers; predictions which at that time were wholly unverified, and were, moreover, regarded by science as chimerical. Prophecy would be impossible in a God-less universe; and were it not that vibration is the law of laws, no mind could come into unison with the Creator or any of His ministers; each living being is minister to the creature immediately inferior. Today witnesseth the faith of those who have believed in my words swallowed up in knowledge: the predictions have numerously been realized; all will be. So it is that today, in the middle of the final year of the century I add

THE MIGHTY CAP-STONE:

—The Division of the Way Hath Come; the Midnight Hour of the Cycle Which, More Than Any Other, Formed Life's Great Divide, Hath Struck.   When first I dictated for this book there lacked, as it were, yet a few seconds to the closing of the Sixth Day. But now for some seconds hath been fulfilled the initiation of that saying of Him who sitteth upon the throne: —"Behold! I make all things new." The Hour hath struck. And now presently "the one overcoming shall inherit all things and I will be his God, and he shall be my son." This is for those who did set their hands to the Plow and their feet to Furrow, and **looked not back, while yet the Sixth Cycle was.** "But as for the cowards [a halt between two opinions] and the unbelievers [in aught above earthly, finite things] and the abominable, and takers of life, and passion and lust-servers, sorcerers, idolaters and swervers from truth, their portion is the [Great Karma of the World], the second death." While the foolish ones were gone to buy oil, the bridegroom came, and they who were prepared entered with him to the feasts, and the door was shut. When the foolish returned the door was not opened unto them. Beloved, remember these words which were spoken by the apostles of the Christ; that they said that in the Last Time before the end of the Age "there will be mockers walking after their own impious lusts (10). These indeed blaspheme what things they do not understand; but that which they know naturally, as do the irrational animals, in these things they are corrupt (19). These are they who separate at the Dividing of the Way, going in the finite direction, not having the Spirit (7), and are placed as an example, to endure the retributive justice of an age-ending fire."

Many have been my references to America as being Atlantis come again; much hath in a general way been said of the beginning, rise, growth and destruction of that ancient prototype; a hint hath been here and there given, rather by inference than by specific statement, that while America should be peer and even more than Atl, just because she is Atl returned on a higher plane, she must endure the woes as well as retrace her pre-carnate glories. The penalty visited upon Poseid was the crowning sentence of that Age. Century after century in the majestic march of Time hath passed since the sun looked down upon a wild waste of ocean waters where but a few days before had been the regal Island-Continent. Another cycle hath reached its end, and its last hour hath chimed. All that which is imperfect in the now-closed Sixth Day is come, in stately, measured but inexorable way to face judgment by the standard, Truth. Spot nor blemish can not hope to stand nor continue before it. Neither can aught be amended so as to now escape its karmic penalty, for the seal of its full time is set upon it. "The one acting unjustly, let him be unjust still; and the filthy one, let him be filthy still; and the righteous one, let him righteousness do still, and the holy one, let him be holy still. Lo, I come speedily, and the reward of me is with me, to give back unto each one as the work of him shall be found." The Great Karma unfailingly setteth each evil-doer back to the point attained ere the animal forces in riot obtained control over the human. Wherefore those who in the Sixth Cycle lost supremacy over their lower selves won no place in the Seventh. In the closing years of the spent cycle one deserted his helpless wife; verily, he really deserted his birthright in the New Age. Another sought, being weak-willed, to drown worries in wine; he but drowned his soul's advanced merits. A wife was faithless to her wedding-vows; the Door of the New Time is fast against her. A thief stole—what? His own life's rewards. One there was who deprived another of physical life; he also erased his own name from TO-DAY'S roll-call. One swore to keep a vow, but broke it often; in this New Day, after the grave shall claim his physical being, he shall not again awaken, having lacked will to live. A man was buried with high honors who at merciless cost to his fellow-men enriched his bank-account; a gravestone near as costly as pure gold rears above his mortal, aye, and under it is also the dead hopes of resurrection. She sold her body; purchased and purchasers form an unhallowed company in Yesterday's catacombs, whence they shall not emerge to see the light of To-Day until, cycles afar hence "death and hell give up" their inhabitants. Such is a brief glimpse into a Closed Record. Turn the page. Another did deeds of love; love and doers thereof live through all the days, forever. One smiled when a smile was heroic and cheered faint souls; one visited the sick and prisoners; one clothed a naked stranger; and one gave half of her last crust, though only to a starving dog. Verily, all these shall receive their reward in the Day now dawning. The bad are not all bad, neither the good wholly good. She who lived a life of shame, yet ever kept hope of better things burning in her inmost heart, and longed for death to release her, since man would not:

"Looked beyond the shadow of the late unhallowed years,
To the far, far distant upland, where yon glimmering light appears."

Verily, she shall be chastened, and made new, in the glory of To-Day; but the chastening is a weary ordeal, and slow. As the Great Karma handles her, so handleth it all others, for it is Christ's mercy, which healeth every soul's-hurt.

During many, many centuries prophecy hath looked forward
to the end of the Age as a time of awful woe, and has pictured
dread scenes of terminal horror. Am I come to say that all
these predictions shall fail? Is the book of the Apocalypse
mere allegory? Would it were! But as the Poseid age was
stricken, this one must also be which has just passed. Shall
America, the Glorious, together with the rest of the world,
meet similar woe? Alas, worse, though not by water but by
fire. Shall all be wiped out of existence, leaving a planet in
ruins? Unto the end of full obedience and the coming into
harmony with divine law shall the lash be applied; words may
not portray the scenes. This is the Message of the End of
the Age:

"The day of vengeance is in mine heart, and the year of my
redeemed is come nigh"—Isaiah. "Behold, the day * * *
that burneth as an oven."—Malachi.

The Hour hath struck. And yet in all of this there is no
mystery, no supernatural penalty, no capricious infliction by
an offended personal God, and nothing of "man's necessity,
God's opportunity." It is all of Man's own doing. He hath
wandered from the Way, and hath for the God-nature in him,
which he should have revered and nourished, substituted
worship of Self and of Mammon; hath cast out Love, and
placed violence, lust, greed and all the riotous animalism in
him in command of his life. **Man is his own judge and executioner.** Man is the type and the universe is the print; Nature
patterns after Man, not Man after Nature. He, a being of
free-will, hath brought all coming woes of judgment to be in-
evitable; he must endure; as he hath sown, so must he reap.
O Man, forgettor of Love, of Mercy, of Right; breeder of Hate,
of Cruelty, and of the inhumanity that hath and still doth
make countless millions mourn, is it possible that thou hast
been blind to the handwriting on the wall? Alas, yes, thou
hast! Rampant is the Spirit of selfishness, of greed, of merciless gain; its hand guides the trains and steamers, clicks the
telegraph keys, operates the telephones and cables, makes a
mockery of free speech, shackles the press so that it dares to

utter only that which cannot offend its master; every human
enterprise, all national policies and international comities, all
things, even the churches, are willing vassals to this fienl,
SELF. What then? Ruin is on all sides, the human race and
all lower creatures its victims. Masons at work on a high wall
shout as a brick falls: "Stand from under!"

Aye, stand from under! A world is falling! Pile no higher
the racial and individual misdeeds now biding expiation; weary
enough the awful reckoning of the Great Karma without addi-
tions to its terrible length that even now stretches ahead, a
seeming eternity. Frenzied millions of men and women, boys
and girls, no longer free save in name, are menaced with starvation. Hungry, cold, half-clad, shelterless only too often,
denied the chance to work, however willing they may be, cor-
poration-owned machinery their competitor; monopoly and
trust-ridden, sleeping or waking. This inhuman picture is the
rule, not the exception. Thou knowest this full well. I state
nothing new in this regard, and the awful facts are under-
drawn instead of exaggerated. All of this, although in far, far
less degree, has been so at the ending of every age, was so in
Poseid and is therefore now repeated. But it can never be so
again after this, for HERE THE WAY DIVIDES. Poseid
survived; so also shall they of the Sixth Age. In the full time
by fire the Reaper shall reap, and no place be found for physical
safety by the unchanged of heart. But the time of it shall be
foreshortened, else no flesh could remain alive. Stand from
under! The roar of armed hosts must succeed the thunderous
mutterings of the times. No more is there any chance to prevent the coming retribution (albeit it may seem unduly de-
ferred), for the causes have had their way. Too late is it to
even modify the result of the misguidance of that Spirit whose
hand sways the helm. A short, but sharp conflict, sanguinary
past belief, even now reddens on the horizon. The trained
armies, millions of men active or in reserve, that are now engaged in conquest, fevered with war, will but little longer, comparatively, submit to having themselves and loved ones ground
under the heel and strangled by the hand of that organized

thing, Capital, which, itself merely the natural fruit of selfishness, none the less is a riotous animal principle, compelling the few to be masters of the many, denying the God-born declaration that all men are created free and equal, and warping it to seem a giant lie. Soon millions of trained soldiers will turn upon the visible representatives—the wealthy and worldly prosperous, who in reality are not more responsible than will be their assailants—of that Relentless Force behind all human enterprise. Later they will break up into lawless bands bent on satisfying Ishmaelitish tendencies, each self-server's hand weaponed against his fellow creatures. Then will the pent-up hate, the savagery and selfishness begotten by ages of selfishness ruled by unbridled animalism break in a storm such as the world hath never yet seen—no, not during all the ages I scan, ages forgotten for untold thousands of years. That loveless conflict will initiate that which, Nature completing, will leave living but one where now are many. Hard and fast after the human conflict will come pestilences unparalleled, sweeping the wide earth over—for in that day none will pause to bury the slain until the evil is wrought, nor then, for the dead of the plagues will be as thousands for every one by violence. And all this because the love that should grace and soften men's hearts, each for all and all for each, dried up and became a mockery in the close of the ended cycle, leaving but scattered oases, few and far between. Nature follows Man. Wherefore the waters of Earth will dry out, rains be withheld, cyclones sweep, and an earthquake come such as was not since a man was on the earth; aye, I am mindful of Poseid! But all of this will occur only through natural causes, and in consonance with the selfishness, lust, greed, anger and general depravity of the Type. As these blaze in the human breast, so shall the air, dry and vaporless under brazen skies, develope solar heats more fierce than history ever knew. A parched earth, furnace-like, piling all flesh mountains high; pestilences stalking unchecked. O Ye! Blind to the Handwriting on the wall, which flickers still, though writ for a spent cycle. Turn now and read, while yet the last midnight stroke reverberates.

The disciples asked the Great Master, saying: "Teacher, when will these things be?" And He said: " * * * When you see surrounded by encampments the Jerusalem, then you may know that has come near the desolation * * * . For days of vengeance these are, to be fulfilled of all the judgments."

Friends, know ye the meaning of the name Jerusalem? That it meaneth "Vision of Peace?" Verily, so it doth. One by one during the years all the signs of the end of the Age but one were fulfilled; but these were "only the beginning of sorrows", for still the Spirit of Liberty abode here and there in the breasts of lovers of their fellowmen. That Spirit wrapped itself in the glorious folds of the Stars and Stripes and proclaimed the imperishable declaration of human equality, granting unto all that freedom which Americans for themselves demanded. But now the "Vision of Peace" is finally encompassed by armies, the last gap being filled with **blue-coated soldiers** forcing Mammon's commercial shackles upon alien peoples in tropical islands. Ah, the Starry Flag droops mournfully low above the freedom-birthright sold for a mess of pottage. My People, O my People! As ye have sown, so must ye reap. The Vision of Spiritual Peace is wholly clouded by the dust of armed camps, and no gap is left unobscured. "Then shall the end come." A Son hath continually called from on High:

"Stand from under! Get into the shelter of that Cross." In all the expiatory time must indeed those who thought no wrong suffer? Ah, thought no wrong. In every life, whether theist's, atheist's or merely one ignorant of any doctrine of belief, there comes a time when the inward Spirit beseeches the soul to go up higher. It pleads again and again and yet again so long as faintest hope remains. Omission too, hath its penalty; "How shall we escape if we neglect so great salvation?"—echoed throughout the past Age. Fire burns a babe's fingers as badly as it does an adult's. There were and are those who lived and live the Cross. These shall not suffer,

not even though bodily death overtake them; they have no
Karma to expiate.

What is the Cross? What is Christ? I have said, long ago,
but I will re-state it:—the Divine stream of Life, the Indefinable God—that is the long arm of the Living Cross. Directed,
purposed Human Will is the short arm. This will-power is
our call upon His Name that is never denied. Jesus, the Man
of Nazareth, gave us pattern. He sacrificed self for us. He
said:—"Follow me." Also:—"If any man will come after me,
let him deny himself, and take up his cross and follow me."
This self is the lower self; it is the animal. All animals are in
man concreted. No hyena is so treacherous, no tiger so ferocious, no hog so brutish, no weasel so destructive; no animal
creature of any sort is so perfect in its own peculiar nature
as is the man who suffers any or all of these animal characteristics within him to run riot; and this is because his human
soul is enslaved to the animal. Animal is only force undirected,
whether it exist in a body or not. Directed, guided by will, it
ceaseth to be animal. But in yielding to that guidance it must
give up its free lawlessness, something never pleasant and often
painful. It is sacrifice, always. Its symbol is the Cross. He
sacrificed self for us on this same cross of the Causeless, Divine
Stream which containeth all thing and floweth no man knoweth
whence nor whither. I would not minimize Calvary; it is very,
very real and the one great fact forever! "Follow me." On
that same Cross, day by day, aye, moment by moment, em-
ploying our wills, as He directed, that we may grow unto His
likeness, we also, following, must sacrifice self, sacrifice the
animal in us,—that is, in God's service we must never cease
to direct those vagrant forces which in running riot turn
Earth into a veritable hell and supplant Love with Self. It is
written that "a little child shall lead them." Verily the "little
child" of the Spirit in the New Time shall be ruler over the
menagerie within the man, and that man shall therefore be
able, even as Quong, the Tchin, to rule any animal outside of
himself. A vast power, this. And because of it in the New
Time no longer shall any beast, whether in human form, or in

lower animal body, or merely apparent as a raging tempest or a disease, be free to do evil.

When the Spirit in Man cometh fully to its own, "he shall rule them as with a rod of iron," this riotous throng. Rule them to their own good; cut them off suddenly, even as Quong cut-off the puma from furthering its own will. He shall destroy that theretofore unbridled animal, by the Cross converting it into a servitor to the Father. All things must become new TO-DAY, because conditions will soon so differ that they who would hold fast to the old will find nothing either in Nature or elsewhere that will longer yield to the old powers.

And now here, of all places, I would indeed not be vague in expression. The Seventh Cycle is that of the Spirit. TO-DAY existence will demand a spiritual eye, and ear, and that every sense be raised to the Heights. The very means of dealing with Nature will be no longer gross, but become as in Hesperus, manageable only by those who, using the Cross in their every life-act, swerve never to either side of the way, never, either in least or greatest deed doing error, even that good may come, knowing it can not bring aught but pain and penalty.

Not one can be lost, finally, of the evil-doers, for God wastes nothing. He converts all things from lower into higher, inexorably, surely. Some must endure the retributive justice of the Great Karma, aye, the majority must experience more or less of this fire of transfiguration; the wrath of God is Love's severity.

Then will be those times when "all things are made new" what now, think ye? Shall not America, and the rest of the world, be more glorious than ever thou hast dreampt? Aye, truly. She shall not indeed have the great population census-takers imagine. There shall be few where were many; tens replacing thousands. But not in numbers is there greatness or magnificance; remember the Saldans and Rai Ernon; which was greater, he or that ill-fated host? Yet never shall a soul be lost; God hath place for everyone.

It is written that after a thousand years Satan shall be loosed for a little season. That is well. For the Race possess-

ing such amazing powers, though few, will be the people, yet
will there be some who will have attained these powers through
mere intellect; they will abuse their privileges, having not the
Spirit, and these sinful ones will the Perfect in Evil assail, that
karma shall overtake them. Having had much given unto them,
of them shall much be demanded, wherefore their karmic atonement will be more intense than words can depict.

The wrath of God is love's severity.   All shall be converted
from lower into higher.

> "A glory shines across the coming years,
> The glory of a race grown great and free.
> 'Twas seen by poets, sages, saints and seers,
> Whose vision glimpsed the dawn that is to be.
> A shining shore is by the Future's sea,
> Whereon each man shall stand among his peers
> As equal; and to none shall bend the knee.
> Awake, my soul, shake off your doubts and fears;
> Behold the hosts of darkness fade and flee
> Before the magic of the Morning's face;
> And hear the sweet and wondrous melody
> That floats to us from far-off golden days—
> It is the choral song of Liberty
> It is the anthem of the coming Race."

ERRATA.

COSIMO is a specialty publisher of books and publications that inspire, inform and engage readers. Our mission is to offer unique books to niche audiences around the world.

COSIMO CLASSICS offers a collection of distinctive titles by the great authors and thinkers throughout the ages. At **COSIMO CLASSICS** timeless classics find a new life as affordable books, covering a variety of subjects including: *Biographies, Business, History, Mythology, Personal Development, Philosophy, Religion and Spirituality*, and much more!

COSIMO-on-DEMAND publishes books and publications for innovative authors, non-profit organizations and businesses. **COSIMO-on-DEMAND** specializes in bringing books back into print, publishing new books quickly and effectively, and making these publications available to readers around the world.

COSIMO REPORTS publishes public reports that affect your world: from global trends to the economy, and from health to geo-politics.

LaVergne, TN USA
30 December 2009
168519LV00002B/147/A